D1789212

A DESCRIPTIVE BIBLIOGRAPHY
OF
ALLAMA MUHAMMAD IQBAL
(1877-1938)

ORIENTALIA LOVANIENSIA
ANALECTA
—————— 94 ——————

A DESCRIPTIVE BIBLIOGRAPHY
OF
ALLAMA MUHAMMAD IQBAL
(1877-1938)

BY

DIETER TAILLIEU
FRANCIS LALEMAN
WINAND M. CALLEWAERT

UITGEVERIJ PEETERS en DEPARTEMENT OOSTERSE STUDIES
LEUVEN
2000

084833254

© 2000, Peeters Publishers & Department of Oriental Studies
Bondgenotenlaan 153, B-3000 Leuven/Louvain (Belgium)
All rights reserved, including the rights to translate or to
reproduce this book or parts thereof in any form.

D. 2000/0602/24
ISBN 90-429-0819-X (Peeters, Leuven)

TABLE OF CONTENTS

FOREWORD

Excellent bibliographical work about Allama Muhammad Iqbal in the Arabic scripts (Urdu, Persian, Arabic and so on) has been published by the Iqbal Academy, Lahore. Our publication covers only what appeared in the Roman script: English, German, French, Dutch, Italian, Polish, Czech, Portuguese, Swedish, Finnish, Turkish, and Russian.

The first book *about* Iqbal, by Z. Khan appeared in 1922 and since then scores of books, hundreds of articles in periodicals and many more articles in newspapers have been produced. They deal with different aspects of Muhammad Iqbal: as a person, a poet, a philosopher and a political thinker. *Iqbalia* started to appear already during Iqbal's lifetime, when attempts were made to arrange and classify his thought and work, and to evaluate his importance as one of the major philosophers of the subcontinent. More than half a century ago B.A. Dar's *Study in Iqbal's Philosophy* appeared (1944). In this work, for the first time, the philosophical views and thoughts were treated exhaustively and in a scientific way. Dar's aim was to explain the philosophical aspects of Iqbal's re-interpretation of the message of Islám in the context of a contemporary situation. This is still the aim of many researchers from all over the world today. Since Iqbal is now considered to be not only a *philosopher of Islam*, but rather a *philosopher of mankind*, the scope of *Iqbalia* has broadened dramatically and interest in Iqbal and his thought among non-Persian and non-Urdu speakers has increased very much.

Not only books about Iqbal have appeared. Also bibliographies have been compiled. In fact many books have some kind of bibliographical list, and we have tried to include all that material in the present publication. I should like to mention especially the excellent *A Bibliography of Articles on Iqbal (1900-1977)* by Malik Mueen Nawas Azhar, published in Lahore in 1978, and the *Analytical Catalogue of Books on Allama Mohammad Iqbal* (1877-1977) by Abdul Hafeez Akhtar, published by the government of Pakistan in 1978. For *Iqbal and the English Press of Pakistan 1948-1971*, I refer to the work by Nadeem Shafiq Malik (1996). For surveys of the work done by the team of the *Iqbal Review*, Lahore, I refer to the publication of A.H. Qarshi and of M. Riaz.

With the generous support of the Ministry of Education, Government of Pakistan the Iqbal Foundation Europe at the KULeuven, Belgium, has endeavoured to combine meticulous and patient work in libraries with the most modern search on internet. The result is an impressive tribute to Iqbal and to the research about him: 2500 entries, the latest entry dated 1998 (A. Schimmel). Even if many superfluous or repetitive articles may have been published, a researcher should look at even small contributions: they may contain valuable information and rare insights. The databank we compiled at the university of Leuven is composed of material taken from published works and from the on-line services of the major university libraries. From this it appeared that hundreds of scholars and authors have contributed to the immense databank about Iqbal. The highest number of contributions is by Annemarie Schimmel, S.A. Vahid and B.A. Dar, followed by A. Bausani, K.A. Waheed, A.J. Arberry and so many others.

For their inspiration and encouragement to start and complete this daring project, I owe special thanks to Prof. Annemarie Schimmel, Bonn, to Dr. Saeed A. Durrani, Birmingham and Mr. Toheed Ahmad, now ambassador in Singapore, and Mr Ambassador Riaz Mohammad Khan, Brussels, while many persons have very kindly made their expertise available. We are very obliged also to the Iqbal Academy, Lahore, and its Director Mr. Suheyl Umar for so kindly putting at our disposal the complete set of the *Iqbal Review* and other publications, and to the numerous authors who responded to our appeal and sent us their lists of publications about Iqbal. David Nelson, librarian of the Van Pelt Library, Philadelphia has been most helpful, not only with good advice. Last but not least I gratefully mention that this enterprise would not have been possible without the driving force of Mr. Syed Hasan Javed, Counsellor, Brussels.

The redaction of the input was not an easy task, partly because personal names in Pakistan cannot easily be classified. We tried to apply a consistent system and apologize if the reader may be at a loss for a while. In our sources we also did not find uniform spellings (e.g. Hasan and Hasan, Sayyid, Syed, and so on). The classification of the keywords too proved to be a headache; the reader may like to look for certain keywords under three additional headings: philosophy, poetry and politics. Unless otherwise specified, all publications are in English. Finally, no bibliography can ever be complete and is in fact outdated on the day it appears. I would be very grateful for all suggestions, corrections and additions that may be useful for bibliographical research about Iqbal in the future.

Leuven, 21st April 1999
winand.callewaert@kuleuven.ac.be
fax 32-16-324945

BIBLIOGRAPHY

1. **A. A.**, "LETTERS OF IQBAL", *IQBAL REVIEW* 1, no. 3: October (1960): pp. 80-82.
    Review of Syed Nazir A. Niyazi (ed.), MAKTUBAT-I-IQBAL, Iqbal Academy, Karachi, 1957. 372 pp.

2. **A. K. M.**, "THE LIFE AND WORKS OF IQBAL", *IQBAL REVIEW* 14, no. 3: October (1973): pp. 45-60.

3. **A. Z. A.**, "IQBAL DAY IN DAMASCUS", *ISLAMIC LITERATURE* 7, no. 10: October (1955): pp. 37-38.

4. **ABBAS, Razia**, "EDUCATION OF THE YOUTH IN THE LIGHT OF IQBAL'S PHILOSOPHY", *IQBAL REVIEW* 30-31, no. 3: October - 1: April (1989-1990): pp. 129-49.

5. **ABBAS, S. G.**, mon., *DR. MUHAMMAD IQBAL: THE HUMANIST - A REASSESSMENT OF THE POETRY AND PERSONALITY OF THE POET-PHILOSOPHER OF THE EAST*, 1st ed., Lahore: Iqbal Academy Pakistan, 1997. xxxi+224 pp.
    Translation into English of CHILD'S PRAYER, MIRZA GHALIB, SHAKESPEARE, DAGH, INDIAN ANTHEM, NATIONAL SONG OF THE INDIAN CHILDREN, RAM, NANAK, HIMALAYA, ON RECEIVING A FLOWER PRESENT, TO THE CUP-BEARER, PRAYER, CORDOVA MOSQUE, NATIONAL ANTHEM, PROTEST, REJOINDER TO PROTEST, LENIN, SONG OF ANGELS, GOD'S COMMAND TO ANGELS, TO JAVED, and IN MEMORIAM OF LATE MOTHER, all facing the original Urdu text.

6. **ABBAS, Yasir**, "POET OF THE EAST, ALLAMA IQBAL", *THE NATION* (Lahore), 27 September 1992.

7. **ABBASI, Muhammad Yusuf**, "THE POPPY LAMPS", *IQBAL REVIEW* 18, no. 4: January (1978): pp. 221-22.
    A free English rendering of Iqbal's inimitable chromatic lyric PHIR CHIRAGH-I LALAH SAY RAUSHAN HU-AY KOH-O DAMAN in his BAL-I JIBRIL.

8. ———, "SOME NEW FACTS ON IQBAL'S APPOINTMENT AS PROFESSOR OF PHILOSOPHY", *JOURNAL OF THE RESEARCH SOCIETY OF PAKISTAN* 14, no. 4: October (1977): pp. 35-40.

9. **ABBOTT, Freeland**, "VIEW OF DEMOCRACY AND THE WEST", *IQBAL: POET-*

PHILOSOPHER OF PAKISTAN, Hafeez MALIK (ed.), New Delhi / New York: Columbia University Press, 1971.

10. **'ABD-AL-RAHMAN, 'Azzam**, mon., *THE ETERNAL MESSAGE OF MUHAMMAD*, Caesar E. FARAH (tr. Arab./E), London, 1979

11. **ABDUL HAI**, mon., *IQBAL AND EDUCATION*, Karachi: Jamia Institute of Education, n.d.
132 pp.

12. ————, "THE MESSAGE OF IQBAL", *IQBAL: A CRITICAL STUDY*, Misbah-ul-Haq SIDDIQUI (ed.), Lahore: Farhan Publishers, 1977, pp. 9-15.
On Iqbal's poetic achievements, his role as a forerunner in the renaissance of Islam, and his involvement in politics and the genesis of Pakistan.

13. **ABDUL HAI, Muhammad**, "BENGALI TRANSLATIONS OF IQBAL AND HIS IMPACT ON BENGALI LITERATURE", *IQBAL REVIEW* 4, no. 1: April (1963): pp. 5-10.

14. **ABDUL HAI, Saiyed**, mon., *IQBAL: HIS CONTRIBUTION*, Dacca: Bureau of National Reconstruction, Government of East Pakistan, 1968. 24 pp.

15. **ABDUL HAKIM, Khalifa**, "ALLAMA MUHAMMAD IQBAL", *PAKISTAN QUARTERLY* 8, no. 2: Summer 1958 (1958): pp. 15-17.

16. ————, "THE CONCEPT OF LOVE IN RUMI AND IQBAL", *ISLAMIC CULTURE* (Hyderabad) 14, no. 3/4: July (1950): pp. 266-73.
Variant Issue ID.: April 1940.

17. ————, "CREATIVE EVOLUTION OF ISLAM", *THE CIVIL AND MILITARY GAZETTE*, 21 April 1953, pp. 1-2.

18. ————, "THE CREATIVE EVOLUTIONIST OF ISLAM", *THE CIVIL AND MILITARY GAZETTE* (Lahore), 21 April 1951, p. i-ii.
Iqbal Day Supplement.

19. ————, "IN MEMORIAM: ALLAMA IQBAL: THE POET-PHILOSOPHER OF THE

EAST", 23 April 1961, p. 1.

20. ———, "IQBAL AND THE MULLAH", *PAKISTAN TIMES*, 27 February 1977, p. 1. Rendered into English by A.G. ZAFAR.

21. ———, "IQBAL'S ATTEMPT AT CREATIVE SYNTHESIS", *IQBAL REVIEW* 13, no. 3: October (1972): pp. 17-23.

22. ———, "IQBAL'S ATTEMPTS AT CREATIVE SYNTHESIS", *PAKISTAN TIMES*, 21 April 1957, pp. 5, 7.

23. ———, "IQBAL'S CONCEPT OF LIFE", *PAKISTAN TIMES*, 20 April 1958, p. 2.

24. ———, mon., *ISLAM AND COMMUNISM*, Lahore: Institute of Islamic Culture, 1976

25. ———, "LETTER ON CONTRIBUTION OF IQBAL TOWARDS THE ACHIEVEMENT OF OUR INDEPENDENCE", *ISLAMIC LITERATURE* 3, no. 4 (1951): pp. 233-36.

26. ———, "RECONSTRUCTION OF RELIGIOUS THOUGHT IN ISLAM: IQBAL'S CONCEPT OF GOD", *PAKISTAN CALLING* 4, no. 2 (1951): pp. 18, 19.

27. ———, "RUMI, NIETZSCHE AND IQBAL", *IQBAL AS A THINKER - EIGHT ESSAYS BY EMINENT SCHOLARS*, Taj Muhammad KHAYAL (ed.), Lahore: Shaikh Muhammad Ashraf, 1944.
From the Quranic qualifications of *a poet* and *a prophet* the author looks for some fundamental concepts in 'the wealth of thoughts and imagery', as it is displayed in Iqbal's works. Iqbal is said to have redefined the concept of *khudi*, which used to have 'an evil odour in Islamic literature', and the traditional conceptions of *momin* (believer) and *taqdir* (predestination). These concepts of Iqbal are influenced by philosophies of both the East and the West, and more in particular by Rumi's mysticism and Nietzsche's philosophy of the Self.
The author aims to contradict the thesis that Iqbal is nothing but an echo of Rumi and Nietzsche, but elaborates on themes of Rumi and Nietzsche, on which Iqbal constructed his own novel ideas with regard to ethics, morality and belief.

28. ———, "SIGNIFICANCE OF LOVE IN IQBAL'S POETRY", *IQBAL REVIEW* [vol. ?], no. [?]: October (1952): pp. 1-48.

29. ———, "TIME AND SPACE IN IQBAL'S PHILOSOPHY", *PAKISTAN CALLING* 4, no. 8: 1 April (1951): pp. 8, 9.
Reprinted in *THE PAKISTAN TIMES*, 21 April 1951/52 (Iqbal Day Supplement).

30. **ABDUL HAQ**, "IQBAL'S CONCEPT OF SPIRITUAL DEMOCRACY", *IQBAL REVIEW* 27, no. 3: October-December (1986): pp. 63-72.

31. **ABDUL HAQ, A. F. M.**, "IQBAL AND INTERNATIONALISM", *IQBAL REVIEW* 3, no. 1: April (1962): pp. 1-5.
Nationalism hinders the development of a world community after the Muslim ideals of harmony and peace, without the limitations of territory, race, wealth, language, etc.

32. **ABDUL HUSSAIN**, "IMPACT OF IQBAL ON BENGALI MUSLIM THOUGHT", *IQBAL REVIEW* 1, no. 1: April (1960): pp. 54-62.

33. ———, "IMPACT OF IQBAL ON BENGALI MUSLIM THOUGHT", *MORNING NEWS* (Karachi), 21 August 1960.

34. ———, "IQBAL IN BENGALI", *MORNING NEWS*, 6 May 1962.

35. **ABDUL KARIM, al-Jilani**, "DOCTRINE OF ABSOLUTE UNITY", *INDIAN ANTIQUARY* (Bombay), 29 November 1900, pp. 237-46.

36. **ABDUL LATIF, Eshack**, "IQBAL: THE INTERNATIONAL POET AND PHILOSOPHER", *IQBAL: DURBARI IQBAL, STUDY GROUP*, 1946, pp. 15-27 [?].

37. **ABDUL LATIF, Sayyid**, "IQBAL AND WORLD ORDER", *OSMANIA MAGAZINE* (Hyderabad) 11, no. 5 (1938).
Published also in ISLAM 3, no.17: 7 Februari (1938), pp. 132-133.

38. ———, mon., *(IQBAL,) INFLUENCE OF ENGLISH LITERATURE ON URDU LITERATURE*, London: Forster Groom, 1924. 141 pp.
Cf. pp. 65, 74*f.*, 104, 110-114, 124, 126, 128, 132*f.*

39. **ABDUL QADRI**, "IQBAL: CONTRIBUTION TO SCIENCE", *DAWN*, 21 April 1966, p. 5.

40. **ABDULLAH, M.**, "IQBAL'S CRITICISM OF MODERNISM", *PAKISTAN TIMES*, 21

April 1916.

41. **ABDULLAH, S. M.**, "IQBAL AND THE ARAB WORLD", *THE PAKISTAN TIMES* (Rawalpindi), 9 November 1977.

42. ———, "IQBAL ON FINE ARTS: HIS THEORY OF AESTHETICS", *THE PAKISTAN TIMES* (Lahore), 21 April 1962, pp. 7-8.

43. ———, "IQBAL ON POETS AND POETRY", *PAKISTAN TIMES*, 21 April 1966, pp. 1, 3.

44. ———, "IQBAL'S CONCEPT OF EDUCATION", *PAKISTAN REVIEW* 7, no. [?]: July (1959): pp. 41.

45. ———, "IQBAL'S CRITICISM OF MODERNISM", *THE PAKISTAN TIMES* (Lahore), 21 April 1961, p. i-iii or 10 [?].
Iqbal Day Supplement.

46. ———, "NACHRUF AUF IQBAL", *MOSLEMISCHE REVUE* (Berlin) [vol. ?], no. [?]: August (1938): pp. 34.
G.

47. ———, "THE NATURE OF DANTE'S INFLUENCE ON IQBAL", *IQBAL REVIEW* 24, no. 1: April (1983): pp. 25-31.
Short article on the nature and extent of Iqbal's borrowings from Dante - in refutation of the assumption that Iqbal's JAVID NAMAH is merely an *imitation*.
Re-issued in [Various authors], *SELECTIONS FROM THE IQBAL REVIEW*, ed. Waheed Qureshi, Lahore, 1983, pp. 459-466.

48. ———, "POETIC ARTISTRY", *CIVIL AND MILITARY GAZETTE* (Lahore), 21 April 1961, p. 1.

49. ———, "SOME NON-MUSLIM ADMIRERS AND CRITICS OF IQBAL", *PAKISTAN TIMES*, 21 April 1977, p. 1.

50. ———, mon., *THE SPIRIT AND SUBSTANCE OF URDU PROSE UNDER THE INFLUENCE OF SIR SAYYID AHMED KHAN* , Muhammad IQBAL (foreword), Lahore:

Sheikh Muhammad Ashraf, 1940. 186 pp.

51. **ABDULLAH, Syed**, "THE NATURE OF DANTE'S INFLUENCE ON IQBAL", *PAKISTAN TIMES*, 11 November 1975, p. 1.

52. **ABID, Ali Abid Syed**, "BABA TAHIR URYAN AND IQBAL", *IQBAL* 5, no. 1: July (1956): pp. 54-81.

53. ———, "IQBAL WAS ESSENTIALLY PRIMARILY A POET", *THE CIVIL AND MILITARY GAZETTE* (Lahore), 21 April 1953, pp. 1, 8.
     Iqbal Day Supplement.

54. **ABID, Mahfooz Jan**, "IQBAL AND MATTHEW ARNOLD - A COMPARATIVE STUDY", *IQBAL REVIEW* 23, no. 3: October (1982): pp. 85-93.

55. **ABID, R. Rizvi**, "DR. MOHAMMAD IQBAL: HIS POETRY CAME TO EPITOMISE ASPIRATIONS OF MUSLIMS", *ILLUSTRATED WEEKLY OF PAKISTAN*, 26 April 1959, p. 12.

56. **ABIDINI SADIQIAN, Bano Maheen Mir**, "A LECTURE ON THE POLITICAL AND INDIVIDUAL ASPECTS OF IQBAL'S PHILOSOPHY", *IQBAL REVIEW* 9, no. 1: April (1968): pp. 46-56.

57. **ABRAMS, M. H.**, *THE MIRROR AND THE LAMP: ROMANTIC THEORY AND THE CRITICAL TRADITION*, New York: Oxford UP, 1953

58. **ADEEB**, "IQBAL'S CONCEPT OF PAKISTAN", *PAKISTAN TIMES*, 21 April 1975, p. 4.

59. **AFZAL, Muhammad**, "BIBLIOGRAPHY ON IQBAL, 1965-1975", University of Karachi.
     M.A. Library Science; Promoter: Anis Khurshid.

60. **'AFZAL, Muhammad**, "IQBAL AND THE SEPARATIST MOVEMENT", University of the Punjab, Dept. Political Science, 1952/1962. iii+38 pp.

61. **AFZAL, Muhammad**, "MY FIRST GLIMPSE OF THE POET", *PAKISTAN TIMES*

(Lahore), 21 April 1952, p. 7.

62. ———, "A SYNTHESIS OF BASIC CONCEPTS IN IQBAL'S PHILOSOPHY (A SYSTEMS APPROACH)", *IQBAL REVIEW* 27, no. 3: October-December (1986): pp. 45-61.

63. **AHANGAR, Muhammad Altaf H.**, "IQBAL'S VIEWS ON IJMA': LEGISLATIVE AND JUDICIAL TRENDS IN PAKISTAN", *ISLAMIC AND COMPARATIVE LAW REVIEW* 15, (1996): pp. 95-110.

64. **AHANGAR, Muhammad Altaf Hassan**, "IQBAL AND QUR'AN: A LEGAL PERSPECTIVE", *IQBAL REVIEW* 35, no. 3: October (1994): pp. 1-22.
As the editor noted (n. 110), the author's conclusion that *so far Iqbal's suggestion to identify foundational legal principles from the Qur'an has least impressed the legislators and jurists of the Muslim countries* (p. 17), is an understatement.

65. **AHANGAR, Muhammad Altaf Hussain**, "IQBAL AND HADITH: A LEGAL PERSPECTIVE", *IQBAL REVIEW* 37, no. 3: October (1996): pp. 89-110.   Special issue on the Reconstruction of Religious Thought in Islam.
Iqbal's negative attitude towards the Hadith as a source of law (because of the presence of contradictory traditions and the late (Abbasid) origin of non-Quranic Islamic law) is not generally followed in contemporary Muslim thought.

66. **AHANGAR, Muhammad Altaf Hussein**, "IQBAL'S THEORY OF IJMA': PERSPECTIVES AND PROSPECTS", *IQBAL REVIEW* 38, no. 1: April (1997): pp. 17-37.
On the relationship between Ijma' and Ummah, Ulama, and Ijtihad.

67. **AHMAD, Absar**, mon., *CONCEPT OF SELF AND SELF-IDENTITY IN CONTEMPORARY PHILOSOPHY: AN AFFIRMATION OF IQBAL'S DOCTRINE*, Lahore: Iqbal Academy, 1986

68. ———, "THE HEGELIAN KEY TO UNDERSTANDING IQBAL", *IQBAL REVIEW* 21, no. 3: October (1980): pp. 31-41.
The author offers a short survey of the Hegelian system of thought, without which, he states, the *quasi-Hegelian* position of Iqbal, both in his criticism of the cosmological argument and in his combined criticism of the ontological and theological arguments, is not intelligible.
Re-issued in [Various authors], *SELECTIONS FROM THE IQBAL REVIEW*, ed. Waheed

Qureshi, Lahore, 1983, pp. 57-67.

69.   ——, "A PLEA FOR PHILOSOPHY'S LIBERATION", *IQBAL REVIEW* 22, no. 3: October (1981): pp. 69-76.

70.   ——, "REFLECTIONS ON QUR'ANIC EPISTEMOLOGY", *IQBAL REVIEW* 25, no. 3: October (1984): pp. 9-24.

71.   **AHMAD, Aftab**, "IQBAL'S CONCEPT OF PAKISTAN", *JOURNAL OF THE REGIONAL CULTURAL INSTITUTE (Iran)* 9, no. 1-2 (1977): pp. 75-80.
According to Iqbal the necessity of a separate Muslim state was due to the dependance of the operation of Islam as a cultural force on its centralization in a specific territory. As such he saw it as the best solution to endemic Hindu-Muslim conflicts. The new country should modernize according to the principle of *ijtihad*, including the rebuilding of the *shari'a* according to modern thought and experience.

72.   **AHMAD, Afzal**, "IQBAL ON THE AIR", *MORNING NEWS* (Karachi), 9 November 1979.

73.   **AHMAD, Aziz**, "IQBAL AND THE RENAISSANCE", *ILLUSTRATED WEEKLY OF PAKISTAN* (Karachi) 4, no. 29: 20 April (1952).

74.   ——, "IQBAL ET LA THEORIE DU PAKISTAN", *REVUE ORIENT* 5 or 17 [?], no. 1 (1961).
F.

75.   ——, "IQBAL: PHILOSOPHER AND POLITICIAN", *DAWN*, 21 April 1948, p. 11.

76.   ——, "IQBAL'S ISLAMIC THOUGHT", *DAWN*, 21 April 1961, p. 7.

77.   ——, "IQBAL'S MESSAGE", *PAKISTAN TODAY* (Dacca) 5, no. 1-2 (1952): pp. 9-12.

78.   ——, "IQBAL'S VIEW ON ISLAMIC ARCHITECTURE", *ILLUSTRATED WEEKLY OF PAKISTAN*, 16 April 1950, p. 17.

79.   ——, mon., *ISLAMIC MODERNISM IN INDIA AND PAKISTAN, 1857-1964*, London: Oxford UP, 1967. 294 pp.

Cf. esp. pp. 123-174.

80. ———, "OUR DEBT TO IQBAL", *ILLUSTRATED WEEKLY OF PAKISTAN*, 22 April 1955, pp. 7-8, 29.

81. ———, "SOURCES OF IQBAL'S IDEA OF THE PERFECT MAN", *IQBAL* 7, no. 1: July (1958): pp. 1-17.

82. ———, "SOURCES OF IQBAL'S PERFECT MAN", *IQBAL* (Lahore) 7, no. 1: July (1958): pp. 1-17.
Variant date: 1968; Variant title: SOURCES OF IQBAL'S IDEA OF THE PERFECT MAN.
A study of the philosophical and literary sources of Iqbal's concept of *the Perfect Man*. 'Sometimes', the author concludes, 'Iqbal's *Perfect Man* is romanticised as *qalandar*, having something of the Sufi mystic and some romanesque elements of Nietzsche's *Also Sprach Zarathustra*, at other times he is *Mu'min*, the *Perfect Man* who has passed the three stages of mystical training, as explained by Jili in his *Insan al-Kamil*, and occasionally there is a glimpse of the Mephistophelian *Superman* in the individual'. The entire construction, however, of the edifice on top of which the *Perfect Man* is in communion with God, men and universe, is strongly Bergsonian.
This article was reproduced in SHEIKH, M. Saeed (ed.), *STUDIES IN IQBAL'S THOUGHT AND ART*, Lahore, 1972, pp. 107-124.

83. **AHMAD, Bashir**, "IQBAL WAS GHALIB INCARNATE", *THE PAKISTAN TIMES* (Rawalpindi), 9 November 1984.

84. ———, "VISION OF IQBAL", *THE PAKISTAN TIMES* (Rawalpindi), 9 November 1985.

85. **AHMAD, Doris**, mon., *IQBAL AS I KNEW HIM*, Lahore: Iqbal Academy, 1981/1986.

86. **AHMAD, H. B.**, "IQBAL'S ROLE IN THE FIELD OF EDUCATION", *WEST PAKISTAN*, May 1960, pp. 3-7.

87. **AHMAD, J. D.**, ed., *IQBAL IN SOME RECENT SPEECHES AND WRITINGS OF MR. M.A. JINNAH*, A. M. JINNAH (mon.), Vol. 2, Lahore: Sheikh Muhammad Ashraf, 1947

88. **AHMAD, J. U.**, "IQBAL IN ENGLISH", *ILLUSTRATED WEEKLY OF PAKISTAN*, 16 April 1950, p. 8.

Iqbal No.

89. **AHMAD, Jalal-ud-Din**, "IQBAL AND RENAISSANCE", *ILLUSTRATED WEEKLY OF PAKISTAN*, 20 April 1952, pp. 32-34.

90. ———, "SOME ENGLISH TRANSLATORS OF IQBAL", *THE CIVIL AND MILITARY GAZETTE* (Lahore), 21 April 1952.

91. **AHMAD, Jamil**, *HUNDRED GREAT MUSLIMS*, Karachi: Ferozsons, 1971. ii+716 pp. Iqbal biography on pp. 338-351.

92. **AHMAD, Jamil-ud-din**, mon., *IQBAL'S CONCEPT OF ISLAMIC POLITY*, Karachi: Pakistan Publications, 1968. 26 pp.

93. **AHMAD, Jamil-ud-Din**, "IQBAL'S VIEW OF ISLAMIC POETRY", *PAKISTAN TIMES*, 21 April 1968, pp. 1, 2.

94. **AHMAD, Javed**, "IQBAL AND HIS PHILOSOPHY", *THE MUSLIM* (Islamabad), 21 April 1984.

95. **AHMAD, Kalimuddin**, "IQBAL'S CONCEPTION OF ART", *IQBAL AS A THINKER - EIGHT ESSAYS BY EMINENT SCHOLARS*, Taj Muhammad KHAYAL (ed.), Lahore: Shaikh Muhammad Ashraf, 1944, pp. 249-66.
This essay analyses Iqbal's conception of art, starting from the dualism between the (creative) artist and the critic. Iqbal is said to have belonged to the first of these categories, although his views on *art* are inseperably connected with his philosophy. This philosophy, heralding personal freedom, is quintessential to the creative spirit of an artist. To Iqbal, the artistic value of poetry lies in the fact that it transcends the philosophical substratum underneath it. Although he used poetry as a medium of expression, Iqbal didn't want to be called a mere *poet* as such. The essay concludes with a reference to the western concept of art, as laid down in Shelley's *Defence of Poetry*.

96. **AHMAD, Khalid**, "ALLAMA IQBAL IN THE SOVIET UNION", *PAKISTAN TIMES*, August 1977, p. 1.

97. ———, "THE PRINCIPLE OF MOVEMENT AND THE PHILOSOPHY OF THE EGO IN IQBAL - IQBAL DAY IN TUNESIA, SPEECH", *IQBAL REVIEW* 10, no. 1: April (1967): pp. 75-90.

98.   **AHMAD KHAN, Hameed**, mon., *BIOGRAPHY OF IQBAL*, Karachi, 1960

99.   **AHMAD KHAN, Hamid**, "HOW IQBAL COMPOSED 'THE MESSAGE OF THE EAST' (PAYAM-I-MASHRIQ)", *IQBAL* 21, no. 1: January-March (1974): pp. 1-12.

100.   ———, "IS IQBAL A 'PAROCHIAL' POET?", *CIVIL AND MILITARY GAZETTE* (Lahore), 21 April 1961, p. 1.

101.   ———, "THE UNIVERSAL NOTE IN IQBAL'S POETRY", *IQBAL* 43, no. 4: October (1996): pp. 25-44.

102.   **AHMAD KHAN, Jaliluddin**, "IQBAL AS A POET WITH A MESSAGE TO THE MODERN WORLD", *IQBAL REVIEW* 4, no. 1: April (1963): pp. 85-94.

103.   **AHMAD KHAN, Mushtaq**, "MAN AND HIS MESSAGE", *THE CIVIL AND MILITARY GAZETTE* (Lahore), 21 April 1960, p. 5.

104.   ———, "POET WHO PREDICTED THIS WAR: IQBAL, THE MAN AND HIS MESSAGE", *BOMBAY CHRONICLE*, 20 April 1941, p. 3.

105.   **AHMAD, Khawaja Jamil**, "IQBAL'S CONCEPTION OF PERFECT MAN", *CIVIL AND MILITARY GAZETTE* (Lahore), 21 April 1952.

106.   ———, "NATIONALISM IN IQBAL'S POETRY", *SIND OBSERVER*, 20 April 1952.

107.   **AHMAD, Khurshid**, "THE FRUSTRATED MAN, A REJOINDER TO A WESTERN CRITIC OF IQBAL", *IQBAL REVIEW* 4, no. 1: April (1963): pp. 95-102. Variant title: ... TO THE WESTERN CRITIC ...

108.   ———, "AN INTRODUCTION TO THE THOUGHT OF IQBAL", *IQBAL REVIEW* 2, no. 3: October (1961): pp. 133. Review of Luce Claude Maitre's *INTRODUCTION TO THE THOUGHT OF IQBAL* (tr. by M.A.M. Dar), Karachi, 1961.

109.   ———, "IQBAL AND HIS MISSION", *DAWN* , 21 April 1962.

110.   ———, "IQBAL AND HYDERABAD (DECCAN)", *IQBAL REVIEW* 2, no. 3: October (1961): pp. 134.

Review of Nazar Hyderabadi, *IQBAL AUR HYDERABAD*, Karachi: Iqbal Academy, n.d.

111. ———, "IQBAL AND MUSLIM RENAISSANCE", *DAWN*, 21 April 1957.

112. ———, "IQBAL AND THE ISLAMIC AIMS OF EDUCATION", *IQBAL REVIEW* 2, no. 3: October (1961): pp. 51-70.

113. ———, "IQBAL AND THE MODERN RENAISSANCE OF ISLAM", *IQBAL REVIEW* 3, no. 1: April (1962): pp. 58-64.

114. ———, "IQBAL AND THE RECONSTRUCTION OF ISLAMIC LAW", *IQBAL REVIEW* 1, no. 1: April (1960): pp. 63-90.
A historical survey of the decline of Muslim law and the difficulties in importing foreign juridical concepts into Islamic societies, is followed by a more or less detailed description of Iqbal's contribution to the renaissance of Islamic law, through his innovative ideas about *Ijtihad* and *Ijma'*, as set forth a.o. in (I) THE RECONSTRUCTION OF ISLAMIC THOUGHT (6th lecture). *The idea of a higher law based on Revelation, eternal and providing the possibilities of growth and evolution, is the most fundamental element of Iqbal's legal philosophy*, the author concludes - *the juristic implications of which are: (1) that 'Law' has its real sanction in this ultimate and higher Law, which is objective and realistic, (2) that the society and state are only political and legal organisations affected for the purpose of the implementation of the higher Law, (3) that an International law, regulating and guiding the different legal orders prevailing in different Nation-States is possible, and (4) that the totalitarian consequences of the Hegelian doctrine of law can be avoided, for (...) the state will be obeyed only as long as it follows the higher Law.*
Re-issued in [Various authors], *SELECTIONS FROM THE IQBAL REVIEW*, ed. Waheed Qureshi, Lahore, 1983, pp. 155-182.

115. ———, "IQBAL ON THE RECONSTRUCTION OF ISLAMIC LAW", *AL-ISLAM*, 15 August 1960, p. 128.

116. ———, "LAST TWO YEARS OF IQBAL", *IQBAL REVIEW* 2, no. 3: October (1961): pp. 134.
Review of *Iqbal Ke Aakhiri do Sal* by Dr. Ashiq Husain Batalavi, Karachi: Iqbal Academy, 1961. A penetrating study of Muslim politics between 1919 and 1938 and Iqbal's role therein.

117. ———, "THE REAL SIGNIFICANCE OF IQBAL", *VOICE OF ISLAM* (Karachi), November 1956, pp. 494-498.

Also published in *MUSLIM NEWS*, 29 June 1962, pp. 6, 7.

118. ———, "STRAY REFLECTIONS", *IQBAL REVIEW* 2, no. 3: October (1961): pp. 130-133.
Review of STRAY REFLECTIONS, ed. by Dr. Javid Iqbal, Lahore, 1961.

119. **AHMAD, Khwaja Jamil**, "IQBAL'S CONCEPTION OF PERFECT MAN", *CIVIL AND MILITARY GAZETTE* (Lahore), 21 April 1952.

120. **AHMAD, M. Aziz**, "IQBAL'S POLITICAL THEORY", *IQBAL AS A THINKER - EIGHT ESSAYS BY EMINENT SCHOLARS*, Various authors (mon.), Lahore: Shaikh Muhammad Ashraf, 1944, pp. 211-45.
Analysis of Iqbal's reflections on *khudi* (the self) in relation to *millat* (society), with *tauhid* (monotheism) as a binding factor. The author stresses the fact that Iqbal was wholeheartedly a *muslim* thinker, pleading for a *millat* based on pure muslim ideas and doctrines: *Iqbal is the mind, and Jinnah is the heart of Muslim India*.

121. **AHMAD, M. B.**, "RUMI (1207-1273) AND IQBAL", *ISLAMIC REVIEW AND ARAB AFFAIRS* 40, no. [?]: April (1952): pp. 31-37.

122. **AHMAD, M. Bashir**, mon., *RUMI & IQBAL*, Lahore, 1952

123. **AHMAD, M. M.**, "IQBAL'S APPRECIATIVE SELF", *IQBAL REVIEW* 2, no. 3: October (1961): pp. 14-17.

124. **AHMAD, M. Nisar**, "VINDICATION OF SIR M. IQBAL'S STATE: FINALITY OF MUHAMMAD'S PROPHETHOOD", *ISLAM* 2, no. 3: 7 July, no. 4: 22 July, and no. 5: 7 August (1936): pp. 22-23, 30-31 and 38-40 resp.
Three parts.

125. **AHMAD, Manzooruddin**, "IQBAL'S THEORY OF MUSLIM COMMUNITY AND ISLAMIC UNIVERSALISM", *THE PAKISTAN TIMES* (Rawalpindi), 9 November 1977.
Discussion of the Iqbalian concept of *millat*, its philosophical and political implications, its link with *Muslim universalism* and both Sayyid Ahmad Khan's and Iqbal's role within the Muslim Renaissance, leading through a re-vitalisation of Muslim philsophy in the Indian subcontinent towards the two-nation theory. With quotations from Iqbal, both in the original and in English rendering.
This article was also published in *IQBAL REVIEW* 23, no. 3: October (1982), pp. 111-132, and later re-issued in [Various authors], *SELECTIONS FROM THE IQBAL REVIEW*, ed.

Waheed Qureshi, Lahore, 1983, pp. 133-154.

126. **AHMAD, Manzur**, "THE LOGICAL DISCREPANCIES OF LOGICAL POSITIVISM", *IQBAL REVIEW* 1, no. 3: October (1960): pp. 58-74.

127. ———, "METAPHYSICS OF PERSIA AND IQBAL", *IQBAL REVIEW* (Karachi) 12, no. 3: October (Iran issue: published on the occasion of the celebration of the 2500th anniversary of the Iranian Monarchy) (1971): pp. 100-117. After a brief introduction, in which *Muslim philosophy* or *Arabic philosophy* is identified as merely *the metaphysics of Persia*, the author analyses Iqbal's two main philosophical works, i.e. THE DEVELOPMENT OF METAPHYSICS IN PERSIA and THE RECONSTRUCTION OF RELIGIOUS THOUGT IN ISLAM, with the aim of finding out whether or not there has been a substantial change in the philosophy of Iqbal from his earlier to his later period. *The assertion, the author concludes, that Iqbal's later philosophy is opposed to his former ideas, breaks down to a difference between two languages, and not between two ontologies.* Failure to identify the so-called 'Persian mysticism' with Iqbalian thought, is reportedly due to (1) failure to see that moral necessities can be safeguarded without necessarily linking them to spiritualistic metaphysics, and (2) not realising that both systems speak a different language altogether. And: *Since the facts these languages are referring to when they present a metaphysics are not verifiable in the same way in which common everyday language statements are verified, delineation of the meaning of the two is a difficult task, and cannot be achieved unless a bigger perspective of the Islamic religion is kept in view, about which Iqbal is concerned in both his former and in his later philosophy.*
Re-issued in [Various authors], *SELECTIONS FROM THE IQBAL REVIEW*, ed. Waheed Qureshi, Lahore, 1983, pp. 69-85.

128. ———, "MODERN CHALLENGES TO RELIGION", *IQBAL REVIEW* 3, no. 1: April (1962): pp. 6-16.
Philosophical approaches to the endangered position of religion in the modern world, in comparison with Iqbal's Reconstruction of Religious Thought in Islam. The author focuses on the impact of philosophy, psychology and socio-economic systems.

129. ———, "RELIGION IN THE LIGHT OF THE PHILOSOPHY OF SELF", *IQBAL REVIEW* 2, no. 1: April (1961): pp. 90-104.

130. ———, "SCIENTIFIC EXPOSITION OF IQBAL", *DAWN* (Karachi), 20 April 1960. An open letter in reply to Dr. Muhammad Rafiuddin's letter on the same subject in *DAWN* of 2 April 1960.

131. **AHMAD, Mian Bashir**, "IQBAL, HIS LIFE, ART AND THOUGHT", *AL-ISLAM* (Karachi) 3, no. 9-10-11 (n.d.): pp. 71-72, 84-88 and 96 resp.

132. ———, "IQBAL'S CONCEPT OF SATAN", *MORNING NEWS*, April 1959. Variant newspaper name: DAWN.

133. ———, "IQBAL'S POLITICAL THEORY", *ISLAMIC CULTURE* (Hyderabad) 18, no. 4 (1944): pp. 377-93. Variant title: IQBAL'S POLITICAL IDEAS.

134. ———, "RUMI AND IQBAL", *ISLAMIC REVIEW* (Woking) 11, no. 4: April (1952). Text of an address delivered on the occasion of the death anniversary of Rumi and Iqbal at the Ankara University, 1952. Also published in *DAWN* (Karachi), 21 April 1959.

135. ———, mon., *RUMI AND IQBAL*, Ankara: Press Office, Embassy of Pakistan, 1952. 72 pp.

136. ———, "RUMI AND IQBAL: A MEDIEVAL AND A MODERN PHILOSOPHER POET", *ISLAMIC REVIEW* 40, no. 4 (1952): pp. 31-37.

137. ———, "RUMI'S INFLUENCE ON IQBAL", *ILLUSTRATED WEEKLY OF PAKISTAN*, 16 April 1950, p. 13.

138. **AHMAD, Mohammad Aziz**, "EVOLUTION OF POLITICAL PHILOSOPHY OF IQBAL", *DAWN* (Karachi), 9 November 1977.

139. **AHMAD, Muhammad Aziz**, "INTRODUCING IQBAL'S ISLAMIC THOUGHT", *MUSLIM WORLD DIGEST* 1, no. 1: October-December (1961): pp. 81-85.

140. ———, "IQBAL AND THE INDIVIDUAL", *DAWN*, 21 April 1974, p. 7.

141. ———, mon., *IQBAL AND THE RECENT EXPOSITION OF ISLAMIC POLITICAL THOUGHT*, Abdul RASHID (preface), Lahore: Sheikh Muhammad Ashraf, 1965. viii+64 pp. Earlier editions (1930 and/or 1950) included 57 (or even 196 [?]) pp.; apart from the 1977 ed. (Lahore: Sheikh Muhammad Ashraf), there appeared also a re-edition of this

monography on Iqbal and Islamic politics in Chicago (Kazi Publications), n.d.

142.　————, "IQBAL'S STUDY OF ISLAM", *DAWN*, 22 April 1962.

143.　**AHMAD, Naeem**, "THE EDUCATIONAL AND SCIENTIFIC SIGNIFICANCE OF THE IDEA OF RESURRECTION IN IQBAL", *IQBAL* (Lahore) 36, no. 3 (1989): pp. 17-24.

144.　————, "IQBAL'S CONCEPT OF ETERNITY", *IQBAL REVIEW* 18, no. 1: April (1977): pp. 1-18.
A short survey of the concept of time throughout man's philosophical history, from Zeno, over classical metaphysics and Newtonian science to Einstein's three-dimensionality, brings the author to a brief analysis of the latter concept, and from there to Iqbal's concept of *Ultimate Reality*, a *Self* who expresses Himself in the laws and behaviour of Nature sempeternally.
Re-issued in [Various authors], *SELECTIONS FROM THE IQBAL REVIEW*, ed. Waheed Qureshi, Lahore, 1983, pp. 25-42.

145.　————, "IQBAL'S CONCEPT OF THE ULTIMATE REALITY", *IQBAL REVIEW* 37, no. 3: October (1996): pp. 59-66.
Special issue on the Reconstruction of Religious Thought in Islam.

146.　————, "THE MIND-BODY PROBLEM AND IQBAL'S POINT OF VIEW", *IQBAL REVIEW* 22, no. 3: October (1981): pp. 33-42.

147.　**AHMAD, Nazir**, "I KNEW IQBAL", *PAKISTAN REVIEW* 19, no. 5 (1971): pp. 5-8, 42.

148.　**AHMAD, Pirzade Muzaffar**, *RAZ-I BEKHUDI*, Delhi, 1918.
Critical of Iqbal's ASRAR-I KHUDI, itself rebutted by Maulana Aslam JAIRAJPURI's article in *AL-NAZIR* (Lucknow), February 1919, reprinted in *THE JAUHAR*, Iqbal No. (Delhi).

149.　**AHMAD, Riaz**, mon., *IQBAL'S LETTERS TO QUAID-I-AZAM: AN ANALYSIS*, SHARIF AL MUJAHID (intr.), Lahore: Friends Educational Service / Quaid-i-Azam Academy, 1976. 68 pp.

150.　**AHMAD, S. F.**, "REVIEW OF 'PAYAM-E-MASHRIQ IN CZECH'", *THE ISLAMIC CULTURE* (Hyderabad, Deccan) 37, no. 1: January (1963).

151. **AHMAD, Saeed**, "IQBAL AND DEPICTION OF NATURE", *THE PAKISTAN TIMES* (Rawalpindi), 1 July 1977, p. 1.

152. ———, "IQBAL AND THE PAKISTAN MOVEMENT", *PERSPECTIVE: A MONTHLY DIGEST PUBLISHED IN PAKISTAN* (Karachi) 4, no. 10 (1971): pp. 5-8.

153. **AHMAD, Sh. Ejaz**, "ALLAMAH IQBAL'S DATE OF BIRTH", *IQBAL* 21, no. 1: January (1974): pp. 51-74.

154. **AHMAD, Shaikh Mahmood**, "INVOCATION", *ISLAMIC CULTURE* (Hyderabad, Deccan) 22, no. 4 (1940/1948): pp. 343-54.
English translation of the first 25 pages of (I) JAVID NAMAH.

155. **AHMAD, Shaikh Mahmud**, tr. P/E, *THE PILGRIMAGE OF ETERNITY* (JAVID NAMAH), Justice S. A. RAHMAN (intr.), Lahore: Institute of Islamic Culture / Bazm-i-Iqbal, 1961. xxv+187 pp.
English verse translation of (I) JAVID NAMA, also published by Kazi Publications (Chicago, 1985).

156. **AHMAD SYED**, "HALI, AKBAR AND IQBAL", *MORNING NEWS*, 16 April 1961.

157. **AHMAD, Syed Hasan**, mon., *IQBAL, HIS POLITICAL IDEAS AT CROSSROADS*, Aligarh, 1979.
Contains reproductions of nine letters of Iqbal, written to Prof. Edward J. Thompson of Oxford University during 1933-34, provided with 68 pages of commentary on these and other letters as well as on Iqbal's speeches and statements. This book is reviewed by SHERWANI, Latif Ahmed, in *IQBAL REVIEW* 24, no. 1: April (1983), pp. 45-48.

158. **AHMAD, Z.**, "RELATIONSHIP BETWEEN EAST AND WEST IN IQBAL'S THOUGHTS", *ISLAMIC REVIEW AND ARAB AFFAIRS* 54, no. [?]: October (1966): pp. 13-16.

159. **AHMAR, Yunus**, "AFGHANISTAN IN IQBAL'S POETRY", *MORNING NEWS* (Karachi), 9 November 1985.

160. **AHMED, A. & KAZIR C.**, "WOMAN THERE WAS", *NATION* (New York) 207, (1968): pp. 474.

Engish translation of a poem.

161. **AHMED, Aftab**, "DISCERNING STUDY OF IQBAL'S POETRY BY FAIZ", *DAWN* (Karachi), 24 April 1987.

162. ———, "IQBAL'S CONCEPT OF A MUSLIM HOMELAND", *DAWN* (Karachi), 9 November 1987.

163. **AHMED, Aziz**, mon., *STUDIES IN ISLAMIC CULTURE IN THE INDIAN ENVIRONMENT*, Lahore: Oxford U.P., 1970

164. **AHMED, G.**, "PRAYER", *U.N. WORLD* 4, (1950): pp. 59.
      English translation of the poem "Prayer" from Iqbal's JAVID NAMAH.

165. **AHMED, Latif**, "PAKISTAN AND IQBAL'S POLITICAL VIEWS", *THE PAKISTAN TIMES* (Rawalpindi), 9 November 1977.

166. **AHMED, Munir D.**, "IQBAL ALS POLITISCHER DENKER", *MUHAMMAD IQBAL UND DIE DREI REICHE DES GEISTES*, Wolfgang KOEHLER (ed.), Hamburg: Deutsch-Pakistanisches Forum, 1977, pp. 227-48.
      Followed by a summary in English: IQBAL AND HIS POLITICAL PHILOSOPHY, pp. 249-256.
      G-E.

167. **AHMED, Nazir**, "MEMORIES OF A NEIGHBOUR", *THE PAKISTAN TIMES* (Rawalpindi), 8 November 1981.

168. ———, "PAINTINGS ON THEMES OF IQBAL", *PAKISTAN TIMES*, 2 September 1977, p. 1.

169. **AHMED, Rizwan**, "IQBAL AND QUAID-I-AZAM: GIANTS OF THOUGHT AND ACTION", *DAWN* (Karachi), 9 November 1977.

170. **AHSAN, A. Shakoor**, "IQBAL ON MUSLIM FRATERNITY", *IQBAL REVIEW* 25, no. 1: April (1984): pp. 1-20.

171. ———, "IQBAL'S GROWING IMAGE IN IRAN", *JOURNAL OF THE RESEARCH*

SOCIETY OF PAKISTAN (Lahore) 21, no. 1: January (1984): pp. 39-58.

172. **AHSAN, 'Abd-ash-Shakoor**, mon., *AN APPRECIATION OF IQBAL'S THOUGHT AND ART*, Lahore: Research Society of Pakistan, University of the Punjab, 1985. 260 pp.

173. **AHSAN, 'Abdul Shakoor**, "IQBAL AND NATURE", *PAKISTAN TIMES*, 21 April 1953, pp. 5, 6, 7.

174. **AHSAN, 'Abdul Shakur**, "WESTERN IMPERIALISM AS HE (IQBAL) SAW IT", *PAKISTAN TIMES* (Lahore), 21 April 1952, p. 8.

175. **AHSAN, Abdush Shakur**, "THE ALLAMA'S GROWING POPULARITY IN IRAN", *PAKISTAN TIMES*, 21 April 1957, pp. 5, 7.

176. ———, "WESTERN IMPERIALISM AS HE SAW IT", *PAKISTAN TIMES*, 21 April 1952, p. 8.

177. **AHSAN, Ali**, "GLEANINGS FROM IQBAL", *MAHMIL* 4, no. 1: November (1942).

178. ———, "IQBAL AND ART", *MAHMIL* 4, no. 1: November (1942).

179. ———, "IQBAL'S IDEAS GIVE RISE TO PAKISTAN AND LITERARY MOVEMENTS", *MORNING NEWS*, 22 November 1954.

180. **AHSAN, Mumtaz Hasan**, "SIDE-LIGHTS ON IQBAL: IQBAL AS A MAN", *PAKISTAN CALLING* 6, no. 8 (1952): pp. 8-9.

181. **AHSAN, Sayyid Ali**, "POETRY AND PHILOSOPHY IN IQBAL", *IQBAL REVIEW* 1, no. 3: October (1960): pp. 21-25.

182. **AHSAN, Shakoor**, "IQBAL'S CONCEPT OF KHUDI", *JOURNAL OF THE RESEARCH SOCIETY OF PAKISTAN* 20, no. 4: October (1983): pp. 51-66.

183. **AHSAN, Shakur**, "ALLAMA'S GROWING POPULARITY IN ISLAM", *PAKISTAN TIMES* (Lahore), 21 April 1957, p. 7.

184. ———, "DR. SIR MUHAMMAD IQBAL: THE POET PHILOSOPHER OF THE

EAST", *N. W. R. MAGAZINE* 2, no. 4 (1950): pp. 11, 12.

185. ———, "A FEW SYMBOLS IN IQBAL'S POETRY", *PAKISTAN TIMES* (Lahore), 21 April 1961, p. 5.
Iqbal Day Supplement.

186. ———, "INTUITION AND INTELLECT IN IQBAL'S POETRY", *PAKISTAN TIMES* (Lahore), 21 April 1951, p. 8.

187. ———, "IQBAL AND NATURE", *IQBAL REVIEW* 13, no. 3: October (1972): pp. 24-32.

188. ———, "IQBAL'S MUSINGS ON KASHMIR", *PAKISTAN TIMES* (Lahore), 21 April 1960, p. 7.

189. ———, "ROMANTIC ELEMENT IN IQBAL'S POETRY", *THE CIVIL AND MILITARY GAZETTE* (Lahore), 21 April 1960, p. 5.

190. ———, "STYLE OF IQBAL'S PERSIAN POETRY", *PAKISTAN TIMES*, 21 April 1962, pp. 7, 8.

191. **AHSAN, Syed Ali**, "THE PROBLEM OF TRANSLATING IQBAL IN BENGALI", *IQBAL, THE POET OF TOMORROW*, Khawaja Abdur RAHIM (ed.), Lahore: Abdul Hameed Khan at Ferozsons Ltd., n.d., pp. 261[263]-267.
Paper read at Lahore on 21 April 1963. After a brief historical introduction of the history of translating literature into Bengali, the author focuses onto the case of rendering Iqbal into Bengali, mentioning Ashraf Ali Khan, Mohd. Shahidullah, Sultan Aminuddin Ahmed and Mizanur Rahman. A second aspect is the connection which Iqbal's (translated) poetry established between Islamic ideology and the emotions and feelings of ordinary life. The author further mentions the approach of (Kavi) Ghulam Mustafa, Abdul Huq, Kazi Akram Hussain and Syed Abdul Mannan: *words to them seem to convey the meaning and the meaning is the meaning of the words only*, or, *in their renderings of Iqbal we do not get projections of the poet's sense-impressions, but only literal reproductions* (p. 267).

192. ———, "RELIGION AND POETRY IN IQBAL", *IQBAL REVIEW* 3, no. 3: October (1962): pp. 6-10.

193. **AHUJA, Y. D.**, "EARLY YEARS OF SHAYKH IQBAL'S LIFE", *ISLAMIC CULTURE*

30, no. 2 (1989).

194. **AJJI**, "A STUDY OF RUMI AND IQBAL", *ISLAMIC REVIEW AND ARAB AFFAIRS* 46, no. [?]: April (1958).

195. **AJMAL, Mohammad**, "MEANING OF PRAYER IN IQBAL", *THE PAKISTAN TIMES* (Rawalpindi), 9 November 1977.

196. **AJMAL, Muhammad**, "IQBAL AND MYSTICISM", *IQBAL REVIEW / IQBALIAT* (Lahore) 29, no. 3: October-December (1988): pp. 11-29.
Short search for an explanation of Iqbal's *ambivalence* towards Sufism in general, and Rumi in particular.

197. ———, "THE POET'S ATTITUDE TOWARDS KNOWLEDGE", *PAKISTAN TIMES* (Lahore), 21 April 1953, pp. 5, 6.

198. ———, "TWO KINDS OF THINKING IN IQBAL'S PHILOSOPHY", *IQBAL REVIEW* 30-31, no. 3: October - 1: April (1989-1990): pp. 59-75.

199. **AKBAR, M.**, "IQBAL: A VIEW", *PAKISTAN REVIEW* 7, no. [?]: October (1959): pp. 33.

200. **AKHTAR, Abdul Hafeez**, comp./ed., *ANALYTICAL CATALOGUE OF BOOKS ON ALLAMA MOHAMMAD IQBAL, 1877-1977*, Karachi: Department of Libraries, Ministry of Education, 1978. iii+97+182 pp.
A catalogue containing seperate English and Urdu parts, each covering works in different languages. Author, title and topical indexes follow both parts.
Published on the occasion of the Iqbal Birthday Centenary Celebrations 1977.

201. **AKHTAR, Hassan**, "ALLAMA IQBAL AND COUNCIL OF STATE AINAH-I-AJAM", *IQBAL REVIEW* 25, no. 3: October (1984): pp. 47-48.

202. **AKHTAR, Muhammad**, "BIBLIOGRAPHY OF BOOKS IN PRINT, APRIL 1993 TO DECEMBER 1994", *IQBAL REVIEW* 36, no. 1: April (1995): pp. 135-43.
Bibliography of English, Persian and especially Urdu books on Iqbal.

203. **AKHTAR, Saleem**, "HERBERT READ ON DR. IQBAL", *IQBAL REVIEW* 24, no. 1: April (1983): pp. 33-37.
Originally published as "READERS AND WRITERS", in *THE NEW AGE*, 25 August

1921.

204. **AKHTAR, Shameem**, "IQBAL'S CONCEPT OF A NEW WORLD ORDER", *PAKISTAN HORIZON* 30, no. 3-4 (1977): pp. 65.

205. **AKHTAR-UN-NISA**, ed., *INDEX OF QUARTERLY IQBAL*, Lahore: Bazm-e-Iqbal, 1994. 210 pp.

206. **AKHTAR, Waheed**, "EXISTENTIALIST ELEMENTS IN IQBAL'S THOUGHT", *IQBAL COMMEMORATIVE VOLUME*, Ali Sardar JAFRI & K.S. DUGGAL (eds.), New Delhi: All India Iqbal Centenary Celebrations Committee, 1977, pp. 103-18.
Iqbal's philosophy reconciles existentialism with a radical new idealism. He made an attempt to reconstruct religious thought in Islam from the existentialist viewpoint before the advent of the new existentialist philosophy of religion (p. 116). The author holds that, though it seems not justifiable to regard Iqbal as an *existentialist in the technical sense of the term*, his philosophy combined *the religious insight of theistic existentialism with the social and historical awareness of humanistic existentialism* (ibid.).

207. **AKS, Ameena**, "IQBAL: A PERSONAL APPRECIATION", *WEEKEND REVIEW* 2, no. 20: 20 April (1968): pp. 15-16.

208. **AL-'ATTAS, Sayyid Muhammad al-Naquib**, "SOME REFLECTIONS ON THE PHILOSOPHICAL ASPECT OF IQBAL'S THOUGHT", *IQBAL REVIEW* 37, no. 3: October (1996): pp. 67-71.   Special issue of
the Reconstruction of Religious Thought in Islam.
Address given at the International Congress, Lahore.

209. **AL-HABROUK, Mohammad Aly**, "MOHAMMAD IQBAL", *IQBAL REVIEW* 8, no. 1: April (1967): pp. 104-8.
This is the English version of the article which appeared in the weekly column "Islamic Personalities" in the daily *AL-GOMHOURIA* on 3 June 1966; the English version was supplied by the Pakistan Embassy, Cairo.

210. **AL-HAMZA**, "THE POET OF FREEDOM", *PAKISTAN TIMES*, 21 April 1961, p. 4.

211. **Al-Islam** (red.[?]), "IQBAL AND THE WEST", *AL-ISLAM*, 15 June 1929, p. 89.

212. **AL-ZIYYAT, Ahmad Hasan**, "IQBAL - THE POET OF ISLAM", *IQBAL REVIEW* 10, no. 1: April (1969): pp. 40-42.

A free English translation of an Arabic article published in *MAJALLA AL-AZHAR*, September 1967.

213. **ALAM, M. Jehangir**, "TWO UNPUBLISHED LETTERS OF IQBAL", *IQBAL REVIEW* 24, no. 1: April (1983): pp. 43-46.
Letters to Mr. M.A. Jinnah (Punjab Provincial Muslim League), dated 8 December 1936 and 13 August 1937, the originals of which are reproduced on pp. 45-46.

214. **ALAVI, Khalid**, "IQBAL AND SUFISM", *IQBAL REVIEW / IQBALIAT* (Lahore) 29, no. 3: October-December (1988): pp. 79-88.
Short paper, delivered at a one day seminar on Iqbal and Mysticism (University of Birmingham, 7 November 1987) on Iqbal's standpoint towards *Tasawwuf* (mysticism), his regarding it both *an experience* and *knowledge*, and his two-fold critcism of mysticism, viz. (1) his critique on *those who cause passivity and create inactiveness among the Muslims* (*"A Sufi [should be] a creative and active agent of Divine will"*), and (2) his critique on the loss of the role of Sufi orders and institutions as centres for spiritual training and purification (*Khanqah*), due to the collaboration of Sufis with the political establishment.

215. **ALAVI, Waris**, "IQBAL AND THE PRICE OF A PHILOSOPHER'S STONE", *IQBAL COMMEMORATIVE VOLUME*, Ali Sardar DUGGAL K. S. JAFRI (eds.), New Delhi: All India Iqbal Centenary Celebrations Committee, 1977, pp. 133-43.
The author criticizes Iqbal's option to write his poetry in Persian in order to disseminate his message to the wide Islamic world. *His romantic sensibility, his sensitiveness to the phenomenological world around, his existential exuberance and his rebellious joy and revolutionary zeal, which gave us our richest legacy, his Urdu poetry, are subdued in his Persian works by the narrow concerns of asectarian leader* (p. 135). Contrary to common opinion, which holds Iqbal's *Javed Nama* to be his masterpiece, the author considers it a failure.

216. **ALEXANDROV, Y.**, tr., *VERSES OF INDIAN POETS*, Moscow, 1956.
Translation of M. IQBAL's poem *The Sun*.

217. **ALI, Abdullah Yusuf**, "THE DOCTRINE OF HUMAN PERSONALITY IN IQBAL'S POETRY", *ESSAYS BY DIVERSE HANDS*, St. John ERVINE (ed.), London: Oxford UP, 1940, Vol. XVIII, pp. 89-105.
This article was re-issued in *TRANSACTIONS OF THE ROYAL SOCIETY OF LITERATURE OF THE U.K.* (NS) 18, 1941, pp. 89-105.

218. **ALI, Ahmad**, "AND OTHER WORLDS BEYOND", *DAWN* (Karachi), 21 April 1949.

English translation of the (I) poem SITARON SE AGE JAHAN AWAR BHI HAIM.

219.　　——, "IQBAL: A PAKISTANI VIEW", *ILLUSTRATED WEEKLY OF INDIA* 95, no. 34: 20 October (1974): pp. 15-19.

220.　　——, "THE POET AND THE CANDLE", *DAWN* (Karachi), 21 April 1948. English translation of part of (I) SHAMA AUR SHA'IR.

221.　　**ALI ASGHAR, Hikmat,** "TRIBUTE FROM THE LAND OF HAFIZ", *PAKISTAN TIMES* (Lahore), 22 April 1947, p. 4.
Text of speeches delivered by Ali Asghar Hikmat, leader of the Iranian delegation, while presenting a carpet for Iqbal's tomb on 17 April 1947.

222.　　**ALI, Ch. Muhammad,** "HOW TO RELEASE [THE] SPIRIT OF THE EAST?", *IQBAL: A CRITICAL STUDY*, Misbah-ul-Haq SIDDIQUI (mon.), Lahore: Farhan Publishers, 1977, pp. 67-86.
This article by the former Prime Minister of Pakistan, taken from *THE CIVIL AND MILITARY GAZETTE* (Iqbal Day Supplement, 1962), is sub-titled 'Iqbal's Diagnosis and Cure', and it deals primarily with a political application of Iqbal's ideas and philosophies.

223.　　——, "WHAT AILS THE SPIRIT OF THE EAST? DIAGNOSIS AND REMEDY", *IQBAL* 1, no. 1: July (1952): pp. 1-18.

224.　　**ALI, Choudhory Muhammad,** mon., *THE TASK BEFORE US, IQBAL DAY ADDRESS AT LAHORE*, Karachi: Pakistan Publications, 1952. 40/42 pp.

225.　　——, "WHAT AILS THE SPIRIT OF THE EAST?", *HINDUSTAN TIMES* (New Delhi), 19 April 1959.
Cf. the article of the same title, in *IQBAL* 1, no. 1: July (1952).

226.　　**ALI MOHAMMAD DAHIR,** "IQBAL - THE REVOLUTIONIST", *OASIS* (Bahawalpur), April 1941, pp. 129-32.

227.　　**ALI, Morad,** "UN PENSEUR MUSULMAN MODERNE: MOHAMMAD IQBAL (1873-1938)", *JOURNAL DE L'INSTITUT DES BELLES LETTRES ARABES* 18, (1955): pp. 339-47.
F.

228.　　**ALI, Rahmat,** "LISTE CHRONOLOGIQUE DES OEUVRES D'IQBAL (1876-1938)",

REVUE DES ÉTUDES ISLAMIQUES 14, no. 1-2 (1940): pp. 83-88.
F.

229. **ALI, S. A.**, "IQBAL: IN SEARCH OF A FAITH", *THE HINDUSTAN TIMES* (New Delhi), 19 April 1959.

230. **ALI SHAH, Syed Ghous**, mon., *IQBAL - THE MEETING POINT OF THE EAST & WEST - TREFFPUNKT ZWISCHEN OST UND WEST*, Annemarie SCHIMMEL (tr. E/G), Stuttgart-Bonn: Burg Verlag, 1987. 40 pp.
Bi-lingual edition of an Allama Muhammad Iqbal Memorial Lecture, delivered at the South Asia Institute of the Heidelberg University, July 6th 1987, by the then Chief Minister of Sind Mr. Ali Shah, also a member of the Governing body of the Iqbal Academy Pakistan, and of the Executice Council of the Markazia-Majlis-e-Iqbal. The lecture was translated into German by Annemarie Schimmel, and edited with a short preface by Abdul Waheed, Ambassador of Pakistan to (then) Western Germany, under the auspices of the German-Pakistan Forum.
E-G.

231. **ALI, Sheikh Mubarak**, mon., *IQBAL - HIS POETRY AND MESSAGE*, Lahore: Qaumi Kutub Khana, 1932. vi+304 pp.
Variant name: Sheikh Akbar ALI, to which are connected two different publishers' names: Mir Muhammad Nawab Din, and Punjab Education Press.

232. **ALI, Syed Anwar**, mon., *REAL ACHIEVEMENT OF THE HUMAN LIFE, PRESENTING: A COMPARATIVE STUDY OF THE LIVES, WORKS AND ACHIEVEMENTS OF THE MUSLIM MYSTICS AND THE MONARCHS*, Karachi: Syed Publications, 1979

233. **Allama Iqbal MUSEUM**, *ALLAMA IQBAL MUSEUM (JAVED MANZIL), LAHORE, A NATIONAL MONUMENT DEDICATED TO THE MEMORY OF ALLAMA IQBAL DURING THE CENTENARY YEAR 1977, TASWIR HUSAIN HAMIDI*: Allama Iqbal Museum [?], 1977

234. **ALLANA, G.**, "IQBAL AS POLITICAL PHILOSOPHER", *IQBAL REVIEW* 14, no. 3: October (1973): pp. 61-68.

235. ———, mon., *OUR FREEDOM FIGHTERS (1562-1947): TWENTY-ONE GREAT LIVES*, Islamabad: National Committee for Birth Centenary Celebrations of Quaid-i-Azam, 1976. 347 pp.

Iqbal biography: pp. 185-198.

236. ———, ed., *PAKISTAN MOVEMENT: HISTORIC DOCUMENTS*, Lahore: Islamic Book Service, 1977.
The 2nd edition was published in Karachi (Paradise Subscription Agency, 1968) and contained 607 pp.
Note esp. Iqbal's correspondence with Jinnah (pp. 138-149).

237. ———, mon., *QUAID-E-AZAM JINNAH: THE STORY OF A NATION*, Lahore: Ferozsons, 1967. 137 pp.
Cf. esp. pp. 216, 254, 257-264, 275, 291, 299-301, 330*f.*, 351-354, 436.

238. **ALLISON, David D.**, ed., *THE NEW NIETZSCHE: CONTEMPORARY STYLES OF INTERPRETATION*, New York: Delta, 1977

239. **AMEN, Ghulam Shabbir**, "'DARE AND LIVE' IS IQBAL'S MESSAGE", *THE CIVIL AND MILITARY GAZETTE* (Lahore), 21 April 1954, p. 4.

240. ———, "GLIMPSES INTO IQBAL'S PHILOSOPHY", *DAWN* (Karachi), 21 April 1949, p. 8.
Extracts from Allama Iqbal's well-known lecture on 'The Reconstruction of Religious Thought in Islam'.

241. **AMIN, Uthman**, "IQBAL'S MESSAGE", *IQBAL REVIEW* 10, no. 1: April (1969): pp. 43-47.

242. **AMINUDDIN, M.**, "INFLUENCE OF MAULANA RUMI ON DR. IQBAL", *DAWN* (Karachi), 9 November 1977.

243. ———, "IQBAL'S CONCEPT OF LIFE", *MORNING NEWS* (Karachi), 9 November 1983.

244. ———, "IQBAL'S CONCEPT OF MAN", *MORNING NEWS* (Karachi), 9 November 1986.

245. ———, "IQBAL'S CONCEPTION OF ART", *DAWN* (Karachi), 9 November 1978.

246. **AMJAD ALI, S.**, "IQBAL IN FOREIGN LANDS", *PAKISTAN QUARTERLY* (Karachi)

3, no. 1 (1953): pp. 30-35.
Author variant: Iqbal Hussain; pseud. A.S.A. or S.A.A.

247. **ANAND, Mulk Raj**, *GOLDEN-BREATH, STUDIES IN FIVE POETS OF THE NEW INDIA*, Wisdom of the East Series, London: Dutton, 1933.
Cf. esp. pp. 61-85.

248. ———, "THE HUMANISM OF MUHAMMAD IQBAL", *MULTI-DISCIPLINARY APPROACH TO IQBAL / IQBAL CENTENARY SYMPOSIUM*, New Delhi, [year?].

249. ———, "IQBAL: A UNIVERSAL POET", *IQBAL, COMMEMORATIVE VOLUME*, Ali Sardar JAFRI and K.S. DUGGAL (eds.), New Delhi: All India Iqbal Centenary Celebrations Committee, 1977, pp. 54-67.
This paper studies the background of Iqbal's thought in the light of his identity as a universal poet, focusing on his initial sadness as reflected in his earliest poetry, his achievement of *an integral synthesis of the dynamic elements in Islam with the co-incidental essences he had absorbed in the West* (pp. 61-62).

250. ———, "THE POETRY OF SIR MUHAMMAD IQBAL", *INDIAN ART AND LETTERS* (London) 5, no. 1 (1931/1937): pp. 5 or 19-39.
Variant date: 1937; also published as a monography (London, 1931) [?].

251. ———, "A UNIVERSAL POET: EXISTENTIALISM TO HUMANISM", *THE PAKISTAN TIMES* (Rawalpindi), 9 November 1977.

252. **ANIKEEV, N. P.**, "[THE EMINENT THINKER AND POET]", *ZNANIYE [The Knowledge]* (Moscow) (1959).
R.

253. ———, "OBSCESTVENNO-POLITICESKIE VZGLJYDY M. IQBALA", *SOVETSKOE VOSTOKOVEDENIA* 3, (1958).
R.

254. **ANIKEEV, N. P. & S. M. KEDROVA**, "[MUHAMMAD IQBAL - SINGER OF A HUMAN BEING]", *VESTNIK ISTORIYI MIROVOI KULTURI [The Herald of the History of World Culture]* (Moscow) 4, (1958).
R.

255. **ANIKEYEV, N. P.**, "THE DOCTRINE OF PERSONALITY", *IQBAL: POET*

PHILOSOPHER OF PAKISTAN, HAFEEZ MALIK (ed.), New York / London: Columbia University Press, 1971, pp. 264-86 [?].

256. **ANJUM, A. R.**, "IQBAL AND MUSLIM CULTURE", *IQBAL* 25, no. 1: January (1978): pp. 69-78.
Also in *EXPLORATIONS* (Lahore) 4, no. 2 (1977), pp. 52-60.

257. **anon.**, "106TH BIRTYH ANNIVERSARY OF ALLAMA IQBAL TODAY", *DAWN* (Karachi), 9 November 1983.

258. ———, "107TH BIRTH ANNIVERSARY: NATION PAYS HOMMAGE TO ALLAMA IQBAL TODAY", *BALUCHISTAN TIMES* (Quetta), 9 November 1984.

259. ———, ed., *10TH EUROPEAN CONFERENCE ON MODERN SOUTH ASIAN STUDIES, VENICE, 1988 - PANEL 5, COLLECTED PAPERS*, Venice: Università di Venezia, Dipartimento di studi eurasiatici, [n.d.]

260. ———, tr., *L'AILE DE GABRIEL*, Paris: Editions Albin Michel, 1977 F.

261. ———, "(ALAMA) IQBAL: HIS APPROACH TO MAN AND SOCIETY", *ILLUSTRATED WEEKLY OF PAKISTAN* (Karachi), 24 April 1960.

262. ———, "(ALAMA) IQBAL'S WARNING AGAINST MATERIALISM", *THE CIVIL AND MILITARY GAZETTE* (Lahore), 21 April 1958.

263. ———, "ALLAMA IQBAL", *BALUCHISTAN TIMES* (Quetta), 9 November 1979.

264. ———, "ALLAMA IQBAL", *BALUCHISTAN TIMES* (Quetta), 9 November 1984.

265. ———, "ALLAMA IQBAL AND ISLAMIC UNITY", *BALUCHISTAN TIMES* (Quetta), 9 November 1987.

266. ———, "ALLAMA IQBAL DESTINED TO MAKE HISTORY", *DAWN* (Karachi), 9 November 1985.

267. **anon.**, "ALLAMA IQBAL IDEALS TRANSFORM CHARACTERS, DESTINIES OF

NATIONS", *BALUCHISTAN TIMES* (Quetta), 9 November 1983.

268. ———, "ALLAMA IQBAL'S BIRTH ANNIVERSARY CELEBRATED THROUGHOUT COUNTRY", *BALUCHISTAN TIMES* (Quetta), 11 November 1984.

269. ———, "ALLAMA IQBAL'S BIRTH DAY PROGRAMME", *MORNING NEWS* (Karachi), 9 November 1986.

270. ———, "ARBERRY, A.J. (Tr.), SIR MUHAMMAD IQBAL - THE TULIP OF SINAI (Book Review)", *MUSLIM WORLD* 39, (1949): pp. 79.

271. ———, ed., *ASPECTS OF IQBAL: A COLLECTION OF SELECTED PAPERS READ ON THE OCCASION OF THE IQBAL DAY CELEBRATIONS ON JANUARY 9TH 1938.*, various authors (mon.), Lahore: Qaumi Kutub Khana, 1938. Collected essays in English and Urdu, re-issued by the Inter-Collegiate Muslim Brotherhood, Lahore 1983.

272. ———, "AVE ATQUE VALE: MEMORIAL NOTICES OF SIR HENRY NEWBOLT, V.P., MR. F. IRVING TAYLOR, SIR M. IQBAL AND OTHERS", *POETRY REVIEW* 29, (1938): pp. 266.

273. ———, "BILGRAMI, GLIMPSES OF IQBAL'S MIND AND THOUGHT (Book Review)", *MUSLIM WORLD* 44, (1955): pp. 188.

274. ———, "BIRTH CENTENARY OF MUHAMMAD IQBAL", *INDO-IRANICA* 26, no. 4: December (1973): pp. 60-64.

275. ———, "CALL TO REBUILD PAKISTAN ON IQBAL'S CONCEPT", *DAWN* (Karachi), 9 November 1987.

276. ———, mon., *CATALOGUE OF RELICS OF ALLAMA IQBAL, PRESERVED IN ALLAMA IQBAL MUSEUM*, Islamabad: Department of Archaeology and Museums, 1982

277. ———, tr. /T, *CAVIDNAME TURK TARIH KURUMU BASIMEVI* (JAVID NAMAH), Ankara, 1958.
Turkish prose translation of (I) JAVID NAMAH.
T.

278.   **anon.**, ed., *CRESCENT AND GREEN: A MISCELLANY OF WRITINGS ON PAKISTAN*, various authors (mon.), London: Cassell, 1955. 170 pp.
Among the topics, note IQBAL AND PHILOSOPHY OF ISLAM (pp. 131-161): namely, IQBAL AND WESTERN PHILOSOPHERS (pp. 131-141), and IQBAL AND DEMOCRACY (pp. 142-161).

279.   ———, "DR. IQBAL", *THE PAKISTAN TIMES* (Rawalpindi), 24 April 1987.

280.   ———, "FAITHFUL ALI BAKSH LOOKS BACK", *THE TIMES OF KARACHI*, 21 April 1954.

281.   ———, "GABRIEL AND SATAN", *THOUGHT* 2, no. 17 (1950): pp. 10.
English translation of poem.

282.   ———, "THE GREATNESS OF IQBAL", *AL-ISLAM* 3, no. 8: 15 April (1955): pp. 59.

283.   ———, "HOMAGE TO IQBAL", *MORNING NEWS* (Karachi), 9 November 1979.

284.   ———, *INTERNATIONAL CONGRESS ON ALLAMA MOHAMMAD IQBAL*, Lahore: University of Punjab, 1977.

285.   ———, "AN INTERVIEW WITH MUNIRA BANU, ALLAMA IQBAL'S ONLY DAUGHTER RELATES WHAT DADDY LOOKED LIKE", *TIMES OF KARACHI*, 21 April 1954.
Special Suppl.

286.   ———, "INTRODUCING IQBAL TO EAST PAKISTAN: PROBLEMS OF TRANSLATION INTO BENGALI", *PAKISTAN TIMES* (Lahore), 21 April 1959, p. 6.

287.   ———, "IQBAL", *SHORT ENCYCLOPEDIA OF PAKISTAN*, MASUD-UL HASAN (comp.), Lahore: Ferozsons for Quaid-i-Azam Centenary Publication, 1975, pp. 80-82.

288.   ———, "IQBAL - A POET OF VISION", *MORNING NEWS* (Karachi), 9 November 1986.

289.   ———, *IQBAL ALBUM*, Mumtaz HASAN (foreword), Karachi: Iqbal Academy, [n.d.].
Unpublished and rare photographs of Iqbal, including several multi-coloured portraits,

printed on "real art paper".

290. **anon.**, "IQBAL ALSO WAS LIKE ANY OTHER CHILD BUT WITH A DIFFERENCE", *TIMES OF KARACHI*, 21 April 1954.

291. ———, "IQBAL AND BENGALI WRITERS", *MORNING NEWS*, 1 May 1960.

292. ———, "IQBAL AND ISLAMIC RENAISSANCE", *THE MUSLIM* (Islamabad), 21 April 1981.

293. ———, "IQBAL AND NIETZSCHE", *RAVI* 32, no. 7-8: May-June (1937): pp. 25-34.

294. ———, "IQBAL AND THE SPELL OF PLATO", *MORNING NEWS*, 19 April 1959.

295. ———, "IQBAL BIRTH DAY TODAY", *MORNING NEWS* (Karachi), 9 November 1985.

296. ———, ed., *IQBAL COMMEMORATIVE VOLUME*, various authors (mon.), New Delhi: All India Iqbal Centenary Celebrations Committee, n.d.

297. ———, ed., *IQBAL CONGRESS PAPERS, PRESENTED AT THE SECOND INTERNATIONAL CONGRESS ON MUHAMMAD IQBAL*, various authors (mon.), Lahore: University of the Punjab, 1983

298. ———, "IQBAL DAY FUNCTIONS", *THE MUSLIM* (Islamabad), 9 November 1982.

299. ———, "IQBAL DAY IN CAIRO", *IQBAL REVIEW* 10, no. 1: April (1969): pp. 40-51. Includes the following contributions: a free English rendering of an article in Arabic (published in *MAJALLA AL-AZHAR*, September 1967), IQBAL - THE POET OF ISLAM by Ahmad Hasan al-ZIYYAT (pp. 40-42); Uthman AMIN, IQBAL'S MESSAGE (pp. 43-47); IQBAL IN ARABIC, Translations of and studies about Iqbal in Arabic; and the poem A MOMENT ON IQBAL'S TOMB.

300. ———, "IQBAL DAY OBSERVED IN BALN WITH GREAT REVERENCE", *BALUCHISTAN TIMES* (Quetta), 11 November 1984.

301. **anon.**, "IQBAL DAY TO BE CELEBRATED BEFITTINGLY", *BALUCHISTAN TIMES*

(Quetta), 9 November 1986.

302.   ———, "IQBAL DAY TODAY", *BUSINESS RECORDER* (Karachi), 9 November 1986.
Cf. also the article of the same title, by the same (or a likewise unknown) author, published
on the same day in *THE MUSLIM* (Islamabad).

303.   ———, "IQBAL DAY TODAY", *THE MUSLIM* (Islamabad), 9 November 1986.
Cf. also the article of the same name, by the same (or a likewise unknown) author,
published on the same day in the *BUSINESS RECORDER*.

304.   ———, "IQBAL, Dr. - THE SECRETS OF THE SELF (Book Review)", *CAMBRIDGE
REVIEW* 42, (1920/1921): pp. 209.

305.   ———, "IQBAL GAVE A MESSAGE OF HOPE AND CEASELESS STRUGGLE",
THE MUSLIM (Islamabad), 16 November 1987.

306.   ———, "IQBAL GAVE NEW DESTINY TO HIS PEOPLE", *ILLUSTRATED WEEKLY
OF PAKISTAN* (Karachi) 13, no. 29: 23 April (1961): pp. 13, 14.

307.   ———, "IQBAL: HIS ART AND THOUGHT (Book Review)", *JOURNAL OF THE
(ROYAL) CENTRAL ASIAN SOCIETY* 37, no. 1: January (1950): pp. 98.

308.   ———, "IQBAL, HIS ART AND THOUGHT, BY S.A. VAHID", *ISLAMIC CULTURE*
35, no. 4 (1961).

309.   ———, "IQBAL IN EAST PAKISTANI LITERATURE", *PAKISTAN TIMES*, 4 May
1962.

310.   ———, mon., *IQBAL, JINNAH AND PAKISTAN: THE VISION AND THE REALITY*,
Lahore: Vanguard, 1984

311.   ———, ed., *IQBAL, MAINSPRING OF MUSLIM RENAISSANCE*, various authors
(mon.), [place ?]: Iqbal Society in the U.K., n.d.

312.   ———, "IQBAL, MOHAMMED, THE RECONSTRUCTION OF RELIGIOUS
THOUGHT IN ISLAM (Descriptive Notices)", *PHILOSOPHICAL REVIEW* 44, (1935):
pp. 407.

313.   ———, "IQBAL - OUR NATIONAL POET", *THE PAKISTAN TIMES* (Rawalpindi), 20 April 1984.

314.   **anon.**, "IQBAL, PAKISTAN AND MUSLIM WORLD", *THE MUSLIM* (Islamabad), 21 April 1982.

315.   ———, "IQBAL: POET AND PHILOSOPHER", *ILLUSTRATED WEEKLY OF INDIA* (Bombay), 1 May 1955, p. 37.

316.   ———, "IQBAL, POET OF SOCIALISM", *LINK* 15, no. 29: 25 February (1973): pp. 33.

317.   ———, "IQBAL'S BIRTH ANNIVERSARY TODAY", *THE FRONTIER POST* (Peshawar), 9 November 1987.

318.   ———, "IQBAL'S CONCEPT OF CULTURE", *IQBAL REVIEW* 37, no. 1: April (1996): pp. 129-31.
        Extracts from the book *Cultural Policy of Pakistan*, National Commission of History and Culture, Islamabad, 1995.

319.   ———, "IQBAL'S EDUCATIONAL PHILOSOPHY (Book Review)", *JOURNAL OF THE (ROYAL) CENTRAL ASIAN SOCIETY* 26, no. 2: April (1939): pp. 340.

320.   ———, "IQBAL'S MESSAGE", *MORNING NEWS* (Karachi), 21 April 1981.

321.   ———, "IQBAL'S MESSAGE", *THE PAKISTAN TIMES* (Rawalpindi), 9 November 1985.
        Published simultaneously in the *MORNING NEWS* (Karachi) of 9 November 1985.

322.   ———, "IQBAL'S THEORY OF ART", *SUNDAY TRIBUNE*, 29 April 1956.

323.   ———, "IQBAL'S VIEWS ON RELIGION", *BALUCHISTAN TIMES* (Quetta), 9 November 1979.

324.   ———, "IQBAL'S WARNING AGAINST MATERIALISM", *THE CIVIL AND MILITARY GAZETTE* (Lahore), 21 April 1958, p. 1.

325.   ———, "IQBAL STUDIES IN THE VOLUMES OF *THE JOURNAL OF THE RESEARCH SOCIETY OF PAKISTAN*", *IQBAL REVIEW* 37, no. 1: April (1996): pp.

127.
List of ten fairly recent (1977-1990) articles on Iqbal and Politics, Philosophy, Poetry and Arabic language.

326.   **anon.**, "IQBAL THE ARCHITECT OF PAKISTAN", *THE CIVIL AND MILITARY GAZETTE* (Lahore), 21 April 1958, p. 3.

327.   ———, "IQBAL: THE POET OF THE EAST", *AL-ISLAM* 3, no. 8: 15 April (1955): pp. 61.

328.   ———, "IQBAL, THE RECONSTRUCTION OF RELIGIOUS THOUGHT IN ISLAM (Book Review)", *JOURNAL OF RELIGION* 15, no. 1: January (1935): pp. 89.

329.   ———, "THE LEGACY OF IQBAL", *MUSLIM WORLD* 44, (1954): pp. 281.

330.   ———, "'Littérature': R. COHEN; F.M. ALBERES; A. GARREAU; G. CIROT Et M. DARBORD; M. IQBAL (Book Review)", *ÉTUDES RELIGIEUSES, PHILOSOPHIQUES, HISTORIQUES ET LITTÉRAIRES* 292, no. [?]: février (1957): pp. 318.
F.

331.   ———, "M.J. VERMASEREN; ESTER PANETTA; PAOLO TOSCHI; GIUSEPPE COCCHIARA; PAOLO TOSCHI; MUHAMMAD IQBAL; ERANOS-JAHRBUCH; RES GESTAE DIVI AUGUSTI (Book Review)", *STUDI E MATERIALI DI STORIA DELLE RELIGIONI* 23, (1951/1952).
I.

332.   ———, "MOHAMMED IQBAL ANNIVERSARY", *ASIAN REVIEW* (NS) 59, no. 219 (1963): pp. 154.

333.   ———, ed., *MUHAMMAD IQBAL*, various authors (mon.), Karachi: Pakistan-German Forum, 1960. 142 pp.
A collection of essays, including Annemarie Schimmel's THE ASCENSION OF THE POET.

334.   ———, "MUHAMMAD IQBAL: DIE WIEDERHERSTELLUNG DES RELIGIOSEN DENKENS IM ISLAM", *AL FADSCHR - DIE MORGENDAMMERUNG* 1-4 [...], no. ... 8 [...] (1991): pp. ... 51.
A German translation of (I) THE RECONSTRUCTION OF RELIGIOUS THOUGHT IN

ISLAM, published as a series in different issues of the journal.
G.

335.   ———, ed., *MUHAMMED IQBAL - THE POET-PHILOSOPHER*, various authors (mon.), Lahore, 1939

336.   **anon.**, "NATION PAYS HOMMAGE TO IQBAL TODAY", *MORNING NEWS* (Karachi), 9 November 1983.

337.   ———, ed., *NINETEENTH PAKISTAN PHILOSOPHICAL CONGRESS - ALLAMA IQBAL SESSION, APRIL 25-27 1978*, various authors (mon.), Hyderabad: University of Sind, 1978.

338.   ———, "ON IQBAL'S TRAIL", *DAWN* (Karachi), 9 November 1977.

339.   ———, ed., *ORIENTAL COLLEGE MAGAZINE: ALLAMA IQBAL CENTENARY NUMBER*, various authors (mon.), Lahore: University Oriental College, 1977.

340.   ———, *PAKISTAN, PAST AND PRESENT*, London: Stacey International, 1977. 288 pp. Topics include Iqbal's philosophy, political and educational views, poetry and life; Iqbal and nationalism, Sufism, etc.

341.   ———, mon., *PAKISTAN UN RAIYAB MILLI SAIRI IKBAL*, Istanbul: Hakkinda Kanferanslar Amil Matboosi, 1952.
T.

342.   ———, ed./tr., *THE POET'S VISION AND MAGIC OF WORDS: AN APPROACH TO IQBAL POETRY*, Lahore: Islamic Book service, 1978

343.   ———, "THE PROFESSOR WHO INTRODUCED IQBAL TO TURKEY", *PAKISTAN TIMES*, 3 September 1961.

344.   ———, "'Questions Religieuses': Pius PARSCH; Mgr. R. KNOX; S.W. BARON; J. DANIÉLOU; Ch. MARSTON; Dom Thierry MAERTENS; J.A. JUNGMANN; H.U. Von BALTHASAR; J. DANIÉLOU; H. BARS; Mystères Chrétiens Et Action Jociste; DIADOQUE De PHOTICE; R.P. MILLOT; F. VAN STEENBERGHEN; Soeur Marie Michel Archange; M. IQBAL; E. DERMENGHEN; M.H. LUZZATO; A. BARREAU; L. CARRAU (Book Review)", *ÉTUDES RELIGIEUSES, PHILOSOPHIQUES, HISTORIQUES ET LITTÉRAIRES* 289, no. [?]: juin (1956): pp. 455.

F.

345. ———, "REVIEW OF THE OXFORD STUDENTS' HISTORY OF INDIA, BY VINCENT A. SMITH ... 1908 3rd Revised Edition Including in Vol. 2 "THE DEVELOPMENT OF METAPHYSICS IN PERSIA" BY SHAIKH MUHAMMAD IQBAL", *IMPERIAL AND ASIATIC QUARTERLY REVIEW AND ORIENTAL AND COLONIAL RECORD* III: 27, no. 53/54: January-April (1909): pp. 190-208.

346. **anon.**, mon., *RUMI VE IQBAL*, Istanbul: Pakistan Safaretu Basic Ataseliya, 1952. Published by the Press Attache of the Embassy of Pakistan in Turkey.
T.

347. ———, "SAIYIDAIN, K.G., IQBAL'S EDUCATIONAL PHILOSOPHY", *MUSLIM WORLD* 30-31, (1940-1941): pp. 88 and 412.

348. ———, *SELECTION AND TRANSLATION OF IQBALIA*, Lahore: Iqbal Academy, 1991

349. ———, ed., *SEMINAR, IQBAL: EAST AND WEST, HELD ON NOVEMBER 4, 1979 AT OSMANIA UNIVERSITY ... UNDER THE AUSPICES OF THE DEPARTMENT OF PHILOSOPHY, OSMANIA UNIVERSITY*, Hyderabad: Max Müller Bhavan / Iqbal Academy, 1994

350. ———, "SIR MUHAMMAD IQBAL", *IQBAL: A CRITICAL STUDY*, Misbah-ul-Haq SIDDIQUI (ed.), Lahore: Farhan Publications, 1977, pp. 211-13.
Anonymous obituary, taken from *THE INDIAN REVIEW*, November 1938.

351. ———, "SIR MUHAMMAD IQBAL'S LECTURES", *ISLAMIC CULTURE* 5, no. 4 (1931).

352. ———, "THE SUBLIME VISION OF IQBAL", *MORNING NEWS* (Karachi), 9 November 1983.

353. ———, *TURKIYE DE DR. MUHAMMAD IQBAL*, Istanbul: Siralar Matbaasi, 1962
T.

354. ———, "THE TWO-NATION THEORY AND IQBAL", *KHYBER MAIL* (Peshawar), 9 November 1986.

355. ———, "THE WEST-ENEMY OF THE EAST", *ISLAM* 2, no. 12: 7 November (1936): pp. 82-84.

356. ———, "ZIA'S CALL TO FOLLOW IQBAL'S MESSAGE", *THE MUSLIM* (Islamabad), 9 November 1984.

357. **anon.**, "ZIA'S CALL TO IMBIBE TRUE SPIRIT OF IQBAL'S MESSAGE", *MORNING NEWS* (Karachi), 9 November 1985.

358. ———, "ZIA TO VISIT MAZAR OF ALLAMA IQBAL", *BALUCHISTAN TIMES* (Quetta), 9 November 1986.

359. ———, "ZIA URGES PEOPLE TO PERCEIVE IQBAL'S MESSAGE IN TOTALITY", *BUSINESS RECORDER* (Karachi), 9 November 1986.

360. ———, "ZIA URGES TO RECONSTRUCT PAKISTAN IN ACCORDANCE WITH IQBAL'S CONCEPT", *BALUCHISTAN TIMES* (Quetta), 9 November 1987.

361. ——— (A Student of Literature), "IQBAL: "THE POET-PHILOSPOHER OF ISLAM" - A CRITIQUE", *IQBAL: A CRITICAL STUDY*, Misbah-ul-Haq SIDDIQUI (ed.), Lahore: Farhan Publishers, 1977, pp. 161-97.
This article, taken from the *HINDUSTAN REVIEW* (1938) and by the hand of an anonimous author, contains a vehement attack against Iqbal's choice of language (i.e. Persian), his poetry, and his political ideas towards a separate homeland for the Indian Muslims. It is followed by a note from the editor M.H. Siddiqui, in which he states to *have intentionally included this article, which is an embodiment of fanaticism and hypocrisy of Hindu parochialism, and simultaneously Allama Iqbal's steadfastness towards demand for Pakistan.*

362. ———, "IQBAL DAY 1955", *ART AND LETTERS* (London) (1955-1956).

363. ———, "IQBAL DAY IN THE U.K.", *THE PAKISTAN REVIEW* (Lahore) 3, no. 6: June (1955).

364. ———, "REVIEW OF 'THE DEVELOPMENT OF METAPHYSICS IN PERSIA'", *THE ATHENAEUM*, 15 November 1908.

365. ———, "REVIEW OF 'THE RECONSTRUCTION OF RELIGIOUS THOUGHT IN

ISLAM'", *THE TIMES* (London), 15 March 1934, sec. Literary Supplement.

366. ———, mon., *IQBAL AND WESTERN PHILOSOPHY, EMINENT MUSULMANS*, Madras: Naterson and Co., 1926. 397 pp.

367. ———, "IQBAL: THE POET-PHILOSOPHER OF ISLAM", *HIDUSTAN REVIEW* 71, no. [?]: September-October (1938): pp. 147-64.

368. **ANSARI, A. A.**, "IQBAL AS POET AND THINKER", *IQBAL REVIEW / IQBALIAT* (Lahore) 27, no. 1: April-September (1986): pp. 121-34.

369. ———, "IQBAL, ISLAM AND THE WEST", *THE ALIGARH CRITICAL MISCELLANY* (Aligarh) 4, no. 2: November (1991): pp. 121-38.
Also published in *ISLAMIC CULTURE* (Hyderabad) 65, no. 2-3 (1991), pp. 1-14.

370. **ANSARI, Asloob Ahmad**, ed., *IQBAL - ESSAYS AND STUDIES*, New Delhi: Ghalile Academy [?], 1978

371. **ANSARI, Aslub Ahmad**, "IQBAL'S RELEVANCE TO OUR TIMES", *ISLAMIC CULTURE* 50, no. 2: April (1976): pp. 81-85.

372. **ANSARI, M. Akram**, "PHILOSOPHY OF EDUCATION", *EDUCATION RESEARCH BULLETIN* [vol. ?], no. [?]: December (1977): pp. 7-10.

373. **ANSARI, M. Aslam**, "NECESSITY OF IQBAL'S PHILOSOPHY OF "SELF" FOR THE MODERN WORLD OF ISLAM", *IQBAL* 44, no. 1: January (1997): pp. 3-11.

374. **ANSARI, Zafar Ishaq**, "IQBAL AND NATIONALISM", *IQBAL REVIEW* 2, no. 1: April (1961): pp. 51-89.

375. **ANSARI, Zoe**, "IQBAL: 'SIRRUL-FIRAQ'", *IQBAL COMMEMORATIVE VOLUME*, Ali Sardar JAFRI & K.S. DUGGAL (eds.), New Delhi: All India Iqbal Centenary Celebrations Committee, 1977, pp. 175-81.
The influence of Islam and Sufi thought on Iqbal should be studied in the wider context of these determining factors: (1) Post-1857 Muslim Panjab and Kashmir, (2) Indian cultural renaissance and the freedom movement, (3) Post-Bismarck Germany and classical German Philosophy, and (4) the European culture with all its positive and negative aspects (p. 175). In a letter to Khwaja Hasan Nizami (1905) Iqbal himself preferred to be called *Sirr-ul-Firaq* (one who discerns the meaning of separatism), rather than *Sirr-ul-Wisal* (one who

discerns the meaning of unison), which also characterizes his preference for pro-alienation characters (like Rumi, Ghazali, ...) over pro-alignment ones (Iraqi, Alkindi, Farabi, etc.) in literature (p. 176). This attitude of Iqbal is then applied to his poetry.

376.   **ANWAR**, "FOLLOW IQBAL'S TEACHINGS, ONLY SOLUTION TO MUSLIM'S PROBLEMS", *PAKISTAN TIMES*, 27 April 1966, p. 3.

377.   **ANWAR, Aleemtanov Kazakh**, "IQBAL'S JAMSHID BOWL", *PAKISTAN TIMES*, 21 April 1974, p. 2.

378.   **ANWAR, Ali Muhammad**, "IQBALS RELIGIOSE IDEEN", 1954. [?].
       A PhD-thesis.
       G.

379.   **ANWAR, Khurshid**, *THE EPISTEMOLOGY OF IQBAL*.
       Book under print in 1996.

380.   ————, "IQBAL'S THEORY OF KNOWLEDGE", *IQBAL REVIEW* 28, no. 1: April-June (1987): pp. 87-105.

381.   **ANWAR, Muhammad**, "DR. MUHAMMAD IQBAL - 'AN ASTRAL STUDY'", *PAKISTAN REVIEW* (Lahore) 15, no. 4 (1967): pp. 37-38, 41.

382.   **ANWAR, Zahir**, "THE VOYAGE OF SELF IN IQBAL", *CHIRAG-I-RAGHUZAR* (Calcutta) [vols. ?], no. [?]: December and January (1977-1978).
       The Muslim Institute, Allama Iqbal - Birth Century Committee.

383.   **AQEEL, Moinuddin**, "IQBAL'S CONCEPT OF NATIONHOOD", *JOURNAL OF THE PAKISTAN HISTORICAL SOCIETY* 31, no. 1 (1983): pp. 14-26.
       Survey of the various forms of nationalism in the 19th and 20th century Islamic world. Iqbal believed the concept of nationalism to be a tool in the hands of Western powers.

384.   **AQIL AHMAD**, "POET OF SELF", *DAWN* (Karachi), 21 April 1954, pp. 5-6.

385.   **ARBERRY, A. J.**, "COMPLAINT AND ANSWER, MUHAMMAD IQBAL", *MUSLIM WORLD* 46, (1956): pp. 171.
       Notes of the quarter.

386. ———, "FREEDOM OF MAN", *THOUGHT* (Delhi) 2, no. 23 (1950): pp. 12.
Extracts from Arberry's translation of (I) RUMUZ-I-BEKHUDI (*THE MYSTERIES OF SELFLESSNESS*, London 1953 - qv.).

387. ———, "A GHAZAL", *THOUGHT* 3, no. 18 (1951): pp. 10.
English translation of a poem.

388. ———, "IQBAL AND MILTON: INTERESTING COMPARISON OF ART AND THOUGHT", *THE CIVIL AND MILITARY GAZETTE* (Lahore), 16 November 1959.

389. ———, "IQBAL COMMEMORATION, 1950", *DAWN* (Karachi), 7 May 1950, sec. Magazine Section, p. 13.

390. ———, tr. P/E, *THE MYSTERIES OF SELFLESSNESS: A PHILOSOPHICAL POEM BY THE LATE SIR MUHAMMAD IQBAL* (RUMUZ-I-BEKHUDI), WISDOM OF THE EAST, London: John Murray, 1953. xvii+92 pp.
English translation of (I) RUMUZ-I-BEKHUDI, with an introduction by the translator, and elaborate footnotes.

391. ———, tr. P/E, *NOTES ON R.A. NICHOLSON'S TRANSLATION OF THE SECRETS OF THE SELF (ASRAR-I-KHUDI)*, Lahore: Shaikh Muhammad Ashraf, 1977

392. ———, "PAKISTAN: IQBAL'S CONCEPT", *PAKISTAN REVIEW* 16, no. 4: April (1968): pp. 32.

393. ———, tr. P/E, *PERSIAN PSALMS* (ZABUR-I-'AJAM), LAHORE: Shaikh Muhammad Ashraf, 1986. 2 vols. / viii+127 pp.
English verse translation of (I) ZABUR-I-AJAM, with a short preface by the translator. Re-edited by Shaikh Muhammad Ashraf, under the title *PERSIAN PSALMS: IQBAL'S ZABUR-I-AJAM* (Lahore, 1968).

394. ———, mon., *PREFACE TO COMPLAINT AND ANSWER*, Lahore, 1961

395. ———, "(Review) IQBAL: HIS ART AND THOUGHT (S.A. VAHID)", *ISLAMIC REVIEW* (Woking) 48, no. 3: March-April (1960): pp. 45-46.
A review of S.A. Vahid, *IQBAL: HIS ART AND THOUGHT*, London, 1959 - qv.

396. ———, "REVIEW ON S.A. VAHID'S BOOK 'IQBAL HIS ART AND THOUGHT'", *ISLAMIC REVIEW* 18, no. 3: March-April (1960): pp. 45-46/47.

Review author variant: Annemarie SCHIMMEL.

397.   ———, ed., *THE SECRETS OF THE SELF* (ASRAR-I-KHUDI), Muhammad IQBAL (mon.), Lahore: Shaikh Muhammad Ashraf, 1950. 48 pp.
Includes IQBAL's own notes on (I) ASRAR-I-KHUDI.

398.   ———, *SUFISM: AN ACCOUNT OF THE MYSTICS OF ISLAM*, London: George Allen & Unwin, 1950

399.   ———, tr. P/E, *THE TULIP OF SINAI*, Muhammad IQBAL (mon.), London: The Royal India Society, 1947. x+36 pp.
English verse translation of (I) LALA-I TUR, from PAYAM-I-MASHRIQ.

400.   ———, "TULIP OF SINAI (Book Review)", *MUSLIM WORLD* 39, (1949): pp. 79.

401.   **ARBERRY, Arthur J.**, tr. U/E, *COMPLAINT AND ANSWER (SHIKWA AND JAWAB-I-SHIKWA), TRANSLATED OUT OF THE URDU INTO ENGLISH VERSE*, Muhammad IQBAL (mon.), Lahore: Shaikh Muhammad Ashraf, 1980. 79 pp.
English verse translation, published under the Heading "NOTES OF THE QUARTER" in *MUSLIM WORLD* 46 (1956), p. 171. Re-edited by Shaikh Muhammad Ashraf (Lahore, 1975).

402.   ———, tr. P/E, *JAVID NAMA BY IQBAL - TRANSLATED FROM THE PERSIAN WITH AN INTRODUCTION AND NOTES*, London: George Allen & Unwin Ltd., 1966. 151 pp.
English verse translation of (I) JAVID NAMA, with a short introduction by the translator, elaborate notes, and a bibliography.

403.   ———, ed., *NOTES ON IQBAL'S ASRAR-I-KHUDI (THE SECRET OF THE SELF)*, Lahore: Shaikh Muhammad Ashraf, 1955/1968. 46/48 pp.
The title on the front cover differs from that on the title page (taken here) in that the former has the plural SECRETS.
With the aid of the symbols N., N. rev., and I., referring to Prof. Nicholson's translation (London, 1920), his second (revised) translation (Lahore, 1940, repr. 1945), and the corrections and annotations in Iqbal's handwriting found in Nicholson's own copy of his first translation respectively, Arberry offers the reader a survey of these three versions.
Re-issued by Kazi Publications (Chicago 1996).

404.   **ARDALAN, Ali Gholi**, "SPEECH, IQBAL DAY IN WASHINGTON", *IQBAL REVIEW*

8, no. 1: April (1967): pp. 52-55.

405. **ARIEL**, "ALLAMA IQBAL SEEN FROM A NEW ANGLE", *DAWN* (Karachi), 9 August 1985.

406. ———, "IQBAL, IJTEHAD AND SECULARISM", *DAWN* (Karachi), 17 April 1987.

407. **ARIFI, Mohib**, "IQBAL AND RADHAKRISHNAN: A COMPARATIVE STUDY (BOOK REVIEW)", *IQBAL REVIEW* 33, no. 1: April (1992): pp. 139-51. Review of Nazeer SIDDIQI, *IQBAL AND RADHAKRISHNAN: A COMPARATIVE STUDY*, New Delhi: Sterling Publishers Private Ltd., n.d.

408. **ARIFUDIN, Muhammad**, "IQBAL'S CONCEPT OF AUSTERITY AS A MEANS TO AN END", *DAWN* (Karachi), 9 November 1979.

409. **ARNOLD, Matthew**, *ESSAYS IN CRITICISM*, First and Second Series 1902, London: Macmillan, 1902

410. **ARNOLD, Thomas W.**, mon., *THE FAITH OF ISLAM*, London, 1928

411. **ARSHED, I. A.**, "ALLAMA IQBAL AS A LOVER OF NATURE", *THE PAKISTAN TIMES* (Rawalpindi), 9 November 1982.

412. ———, "ALLAMA IQBAL ON PRE-DESTINATION", *THE PAKISTAN TIMES* (Rawalpindi), 21 April 1986.

413. ———, "EDUCATIONAL VIEWS OF IQBAL", *THE PAKISTAN TIMES* (Islamabad - Lahore), 9 November 1986.

414. ———, "FROM PANTHEISM TO HUMANISM", *THE PAKISTAN TIMES* (Rawalpindi), 9 November 1985. Re-issued in *THE BALUCHISTAN TIMES*, 9 November 1986.

415. ———, "IBLIS KI MAJLIS-I-SHOORA - AN APPRAISAL", *NATION* (Islamabad), 9 November 1993.

416. ———, "IQBAL'S KHIZR-I-RAH - AN ANALYSIS", *THE PAKISTAN TIMES*

(Rawalpindi), 8 November 1985.

417. ———, "IQBAL'S LOVE FOR THE PROPHET", *THE PAKISTAN TIMES* (Rawalpindi), 21 April 1985.

418. ———, "IQBAL'S VIEW OF DEATH", *THE PAKISTAN TIMES* (Rawalpindi), 20 April 1984.

419. ———, "THE POET IN POLITICS", *THE PAKISTAN TIMES* (Rawalpindi), 9 November 1983.

420. ———, "POLITICO-ECONOMIC VIEWS OF IQBAL", *THE NATION* (Islamabad / Lahore), 9 November 1992.

421. **ASAD, Muhammad**, "IQBAL'S ROLE IN MUSLIM THOUGHT", *VOICE OF ISLAM*, March 1957, pp. 633-34.
Re-issued in *Al-ISLAM* (Karachi) 4, no. [?]: 1 May (1957), p. 146.

422. **ASHRAF, Muhammad**, tr. U/E, *THE DEVIL'S CONFERENCE* (IBLIS KI MAJLIS-I-SHURA), SHAIKH ABDUL QADIR (intr.), Gujarat (Pakistan): Urdu House, 1951. xiii+158 pp.
English translation of (I) IBLIS KI MAJLIS-I-SHURA, with notes and an introduction by Shaikh Abdul Qadir.

423. ———, tr., *THUS CONFERRED SATAN* (IBLIS KI MAJLIS-I-SHURA), 'Allama Muhammad IQBAL (mon.), 2nd rev. ed., Lahore: Book House, 1974. 350+10 pp.

424. **ASHRAF, S. Ehsan**, mon., *A CRITICAL EXPOSITION OF IQBAL'S PHILOSOPHY*, Patna: Associated Book Agency, 1978. viii+216 pp.
Includes bibliography (pp. 206-213) and index.

425. **ASIF, Khwaja**, "IQBAL - SOME CHILDHOOD MEMORIES", *THE MUSLIM* (Islamabad), 21 April 1983.

426. **ASLAM, Muhammad**, "BIBLIOGRAPHY ON IQBAL (1965-1975)", University of Karachi, 1976. (35 +) 60 pp.
Thesis (M.A. - Library Science), University of Karachi.

427. **ASLAM, Qazi Muhammad**, "IQBAL AT A COLLEGE RECEPTION IN LAHORE", *IQBAL REVIEW* 11, no. 3: October (1970): pp. 17-27.
Biographical anecdote about Iqbal, shortly after his receiving a knighthood, from an eye-witness, including a reconstruction of a speech given by Iqbal at the Brett Philosophical Society, Lahore, 1921.
Re-issued in [Various authors], *SELECTIONS FROM THE IQBAL REVIEW*, ed. Waheed Qureshi, Lahore, 1983, pp. 531-539.

428. **ASLAM, Shereen**, "PAN-ISLAMISM AND IQBAL", *IQBAL REVIEW* 35, no. 3: October (1994): pp. 23-38.

429. **ATAULLAH, Sheikh**, ed., *IQBAL NAMA: COLLECTION OF IQBAL'S LETTERS (IN URDU)*, Lahore, 1945/1951.
2 vols.

430. ———, "IQBAL'S UNDYING ATTACHMENT TO HIS KASHMIR HOMELAND", *THE CIVIL AND MILITARY GAZETTE* (Lahore), 20 April 1952, p. 2.
Iqbal Day Suppelement.

431. ———, "A LESSON STILL TO BE LEARNED, UNITY IS THE ONLY SOLUTION TO ALL OUR PROBLEMS, SAID IQBAL 18 YEARS AGO", *THE CIVIL AND MILITARY GAZETTE* (Lahore), 21 April 1951.

432. **ATIQ-UZ-ZAMAN, Khan**, "IQBAL AS A PROSE WRITER WITH SPECIAL REFERENCE TO IQBAL-NAMA", *ILLUSTRATED WEEKLY OF PAKISTAN*, 4 September 1949, p. 20.

433. ———, "IQBAL AS HIS OWN COMMENTATOR", *ILLUSTRATED WEEKLY OF PAKISTAN*, 11 September 1949, p. 29.

434. ———, "SOME NEGLECTED ASPECTS OF IQBAL", *ILLUSTRATED WEEKLY OF PAKISTAN*, 21 August 1949, p. 20.

435. **AUJ, Nurul Zaman Ahmed**, "THREE UNPUBLISHED LETTERS OF IQBAL", *THE NATION* (Islamabad / Lahore), 21 April 1992.

436. **AVERY, Peter**, "IQBAL: A GREAT SOUL OF RARE COMBINATION", *WEEKLY MAIL* (Dacca), 21 April 1961.

437. ———, "IQBAL AND THE MESSAGE OF PERSIAN METAPHYSICS", *IQBAL REVIEW* 10, no. 1: April (1969): pp. 60-63.
Iqbal Day in London.

438. ———, "IQBAL IN THE EYES OF OTHERS", *IQBAL: A CRITICAL STUDY*, Misbah-ul-Haq SIDDIQUI (ed.), Lahore: Farhan Publishers, 1977, pp. 31-36.
The author presents Iqbal's philosophy as essentially a *philosophy of love*, and views this in the light of the Persian tradition of mystics.

439. ———, "THE MESSAGE OF METAPHYSICS", *THE CIVIL AND MILITARY GAZETTE* (Lahore), 21 April 1961, p. 3.

440. **AZAD, Jagan Nath**, "AESTHETICS IN IQBAL'S POETRY", *IQBAL REVIEW* 38, no. 1: April (1997): pp. 49-68.

441. ———, "HAFIZ AUR IQBAL BY DR YUSUF HUSAIN", *IQBAL REVIEW* 20, no. 1: April (1981): pp. 81-83.
Review.

442. ———, "IQBAL AND SCHOPENHAUER", *CULTURAL FORUM* 15, no. 3-4: April-July (1973): pp. 70-73.

443. ———, "IQBAL: HIS ART AND THOUGHT", *THE MUSLIM* (Islamabad), 9 November 1980.

444. ———, "IQBAL, ISLAM AND THE MODERN AGE", *IQBAL* (Lahore) 26, no. 1: January (1979): pp. 31-61.
Previously published, without the original Urdu/Persian text of quotations from Iqbal's writings, in Ali Sardar JAFRY and K.S. DUGGAL (eds.), *IQBAL, COMMEMORATIVE VOLUME*, New Delhi: All India Iqbal Centenary Celebrations Committee, 1977, pp. 73-92.

445. ———, "IQBAL: POET AND POLITICIAN", *THE PAKISTAN TIMES* (Rawalpindi), 9 November 1984.

446. ———, "IQBAL: POET-SON OF INDIA", *INDIAN AND FOREIGN REVIEW* (New Delhi) 10, no. 12 or 13 [?]: 15 April (1973): pp. 19-21.

447. ———, mon., *IQBAL'S MIND AND ART*, Lahore: National Book House, 1981. 232 pp.

Variant title: IQBAL: MIND AND ART.

448. ———, "IQBAL'S PHILOSOPHY OF LIFE", *ILLUSTRATED WEEKLY OF INDIA* 94, no. 34: 26 August (1973): pp. 28-31.
Re-issued in *THE PAKISTAN TIMES* (Rawalpindi), 9 November 1977.

449. ———, "PANDIT ANAND NARAIN MULLA AS A TRANSLATOR OF IQBAL", *IQBAL REVIEW* 23, no. 1: April (1982): pp. 37-45.
On the famous Urdu poet and his translation of Iqbal's ASRAR-I KHUDI, RUMUZ-I BEKHUDI and the quatrains LALAH-I TUR (from PAYAM-I MASHRIQ) into English.

450. **AZAD, Jagannath**, mon., *IQBAL, HIS POETRY AND PHILOSOPHY*, Mysore: Prasaranga, 1981

451. **AZAM, Ikram**, "IQBAL'S FUTURISTICS: HIS VISION OF PAKISTAN", *THE MUSLIM* (Islamabad), 23 September 1983.

452. **AZAM, Muhammad**, "A FEW MOMENTS WITH ALLAMA IQBAL", *PAKISTAN REVIEW* 14, no. 8: August (1966): pp. 21-22.

453. **AZAM, Shabbir**, "ALLAMA IQBAL AS A PHILOSOPHER", *PAKISTAN TIMES*, 23 January 1977, p. 1.

454. ———, "THE FALL OF ADAM", *THE PAKISTAN TIMES* (Rawalpindi), 21 April 1981.

455. ———, "IQBAL'S REVOLUTIONARY MESSAGE", *PAKISTAN TIMES*, 13 March 1977, p. 1.

456. ———, "SELF - THE KEY OF IQBAL'S MESSAGE", *THE PAKISTAN TIMES* (Rawalpindi), 8 November 1981.

457. **AZEEZ, A. M. A.**, "IQBAL: A POET OF ISLAM", *PAKISTAN TODAY* 2, no. 1-2 (1952): pp. 9-12.

458. ———, "IQBAL: A POET OF ISLAM", *PAKISTAN REVIEW* 2, no. 4 (1954): pp. 22-23, 30.
Variant name: AZIZ, Ahmad.

459. **AZEEZ, S. A.**, "SORROWS OF IQBAL", *THE CIVIL AND MILITARY GAZETTE* (Lahore), 21 April 1954, p. 4.

460. **AZHAR, A. D.**, "AN EVENING - ON THE BANKS OF THE NECKAR, BY IQBAL, TRANSLATED BY A.D. AZHAR", *IQBAL REVIEW* 3, no. 1: April (1962): pp. 47. English translation of the (I) poem EK SHAM.

461. ———, "IQBAL AS A SEER", *IQBAL REVIEW* 2, no. 3: October (1961): pp. 1-13.

462. **AZHAR, M. A.**, "IQBAL", *PAKISTAN REVIEW* 1, no. [?]: May (1953): pp. 23-24.

463. **AZHAR, Malik Mueen Nawaz**, comp., *A BIBLIOGRAPHY OF ARTICLES ON IQBAL (1900-1977)*, Bashir Ali KHAN (foreword), 1st ed., Lahore: Islamic Book Service, 1978. 64 pp.

464. **AZHAR, Mirza Ali**, "IQBAL: POET-PHILOSOPHER OF PAKISTAN", *DAWN* (Karachi), 21 April 1953, p. 5. Variant date: 1959.

465. ———, "IQBAL - THE PHILOSOPHER POET OF PAKISTAN", *PAKISTAN REVIEW* 1, no. 5 (1953): pp. 23-24.

466. **AZIM, Syed Viqar**, "IQBAL: POET AND PHILOSOPHER", *THE CIVIL AND MILITARY GAZETTE* (Lahore), 21 April 1962.

467. **AZIZ, K. K.**, *THE HISTORICAL BACKGROUND OF PAKISTAN, 1857-1947, AN ANNOTATED DIGEST OF SOURCE MATERIAL*, Karachi: The Pakistan Institute of International Affairs, 1970. xi+626 pp.

468. **AZIZ, Naila**, "A PAINTER'S PERCEPTION OF IQBAL'S VISIONS", *THE PAKISTAN TIMES* (Rawalpindi), 21 April 1981.

469. **AZRAF, D. M.**, "IQBAL AND THE PROCESS OF HISTORY", *IQBAL REVIEW* 3, no. 3: October (1962): pp. 26-39. Variant name: Muhammad ASHRAF. Reconstruction of Iqbal's views on the processes of history on the basis of his ideas about evolution, politics and the principle of movement in Islam.

470. **BÜRGEL, J. Christoph**, tr., *STEPPE IM STAUBKORN, TEXTE AUS DER URDU-DICHTUNG MUHAMMAD IQBALS*, Muhammad IQBAL (mon.), SEGES - Philologische Und Literarische Studien Und Texte 28, Freiburg: Universitätsverlag Freiburg (Schweiz), 1982. 194 pp.
Thematically arranged anthology on (I) Islam, (II) Indien, (III) Europa, (IV) Staat und Gesellschaft, (V) Selbstaussagen Iqbals, (VI) Dichtung und schöne Künste, (VII) Mensch, (VIII) Natur, (IX) Mystik und Liebe, and (X) Ghaselen und Vierzeiler, with an Appendix of poetry translated from Persian.
G.

471. **BABAR, Farhat Ullah**, "IQBAL AND INDIVIDUALISM", *THE FRONTIER POST* (Peshawar), 20 November 1987.

472. **BABAR, Farhatullah**, "MOVING-SPIRIT IN IQBAL'S PHILOSOPHY", *THE MUSLIM* (Islamabad), 21 April 1980.

473. **BABREE, Laeeq**, "ALLAMA IQBAL AND LOUIS MASSIGNON", *JOURNAL OF THE REGIONAL CULTURAL INSTITUTE (Iran)* 9, no. 1-2 (1977): pp. 81-85.
On the differring interpretations of Sufism as an inner retreat and as a method of integral introspection by Iqbal and Massignon respectively, and on their common admiration for Hallaj.

474. **BADAR, Khawaja**, *"BANDAGI-NAMAH OF IQBAL"*, *IQBAL* 12, no. 3: January (1964): pp. 64-73.
BANDAGI-NAMAH along with GULSHAN-I-RAZ-I-JADID form the closing parts of Iqbal's ZABUR-I-'AJAM, but both these *mathnavi*s were omitted in Arberry's translation. The present English translation completes that published in *IQBAL* 5, no. 3.

475. **BAHADUR ALI**, "IQBAL'S PHILOSOPHY OF RELIGION", *VOICE OF ISLAM*, July 1958, pp. 442-46.

476. **BAHAR, A. C.**, "MILTON AND IQBAL", *MODERN REVIEW* 123, no. 12: December (1968): pp. 918-23.

477. **BAHAR, Khalidah**, "IQBAL ON TIME", University of the Punjab, Dept. Philosophy, 1968. ix+66 pp.
M.A. Philosophy; Promoter: K.G. Sadiq.
Contents: (1) The concept of Time, (2) Sources of Iqbal's concept of Time, (3) Iqbal's

concept of Time, and (4) Conclusion.

478. **BAHARUDDIN, Azizan**, "REASON AND FAITH IN THE NATURAL THEOLOGY OF IQBAL", *IQBAL REVIEW* 33-34, no. 3: October, no. 1: April, and no. 3: October (1992): pp. 17-39, 51-81 and 51-68 resp.
Part I deals with the themes of Iqbal's natural theology; intuition and the possibility of intuitive knowledge, its relation to consciousness and time. Part II deals with God and nature; proofs of the existence of God; Panentheism; God's qualities of infinity and creativity; man's freewill, determination, destiny and the problem of Good and Evil; teleology; God's omniscience; Good and Evil; evolution and its method at the human or moralistic level. Part III deals with Iqbal's thinking on religion and science.

479. **BAHRAMI, Ahmad Ali**, "IQBAL, THE GREAT SERVANT OF HUMANITY", *IQBAL REVIEW* (Karachi) 16, no. 3: October (1975): pp. 55-60.
English translation of a speech delivered during the Iqbal Day programma in Peking. Published here by courtesy of the Embassy of Pakistan.

480. **BAHRAMI, Ahmad Ali H. E.**, "IQBAL THE GREAT SERVANT OF HUMANITY", *THE PAKISTAN TIMES*, 16 January 1977, p. 1 or 3-7.

481. **BAIG, M. Safdar Ali**, "DOCTOR IQBAL'S OPTIMISM", *ISLAMIC CULTURE* 44, no. 2: April (1970): pp. 91-100.
Also in *RESEARCH* 4, April 1970, pp. 91-100.

482. ———, "GLORY OF IQBAL, BY MAULANA SAYYID ABUL HASAN ALI NADWI", *ISLAMIC CULTURE* 50, no. 2 (1976).

483. ———, "POET IQBAL'S DYNAMISM", *TRIVENI* 36, no. 3: October (1967): pp. 35-41.

484. **BAJNURI, 'Abdur Rahman**, "THE ASRAR AND RUMUZ", *EAST AND WEST* [vol. ?], no. [?]: August (1931).
Urdu translation of both appears in *NAYRANG-I KHAYAL* (Lahore), Iqbal No. (September-October) 1932.

485. **BAKAR, S. N.**, "IQBAL AND (THE) MODERN AGE", *DAWN*, 22 April 1951, p. 7.

486. **BALJON, J. M. S.**, "IQBAL AND THE IDEAL OF PAKISTAN", *IQBAL* 24, no. 4: October (1977): pp. 101-6.

487. **BALOCH, S. K.,** "IDEALISM IN IQBAL'S POETRY", *PAKISTAN REVIEW* 16, no. 4: April 1968 (1968): pp. 22-25.

488. ———, "IQBAL: THE POET-PHILOSOPHER OF PAKISTAN", *PAKISTAN REVIEW* (Lahore) 19, no. 4 (Special Iqbal Number) (1971): pp. 13-18, 28.

489. **BALOUCH, Saad Ullah Khan,** "ISLAMIC IDEALISM IN IQBAL'S POETRY", *PAKISTAN TIMES*, 21 April 1969, pp. 3-4.

490. **BALQIS, Jamal Afsar,** "IQBAL'S THEORY OF KNOWLEDGE AND ITS AMPLIFICATION FOR EDUCATION", University of the Punjab, n.d. M.A. Education.

491. **BANNERTH, E.,** "ISLAM IN MODERN URDU POETRY: A TRANSLATION OF DR. M. IQBAL'S *SHIKWA* AND *JAWABI SHIKWA*", *ANTHROPOS* 37-40, (1942-1945).

492. **BAQA, Muhammad Sharif,** mon., *THE POET-PHILOSOPHER OF PAKISTAN*, Barking: Jadid Urdu Digest Publications, n.d. [?]

493. **BAQA, Sharif,** "IQBAL AND ISLAM", *THE PAKISTAN TIMES* (Lahore), 9 November 1986.

494. **BAQIR, Muhammad,** mon., *A CATALOGUE OF THE IQBAL EXHIBITION 1963,* Lahore: Punjabi Adabi Academy, 1963

495. ———, "EARLY CAREER OF ALLAMA IQBAL", *PAKISTAN TIMES*, 21 April 1961, pp. 1, 2. Variant pages: 81-85 [?].

496. ———, "IQBAL: AN ADVOCATE OF ISLAMIC VALUES", *PAKISTAN TIMES*, 21 April 1966, pp. 1-3.

497. ———, "IQBAL: AN UNRELENTING ADVOCATE OF ISLAMIC VALUES", *IQBAL REVIEW* 9, no. 1: April (1968): pp. 34-36.

498. ———, "IQBAL: GREATEST SOCIAL PHILOSOPHER", *THE CIVIL AND MILITARY GAZETTE* (Lahore), 21 April 1955, p. 6.

499.   ———, "IQBAL ON SOCIAL DEMOCRACY", *PAKISTAN TIMES*, 21 April 1972, p. 4.

500.   ———, "IQBAL'S CONCEPT OF AN IDEAL SOCIETY", *IQBAL REVIEW* 23, no. 3: October (1982): pp. 35-36.

501.   ———, "IQBAL WAS MORE HUMAN THAN STRESS ON HIS PHILOSPOHY HAS LEFT HIM", *THE CIVIL AND MILITARY GAZETTE* (Lahore), 21 April 1953, p. 4.

502.   ———, mon., *LAHORE: PAST AND PRESENT*, Lahore: Publishers United, 1952. 556 pp.
Cf. esp. pp. 237, 256, 260, 287. The same book contains the paper MAUSOLEUM OF IQBAL, pp. 429-432.

503.   ———, "A STUDY OF IQBAL'S THOUGHT ON GOVERNMENTAL FORMS", *PAKISTAN TIMES* (Lahore), 21 April 1961, p. 4.
Iqbal Day Supplement.

504.   ———, "TWO EPISTLES ON ALLAMA IQBAL", *IQBAL* 36, no. 1 (1989): pp. 16-18. Epistle by Abdul Jalil Mir (Post Master General of Pakistan, retired) to Dr. William Lillie, who was a colleague of Maulavi Mir Hasan, a teacher of Iqbal, and his reply (dated 9 May 1978 and 4 June 1978, respectively).

505.   **BAQIR, Naseem Ajmi**, "IQBAL'S CONCEPTION OF FINE ARTS", *CAR(A)VAN*, March 1958, pp. 22-30.
See also (variant name) BASHIR NASEEM, Ajmi.

506.   **BAQIR, Zainal Abidin M.**, "IQBAL'S METHOD OF RECONSTRUCTION", *IQBAL REVIEW* 37, no. 3: October (1996): pp. 13-33.   Special   issue on the Reconstruction of Religious Thought in Islam.

507.   **BARANI, Z. A.**, "A FEW MOMENTS WITH IQBAL", *DAWN*, 21 April 1950, p. 10.

508.   **BASHIR, Ahmed**, "IQBAL ACADEMY", *THE MUSLIM* (Islamabad), 21 April 1980.

509.   **BASHIR, Javed Kamran**, mon., *IQBAL AND SECULAR NATIONALISM (POST-1908 PHASE)*, Lahore: Progressive Publishers, 1977

510.   **BASHIR NASEEM, Ajmi**, "IQBAL AND THE EDUCATION SYSTEM OF TODAY",

CAR(A)VAN, November 1957, pp. 26-31.
See also (variant name) BAQIR, Naseem Ajmi.

511. **BATTERSBY, Abdulla**, "IQBAL: POET, POLITICIAN AND PHILOSOPHER", *THE CIVIL AND MILITARY GAZETTE* (Lahore), 20 April 1952, p. 1.
Variant name: BATTERSLEEY.

512. **BAUSANI, A.**, "M. IQBAL, "RECONSTRUIRE LA PENSÉE RELIGIEUSE DE L'ISLAM", Trad. E. MEYEROVITCH (Book Review)", *STUDI E MATERIALI DI STORIA DELLE RELIGIONI* 27, (1956): pp. 165.
F or I [?].

513. **BAUSANI, Alessandro**, "CLASSICAL MUSLIM PHILOSOPHY IN THE WORK OF A MUSLIM MODERNIST: MUHAMMAD IQBAL (1877-1938)", *ARCHIV FÜR GESCHICHTE DER PHILOSOPHIE* (Berlin) 42, no. 3 (1960): pp. 272-88.

514. ———, "THE CONCEPT OF TIME IN THE RELIGIOUS PHILOSOPHY OF (MUHAMMAD) IQBAL", *DIE WELT DES ISLAM* (Leiden) (NS) 3, (1954): pp. 158-86.

515. ———, "DANTE AND IQBAL", *PAKISTAN QUARTERLY* 1, no. 6: Summer (1951): pp. 51-54, 72.
Re-issued in *EAST AND WEST* (Rome), 2, 1951-52, pp. 77-81; and in *PAKISTAN MISCELLANY*, Karachi: Pakistan Publications, 1952, pp. 75-83. Further also published in *CRESCENT AND GREEN*, London: Cassell, 1955, pp. 162-170; and in *THE CIVIL AND MILITARY GAZETTE*, 21 April 1960, p. 8.

516. ———, "IL "GULSAN-I RAZ-I GADID" DI MUHAMMAD IQBAL", *ANNALI DELL' ISTITUTO ORIENTALE DI NAPOLI* (NS) 8, (1958): pp. 125-72.
Italian translation of part of (I) ZABUR-I-AJAM.
I.

517. ———, tr. P/I, *IL POEMA CELESTE. TRADUZIONE DAL PERSIANO E NOTE A CURA DI A.B.* (JAVID NAMAH), Scrittori D'Oriente Giuseppe TUCCI / Istituto Italiano per il Medio ed Estremo Oriente 3, Bari: Leonardo da Vinci editrice, 1965. 326 pp.
Contents: (I) Il poema celeste, (II) Il messaggio d'Oriente, (III) Il segnale della carovana, (IV) I salmi di Persia, (V) L'ala di Gabriele, (VI) Il colpo di Mosè, (VII) Il dono del Hijâz.
I.

518. ———, "INDIVIDUAL IN DEMOCRACY AND IQBAL: CONCEPTION OF KHUDI",

CRESCENT AND GREEN, London: Cassell & Co., 1955, pp. 142-61.

519. ———, "IQBAL", *PAKISTAN QUARTERLY* 2, no. 3: Summer (1952): pp. 16-19.

520. ———, "IQBAL: HIS PHILOSOPHY OF RELIGION AND THE WEST", *PAKISTAN QUARTERLY* 2, no. 3 (1952): pp. 16-19, 54.
Later in *CRESCENT AND GREEN*, London: Cassell & Co., 1955, pp. 131-141.

521. ———, "IQBAL UND DANTE. BETRACHTUNGEN ÜBER IQBALS DSCHAVIDNAMA", *IQBAL UND EUROPA - VIER VORTRÄGE*, J. C. BURGEL (ed.), Bern: P. Lang, 1980, pp. 51-66.
German translation of Bausani's article DANTE AND IQBAL, which first appeared in *PAKISTAN QUARTERLY* 1, no. 6 (1951), with many reprints.
G.

522. ———, "THE LIFE AND WORK OF IQBAL", *IQBAL REVIEW* (Karachi) 14, no. 3: October (1973): pp. 45-60.
Variant date 1976.
English rendering (with some corrections suggested in footnotes) by A.K.M. of Bausani's introduction to his Italian translation of the JAVID NAMAH, which was published in 1952 as IL POEMA CELESTE.

523. ———, "MOHAMMAD IQBAL'S MESSAGE IN EAST AND WEST", *ORIENTAL MODERN* [vol. ?], (1950): pp. 137-40.

524. ———, tr. P,U/E, *MUHAMMAD IQBAL. POESIE. TRADUZIONE DAL PERSIANO E DALL'URDU CON INTRODUZIONE E NOTE DI A.B.*, Parma: Guanda, 1957. 107 pp.
I.

525. ———, "MUHAMMAD IQBAL'S MESSAGE (1873-1938) ", *EAST AND WEST* (Rome) 1, (1950-1951): pp. 137-39.

526. ———, tr. P/I, U/I, *POESIE DI MUHAMMAD IQBAL*, Collana Fenice / Collezione Fenice, dir. Attilio Bertolucci 31, Parma: Vgr Guanda, 1956. viii+108 pp.
Italian prose translation of selected poems: Il Tulipano del Sinai (Quatrine), La Prima Rosa, La Conquista della Natura, Il Profumo della Rosa, Il Canto del Tempo, La Primavera, Vita Eterna, Pensieri di Stelle, La Vita, Il Canto delle Stelle, Lo Zefiro del Mattino, La Goccia d'Acqua, Dialogo fra Uomo e Dio, Solitudine, La Huri e il Poeta, Ghazal, L'Eterna Rivoluzione (da MESSAGGIO D'ORIENTE); La candela e la farfalla, La

Luna Nuova, L'Uomo e la Natura, La Lucciola, Che cos'e davvero la Bellezza, Sicilia, In occosaione del dono d'un fiore, La Luna, Preghiera (da IL SEGNALE DELLA CAROVANA); Al Lettore (da I SALMI DI PERSIA); Frammenti di un Dialogo con Dio, Varie, Poemetti brevi, Ode alla Moschea di Cordova, Alla Spagna, Intermezzo, Lenin e Dio, Gusto e Passione, La Terra e di Dio, Gli Angeli prendono congedo da Adamo, La Spirito della Terra da il benvenuto all'avvento di Adamo, Frammento, Messaggio di Stella, Sulla Tomba di Napoleone, Separazione (da L'ALA DI GABRIELE); Il Destino, Rassegnazione, La Morte, La Meta, L'Ospite Caro, Le Piramidi, Aurora nel Giardino (da LA SPADA DI MOSE); Poemetti, La Cammella, Al Re Faruq, Il Credente, Di a *Iblis* ... (da IL DONO DEL HEGIAZ).
I.

527.   ———, "SATAN IN IQBAL'S PHILOSOPHICAL AND POETICAL WORKS", *IQBAL REVIEW* 9, no. 3: October (1968): pp. 68-118.
English rendering (tr. R.A.Butler) of Bausani's major article SATANA NELL' OPERA FILOSOFICO-POETICA DI MUHAMMAD IQBAL (Roma 1955). This English version was once more re-issued as part of [Various authors], *SELECTIONS FROM THE IQBAL REVIEW*, ed. Waheed Qureshi, Lahore, 1983, pp. 286-336.
Bausani sets the scene by presenting translations of all major parts of Iqbal's works referring to Satan, viz. parts from PAYAM-I-MASHRIQ (TASKHIR-I-FITRAT) (1923), JAVID NAMAH (1932), BAL-I-JIBRIL (1935), ZARB-I-KALIM (1937), and ARMUGHAN-I-HIJAZ (1938), and then proceeds to carefully analyse the Iqbalian concepts of *Satan*, with reference to his works, Islamic tradition, and Western sources.
Iqbal's views on Satan fall roughly into five categories: (1) Satan appears under two seemingly irreconcilable aspects: on the one hand as man's enemy, on the other as man's friend; (2) Satan has above all one enemy: *it is the prophetic conception of life which considers the prophet superior to the saint, law superior to theology, social institution superior to mysticism*; (3) the Iqbalian Satan is unlinked with the sinful aspect of Christianity; (4) Iqbal holds that, in the old controversy between the Fire and the Earth, in the end the Earth, in order to be worshipped by the Fire, needs purification and transfromation through the very Fire; and (5) Satan represents the strength of logic, intellect and systematic doubt - as against the concept of *'Ishq* (Love). Having meticuously gone through all five of these categories, Bausani concludes that Iqbal's views on Satan represent a confluence of (1) the Greek element of *Prometheus*, seen through the filter of Milton, (2) the ancient Hebrew and the genuine Islamic element of Satan as God's instrument and intendant, (3) the Christian and gnostic element as *the positively evil power*, as found in Zoroastrianism, Avesta and Mazdaism, (4) the realisation, implicitly found with authors of the Islamic mystical tradition (Ghazali, Rumi) and in post-Kantian idealism, that in the Hebraic-Islamic God there is an element of what Christianity calls *satanic*; and (5) a *typically Iqbalian pragmatic-political development* of Satan as *Opium of the People*.

With elaborate footnotes and references.

528.   ——, "SATANA NELL'OPERA FILOSOFICO-POETICA DI MUHAMMAD IQBAL
(1873-1938)", *RIVISTA DEGLI STUDI ORIENTALI* (Roma) 30, no. 1-2 (1955): pp. 55-
102.
This article was translated into English by R.A. Butler, and published in *IQBAL REVIEW*
(*abstract* qv.).
I.

529.   ——, "SETTE POESIE INEDITE DI MUHAMMAD IQBAL", *IL PUNTO NELLE
LETTERE E NELLE ARTI* (Roma) 2, no. 3 (1953): pp. 16-21.
Italian translation of 6 unpublished poems by Iqbal.
I.

530.   ——, *STORIA DELLE LETTERATURE DEL PAKISTAN*, Milano, 1958

531.   **BAWHAB, A. B. A.**, "HENRI BERGSON AND MUHAMMAD IQBAL", *IQBAL
REVIEW / IQBALIAT* (Lahore) 29, no. 3: October-December (1988): pp. 103-14.
Short lecture, delivered at the one day Seminar on Iqbal and Mysticism (University of
Birmingham, 7 November 1987), on the philosophies of Bergson and Iqbal and centred
around the statement that *Bergson preached morality without naming religion, and Iqbal
preached religious morality*.

532.   **BEDI, B. P. L.**, "IQBAL, MAKER OF NEW MAN", *IQBAL REVIEW* 8, no. 1: April
(1967): pp. 31-33.
Article specially written for the occasion of IQBAL DAY at Delhi.

533.   **BEG, A. A.**, "IQBAL: A BRIDGE BETWEEN THE EAST AND WEST", *PAKISTAN
REVIEW* 3, no. [?]: April (1955): pp. 19-22.

534.   **BEG, Abdullah Anwar**, "DR. MUHAMMAD IQBAL", *PAKISTAN REVIEW* (Lahore)
19, no. 4 (1971): pp. 8-12, 39.
Special Iqbal Number.

535.   ——, "IQBAL AND THE NEW WORLD", *TIMES OF KARACHI*, 21 April 1954.
Special Suppl.

536.   ——, "IQBAL: POET OF HUMANITY", *PAKISTAN REVIEW* 8, no. 6: June (1960):

pp. 19-22.

537.   ———, "IQBAL - THE POET OF THE EAST", *THE PAKISTAN TIMES* (Rawalpindi), 21 April 1983.

538.   ———, "IQBAL, THE POET-PHILOSOPHER", *PAKISTAN REVIEW* 2, no. 4: April (1954): pp. 31-33, 36.

539.   ———, "THE PHILOSOPHY AND POETIC THOUGHT OF IQBAL", *EVENING TIMES*, 21 April 1952, pp. 3, 4.

540.   ———, "POET OF HUMANITY", *PAKISTAN REVIEW* 3, no. 6: June (1960): pp. 19-22.
        Cf. also the article of the same title in *THE CIVIL AND MILITARY GAZETTE* (Lahore), 21 April 1960, p. 5.

541.   ———, "THE POET OF ISLAM", *ISLAMIC LITERATURE* 15, no. 3: March (1969): pp. 53-62.

542.   ———, "THE POET OF THE EAST", *ISLAMIC LITERATURE* 13, no. 4: April (1967): pp. 5-10.
        Re-issued in *PAKISTAN REVIEW* 16, no. 4: April (1968), pp. 4-8.

543.   ———, mon., *THE POET OF THE EAST: THE LIFE AND WORK OF DR. SHEIKH SIR MUHAMMAD IQBAL, THE POET-PHILOSOPHER, WITH A CRITICAL SURVEY OF HIS PHILOSOPHY, POETICAL WORKS AND TEACHINGS*, R. A. NICHOLSON (introd.), Lahore: Sh. Muhammad Ashraf, 1939. xxvii+425 pp. / 323 pp.
        Later issues include Lahore: Qawmi Kutub Khana, 1940; Lahore: Islamic Publications, 1956; and Lahore: Khawar Publishing Cooperative Society / Sheikh Muhammad Ashraf, 1961.
        The book includes three parts: (I) The Life of Iqbal, (II) The Poetical Works of Iqbal, and (III) Iqbal and his Teachings.

544.   **BEGUM, Atiya**, mon., *IQBAL*, Academy of Islam (International) 161, Bombay: Victoria Printing Press, 1947. 88 pp.
        Biography including many photographs and reproductions of Iqbal's letters.

545.   **BEGUM, Atiya Faizi**, "IQBAL", *THE CIVIL AND MILITARY GAZETTE* (Lahore), 21

April 1951, p. 4.

546.   ———, mon., *IQBAL*, Lahore: Aina-i-Adab, 1969. 93 pp.
Includes reproductions of selected (I) letters in the original English.
Originally published in Bombay: Academy of Islamic Publications / Victory Printing Press, 1947, and containing 88 pp.; re-edited by Iqbal Academy (Lahore, 1981).

547.   ———, "IQBAL, A REFLECTION", *DAWN*, 30 April 1967, p. 15.

548.   ———, "IQBAL AS I KNEW HIM", *PAKISTAN TIMES*, 21 April 1950, pp. 6, 10-11.
Special Iqbal Day Suppl.

549.   ———, "MY IMPRESSION OF IQBAL", *ILLUSTRATED WEEKLY OF PAKISTAN*, 16 April 1950, p. 31.

550.   ———, "POET AS A YOUNG MAN", *PAKISTAN TIMES* (Lahore), 21 April 1956, p. 6.

551.   ———, "WHEN SOFT MUSIC CONFUSED IQBAL", *DAWN* (Karachi), 21 April 1952, p. 6.

552.   **BENABOUD, M.**, "COMPREHENSIVE NATURE OF IQBAL'S PHILOSOPHY", *ISLAMIC STUDIES* 16, no. 1 (1977): pp. 317-27.

553.   **BHAJJAN, S. V.**, "IQBAL THE POET", *BULLETIN (HENRY MARTYN INSTITUTE OF ISLAMIC STUDIES)* 54, no. 4: January (1966): pp. 15-34.

554.   **BHATTI, Abdul Majid A.**, "A LINE FROM IQBAL", *PAKISTAN REVIEW* 2, no. 4: April (1954): pp. 34-36.

555.   **BHUTTA, Zafar Ahmad**, "IQBAL AND HIS SIGNATURES", *PAKISTAN TIMES* (Lahore), 21 April 1959, p. 5.

556.   **BILGRAMI, H.H.**, mon., *GLIMPSES OF IQBAL'S MIND & THOUGHT: ITS CAUSES & CONSEQUENCES*, Chicago: Kazi Publications, 1985. 213 pp.

557.   **BILGRAMI, H. H.**, mon., *GLIMPSES OF IQBAL'S MIND AND THOUGHT (BRIEF LECTURES ON IQBAL, DELIVERED AT LONDON, CAMBRIDGE AND OXFORD)*, Lahore: Orientalia, 1954. vii+124 pp.

A collection of 6 articles on different apects of Iqbal and Iqbal's philosophy.

(1) SHEIKH MUHAMMAD IQBAL (1877-1938): A general and introductory essay on the life, the works and the politico-philosophical impact of Iqbal. *Talk delivered at Balliol College, Oxford, July 15th 1951.*

(2) IQBAL'S APPROACH TO THE SPIRIT OF ISLAMIC CULTURE: Starting from a definition of *Islam* and *Culture*, Bilgrami proceeds to analyse Iqbal's concept of *tauhid*, the finality of prophethood, the 'gaze on the concrete', and the concept of *Ijtihad. Adress delivered on the occasion of Iqbal Day 1952, at the Islamic Culture Centre, London.*

(3) IQBAL'S THEORY OF KNOWLEDGE AND ITS SIGNIFICANCE IN HIS POETRY: An analysis of Iqbal's views on the concept of *'ilm*, and where Iqbal differs from Ghazzali's theory of knowledge. Bilgrami states: 'To Iqbal, knowledge is not merely the basis of a moral and ethical system, but the foundation-stone of the whole life'. *Talk given to the Oxford University Group of Study of Religions, at All Souls, on an unknown date. The second part of the text, on how Iqbal's theory of knowledge has found expression in his poetry, was later added by the author.*

(4) IQBAL'S PHILOSOPHY OF 'AMAL: A discussion of Iqbal's thought with regard to the motives, directives and purposes which govern the lives and actions of human beings. The main point is that, according to Iqbal, the concept of 'good', and the factor of 'faith' therein, determines man's behaviour. *Lecture given at Pembroke College, Cambridge (date unknown).* The same article appeared in *ISLAMIC LITERATURE*, August 1952, qv.

(5) IQBAL'S CONCEPT OF DEMOCRACY, BASED ON ISLAMIC PRINCIPLES: The author warns his audience against misunderstanding the seemingly dual approach of Iqbal towards certain concepts and phrases. As to the concept of *democracy*, Iqbal has certainly praised it and criticised it at the same time. To Iqbal *Islamic democracy* means the following: -1- *Tauhid* (the oneness of God) as a fundamental basis, -2- obedience to the Law, as given to mankind by the Prophets, -3- implication of a fundamental *tolerance*, -4- a concemnation of nationalism, -5- the application of the islamic concept of *Ijtihad. Lecture given on Iqbal Day 1953 at the Iqbal Society, London.*

(6) THE MAIN SOURCE OF IQBAL'S INSPIRATIONS: A short adress on Iqbal's inspiration from the Quran, ending with a quotation of a poem from Iqbal's BAL-I-JIBRIL, both in Urdu and in English. *Talk given at the East London Mosque, 1949.*

This book was re-issued as a paperback by Shaikh Muhammad Ashraf (Lahore 1966).

558. ———, "IQBAL: HIS APPROACH TO THE SPIRIT OF ISLAMIC CULTURE", *THE INDIAN ART AND LETTERS* (London) 23, no. 1 (1949): pp. 16-23.

559. ———, "IQBAL: HIS THEORY OF KNOWLEDGE AND ITS VALUE IN LIFE AND POETRY", *DAWN*, 21 April 1950, pp. 10-11.

560. ———, "IQBAL'S APPROACH TO THE SPIRIT OF ISLAMIC CULTURE", *VOICE OF ISLAM*, July 1953, p. 372.

Address delivered on the occasion of Iqbal Day, 21 April 1953, at the Islamic Culture Centre, London.

561. ———, "IQBAL'S CONCEPT OF DEMOCRACY BASED ON ISLAMIC PRINCIPLES", *ISLAMIC LITERATURE* (Lahore) 6, no. 4: April (1954): pp. 197-202. Re-issued in *ISLAMIC LITERATURE*, April 1958, pp. 17-22.

562. ———, mon., *IQBAL'S MIND AND THOUGHT*, Lahore, 1954. Six articles on different aspects of Iqbal.

563. ———, "IQBAL'S PHILOSOPHY OF 'AMAL", *ISLAMIC LITERATURE* (Lahore) [vol. ?], no. [?]: August (1952).
This article was reprinted in Bilgrami's collection of six lectures (*GLIMPSES OF IQBAL'S MIND AND THOUGHT*, Lahore: Orientalia, 1954 - qv.).

564. ———, "IQBAL'S THEORY OF KNOWLEDGE AND ITS SIGNIFICANCE IN HIS POETRY", *ISLAMIC LITERATURE* (Lahore) 3, no. 5: May (1951): pp. 244-54.

565. ———, "SHAIKH MUHAMMAD IQBAL", *IQBAL, MAINSPRING OF MUSLIM RENAISSANCE*, Various authors (mon.), [place ?]: Iqbal Society in the U.K., n.d., pp. 9-13.

566. ———, "SPIRIT OF ISLAMIC CULTURE, IQBAL'S APPROACH", *DAWN*, 21 April 1958, p. 5.

567. **BILIMORIA, Purusottoma**, "IQBAL'S GOD AND GITA'S LORD", *IQBAL REVIEW* 28, no. 1: April-June (1987): pp. 39-53.

568. **bin SAYEED, Khalid**, mon., *PAKISTAN, THE FORMATIVE PHASE: 1857-1948*, George CUNNINGHAM (foreword), 2nd ed., Lahore: Oxford UP, 1968. 341 pp. See esp. pp. 1, 11, 93-94, 103-106, 108, 117, 176, 283, 295.

569. **BIRTHA, Rachel**, "ROLE SEEN FOR U.S. SCHOLARS IN INTERPRETING IQBAL", *PAKISTAN TIMES*, 10 April 1977, p. 1.

570. **BIRUNI, A. H. AL S. M. IKRAM**, *MAKERS OF PAKISTAN AND MODERN MUSLIM INDIA*, Lahore: Muhammad Ashraf, 1950/1952. 261 pp.

Cf. esp. pp. 169-190.

571.   **BISWAS, Anil**, "IQBAL'S GHAZAL AND MUSIC", *THE PAKISTAN TIMES* (Rawalpindi), 2 December 1977.

572.   **BISWAS, Lakshmi**, mon., *TAGORE AND IQBAL: A STUDY IN PHILOSOPHICAL PERSPECTIVE*, R. P. SRIVASTAVA (ed.), Delhi: Capital Publishing House, 1991. iv+308 pp.

573.   **BOKHARI, A. S.**, "SIR MUHAMMAD IQBAL", *STATESMAN* (Calcutta/Delhi), 22 April 1939.

574.   **BONUCCI, A.**, "[Title ?]", *REVISTA TRIMESTRALE FILOSOFIA (E RELIGIONI PERUGIA)* 2, (1921): pp. 223-25.
       I.

575.   **BOXANYI, A.**, "IQBAL'S PHILOSOPHY", *PACIFIC REVUE DES ASIATIQUES* (Paris) (1953-1954).
       Variant name: BOKHARI, A.S.

576.   **BROHI, A. K.**, mon., *IQBAL AND QURANIC WISDOM*, Lahore: Islamic Book Foundation, n.d. 175 pp.

577.   ———, mon., *IQBAL AND THE CONCEPT OF ISLAMIC SOCIALISM*, Karachi: Begum Aisha Bowany Wakf, 1977. 10 pp.
       An address delivered by the author on 23 April 1967 at Lahore, on the occasion of Iqbal Day Celebrations organized by the Central Iqbal Committee.

578.   ———, "IQBAL AS A PHILOSOPHER POET", *IQBAL REVIEW* 2, no. 1: April (1961): pp. 1-21.

579.   ———, "IQBAL'S CONCEPT OF AN ISLAMIC STATE", *IQBAL, THE POET OF TOMORROW*, Khawaja Abdur RAHIM (ed.), Lahore: Abdul Hameed Khan at Ferozsons Ltd., n.d., pp. 55[59]-68.
       As indicated in the footnote on p. 59, this paper was originally read as presidential address at the morning session of 21 April 1961.
       With regard to the origin of Pakistan in the light of political history and Islam, the author concludes that (p. 69) *Pakistan is a legacy left to us by Iqbal and the one way to show reverence to him is to safeguard its sanctity, its integrity and to labour for its continued*

progress and prosperity.

580. ———, "IQBALIAN IJTEHAD AND THE CONCEPT OF ISLAMIC SOCIALISM", *IQBAL REVIEW* 9, no. 1: April (1968): pp. 37-45.
Address delivered on 23 April 1967, published also by the Central Iqbal Committee, Lahore.

581. ———, "REDEEMER OF MUSULMANS", *PAKISTAN STANDARD*, 24 April 1955.

582. **BROMS, Henri**, mon., *MUHAMMAD IQBAL*, Helsinki, 1954. 32 pp.
Fi.

583. **BROWNE, E. G.**, "THE SECRETS OF THE SELF (ASRAR-I-KHUDI)", *THE JOURNAL OF THE ROYAL ASIATIC SOCIETY* (London) (1921): pp. 146-47.
A Review of Nicholson, *SECRETS OF THE SELF*, London: MacMillan, 1920 - qv.

584. **BURGEL, J. C.**, "DIE GRIECHISCHE ZIEGE UND DAS SCHAF VON SCHIRAS: BEMERKUNGEN ZU GEDANKEN MUHAMMAD IQBALS ÜBER PLATO UND HAFIS", *STUDIEN ZUR GESCHICHTE UND KULTUR DES VORDEREN ORIENTS: FESTSCHRIFT FÜR BERTOLD SPULER ZUM SIEBZIGSTEN GEBURTSTAG*, Hans R. ROEMER & Albrecht NOTH (eds.), Leiden: Brill, 1981.
G.

585. ———, ed., *IQBAL UND EUROPA: VIER VORTRÄGE*, A. BAUSANI & J.C. BURGEL & J. MAREK & A. SCHIMMEL (mon.), Schweizer Asiatische Studien Studienhefte 5, Bern / Frankfurt am Main / Las Vegas: Peter Lang, 1980. 85 pp.
This book contains 4 lectures (*abstract* qv.), which, according to the editor's preface (p. 10), were delivered during the Summer term of 1977, in a cooperation of the Collegium Generale of the University of Bern and the Schweizerische Gesellschaft fur Asienkunde:
(1) J.C. Burgel: IQBAL UND GOETHE;
(2) Annemarie Schimmel: MUHAMMAD IQBAL, DER GEISTIGE VATER PAKISTANS;
(3) Alessandro Bausani: IQBAL UND DANTE, BETRACHTUNGEN ÜBER IQBALS DSCHAWIDNAMA;
(4) J. Marek: MUHAMMAD IQBALS SOZIALE IDEEN.
G.

586. ———, "IQBAL UND GOETHE", *IQBAL UND EUROPA: VIER VORTRAGE*, J. C. BURGEL (ed.), Bern / Frankfurt am Main / Las Vegas: Peter Lang, 1980, pp. 11-32.

On Goethe's and Iqbal's common admiration of Hafez; Goethe's praise of the *"pure* East" and Iqbal's politico-religious conception of *Paki*stan; etc.
G.

587. ———, "THE PIOUS ROGUE: A STUDY IN THE MEANING OF QALANDAR AND REND IN THE POETRY OF MUHAMMAD IQBAL", *EDEBIYAT - THE JOURNAL OF MIDDLE EASTERN LITERATURES* (Reading, Berkshire, U.K.) 4, no. 1 (1979): pp. 43-64.

588. **BURKI, Riffat Hassan Dawar**, "IQBAL'S 'KHUDI' - ITS MEANING AND STRENGTHENING FACTOR", *IQBAL* (Lahore) 23, no. 3: July (1976): pp. 1-26.

589. **BURKI, Riffat J.**, "IQBAL AS A PHILOSOPHER: A VINDICATION", *PAKISTAN REVIEW* (Lahore) 19, no. 4 (1971): pp. 19-21, 28.
Special Iqbal Number.

590. **BURKI, Riffat Jehan Dawar**, "INTUITION IN IQBAL'S PHILOSOPHY", *IQBAL REVIEW* 11, no. 3: October (1970): pp. 58-67.

591. ———, "INTUITION IN IQBAL'S PHILOSOPHY", *PAKISTAN TIMES*, 21 April 1973, p. 4.

592. ———, "IQBAL AND BERGSON: CONCEPT OF TIME", *IQBAL REVIEW* 12, no. 1: April (1971): pp. 6-11.

593. ———, "IQBAL AND SOCIAL SYSTEM; JUSTICE", *PAKISTAN TIMES*, 21 April 1969.

594. ———, "IQBAL AND TAUHID", *IQBAL REVIEW* 14, no. 3: October (1973): pp. 9-15.

595. ———, "IQBAL'S CONCEPT OF THE *MARD-I-MU'MIN* AND RUMI'S INFLUENCE", *IQBAL REVIEW* 13, no. 1: April (1972): pp. 1-17.

596. ———, "IQBAL'S VISION OF NEW SOCIETY", *DAWN*, 21 April 1958, p. 9.

597. ———, "THE POET'S ROLE AS A PHILOSOPHER", *PAKISTAN TIMES*, 21 April 1969, pp. 1, 2.

598. ————, "SPIRITUAL FOUNDER OF PAKISTAN. ALLAMA IQBAL AS A PHILOSOPHER ", *PAKISTAN TIMES*, 21 April 1974, p. 1.

599. BURNEY, Sayed Muzaffar Husain, *IQBAL AND NATIONAL INTEGRATION*, Chandigarh: Haryana Sahitya Akademi, 1984

600. ————, mon., *IQBAL - POET-PATRIOT OF INDIA*, Syeda SAIYIDAIN (tr.), New Delhi / Ghazibad: Vikas Publishing House, 1987. 136 pp.
From the poetical works of Iqbal, Burney deducts various aspects in the philosophy of the author, such as his patriotism (India before partition), his adherence to and admiration of certain aspects of traditional Indian philosophy and thought, his involvement in the freedom movement and his opinion about the rise of Pakistan as an independent country. The general idea of the work is to remove Iqbal from his traditional role as the 'father of the nation of Pakistan' and to qualify the author as an all-India thinker and poet.
Including notes and a basic bibliography.

601. BUTT, Nisar Aziz, "IQBAL'S PHILOSOPHY OF EVILS", *DAWN*, 4 May 1967, p. 7.

602. CALLEWAERT, W. M., "IQBAL (1877-1938)", *INFORIENT* (Leuven) 9, no. 1: May (1990): pp. 95-108.
A short introduction into the life and works of Iqbal - followed by an integral rendering (in the original English) of Iqbal's *Pakistan Adress*, delivered at Allahabad, December 30th 1930, on the necessity of setting up a seperate state for India's Muslim population.
D/E.

603. CARDILLO, V., "MUHAMMAD IQBAL E LA VICE-GERENZA DI DIO", *GENTES* [vol. ?], no. [?] (1962): pp. 5-6.
I.

604. Central Iqbal Committee, "ALLAMA IQBAL WAS NOT A QADIANI", *PAKISTAN TIMES*, 13 April 1954.
Refutation of the allegation that Iqbal was a Qadiani.

605. CHABRIA, R. G., "DIALOGUE WITH SELF. A COMPARATIVE APPROACH TO IQBAL'S 'ASRAR-I-KHUDI' AND AUROBINDO'S 'SAVITRI'", *ARYAN PATH* 47, no. 3: May-June (1976): pp. 116.

606. CHAGHTAÏ, Mirza Saïd-uz-Zafar & Suzanne BUSSAC, tr., *L'AILE DE BAGRIEL (BÂL-É-DJIBRÎL)*, Muhammad IQBAL (mon.), Spiritualités Vivantes, Série Islam /

Collection Unesco D'Oeuvres Représentatives, Série Pakistanaise, Paris: Éditions Albin Michel, 1977. 157 pp.
Translation into French of Iqbal's (Urdu) BAL-I JIBRIL.
F.

607. **CHAGHTAI, Abdullah**, "HE CARRIED THE POET'S MESSAGE TO THE ARABS", *THE CIVIL AND MILITARY GAZETTE* (Lahore), 21 April 1960, p. 3.
Variant name: CHUGHTAI.

608. ———, "IQBAL AND ART", *THE CIVIL AND MILITARY GAZETTE* (Lahore), 21 April 1961, p. 4.

609. **CHAGHTAI, Muhammad Abdullah**, "ALLAMA IN LONDON", *PAKISTAN TIMES* (Lahore), 21 April 1956, p. 6.

610. ———, "REMINISCENCES", *IQBAL* (Lahore) 7, no. 1: July (1958): pp. 72-81.

611. **CHAGLA, A. G.**, "SOME ASPECTS OF IQBAL'S THOUGHT", *TRIVENI* (Bangalore) 18, no. 2: June (1946): pp. 93-102.

612. **CHAGLA, Ahmed G.**, "IQBAL'S GHAZALS", *ARYAN PATH* 17, no. 12: December (1946): pp. 460.

613. **CHAKRAVARTY, Amiya**, "IQBAL AND HIS POETIC FAITH", *RAVI* 32, no. 7-8: May-June (1936): pp. 3-7.

614. ———, "IQBAL, INDIA'S MUSLIM POET", *ASIA* (New York) - *JOURNAL OF THE AMERICAN ASIATIC ASSOCIATION* 38, no. 9: September (1938): pp. 559-62. Extracts of this article were re-issued in *MODERN REVIEW* (Calcutta) 14, no. 5: November (1938), pp. 632-634; and in *THE STATESMAN*, Magazine Section, 1939.

615. ———, "SIR MUHAMMAD IQBAL", *VOICE OF ISLAM* (Singapore), January 1939-28 February 1939, pp. 19-23.
Re-issue of an article from *ASIA* (New York) 38, no. 9 (1938) - qv.

616. **CHATTERJEE, G. P.**, mon., *ARCHITECTS OF PAKISTAN*, Kushtia (East Pakistan) / Lahore: New Book Stall - Sheikh Muhammad Ashraf, n.d.

Cf. esp. pp. 23-41.

617. **CHAUDHRI, Ashraf**, "IQBAL AND KASHMIRI MUSLIMS", *DAILY NEWS* (Islamabad), 9 November 1993.

618. **CHAUDHRI, Ghulam Ali**, "IQBAL AND JINNAH ON PALESTINE", *IQBAL REVIEW* 32, no. 3: October (1991): pp. 87-104.

619. **CHAUDHRI, Muhammad Ashraf**, mon., *THE MUSLIM UMMAH AND IQBAL*, Islamabad: National Institute of Historical and Cultural Research, 1994.
Cf. in particular Chapter 3, Iqbal's concept of man and society; and Chapter 4, the unit of social structure in the philosophy of Iqbal: ego.

620. **CHAUDHRY, Ghulam Ali**, "ABDUL WALI KHAN TRADUCES IQBAL", *JOURNAL OF THE RESEARCH SOCIETY OF PAKISTAN* 29, no. 1: January (1992).

621. **CHAUDRY, A. K. M. Kabir**, "SOME ASPECTS OF IQBAL'S POETRY", *IQBAL, THE POET OF TOMORROW*, Khawaja Abdur RAHIM (ed.), Lahore: Abdul Hameed Khan at Ferozsons Ltd., n.d., pp. 241[243]-249.
According to the footnote on p. 243, *Mr. A.K.M. Kabir Chaudry, who is among the intellectual leaders of East Pakistan, read this paper on Iqbal Day at Lahore on April 21, 1963. He concludes that Iqbal certainly was no opium-eater in Art. He wrote because he felt that he had something definite to say. And of all his messages the ringing words regarding the development of personality and the need for complete freedom for making that possible would always be cherished by humanity through the ages.*

622. **CHAUHAN, M. Rafiq**, "SOME ASPECTS OF IQBAL'S CONTRIBUTION TO THE CAUSE OF ISLAM", *IQBAL REVIEW* 18, no. 4: January (1978): pp. 183-93.

623. **CHAWDHURY, Kabir**, "IQBAL: AN APPRECIATION", *IQBAL REVIEW* 2, no. 3: October (1961): pp. 79-85.

624. **CHELYSHEV, Y.**, "MOHAMMAD IQBAL - CLASSIC OF WORLD LITERATURE", *IQBAL COMMEMORATIVE VOLUME*, Ali Sardar JAFRI & K.S. DUGGAL (eds.), New Delhi: All India Iqbal Centenary Celebrations Committee, 1977, pp. 267-80.
This article bears the sub-title A TYPOLOGICAL ANALYSIS OF IQBAL'S AND PUSHKIN'S POETRY, dealing with their concept of man, the social trend and east-west synthesis in their poetry, etc.

625.   ———, "MUHAMMAD IQBAL - A WORLD CLASS", *THE WORK OF MUHAMMAD IQBAL: ARTICLES BY SOVIET SCHOLARS*, Abdur Rauf MALIK (ed.), Lahore: People's Publishing House, 1983, pp. 21-31.

626.   **CHISHTI, Yusuf Salim**, "IQBAL'S PHILOSOPHY OF FAQR", *IQBAL REVIEW* 3, no. 3: October (1962): pp. 40-59.

627.   **CHOPRA, Hari Lal**, "IQBAL - THE POET", *INDO-IRANICA* (Iran Society, Calcutta) 10, no. 3: September (1957): pp. 24-27.
        Variant journal title: INDO-ISLAMICA.

628.   **CHOPRA, Hira Lall**, "IMMORTAL POET IQBAL", *THE TIMES OF KARACHI*, 8 May 1955.
        Text of a speech delivered on Iqbal Day, 21 April 1955, at the Pakistan High Commission, Calcutta.

629.   ———, "IQBAL AND HIS MESSAGE", *INDO-IRANICA* 8, no. 3: September (1955): pp. 20-28.

630.   ———, "IQBAL AND INDIA", *INDO-IRANICA* 15, no. 2: June (1962): pp. 27-33.

631.   ———, "IQBAL - SOME REMINISCENCES", *CHIRAGH-I RAGHUZAR* (Calcutta), January 1978.
        Variant date: 1977.
        The Muslim Institute, Allama Iqbal Birth Centenary Committee.

632.   **CHRISTOPHER, C. B.**, "INDIVIDUAL AND SOCIETY: A STUDY OF THE SOCIAL PHILOSOPHY OF IQBAL", *PAKISTAN REVIEW* 3, no. [?]: April (1955): pp. 26-28.

633.   **CHUGHTAI, Abdur Rahman**, mon., *IQBAL: POET OF THE EAST* (AML-E-CHUGHTAI), Lahore: Nisar Art Press, 1968. 227 pp.
        English and Urdu.

634.   **CHUGHTAI, Arif**, "CHUGHTAI AND IQBAL", *IQBAL COMMEMORATIVE VOLUME*, Ali Sardar JAFRI & K.S. DUGGAL (eds.), New Delhi: All India Iqbal Centenary Committee, 1977, pp. 207-16.
        In this article, *the relation of Dr Mohammad Iqbal and Khan Bahadur Abdur Rahman Chughtai*, who was *a friend and associate of the late poet*, a true *Moslem renaissance painter*, is studied within the context of the historical developments of the region

(Pakistan).

635. **Civil and Military Gazette** (red.), "MISREPRESENTATION OF IQBAL'S MESSAGE DEPLORED", *CIVIL AND MILITARY GAZETTE*, 24 February 1962, p. 4.
Staff Reporter's Report of a public meeting held in the Y.M.C.A. Hall, Lahore, on 23 Frebruary 1962.

636. **CLAVEL, Leotiny S.**, "ISLAMIC ALLUSIONS IN THE POETRY OF IQBAL", *ASIAN STUDIES* (Quezon City, Philippines) 8, (1970): pp. 378-85.

637. **COPPOLA, Carlo**, "IQBAL AND THE PROGRESSIVE MOVEMENT", *JOURNAL OF SOUTH ASIAN AND MIDDLE EASTERN STUDIES* 1, no. 2 (1977): pp. 49-57.

638. **CORNELIUS, Justice A. R.**, "IDEOLOGICAL FOUNDATION FOR DEMOCRACY IN ISLAM", *IQBAL, THE POET OF TOMORROW*, Khawaja Abdur RAHIM (ed.), Lahore: Abdul Hameed Khan at Ferozsons Ltd., n.d., pp. 93[97]-107. Paper read as inaugural address by Chief Justice A.R. Cornelius on 21 April 1964, who admits that (p. 97) *to savour to the full the quality of a poet such as Iqbal, it is clearly necessary that one should have an appreciation and acceptance from the heart of the dogma and the ethic of Islam. How then can I, a Christian, attempt to speak of him?* The author's acquaintance with the constitution of Pakistan, however, qualifies him to appreciate at least some aspects of Iqbal's message. So it is apparent that (p. 103) *the poet must have been well aware of the need to provide his choice of the republican form of Government with a respectable heredity, a kind of ideological lineage, drawn from the fundamental principles of Islam.*

639. **COURTOIS, Victor S. J.**, "SIR MUHAMMAD IQBAL, POÈTE, PHILOSOPHE ET APOLOGISTE INDIEN", *TERRE D'ISLAM* 13, no. 4 (1938): pp. 3-4.
Review of (I) THE RECONSTRUCTION OF RELIGIOUS THOUGHT IN ISLAM. F.

640. **DADASHI, Yakub**, "WHAT TURKEY THINKS OF ALLAMA IQBAL", *DAWN* (Karachi), 21 April 1954, p. 5.
Variant name: DASHI, M. Yakub.

641. **DAMAL, A. K.**, "A CHRONOLOGICAL BIOGRAPHY", *THE PAKISTAN TIMES* (Rawalpindi), 9 November 1977.

642. **DANEK, Vaclav & Jan MAREK**, tr. U/Cz, P/Cz [?], *HLAS KARAVANNIHO ZVONKU,*

Muhammad IKBAL (mon.), Praha: [Vydal] Odeon, 1977. 152(+7) pp.
Vychazi k stemu vyroci basnikova narozeni - svetovemu kulturnimu vyroci UNESCO.
Contents: Hlas Karavanniho Zvonku (pp. 7-37); Tajemstvi Vlastniho Ja (pp. 39-64);
Poselstvi z Vychodu (pp. 65-97); Kniha o Vecnosti (pp. 99-105); Perske Zalmy (pp. 107-109); Kridlo Gabrielovo (pp. 111-113); Uder Mojzisovy Hole (pp. 115-132); Darek z
Hidzazu (pp. 133-134); as well as Jan Marek, BASNIK DVOU SVETU (pp. 135-145),
and Poznamky (pp. 146-*153).
Cz [?].

643. **DAR, B. A.**, *ARTICLES ON IQBAL*.
Book under print in 1996.

644. ———, "DISCUSSION", *IQBAL* 20, no. 1: July-October (1972): pp. 62-74.
Discussion of James B. Prior's article "IQBAL'S VIEW OF 'ISLAMIC NATIONALISM'
IN JAVIDNAMEH", published in *IQBAL*, July-September 1971.

645. ———, "DR. MOHAMMAD MARUF (Ed.), CONTRIBUTION TO IQBAL'S
THOUGHT - REVIEW", *IQBAL* 25, no. 1: January (1978): pp. 88-91.

646. ———, "DR. MUHAMMAD MARUF, IQBAL'S PHILOSOPHY OF RELIGION -
REVIEW", *IQBAL* 25, no. 1: January (1978): pp. 92-94.

647. ———, "FOR THE COMPANIONS OF THE WAY", *IQBAL* 25, no. 3: July (1978): pp.
63-72.
English rendering of the last Persian part of ARMUGHAN-I HIJAZ, entitled YARAN-I
TARIQ (pp. 187-210), with explanatory notes.

648. ———, "GHALIB AND IQBAL", *IQBAL REVIEW* 10, no. 3: October (1969): pp. 25-43.

649. ———, "HISTORICAL BACKGROUND OF IQBAL'S EARLY POEMS", *IQBAL*
(Lahore) 21, no. 3: July-September (1974): pp. 19-56.
On the influence exerted on Iqbal's early poetry by the antagonism between Hindus and
Muslims.

650. ———, "INSPIRATION FROM THE WEST", *IQBAL: POET-PHILOSOPHER OF
PAKISTAN*, Hafeez MALIK (ed.), New Delhi / New York: Columbia UP, 1971.

651. ———, "IQBAL AND BERGSON", *IQBAL* (Bazm-i-Iqbal, Lahore) 3, no. 1: July (1954):
pp. 34-86.

On Iqbal's treatment of Bergson's philosophy. With exhaustive quotes from Iqbal's works, both in the original and in English translation.
This article was reproduced in SHEIKH, M. Saeed, *STUDIES IN IQBAL'S THOUGHT AND ART*, Lahore, 1972, pp.191-247.

652. ——, "IQBAL'S CONCEPTION OF MAN AND SOCIETY", *IQBAL* (Lahore) 22, no. 1: January (1975): pp. 51-59.

653. ——, mon., *IQBAL'S PHILOSOPHY OF INDIVIDUAL*, Lahore: 1938

654. ——, "IQBAL'S PROSE WORKS", *IQBAL* 19, no. 1: July-September (1971): pp. 85-94.

655. ——, "MIRACLE OF ISLAM. AN ACCOUNT BASED ON IQBAL'S NARRATION", *IQBAL* (Lahore) 24, no. 1: January (1977): pp. 41-56.

656. ——, "NEW IQBAL MATERIAL", *IQBAL REVIEW* 10, no. 3: October (1969): pp. 83-96.

657. ——, "REFLECTIONS OF MIHRAB GUL AFGHAN", *IQBAL* 19, no. 3: January-March (1972): pp. 34-48.
English translation of Iqbal's poem MIHRAB GUL KHAN KE AFKAR in ZARB-I KALIM, pp. 166-182.

658. ——, "REVIEW [ON] STUDIES IN IQBAL BY SYED ABDUL VAHID", *IQBAL REVIEW* 9, no. 1: April (1968): pp. 141-44.

659. ——, "RIAZ HUSSAIN, THE POLITICS OF IQBAL - REVIEW", *IQBAL* 25, no. 1: January (1978): pp. 85-88.

660. **DAR, Bashir Ahmad**, tr. P/E, *ADDRESS TO JAVID: A WORD TO THE NEW GENERATION, WITH INTRODUCTION AND NOTES, RENDERED INTO ENGLISH*, Karachi, 1971. 34 pp.

661. ——, "ADDRESS TO JAVID; TALK TO THE NEW GENERATION", *IQBAL REVIEW* 12, no. 1: April (1971): pp. 12-38.
English translation of (I) JAVID-NAMA, with an introduction and notes.

662.   ———, "GULSHAN-I-RAZ-I-JADID: THE NEW GARDEN OF MYSTERY", *IQBAL* 5, no. 3: January (1957): pp. 1-48.
English translation of (I) GULSHAN-I-RAZ-I-JADID.

663.   ———, "THE IDEA OF SATAN IN IQBAL AND MILTON", *IQBAL* 1, no. 1: July (1952): pp. 83-108.

664.   ———, "INTELLECT AND INTUITION IN BERGSON AND SUFIS", *IQBAL* 4, no. [?] (1956).

665.   ———, "IQBAL AND NIETZSCHE", *MAH-I-NAU (Urdu)* 30, no. [?]: September (Iqbal Number) (1977): pp. 24-32.

666.   ———, mon., *IQBAL AND POST-KANTIAN VOLUNTARISM*, Lahore: Bazm-i-Iqbal, 1956. vi+498 pp.
A comparative study of Iqbal and the following Western philosophers: Kant, Fichte, Schopenhauer, Milton, Goethe, Bergson, Nietzsche, James Ward, McDougall, Lloyd Morgan, W. James, Carlyle, Browning, Bernard Shaw.
The 1965 edition has iv+546 pp.

667.   ———, "IQBAL, MUHAMMAD", *THE ENCYCLOPEDIA OF PHILOSOPHY*, Paul EDWARDS (ed.-in-chief), New York: Macmillan and Free Press, 1967, Vol. 4, pp. 212-13.

668.   ———, tr. P/E, *IQBAL'S "GULSHAN-I-RAZ-I-JADID" (NEW GARDEN OF MYSTERY) AND "BANDAGI NAMAH" (BOOK OF SERVITUDE), RENDERED INTO ENGLISH*, Lahore: Institute of Islamic Culture, 1964. x+77 pp.
Reprint available in 1996.

669.   ———, mon., *IQBAL'S PHILOSOPHY OF SOCIETY: AN EXPOSITION OF RUMUZ-I-BEKHUDI*, Lahore: Sheikh Muhammad Ashraf, 1933/1944.

670.   ———, comp./ed., *LETTERS AND WRITINGS OF IQBAL*, Mumtaz HASAN (intr.), Lahore: Iqbal Academy, 1981. viii+129 pp.
A collection of letters and essays by Iqbal hitherto unpublished in the English original, and therefore a useful addition to Shamloo's *SPEECHES AND STATEMENTS OF IQBAL* (qv.) and Vahid's *THOUGHTS AND REFLECTIONS OF IQBAL* (qv.). Exception is the master-plan of the book Iqbal was intending to write, which was reproduced first in *TOLU-I-ISLAM*, and later in Vahid's *THOUGHTS* etc., but with many undeciphered words

and phrases.

With a foreword by Mumtaz Hasan, a short preface by B.A. Dar, elaborate bibliographical footnotes, and an index. The first edition was published in Karachi (1967), and has iv+129 pp.

671.　———, comp., *LETTERS OF IQBAL*, Lahore: Iqbal Academy Pakistan, 1977/1978 [?]. 270 pp.
This collection of Iqbal's letters comprises only those written in English, several of which hitherto remained unpublished. Introductory notes and footnotes by the compiler elucidate the letters.

672.　———, mon., *MULTI-DISCIPLINARY APPROACH TO IQBAL*, New Delhi: Publications Division, 1977

673.　———, tr., *'NEW GARDEN OF MYSTERY' AND 'BOOK OF SERVITUDE'* (GULSHAN-I RAZ-JADID and BANDAGI-NAMAH), Lahore: Institute of Islamic Culture, 1964. 58 pp.
English translation of (I) GULSHAN-I RAZ-JADID and (I) BANDAGI NAMAH.

674.　———, "THE PROBLEM OF STYLE AND TECHNIQUE IN IQBAL", *ASPECTS OF GHALIB - FIVE ESSAYS*, Various authors (mon.), Karachi: Pakistan American Cultural Centre, 1970.
Essay on the style and technique in Iqbal's poetry, with reference to the same in Ghalib, as exemplified in another essay by Ahmed Ali in the same book. Further contributions to the volume are on Ghalib: (3) THE USES OF POETRY FOR HISTORICAL UNDERSTANDING - THE CASE OF GHALIB, by A.T. Embree; (4) GHALIB: MAN AND POET, by Hamid Ahmad Khan; (5) GHALIB, AN INDIVIDUALIST, by Mumtaz Hasan.

675.　———, mon., *A STUDY IN IQBAL'S PHILOSOPHY*, Lahore: Shaikh Muhammad Ashraf, 1944. 10+422 pp.
The first ever thorough attempt at a philosophical interpretation of Iqbal's thought in the English language. The aim of the author is to explain generally the philosophical aspects of Iqbal's re-interpretation of the message of Islam, in the context of a contemporary situation. The first chapter deals with Iqbal's aesthetics, and more in particular with the divide between *art for art's sake* and *art for life's sake*, to conclude with Iqbal's opinion about *form* and *content* in art. In chapter 2 the author deals with Iqbal's main predecessors, viz. Rumi, Nietzsche, Bergson and James Ward. In the third chapter Dar offers a detailed analysis of Iqbal's philosophy of the Self (*khudi*), with reference to a.o. Kant, Bradley, McTaggart, Hujwari, Hallaj, Ghazali, Fichte, Plato, Ibn 'Arabi, Shankaracarya, the Buddha

and Schopenhauer. From there, he opens a discussion of *society* as envisaged by Iqbal, en-route considering the role of the individual in society, the finality of prophethood, the idea of sovereignty, and the Islamic State. *It is clear that the message of Iqbal has intimate bearing on problems we are facing today in Pakistan,* Dar states (1971), and he expresses the wish that *a book dealing with these problems, in the framework of Islamic ideology as envisaged by Iqbal, can serve some purpose.*

Appendices to the original edition include two short articles by Iqbal: (I) SELF IN THE LIGHT OF RELATIVITY and (I) McTAGGART'S PHILOSOPHY. Also appended is a detailed and step-by-step REPLY TO MR. W.C. SMITH'S CRITICISM OF IQBAL, which was stated in Smith's *MODERN ISLAM IN INDIA* (Minerva Book Shop, Lahore 1943). Smith, *a socialist by conviction but with a socialism which seems to be marred by his Christian outlook on life* (sic) had isolated two divergent tendencies in Iqbal's personality, viz. a *progressiveness*, where Iqbal is reported to have been *least religious* and*most modern,* and a *reactionary attitude*, where Iqbal was *most religious* and *conservative*.

Also published by Ilmi Printing Press (Lahore), 1954; and revised and re-edited by Shaikh Ghulam Ali (Lahore, 1971. xxiv+329 pp.), with a foreword by Mr. Mumtaz Hasan, a new introduction by the author, a basic bibliography and an index.

676. ———, tr. P/E, *WHAT SHOULD THEN BE DONE O PEOPLE OF THE EAST - AN ENGLISH RENDERING OF IQBAL'S PAS CHIH BAYAD KARD AY AQWAM-I-SHARQ,* Lahore: Iqbal Academy, 1977. 146 pp.

677. **DAR, M. Ashraf**, "REVIEW [OF] SPEECHES, WRITINGS AND STATEMENTS OF IQBAL BY LATIF AHMAD SHERWANI", *IQBAL REVIEW* 19, no. 3: October (1978): pp. 77.

678. ———, "REVIEW [OF] WHAT SHOULD BE DONE, O PEOPLE OF THE EAST BY B.A. DAR", *IQBAL REVIEW* 19, no. 3: October (1978): pp. 77.

679. **DARLING, M.**, "REMINISCENCES OF IQBAL", *Iqbal Day 1959*. An Iqbal Day adress, delivered at London, April 1959 - unpublished.

680. **DARNAUD, Michel**, "M. IQBAL, 'LA MÉTAPHYSIQUE EN PERSE' (Book Review)", *CAHIERS INTERNATIONAUX DE SOCIOLOGIE* (NS) 71, no. juillet-décembre (1981): pp. 374.
Numéro Spécial: les Sociologies / Comptes Rendus / Culture et Politique.
F.

681. **DAS, Sundar**, "THE PHILOSOPHY OF SIR MUHAMMAD IQBAL", *INDIAN*

REVIEW (Madras) 39, no. 2 (1938): pp. 737-41.

Variant name: Shunder DAS.

Appraisal of Iqbal as a *Poet of Humanity* (says the author: *in spite of his communal activities during the closing few years of his life, which I believe became inevitable under the political exigencies of the time*), by way of isolating some general humanistic motives in Iqbal's poetry.

Reprinted in Various authors, *IQBAL: A CRITICAL STUDY*, Lahore: Farhan Publishers, 1977 - qv.

682. **Dawn** (Editorial), "IQBAL", *DAWN*, 21 April 1950, p. 7.

683. **DE SMEDT, Richard V.**, mon., *PHILOSOPHICAL ACTIVITY IN PAKISTAN*, Lahore: Pakistan Philosophical Congress, 1961. 132 pp.
Cf. esp. pp. 6-8, 37, 46, 56, 73, 89, 126.

684. **DE VITRAY-MEYEROVITCH, Eva**, tr., *LA MÉTAPHYSIQUE EN PERSE*, M. IQBAL (mon.), Paris: Sindbad, 1980. 146 pp.
F.

685. **DESNAVI, Misbah**, "ALLAMA IQBAL AND SULAIMAN NADVI", *DAWN* (Karachi), 9 November 1983.

686. ———, "IQBAL AND SULAIMAN NADVI HAD COMMON OBJECTIVE", *MORNING NEWS* (Karachi), 9 November 1983.

687. **DEV, G. C.**, *IDEALISM AND PROGRESS*, Calcutta, 1952

688. ———, "IQBAL AND THE FUTURE", *PAKISTAN OBSERVER*, 21 April 1961.

689. **DHAWAN, Madan Lal**, mon., *IQBAL AND HIS EQUALS*, Delhi: Bhavna Prakashan, 1986

690. **DICKIE, James**, "MUHAMMAD IQBAL: A REAPPRAISAL", *ISLAMIC REVIEW AND ARAB AFFAIRS* 53, no. 4: April (1965): pp. 31-34.
Published also in *IQBAL REVIEW* 9, no. 1: April (1968), pp. 67-74.

691. **DICKINSON, L.**, "THE SECRETS OF THE SELF (ASRAR-I-KHUDI)", *THE NATION*

(London), 24 December 1920, p. 458.

692. **DINSAWI, M. Bashir ul-Haq**, "DR. MUHAMMAD IQBAL AND THE AHMADDIYYA MOVEMENT", *REVIEW OF RELIGIONS* 35, (1936).

693. **DJOHAN, Bahder**, "SPEECH, IQBAL DAY IN INDONESIA", *IQBAL REVIEW* 8, no. 1: April (1967): pp. 41-45.

694. **DORRAJ, Manochehr**, "THE INTELLECTUAL DILEMMAS OF A MUSLIM MODERNIST: POLITICS AND POETICS OF IQBAL", *THE MUSLIM WORLD* 85, no. 3-4 (1995): pp. 266-79.

695. **DOUGLAS, William O.**, "SPEECH, IQBAL DAY IN WASHINGTON", *IQBAL REVIEW* 8, no. 1: April (1967): pp. 65-66.

696. ———, "STATEMENT ON IQBAL", *THE TIMES OF KARACHI*, 24 April 1959. Text of a statement made by the U.S. Supreme Court Judge at the Pakistan Day Meeting at the Islamic Centre, Washington D.C., 21 April 1959.

697. **DURRANI, F. R. Khan**, "IQBAL'S DOCTRINE OF SELF", *ASPECTS OF IQBAL*, Altaf H. SHAUKAT (ed.), Lahore: Qumi Kutub Khana, 1938.

698. **DURRANI, S. A.**, "*GHAZALS* OF IQBAL", *IQBAL REVIEW* 30-31, no. 3: October and 1: April (1989-1990): pp. 77-82. English translation of Ghazals, which are included in the original.

699. ———, "IQBAL AND MYSTICISM", *IQBAL REVIEW* 29, no. 3: October (1988): pp. 1-9. Opening address, delivered at the one day Seminar on Iqbal and Mysticism (University of Birmingham, 7 November 1987).

700. **DURRANI, Saeed A.**, "IQBAL: HIS LIFE AND WORKS", *IQBAL REVIEW* 31, no. 3: October (1992): pp. 105-36. Transcript of an Invited Lecture presented at the Pakistan Day Symposium, held on 11 January 1990 at the Department of Oriental Studies, Catholic University of Leuven, Belgium. The article includes six figures.

701. ———, "SIR THOMAS ARNOLD AND IQBAL", *IQBAL REVIEW* 32, no. 1: April (Special issue on Sir Thomas W. Arnold) (1992): pp. 13-29.

Text of a speech, delivered at the *Sir Arnold Day* conference (University of Birmingham, 19 November 1988), mainly on the influence of Arnold as a teacher on the young Muhammad Iqbal, with reference to parts of BANG-I-DARA.

702. **editor [?]**, "JINNAH PAYS TRIBUTE TO IQBAL", *IQBAL* 42, no. 4 (1995): pp. 1-10 (95-102).
Collection of newspaper records on Jinnah's condolence message on 21 April 1938.

703. **EDSMAN, Carl-Martin**, mon., *IQBAL AND THE WEST - SWEDEN'S TRIBUTE TO THE MEMORY OF DR. MOHAMMAD IQBAL*, Stockholm, 1978

704. ———, "IQBAL OCH VASTERLANDET (IQBAL AND THE WEST)", *SVENSK MISSIONSTIDSKRIFT* 71, no. 3 (1983): pp. 51-59.
A Swedish translation of the author's article IQBAL AND THE WEST (qv.), with an English summary.
S.

705. **EL-SEBAI, Yousuf**, "IQBAL AS A POET, A PHILOSOPHER AND A POLITICIAN - IQBAL DAY IN CAIRO, ADDRESS", *IQBAL REVIEW* 8, no. 1: April (1967): pp. 93-94.

706. **ELAHI, Maqbool**, "LONGING FOR SOLITUDE AND COMPANIONSHIP", *THE PAKISTAN TIMES* (Rawalpindi), 21 April 1979.

707. ———, tr., *SECRETS OF THE SELF*, Muhammad IQBAL (mon.), Lahore: Iqbal Academy Pakistan, 1986. 143 pp.
A versified translation of (I) ASRAR-I-KHUDI.

708. **ELSON, Edward L. R.**, "SPEECH, IQBAL DAY IN WASHINGTON", *IQBAL REVIEW* 8, no. 1: April (1967): pp. 56-59.

709. **EMBREE, Ainslie**, "IQBAL", *THE McGRAW-HILL ENCYCLOPEDIA OF WORLD BIOGRAPHY*, New York: McGraw-Hill, 1973, Vol. 5, pp. 479-80.

710. **ENGINEER, Asghar Ali**, "A CRITICAL APPRAISAL OF IQBAL'S 'RECONSTRUCTION OF RELIGIOUS THOUGHT IN ISLAM'", *IQBAL COMMEMORATIVE VOLUME*, Ali Sardar JAFRI & K.S. DUGGAL (eds.), New Delhi: All India Iqbal Centenary Celebrations Committee, 1977, pp. 119-32.
The author concludes his analysis of Iqbal's RECONSTRUCTION OF RELIGIOUS

THOUGHT IN ISLAM as follows: *In fact, Iqbal was too conservative [...] to undertake any real re-structuring of religious thought. His only real concern was to check the liberal and permissive trends among the Muslim intelligentsia. In other words, Iqbal was not prepared to commit the sin of carving out a new path. He shuddered at his own free thinking* (p. 132).

711. ———, "SOME SOCIO-POLITICAL MOTIVATIONS OF IQBAL'S TRADITION AND ITS CONTEMPORARY LITERARY RELEVANCE", *MULTI-DISCIPLINARY APPROACH TO IQBAL* (n.d.).
Iqbal Centenary Symposium, New Delhi.

712. **ENNAIFER, Hmida**, "IQBAL ET LE QUESTIONNEMENT DE LA PROPHETIE", *IBLA: Revue De L'Institut Des Belles-Lettres Arabes* (Tunis) 59, no. 2 (178) (1996): pp. 233-51.
F.

713. **ENVER, Ishrat Hasan**, "ETHICS OF IQBAL", *ISLAMIC LITERATURE* (Lahore) [vol. ?], no. [?]: September (1956): pp. 43-45.

714. ———, mon., *THE METAPHYSICS OF IQBAL*, Syed Zafarul HASAN (intr.), Lahore: Shaikh Muhammad Ashraf, 1944. xiv+91 pp.
A Ph.D.-thesis from Aligarh University, including a bibliography (pp. 85-88).
Reprinted in 1963, then containing xiv+105 pp.; re-issued by Kazi Publications (Chicago 1985).

715. ———, "TESTING IQBAL'S PHILOSOPHICAL TEST OF REVELATIONS OF THE RELIGIOUS EXPERIENCE", *IQBAL* 41, no. 3 (1994): pp. 1-17.
Variant name: ENVAR.

716. **'ERFAN, N.**, "WHAT IS COMMON BETWEEN EXISTENTIALISTS AND IQBAL", *THE PAKISTAN PHILOSOPHICAL JOURNAL* (Lahore) 6, no. 3: January (1963).

717. **ERFAN, Niaz**, "IQBAL AND EXISTENTIALISM", *IQBAL* 14, no. 3: January (1966): pp. 65-71.
Variant name: IRFAN.
A short note on the common aspects and the differences between Iqbal's philosophical thought and existentialism.
Reproduced in SHEIKH, M. Saeed (ed.), *STUDIES IN IQBAL'S THOUGHT AND ART*,

Lahore, 1972, pp. 252-259.

718. ———, "IQBAL ON SOCIAL PROBLEMS", *IQBAL REVIEW* 18, no. 4: January (1978): pp. 37-70.

719. **ESPOSITO, John L.**, "MALIK, HAFEEZ, ED., IQBAL: POET-PHILOSOPHER OF PAKISTAN (Book Review)", *JOURNAL OF BIBLE AND RELIGION* 43, no. 2: June (Supplement) (1975): pp. 452.
American Academy of Religion.

720. **Evening Star** (red.), "THE HOUSE WHERE [THE] IDEA OF PAKISTAN TOOK SHAPE", *EVENING STAR*, 21 April 1962, p. 2.

721. **FÜCK, J.**, "IQBAL, M.: BOTSCHAFT DES OSTENS. AUS DEM PERSISCHEN VOM A. SCHIMMEL (Book Review)", *ORIENTALISTISCHE LITERATURZEITUNG* 60, no. 7-8: Juli-Augustus (1965): pp. 389.
G.

722. **FAHID, S. I.**, "Untitled - IQBAL DAY IN MOROCCO", *IQBAL REVIEW* 8, no. 1: April (1967): pp. 171-75.

723. **FAIZ, Faiz Ahmad**, "IQBAL DAY AT KARACHI: IQBAL AS A POET", *IQBAL REVIEW* 8, no. 1: April (1967): pp. 119-33.

724. ———, "MUHAMMAD IQBAL", *PAKISTAN: PAST & PRESENT*, Hamid JALAL & Aimee MERRIAM & Abdul QAYYUM & Tom STACEY (eds.), London: Stacey International, 1977, pp. 239-42.

725. **FAIZ, Javed**, "IQBAL ON IJTEHAD", *THE PAKISTAN TIMES* (Rawalpindi), 21 April 1981.

726. **FAIZI, Hasan F. S.**, "THE POET'S GREATNESS", *THE DAWN* (Karachi), 21 April 1960, p. 5.

727. ———, "RELEVANCE OF IQBAL'S MESSAGE", *PAKISTAN TIMES*, 21 April 1974, p. 1.

728. **FAKHAR-UN-NISA**, "CONTRIBUTION OF IQBAL TO THE CREATION OF

PAKISTAN", University of the Punjab, 1958. 34 pp.

M.A. Political Science; Promoter: Shaukat Ali.

Contents: (1) Introduction: A brief account of Iqbal's intellectual and political background, (2) Iqbal's poetry as a source of awakening among Muslims of the subcontinent, particularly his concept of millat, (3) Allahabad Resolution and Iqbal's Speech, (4) Iqbal's correspondence with Jinnah on the question of Pakistan, and (5) Conclusion.

729. **FARIDI, Sibte Farooq**, "ALLAMA IQBAL: HIS APPROACH TO MAN AND SOCIETY", *THE ILLUSTRATED WEEKLY OF PAKISTAN* (Karachi), 21 April 1960, pp. 9-10.
Frequently referred to as Anonymous.

730. **FAROOQ, Muhammad**, "IQBAL'S CONCEPT OF 'EGO' AND LEIBNIZ MONADDOGY", University of the Punjab, Dept. Philosophy, n.d. ?
Promoter: Naeem Ahmad.

731. **FAROOQI, Abadullah**, "EDUCATIONAL IDEAS OF IQBAL", *IQBAL REVIEW* 4, no. 1: April (1963): pp. 35-50.

732. ———, "IQBAL'S PALESTINE STATEMENT", *PAKISTAN TIMES*, 21 April 1965, p. 2.

733. ———, "ISLAMIC SOCIALISM AND IQBAL", *IQBAL REVIEW* 15, no. 1: April (1974): pp. 1-7.
Short essay on the concept of *Islamic socialism*, with emphasis on its Quranic sources, its universalism and its basis in economic equality.

734. ———, "(THE) PILGRIMAGE OF ETERNITY", *PAKISTAN TIMES*, 21 April 1969, p. 4.

735. ———, "(THE) PROBLEM OF GOOD AND EVIL AS VIEWED BY IQBAL", *IQBAL REVIEW* 13, no. 3: October (1972): pp. 33-43.

736. **FAROOQI, Abbadullah**, "THE IMPACT OF KHOWAJA HAFIZ ON IQBAL'S THOUGHT", *IQBAL REVIEW* 14, no. 1: April (1973): pp. 33-60.
Mystic introspection is central to both Iqbal and Hafiz, but to the former it is but an urge to dynamic energy and a warning against mysticism as an opiate, whereas to the latter it is the very goal in itself. Although Iqbal adopts an uncompromising attitude towards the

pantheistic creed of Hafiz, the impact of the Persian poet upon Iqbal is unmistakable.

737.   ———, "IQBAL AND TAGORE", *PAKISTAN REVIEW* (Lahore) 19, no. 4 (1971): pp. 22-25.
Special Iqbal Number.

738.   **FAROOQI, H. A.**, "A COMPARATIVE STUDY OF IQBAL'S THOUGHT", *PAKISTAN TIMES*, 21 April 1964, p. 2.

739.   **FAROOQI, Hafiz Abbadullah**, "IQBAL AND BERGSON ON TIME", *IQBAL* 15, no. 1: July 1966 (1966): pp. 56-59.
A short note on Bergson's and Iqbal's treatment of the concepts of *time* and *duration*. Reproduced in SHEIKH, M. Saeed (ed.), *STUDIES IN IQBAL'S THOUGHT AND ART*, Lahore, 1972, pp. 248-251.

740.   ———, "IQBAL'S CONCEPT OF STATE", *IQBAL* 15, no. 3: January (1967): pp. 53-60.

741.   ———, "IQBAL'S PHILOSOPHY OF LIFE", *IQBAL REVIEW* 14, no. 3: October (1973): pp. 27-44.
On the four movements which, according to Iqbal, have made heavy onslaughts upon life and have made it appear insignificant: Platonism, Buddhism, Vedanta and Christianity.

742.   ———, "IQBAL'S THEORY OF KNOWLEDGE", *IQBAL REVIEW* 16, no. 1: April (1975): pp. 21-31.

743.   **FAROOQI, M. Abadullah**, "IQBAL'S ESTIMATE OF GURU NANAK", *IQBAL REVIEW* 3, no. 3: October (1962): pp. 77-87.
Nanak did not believe in formal religions and their formal rituals, whereas Iqbal adhered to the formal practices of Islam.

744.   **FAROOQI, Muhammad Ahsan**, "THE POETIC ART OF IQBAL", *IQBAL REVIEW* (Karachi) 2, no. 3: October (1961): pp. 24-50.

745.   **FARUQI, Abbadullah**, "A COMPARATIVE STUDY OF IQBAL'S THOUGHT", *PAKISTAN REVIEW* 14, no. 4: April (1966): pp. 11-19.

746.   ———, "IQBAL AND THE DOCTRINE OF REINCARNATION", *STUDIES IN ISLAM* (New Delhi) 5, no. 2-3: April-July (1968): pp. 120-128.

Iqbal number.

747. ———, "IQBAL'S ANTIPATHY TO HINDU PHILOSOPHICAL THOUGHT", *IQBAL* 17, no. 3: January (1969): pp. 70-76.

748. ———, "IQBAL'S CONCEPTION OF GOD", *ISLAMIC LITERATURE* 11, no. 2: September (1965): pp. 27-32.

749. ———, "ZOROASTRIANISM AND IQBAL", *IQBAL REVIEW* (Karachi) 5, no. 3: October (1964): pp. 1-20.

750. **FARUQI, Burhan Ahmad**, "ASSESSMENT OF OUR PAST AND PRESENT, IQBAL'S CONTRIBUTION", *THE CIVIL AND MILITARY GAZETTE* (Lahore), 21 April 1951/1959, pp. 4-5.

751. **FARUQI, Hafiz Abbadullah**, "IQBAL'S REVOLUTION IN TRADITIONAL SUFISM", *IQBAL* (Lahore) 23, no. 3: July (1976): pp. 101-16.

752. **FARUQI, K. A.**, "IQBAL - THE HUMANIST", *INDIAN LITERATURE* (New Delhi) 22, no. 3 (1979): pp. 97-107.

753. **FARUQI, Shamsur Rahman**, "IQBAL FROM THE INSIDE", *INDIAN LITERATURE* (New Delhi) 28, no. 5: September-October (1985): pp. 207-11.
A short essay on Masood Husain Khan's and Iqbal ka Fan's criticism on Muhammad Iqbal's poetry.

754. **FATIMI, S. Qudratullah**, "ISLAMIC UNIVERSALISM AND TERRITORIAL NATIONALISM IN IQBAL'S THOUGHT", *IQBAL REVIEW* 17, no. 3: October (1976): pp. 39-64.
An essential study of Iqbal vs. *Islamic Universalism* and *Territorial Nationalism* - two complementary political forces in the modern Muslim world, taken from Jamal al-Din al-Afghani's thinking and interpretation of Islamic teachings - and *having found their most eloquent expression in the prose and poetical compositions of Allamah Muhammad Iqbal*. The author starts from a brief survey of Afghani's contributions to modern Muslim thought, and from there proceeds to present Iqbal as a *spiritual disciple* of Afghani's, arriving at an analysis of the progress of these two complementary trends in Iqbal's thought. The conclusion is a survey of the *phased development of Iqbal's political thought with relevance to his writings*, also drawn into a table, appended to the article. The main elements   are:

(1) a first period, up to 1905 (i.e. before Iqbal's journeys to Europe), in which Iqbal proclaims a *Pan-Indian Nationalism*, based on a popular theosophical interpretation of Wahdat al-Wujud, and expounded in a.o. the first part of BANG-I-DARA.
(2) a transitional period, marked by Iqbal's stay in Europe (1905-1908), during which Iqbal suffers from a mental conflict, discovers Western philosophy and discusses Wahdat al-Wujud with Western teachers. This period is to be seen in a.o. the second part of BANG-I-DARA and in THE DEVELOPMENT OF METAPHYSICS IN PERSIA.
(3) the second main period (1908-1926), based on a repudiation of Wahdat al-Wujud, marked by an emerging *Pan-Islamism*, as expounded in a.o. STRAY REFLECTIONS, ASRAR-I-KHUDI, RUMUZ-I-BEKHUDI, PAYAM-I MASHRIQ, and the third part of BANG-I-DARA.
(4) a third and final period (from 1926 onwards), during which Iqbal enters into active political life, proclaiming *Islamic Universalism* and *Territorial Nationalism* complemented, and a *Pakistani Nationalism tempered by 'Pan-Humanism'* - based on an assertion of Wahdat al-Wujud as enunciated by Hallaj and Rumi, and expounded in a.o. ZABUR-I-'AJAM, the SIX LECTURES, and JAVID NAMAH.
With a comprehensive bibliography, and an appendix (table). Re-issued in [Various authors], *SELECTIONS FROM THE IQBAL REVIEW*, ed. Waheed Qureshi, Lahore, 1983, pp.189-214 + inlay.

755. **FAUZ, Nasim Nasho**, "IQBAL'S CONCEPT OF ISLAMIC CULTURE", *DAWN* (Karachi), 9 November 1978.

756. **FAYYAZ, Muhammad**, "SELF AND SYNTHESIS", *IQBAL REVIEW* 28, no. 3: October-December (1987): pp. 41-59.

757. **FAZAL-I-HAMID**, "IQBAL A POET, FIRST AND LAST", *PAKISTAN TIMES*, 3 June 1966, pp. 1, 2.

758. **FERNANDEZ, A.**, "MAN'S DIVINE QUEST. APPRECIATION OF THE PHILOSOPHY OF THE EGO ACCORDING TO SIR MUHAMMAD IQBAL", *ANNALI LATERANENSI* (Roma) 20, (1956): pp. 265-334.

759. **FEROZ, S.**, "IQBAL AND THE SELF", *PAKISTAN REVIEW* 3, no. [?]: April (1955): pp. 29-30.

760. **FEROZUDDIN, Khadija**, "THE POET'S CALL FOR ACTION", *THE PAKISTAN TIMES* (Lahore), 21 April 1954, p. 5.

Special Supplement.

761. **FIGAR, Abdur Rahman**, "IQBAL'S PHILOSOPHY OF REVOLUTION", *PAKISTAN QUARTERLY* 9, no. 4: Winter (1959): pp. 26-29.

762. **FIRAQI, Tehsin**, ed., *BEDIL IN THE LIGHT OF BERGSON*, 'Allama Muhammad IQBAL (mon.), Lahore: Universal Books / Iqbal Academy Pakistan, 1988. 44+38+60 pp. English introduction and notes, reproduction of Iqbal's manuscript, and Urdu (?) introduction with notes.

763. ———, "BEDIL IN THE LIGHT OF BERGSON (AN UNPUBLISHED ARTICLE OF IQBAL)", *IQBAL REVIEW* 27, no. 3: October-December (1986): pp. 1-44.

764. **FISCHER, Humphrey**, "AHMADIYYAH THOUGHT AND EVOLUTION", *THE MUSLIM WORLD* (Hartford, Connecticut) [vol. ?], (1959): pp. 275*ff.*

765. **FITCH, Nancy C.**, "HAFEEZ MALIK, ED., IQBAL: POET-PHILOSOPHER OF PAKISTAN ...", *JOURNAL OF SOUTH ASIAN LITERATURE* (Rochester, MI) 10, no. 1 (1974): pp. 179-83.

766. **FORESTER, E. M.**, "(A) COMMANDING GENIUS", *PAKISTAN TIMES*, 21 April 1956, p. 5.
Variant name: FOSTER, E.M.
Text of a BBC radio talk broadcast in 1946.

767. ———, "(Review) THE SECRETS OF THE SELF (ASRAR-I-KHUDI)", *THE ATHENAEUM*, December 1920, pp. 803-4.
Variant name: FORSTER; variant date: 1921.
Review of NICHOLSON's *THE SECRETS OF THE SELF*.

768. **FORSTER, E. M.**, "IQBAL: POET-PHILOSOPHER", *LISTENER* 35, no. 906: 23 May (1946): pp. 686.
Journal dedicated to Music and Performing Arts.

769. ———, "MUHAMMAD IQBAL", *TWO CHEERS FOR DEMOCRACY*, London, 1961.

770. ———, "THE POETRY OF IQBAL (Book Review)", *THE ATHENAEUM* (London), 10 December 1920, p. 803.

Vol. 4728.

771. **FORSTER, F. M.**, "IQBAL", *PAKISTAN REVIEW* 1, no. 1: January (1953): pp. 12-13. Reproduced from *TWO CHEERS FOR DEMOCRACY*, London 1952.

772. **FRANDON, I.-M.**, "M. IQBÂL. MESSAGE DE L'ORIENT (Book Review)", *REVUE DE LITTÉRATURE COMPARÉE* 33, (1959): pp. 585.
F.

773. **FUCK, J.**, "DER SUNNITISCHE ISLAM", *HANDBUCH DER ORIENTALISTIK*, B. SPULER (ed.), Leiden: E.J. Brill, 1961, Vol. I, pp. 8.
G.

774. **FUCK, Johannes W.**, "MUHAMMAD IQBAL UND DER INDO-MUSLIMISCHE MODERNISMUS", *WESTOSTLICHE ABHANDLUNGEN, RUDOLF TSCHUDI ZUM 70. GEBURTSTAG ÜBERREICHT*, Various authors (mon.), 1954, pp. 356-65.
Reprinted in Wolfgang KOEHLER (ed.), *MUHAMMAD IQBAL UND DIE DREI REICHE DES GEISTES*, Hamburg: Deutsch-Pakistanisches Forum, 1977, pp. 79-96.
G.

775. **FYZEE, Asaf A. A.**, "IQBAL'S CONCEPTION OF ETHICS (Book Review)", *ARYAN PATH* 32, no. 6: June (1961): pp. 271.

776. **G.M.**, "SHEIKH MUHAMMAD IQBAL (Book Review)", *RIVISTA DI FILOSOFIA* 13, no. 1: genn.-mar. (1921): pp. 94.

777. **GAFAROV, A.**, "MUHAMMAD IQBAL AND PERSIAN-LANGUAGE POETS IN INDIA AND PAKISTAN", *THE WORK OF MUHAMMAD IQBAL: ARTICLES BY SOVIET SCHOLARS*, Abdur Rauf MALIK (ed.), Lahore: People's Publishing House, 1983, pp. 153-65.

778. **GANDAPUR, Amanullah Khan**, "IQBAL AND MOSQUERADED DETRACTOS", *THE PAKISTAN TIMES* (Rawalpindi), 9 November 1985.

779. **GANDHI, Rajmohan**, mon., *EIGHT LIVES*, New Delhi, 1986

780. **GAREWAL, Sher Muhammad**, "ANJUMAN-I-HIMAYAT-I-ISLAM AND ALLAMA

IQBAL", *THE PAKISTAN TIMES* (Rawalpindi), 9 November 1982.

781. ———, "IQBAL'S ROLE IN GROWTH OF MUSLIM NATIONHOOD", *THE PAKISTAN TIMES* (Rawalpindi / Lahore), 9 November 1985.
Also published in *THE BALUCHISTAN TIMES* (Quetta), 9 November 1986.

782. ———, "IQBAL'S ROLE IN PUNJAB POLITICS", *JOURNAL OF THE RESEARCH SOCIETY OF PAKISTAN* 25, no. 2: April (1988): pp. 26-44.

783. **GHAFFAR, Abdul**, "THE DIVINE COMEDY OF MODERN INDIA: AN EVALUATION OF IQBAL", *CONTEMPORARY INDIA* (Lahore) 2, (1936): pp. 255-60.

784. **GHAFOOR, Abdul**, "ALLAMA IQBAL, TAGORE AND NAZRUL ISLAM: A SYMPHONY OF SOULS", *DAWN* (Karachi), 9 November 1978.

785. **GHALUM, Iqbal Ahmad**, "IQBAL DAY IN KUWAIT: SOME ASPECTS OF IQBAL'S LIFE", *IQBAL REVIEW* 10, no. 1: April (1969): pp. 52-53.
Article read at Iqbal Day (27 April 1967) held in Pakistan Urdu School, Kuwait.

786. **GHANI, A. R. & Kh. NUR ELAHI**, *AN IQBAL BIBLIOGRAPHY*, Lahore: Bazim-i-Iqbal, 1953. 16 pp.

787. ———, "AN IQBAL BIBLIOGRAPHY", *IQBAL* (Lahore) 3, no. 1: July (1954): pp. 114-29.
Variant title: IQBAL'S BIBLIOGRAPHY.

788. **GHANI, A. R. & Khwaja NUR ILAHI**, comp., *BIBLIOGRAPHY OF IQBAL*, Lahore: Bazm-i-Iqbal, 1950.
vii+26 pp.

789. **GHANI, Abdul & Khwaja NUR ILAHI**, comp., *BIBLIOGRAPHY OF IQBAL*, Lahore: Bazm-i-Iqbal, 1955. 16 pp.
A comprehensive bibliography of both Iqbal's works and books, articles, etc. on Iqbal; all critical material included in English.

790. **GHAREEB, Mamoun**, "IQBAL: THE PHILOSOPHER AND THE POET", *IQBAL REVIEW* 9, no. 1: April (1968): pp. 18-21.

791.   **GHAZNAVI, Masood**, "MALIK, Ed.: IQBAL: POET-PHILOSOPHER OF PAKISTAN (Book Review)", *MIDDLE EAST JOURNAL* 27, no. 1: Winter (1973): pp. 86.

792.   **GHOSE, Sisirkumar**, *TAGORE, SRI AUROBINDO AND IQBAL: THREE LECTURES*, Srinagar: University of Kashmir, 1979

793.   **GHOURI, H. R.**, "IQBAL'S POETRY OF INTELLECT: A LITERARY CONTEXT", *EDUCATIONAL RESEARCH BULLETIN* [vol. ?], no. [?]: December (1977).

794.   **GHULAM, Iqbal Ahmad**, "SOME ASPECTS OF IQBAL'S LIFE", *IQBAL REVIEW* 10, no. 1: April (1969): pp. 52-53.

795.   **GHULAM RIZA TAJ BAKSH**, "SPEECH ON IQBAL", *IQBAL REVIEW* 9, no. 1: April (1968): pp. 62-66.

796.   **GIBB, H. A. R.**, "IQBAL, SIR MUHAMMAD (1876-1938)", *DICTIONARY OF NATIONAL BIOGRAPHY, 1931-1940*, London: Oxford UP, 1949, pp. 266-73 and 461-2.

797.   ———, *MODERN TRENDS IN ISLAM*, Chicago: University Press, 1947. 141 pp. See esp. pp. ix, 12, 59, 61, 77, 84, 100-103, 110, 127.

798.   **GILANI, A. R.**, "ALLAMA IQBAL AND QURANIC WISDOM", *THE PAKISTAN TIMES* (Rawalpindi), 9 November 1982.

799.   **GILANI, Saleem A.**, tr. U/E, *THE MOSQUE OF CORDOBA - ENGLISH RENDERING WITH COMPARATIVE URDU TEXT*, Muhammad IQBAL (mon.), 1st ed., Lahore: Iqbal Academy Pakistan, 1995. 45 pp.
Includes three pictures, the original Urdu text facing the English translation, and bibliography.

800.   **GIMMI, S. K.**, "IQBAL'S THEORY OF RELIGIO-POLITICAL POWER", *THE PAKISTAN TIMES* (Rawalpindi), 9 November 1983.

801.   ———, "IQBAL'S VISION OF PAKISTAN", *THE PAKISTAN TIMES* (Rawalpindi), 9 November 1985.
Re-issued in *THE BALUCHISTAN TIMES* (Quetta), 9 November 1986.

802.   **GIMMI, Salim Khan**, "IQBAL AND KASHMIR", *THE NATION* (Lahore), 9 November

1986.
Iqbal Day Supplement.

803. **GLEBOV, N.**, "[A POET OF THE EAST]", *SOVREMENNY VOSTOK [Contemporary East]* (Moscow) 5, (1958).
R.

804. **GORDON-POLONSKAYA, L. R.**, "IDEOLOGY OF MUSLIM NATIONALISM", *IQBAL: POET-PHILOSOPHER OF PAKISTAN*, Hafeez MALIK (ed.), New York: Columbia UP, 1971, pp. 108-35.

805. ———, "IQBAL AND SOCIAL JUSTICE", *IQBAL COMMEMORATIVE VOLUME*, Ali Sardar JAFRI & K.S. DUGGAL (eds.), New Delhi: All India Iqbal Centenary Celebrations Committee, 1977, pp. 144-49.
Iqbal's progressive social thoughts called for a *revolutionary transformation of life* (p. 144), first of all the liberation of his country from colonial hegemony, for which he, after the October Revolution in Russia, did not only address the Muslim intelligentsia, but exhorted those to unite with the toiling masses. Against the atheistic character of the October Revolution, however, he considered the reconstruction of Islam a necessary preliminary to revolutionary changes.

806. **GOUDAT, Saleh**, "IDEAL STATE AND IQBAL - IQBAL DAY IN CAIRO, ADDRESS", *IQBAL REVIEW* 8, no. 1: April (1967): pp. 97-98.

807. **GROVER, Verinder**, ed., *POLITICAL THINKERS OF MODERN INDIA*, Vol. 26, 1993

808. **GRUNEBAUM, G. E. von**, "BILGRAMI, H.H., GLIMPSES OF IQBAL'S MIND AND THOUGHT (Book Review)", *JOURNAL OF NEAR EASTERN STUDIES* 15, no. [?]: January-October (1956): pp. 260.

809. **GULATI, Azad**, "IQBAL AUR MAGHRIBI MUFAKREEN, BY PROF. JAGAN NATH AZAD", *IQBAL REVIEW* 26, no. 3: October-December (1985): pp. 138.
Book review of Jagan Nath Azad, *Iqbal aur Maghribi Mufakreen*, Delhi: Maktaba-e-Jamia, n.d., 190 pp.

810. ———, "ON IQBAL: MIND AND ART, BY G.N. AZAD", *IQBAL REVIEW* 27, no. 1: April-May-June (1985): pp. 126-27.

811. **GUMBRETIERE, Andre**, "ELEMENTAL DYNAMICS IN IQBAL'S POETRY

(ASTRO-ANALYSIS)", *THE TIMES OF KARACHI*, 21 April 1956, p. 3.

812.   ———, "LE RÉFORMISME MUSULMAN EN INDE", *REVUE ORIENT* 16 and 18, no. 4 and 2 (1960-1961).
F.

813.   ———, "UNE DYNAMIQUE DE L'EAU ET DU FEU: LE POÈTE MUHAMMAD IQBAL ", *JOURNAL DES POÈTES DE BRUXELLES* [vol. ?], no. [?]: April (1958).
F.

814.   **GUNAWARDHANS, Theja**, "WHOLENESS AT ALL LEVELS IN IQBAL'S PHILOSOPHY", *JOURNAL OF THE RESEARCH SOCIETY OF PAKISTAN* 14, no. 4: October (1977): pp. 41-56.

815.   **HABIB, Kamal**, "STUDIES IN IQBAL'S LONG POEMS", *IQBAL REVIEW* 6, no. 1: April (1965): pp. 1-32.

816.   **HABIB, Kamal Muhammad**, "A *BANG-I DARA* POEM STUDIED: "*MUHABBAT*" (LOVE)", *IQBAL REVIEW* 17, no. 1: April (1976): pp. 47-55.
This article is based upon the author's analysis of the poem in *IQBAL: A STUDY OF HIS POETIC THOUGHTS, DICTION AND IMAGERY*.

817.   ———, "IQBAL AND TAGORE: AN ESSAY ON TWO CONTRASTING SENSIBILITIES", *VISION* (Karachi), October and November 1967, pp. 13-20 and 13-20 resp.

818.   ———, "IQBAL AS THE POET OF TIME: A LITERARY STUDY", *IQBAL REVIEW* 18, no. 4: January (1978): pp. 149-70.

819.   ———, "IQBAL'S POETIC ACHIEVEMENT", *PAKISTAN REVIEW* 14, no. 4: Spring (1967): pp. 30-36 and 65-71.
Variant journal title: PAKISTAN QUARTERLY.

820.   ———, "IQBAL TOWARDS AN ETHICAL THEORY OF POETRY", *IQBAL REVIEW* 16, no. 1: April (1975): pp. 49-65.

821.   ———, "SOME ASPECTS OF IQBAL'S POETRY: A DISCUSSION OF HIS

IMAGERY AND SYMBOLS", *VISION* (Karachi) 17, no. 7: August (1968): pp. 7-17.

822. **HABIB, Nasira**, ed., *VERSATILE IQBAL*, Various authors (mon.), Lahore: Bazm-i-Iqbal, 1985

823. **HADI HUSSAIN**, "CONCEPTION OF POETRY AND THE POET", *IQBAL: POET-PHILOSOPHER OF PAKISTAN*, Hafeez MALIK (ed.), New York / London: Columbia UP, 1971, pp. 327-46 (?).

824. **HADI HUSSAIN, M.**, "THE BOOK OF SERVITUDE", *IQBAL REVIEW* 7, no. 1: April (1966): pp. 83-94.
English translation of (I) BANDAGI-NAMAH.

825. ———, "THE CONQUEST OF NATURE", *IQBAL REVIEW* 6, no. 3: October (1965): pp. 37-40.
English translation of (I) TASHKHIR-I-FITRAT (from PAYAM-I-MASHRIQ).

826. ———, "IQBAL: POET AND THE POLITICAL SAGE", *THE MUSLIM* (Islamabad), 21 April 1983.

827. ———, "THE NEW ROSE GARDEN OF MYSTERY", *PAKISTAN REVIEW* 16, no. 5: May (1968): pp. 28-29.
English translation of (I) GULSHAN-I-RAZ JADID.

828. ———, tr., *'THE NEW ROSE GARDEN OF MYSTERY' AND 'THE BOOK OF SLAVES'* (GULSHAN-I-RAZ-JADID and BANDAGI-NAMAH), S. A. VAHID (intr.) 30, Lahore: Shaikh Muhammad Ashraf, 1980. xvi+66 pp.
English verse translation of (I) GULSHAN-I-RAZ-JADID and (I) BANDAGI-NAMAH; also published by Kazi Publications (Chicago, 1985).

829. ———, "PROLOGUE TO IQBAL'S *ASRAR-I-KHUDI*", *IQBAL REVIEW* 14, no. 3: October (1973): pp. 1-8.
Translation by M. Hadi Hussain.

830. ———, "SAKI-NAMAH, FROM IQBAL'S BAL-I JIBRIL", *IQBAL REVIEW* 21, no. 1: April (1980): pp. 69-75.
Translation.

831. ———, "SATAN'S ADVISORY COUNCIL", *IQBAL REVIEW* 20, no. 3: October

(1979): pp. 95-100.
Translation of Iqbal's poem IBLIS KI MAJLIS-I SHURA, from ARMUGHAN-I HIJAZ.

832. **HADI HUSSAIN, Muhammad**, tr., *A MESSAGE FROM THE EAST: A SELECTIVE VERSE RENDERING OF IQBAL'S 'PAYAM-E-MASHRIQ'*, IQBAL ACADEMY 15, Karachi: Iqbal Academy, 1971. x+127 pp.
English versified translation of (I) PAYAM-E-MASHRIQ. The 2nd ed. (Lahore: Iqbal Academy Pakistan for National Committee for Birth Centenary Celebrations of Allama Muhammad Iqbal, 1977, xxiv+189 pp. and portrait) includes a foreword by Dr. S.A. Rahman.

833. **HAIDAR, Syed Afzal**, "IQBAL AND HIS CREATIVE AWARENESS", *THE FRONTIER POST* (Peshawar), 9 November 1987.

834. **HAIDER, Ghulam**, "DR. IQBAL'S CONTRIBUTION TO THE CREATION OF PAKISTAN", University of the Punjab, 1958.
M.A. Political Science.

835. ———, "THE IDEA OF PAKISTAN BY IQBAL HAS PUT THE MUSLIM IMAGINATION AFIRE", University of the Punjab, 1958. 39 pp.
M.A. Political Science; Promoter: Shaukat Ali.
Contents: (1) Iqbal and his nationalistic fervour, (2) Iqbal and the Muslim Renaissance in the 20th century, (3) The flow of political conditions in India as they moved to the demand of a Muslim state by Dr. Iqbal, (4) Opposition to the Muslim demand for seperate homeland: the activities of Dr. Iqbal to make (it) a living reality, and (5) Partition of India into the Dominion of India and Pakistan.

836. **HAKIM-UL-UMMAT**, "KNOWLEDGE AND EDUCATION AS PERCEIVED BY HAKIM-UL-UMMAT", *THE PAKISTAN TIMES* (Islamabad / Lahore), 9 November 1986.

837. **HALEPOTA, A. J.**, "AFFINITY OF IQBAL WITH SHAH WALIYULLAH", *IQBAL REVIEW* 15, no. 1: April (1974): pp. 65-72.
Text of a lecture read in a meeting held under the auspices of the Iqbal Academy, Karachi, on the occasion of the 36th Death Anniversary of Allama Iqbal, 21 April 1974. The author presents Shah Waliyullah as a direct predecessor of Iqbal, and looks for some points of resemblance between the thought of Waliyullah and Iqbal, mainly based on Iqbal's RECONSTRUCTION OF RELIGIOUS THOUGHT IN ISLAM. The main points of agreement are said to be situated in (1) the fact that both authors built their philosophical systems on *Wahdat-al-Wujud* (Waliyullah is said to have brought the *Wahdat-al-Wujud* of

Ibn 'Arabi and the *Wahat-al-Shuhud* of Imam Rabbani *into such harmony, that both the systems seem to supplement each other*), (2) their concepts of evolution, change and development, reportedly based on Jahiz, Ibn Miskawaih and Rumi, (3) their views on reality, God and world, (4) their concept of the universe and nature as *Sunnatallah* ("habit of Allah"), (5) their views on the study of nature as a form of *'Ibadah* (worship), (6) their refusal to separate the Sacred from the profane, (7) their definition of *Tilism Ilahi*, (8) their views on the nature and function of *'Ibadah*, (9) their psychological analysis of prayer, (10) their definition of the different stages of history of mankind, and (11) their concept of the international unity of mankind.

838.   **HALIM, Yousouf Hussain**, "SOME REMINISCENCES", *PAKISTAN TIMES* (Lahore), 21 April 1961, p. 6.

839.   **HAMEED, Abdul**, "IQBAL'S CONCEPTION OF HISTORY AGAINST MARXIST AND HEGELIAN BACKGROUND", *THE CIVIL AND MILITARY GAZETTE* (Lahore), 20 April 1952, p. 4.
Supplement.

840.   ———, "THE LEGACY OF IQBAL", *PAKISTAN TIMES*, 14 August 1977, p. 4.

841.   ———, "THE POET OF THE EAST LOOKED UPON CAPITALISM, COMMUNISM AND FASCISM AS THREE FACETS OF THE SAME MATERIALISTIC CULTURE OF THE WEST", *THE CIVIL AND MILITARY GAZETTE* (Lahore), 21 April 1956, pp. 2, 3.

842.   **HAMID IRFANI**, "IQBAL, MALIK KUSHSHOARA BAHAR AND PAKISTAN", *THE PAKISTAN TIMES* (Rawalpindi / Lahore), 9 November 1985.

843.   **HAMID IRFANI, Khawaja Abdul**, ed., *THE SAYINGS OF RUMI AND IQBAL*, Sialkot: Bazm-e-Rumi, 1976

844.   **HAMID, K. A.**, "IQBAL'S VIEW ON THE HUMAN EGO AS A CREATIVE AGENT", *VERSATILE IQBAL*, Nasira HABIB (ed.), Lahore: Bazm-i-Iqbal, 1985.
Previously published in: *IQBAL* (Lahore) 26, no. 3: July (n.d.), pp. 39-43.

845.   **HAMID, Kh. Abdul**, "IQBAL'S PHILOSOPHY OF HUMAN EGO", *VISHVABHARATI QUARTERLY* 9, no. 4: September 1943 (1944).

846.   **HAMID, Khwaja Abdul**, "DEVELOPMENT OF IQBAL'S POETIC THOUGHT",

POEMS FROM IQBAL, V. G. KIERNAN (tr.), Bombay: Kutub Publishers Ltd., 1947, pp. 125-33.
Introductory essay. Variant title: REMARKS ON THE DEVELOPMENT ...

847.   ———, "THE DEVELOPMENT OF IQBAL'S POETIC THOUGHT", *IQBAL* 42, no. 1 (1995): pp. 3-14.
Reprint; originally published in 1947.

848.   **HAMID, Muhammad**, mon., *IQBAL: THE POET OF FIFTEENTH CENTURY HIJRAH*, Lahore: Sang-e-Meel Publishers, 1980. 140 pp.
Variant title: THE POET PILOSOPHER OF THE FIFTEENTH CENTURY.

849.   **HAMID-UD-DIN, M.**, "IQBAL AND THE WEST", *PAKISTAN REVIEW* 5, no. [?]: December (1957): pp. 26, 27.

850.   **HAQ ANSARI, M. Habibul**, "IQBAL'S INNATE BIOLOGISM", *INTERNATIONAL STUDIES IN PHILOSOPHY* 28, no. 2 (1996): pp. 1-17.
A study of Iqbal's conception of the developed world, as seen in his poetical and metaphysical works, with emphasis on the concepts of the dynamism of the universe, the unity of the biosphere, biotic circulation in the world's history, evolution, humanity and the emergence of a noosphere.

851.   **HAQ, Jalalul**, "IQBAL'S APPROACH TO RELIGION", *IQBAL* 24, no. 4: October (1977): pp. 107-15.
Published also in *MULTI-DISCIPLINARY APPROACH TO IQBAL*, n.d., Iqbal Centenary Symposium [?].

852.   **HAQ, Justice Anwarul**, "IQBAL'S CONCEPTION OF THE HUMAN EGO", *IQBAL, THE POET OF TOMORROW*, Khawaja Abdur RAHIM (ed.), Lahore: Abdul Hameed Khan at Ferozsons Ltd., n.d., pp. 69[73]-76.
As indicated in the footnote on p. 73, this paper was originally read as presidential address at the afternoon Special Session of Iqbal Day of 21 April 1961. It discusses the six factors and forces fortifying, according to Iqbal, the human ego or personality (namely love, *faqr*, courage, tolerance, *kasbe-hilal*, and original and creative activity) and their four negative counterparts (fear, beggary or *sawal*, slavery, and pride of extraction or *nasab parasti*). The practical implication of Iqbal's philosophy of *khudi* is then reflected in the author's conclusion: *It is, therefore, imperative to us, who are fortunate to have the precious heritage of Iqbal's philosophy, to understand this philosophy and to try to act upon it in our daily lives. Who knows that the salvation of the world may yet lie with those who*

imbibe the teachings of Iqbal and of the Quran which is the source of Iqbal's inspiration?

853. **HAQ, Maulvi Abdul**, "SIR MUHAMMAD IQBAL", *INDIAN REVIEW* (Madras) 26, (1925): pp. 785-90.

854. **HAQ, Qazi Mahmud & M. I. WALEY**, mon., *ALLAMA SIR MUHAMMAD IQBAL: POET-PHILOSOPHER OF THE EAST*, London: British Museum Publications for the British Library, 1977. 30 pp.
Published in connection with a centenary exhibition; bibliography included.

855. **HAQ, S. M. Izrahul**, "IQBAL'S CONCEPT OF PAKISTAN", *THE PAKISTAN TIMES* (Rawalpindi), 21 April 1982.

856. **HAQ, Shuja Al**, "SUFISM AND ITS DEVELOPMENT IN THE PANJAB", University of London, 1992. 370 pp.

857. **HAQ, Syed Moinul**, comp., *PROCEEDINGS OF THE PAKISTAN HISTORY CONFERENCE, 16TH SESSION, KARACHI, 26-28 APRIL 1968*, Karachi: Pakistan Historical Society, 1968. 258 pp.
On Iqbal philosophy, see pp. 148-164.

858. **HAQUE, Izharful**, "ISLAMIC STATE OF IQBAL'S VISION", *THE PAKISTAN TIMES* (Rawalpindi), 21 April 1985.

859. **HAQUE, Izrahul**, "QUAID'S TRIBUTE TO IQBAL", *THE PAKISTAN TIMES* (Rawalpindi), 9 November 1983.

860. ———, "THE VISUALISER OF PAKISTAN", *THE PAKISTAN TIMES* (Rawalpindi), 9 November 1982.

861. **HAQUE, S. M. Izharul**, "ALLAMA IQBAL'S LETTERS TO QUAID-I-AZAM", *THE PAKISTAN TIMES* (Rawalpindi), 21 April 1986.

862. **HAQUE, S. M. Izrahul**, "IQBAL IN THE EYES OF THE QUAID", *THE PAKISTAN TIMES* (Islamabad), 9 November 1986.

863. ———, "IQBAL'S LOVE FOR THE PROPHET", *THE PAKISTAN TIMES* (Rawalpindi /

Lahore), 9 November 1985.

864.   ———, "IQBAL'S POLITICAL FORSIGHTEDNESS", *THE PAKISTAN TIMES* (Rawalpindi), 21 April 1983.

865.   **HARDY, John L.**, "IQBAL: POET OF THE EAST", *THE SCOTSMAN* (Edinburgh), 26 April 1954.
A letter.

866.   **HARLEY, A. H.**, "IQBAL", *CHAMBER'S ENCYCLOPAEDIA* , London: George Newmen Ltd., 1950, Vol. 7, pp. 399.

867.   **HARRÉ, R.**, "IQBAL: A REFORMER OF ISLAMIC PHILOSOPHY", *HIBBERT JOURNAL* (London) 56, no. 4: October and [?]: July (1957-1958): pp. 333-39. This article aims at contradicting the opinion that the Islamic resurgence of the mid-20th century is a purely political movement. On the contrary, the author states, Iqbal has fundamentally opposed the orthodox Islamic philosophy; this opposition *hangs not upon a piecemeal revision of the traditional conceptual scheme, but on the recommendation of one compound: partly of elements from the early centuries of Islamic culture, and partly of elements derived from an evolutionary view of the world, owing much to Bergson and Whitehead.*
Iqbal's novel interpretation *("reconstruction")* of Quranic doctrines, then, is based primarily on three interconnected principles: (1) that there are three fundamentally different *areas of experience* - inanimate matter, living organisms, and minds - the study of which gives rise to three groups of sciences, the physical, the biological and the psychological, together producing a total world-picture called *religion*; (2) that neither blind obedience to *fate* nor belief in predestination, which is supposed to justify the acceptance of *Qismat*, can offer any theoretical ground for immortality, and that it is thus proper for an individual to be active; and (3) that everything in the three realms is subjected to *change* (in other words: even God is changing) and Muhammad was the last prophet, *not because he gave a final description of the three realms of experience, but because he recommended a method of enquiry that enables a day-to-day record of the change to be kept.*
Re-issued in *IQBAL REVIEW* 10, no. 3: October (1969), pp. 1-8; and once more in [Various authors], *SELECTIONS FROM THE IQBAL REVIEW*, ed. Waheed Qureshi, Lahore, 1983, pp. 273-279.
Variant Name (cf. Waheed QURESHI, 1983): R. HAREE [sic].

868.   **HARRE, R.**, "IQBAL: A REFORMER OF ISLAMIC PHILOSOPHY", *AL-ISLAM*, 1[5] October and 1[5] November 1960, p. 155 and [?] resp.

869.   HARRIS, M. A., "ALLAMA IQBAL'S CONCEPTION OF ART", *ILLUSTRATED WEEKLY OF PAKISTAN* 4, no. 29: 20 April (1952): pp. 33, 34.

870.   ———, "IQBAL'S CONCEPTION OF ART", *IQBAL: A CRITICAL STUDY*, Misbah-ul-Haq SIDDIQUI (ed.), Lahore: Farhan Publishers, 1977, pp. 47-50.
       Short article on Iqbal's conception of Art, compared with Tolstoy and I.A. Richards' theory of *Balance of Propensities.*

871.   HARVEY, Pharis J., "IQBAL'S DEATH: A CHILD CRUSADER AGAINST CHILD LABOR", *THE CHRISTIAN CENTURY: UNDENOMINATIONAL* 112, no. 18 (1995): pp. 557-58.

872.   HASAN, Ahmad, "ALLAMA IQBAL IN LUCKNOW", *THE MUSLIM* (Islamabad), 21 April 1981.

873.   HASAN, M., "IQBAL: POET-PHILOSOPHER OF SOUTH ASIA", *CREATIVE MOMENT* (Sumter, SC) 11-12, (1978): pp. 22-28.

874.   HASAN, Masud-ul, mon., *LIFE OF IQBAL*, 1st ed., Vol. I-II, Lahore: Ferozsons, 1978. x+506 pp. and xiv+446 pp. resp.
       Two vols.: (*Book 1*) General Account of his Life, (*Book 2*) His Works, Personality, Anecdotes, Thoughts and Times. Contents:
       Book 1: (I) Years of childhood, (II) Years of early youth, (III) Higher studies in England, (IV) Atiya Begum, (V) Pre-war years 1908-1914, (VI) War years 1914-1918, (VII) After the war, (VIII) Letters of Iqbal to Girami, (IX) Return to the Legislative Council, (X) General activities 1927-28, (XI) In South India and Aligarh, (XII) General activities 1929-30, (XIII) Allahabad Muslim League Session 1930, (XIV) General activities 1931, (XV) Political activities 1932, (XVI) General activities 1933, (XVII) Round Table Conference 1930-33, (XVIII) Travels abroad 1931-33, (XIX) General activities 1934-36, (XX) The Qadianis and the Muslims, (XXI) General activities 1937, (XXII) The last year, (XXIII) Passing away of Iqbal 21st April 1938.
       Book 2: (I) Early poetry, (II) Urdu poetry 1908-1924, (III) Development of Metaphysics in Persia, (IV) Asrar-i-Khudi and Rumuz-i-Bekhudi, (V) Payam-i-Mashriq, (VI) Zabur-i-Ajam, (VII) Reconstruction of Religious Thought in Islam, (VIII) Javid Nama, (IX) Musafir and Pas Cheh Bayd Kard, (X) Bal-i-Jibril (Wing of the Gabriel), (XI) Zarb-i-Kalim, (XII) Armughan-i-Hijaz, (XIII) Personality of Iqbal, (XIV) Self Assessment of Iqbal, (XV) Philosophy of Iqbal, (XVI) Poetry of Iqbal, (XVII) Anecdotes of Iqbal, (XVIII) Tributes to Iqbal, (XIX) Thoughts of Iqbal, (XX) Times of Iqbal; (XXI) Bibliography.

875. ———, mon., *LIFE OF IQBAL: HIS WORKS, PERSONALITY, ANECDOTES, THOUGHTS AND TIMES*, Lahore: Ferozsons, 1978. 305 pp.

876. **HASAN, Masud ul**, mon., *STORIES AND BIOGRAPHIES FROM IQBAL*, Lahore: Ferozesons, 1978.
Cf. of the same author, *LIFE OF IQBAL*.

877. **HASAN, Mohammad**, "IQBAL: A NEW VISION FOR A DESPERATE WORLD", *INDIAN AND FOREIGN REVIEW* (New Delhi) 15, no. 3 (1977): pp. 15-17.

878. ———, mon., *A NEW APPROACH TO IQBAL*, New Delhi: Ministry of Information and Broadcasting, Publications Division, 1987. viii+102 pp.

879. **HASAN, Mumtaz**, "ALLAMA IQBAL INSPIRES SUFFERING HUMANITY", *DAWN*, 21 April 1966, p. 5.

880. ———, "A DAY IN THE LIFE OF MUHAMMAD IQBAL", *MUHAMMAD IQBAL*, Various authors (mon.), Karachi: Pakistan-German Forum, 1960, pp. 133-39.

881. ———, "IQBAL, A RECOLLECTION", *IQBAL STUDIES*, Muhammad Ziaul ISLAM (ed.), Karachi: Bazm-i-Iqbal, 1949.
Published also in *AL-ISLAM*, 1 January 1958, p. 84.

882. ———, "IQBAL AND THE PHILOSOPHY OF THE WEST", *NAYRANG-I KHAYAL* [vol. ?], (n.d.).
Iqbal Number.

883. ———, "IQBAL: ARCHITECT OF PAKISTAN", *EVENING TIMES*, 21 April 1952, pp. 2, 5.

884. ———, "IQBAL AS A SEER", *IQBAL REVIEW* 7, no. 1: April (1966): pp. 43-62.
Text of a speech delivered on the occasion of the presentation ceremony of IQBAL IN PICTURE, compiled by Fakir Syed Wahiduddin, to the Museums Association of Pakistan; later once more re-issued in [Various authors], *SELECTIONS FROM THE IQBAL REVIEW*, ed. Waheed Qureshi, Lahore, 1983, pp. 345-364.

885. ———, "IQBAL AS AN EXPONENT OF ISLAMIC THOUGHT", *PAKISTAN*

OBSERVER, 21 April 1960.

886.   ——, "IQBAL EXHIBITION WELCOME ADDRESS", *IQBAL REVIEW* 7, no. 3: October (1966): pp. 18-21.
Speech held on the occasion of Iqbal Day at Karachi on 16 April 1966, when an exhibition of Iqbal material was arranged. It was inaugurated by H.E. Mr. Hoshang Ansari, Ambassador of the Royal Iranian Embassy in Karachi.

887.   ——, "IQBAL'S TRIBUTE TO GOETHE", *IQBAL* 21, no. 1: January-March (1974): pp. 13-40.

888.   ——, "A NATION IS BORN", *MUHAMMAD IQBAL UND DIE DREI REICHE DES GEISTES*, Wolfgang KOEHLER (ed.), Hamburg: Deutsch-Pakistanisches Forum, 1977, pp. 257-65.
Followed by a summary in German: GEBURT EINER NATION, pp. 265-266. E-G.

889.   ——, "RECONSTRUCTION OF ISLAMIC THOUGHTS: IQBAL ON IJTIHAD", *DAWN*, n.d., p. 1.

890.   ——, "SIDELIGHTS ON IQBAL: IQBAL AS A MAN", *PAKISTAN CALLING* 6, no. 8 (1952): pp. 8, 9.

891.   **HASAN, Mumtaz & M. MOIZUDDIN**, comp./eds., *TRIBUTE TO IQBAL*, Lahore: Iqbal Academy, 1982

892.   **HASAN, Nazeer**, "IQBAL'S CONCEPTION OF ART", *EASTERN WORLD* (London) 7, no. [?]: February (1953): pp. 27-29.

893.   **HASAN, Parveen Feroze**, "THE POLITICAL PHILOSOPHY OF IQBAL", University of the Punjab, Dept. of Philosophy, 1967. 459 pp.
Ph.D. dissertation; promoter: Munir-ud-Din Chughtai; cf also HASSAN, Parveen Feroze. Influence onto Iqbal is sought in Greek thought (Plato and Aristotle), Dante, Goethe, Nietzsche, Bergson, Ibn Arabi, Rumi, Al-Jili, Shaikh Ahmad Sirhindi. Contents: (1) The life and works of Iqbal, (2) Impacts and impressions: Western and Oriental, (3) Hakimiyat (Sovereignty of Allah), (4) The prophet as the ideal leader, (5) Ijtihad (Independant reasoning), (6) The political significance of khudi, moman and millat, (7) Nationalism, (8) Muslim universalism, (9) Communism, (10) Democracy, (11) Iqbal and practical politics, and Conclusion.

Including a bibliography of 54 pages (pp. 405-459).

894. **HASAN, Rafia**, "THE MAIN PHILOSOPHICAL IDEAS IN THE WRITINGS OF MUHAMMAD IQBAL (1877-1938)", University of North Carolina - PhD Thesis, 1967-1968.

895. **HASAN, Reyazul**, "GOETHE AND IQBAL", *THE PAKISTAN TIMES* (Rawalpindi), 9 November 1977.

896. ———, "IL POETA MUSULMANO INDIANO MOHAMMAD IQBAL", *ORIENTE MODERNO* (Roma) 20, (1940): pp. 605-23.
I.

897. ———, "IQBAL ON THE INDIVIDUAL", *THE MORNING NEWS*, 14 August 1962.

898. ———, "IQBAL'S *TULIP OF SINAI* - PROF. A.J. ARBERRY'S TRANSLATION", *IQBAL REVIEW* 16, no. 1: April (1975): pp. 43-48.
Critique on Arberry's translation, which, according to the author, *at places has been done at the expense of meaning*. Re-issued in [Various authors], *SELECTIONS FROM THE IQBAL REVIEW*, ed. Waheed Qureshi, Lahore, 1983, pp. 453-458.

899. ———, "MUHAMMAD IQBAL", *ORIENTE MODERNO* 20, no. 2 (1940).

900. ———, "A UNIQUE LETTER OF IQBAL", *IQBAL REVIEW* 9, no. 1: April (1968): pp. 75-79.

901. **HASAN, Riffat**, "IQBAL AND SOCIALISM", *IQBAL: A CRITICAL STUDY*, Misbah-ul-Haq SIDDIQUI (ed.), Lahore: Farhan Publishers, 1977, pp. 118-22.
Iqbal's sympathy for Socialism, the author states, *flowed out from his passionate dislike for injustice and despotism*. And: *Iqbal's Socialism was one which has as its ideal "not a mechanical equality of all over less of society, but rather a potential equality in the sense of the maxim of Saint Simon's followers - from each according to his capacity, to each according to his merit - which has as its fundamental tenet not common ownership, but the elimination of all unearned increment"*. The author concludes that, according to Iqbal, *original Islam had been a socialistic movement*.
Article taken from *THE PAKISTAN TIMES*, 21 April 1968, p. 4.

902. ———, "IQBAL'S POLITICAL PHILOSOPHY AND THE CONCEPT OF ISLAM",

THE MUSLIM (Islamabad), 9 November 1983.

903.   ———, "SOME THOUGHTS ON IQBAL'S AESTHETICS", *PAKISTAN REVIEW* 16, no. 4: April (1968): pp. 18-20.

904.   **HASAN, S. Sibte**, "IQBAL'S CONCEPT OF MAN", *THE MUSLIM* (Islamabad), 21 April 1980.

905.   **HASAN, Zeenat Fida**, "IQBAL'S CAMPAIGN AGAINST MUSLIM PSEUDOMYSTICISM", *THE CIVIL AND MILITARY GAZETTE* (Lahore), 21 April 1955, p. 5.

906.   **HASHIMI, Syed Moulvi Sahib**, "IQBAL", *POETRY REVIEW* 27, (1936): pp. 293.

907.   **HASHIMY, S. Y.**, ed., *ISLAM AS AN ETHICAL AND POLITICAL IDEAL: IQBAL'S MAIDEN ENGLISH LECTURE (1908), EDITED WITH CRITICAL INTRODUCTION, COPIOUS NOTES AND APPENDIX*, 2nd rev. ed., Lahore: Islamic Book Service , 1977. 117 pp.
Originally published in Lahore:Orientalia, 1955, 147 pp.

908.   **HASHMEY, N. H.**, "PESHAWAR'S UNIQUE IQBAL DAY", *THE PAKISTAN TIMES* (Rawalpindi), 20 April 1984.

909.   **HASHMI, Anwar-ul-Haq**, "IQBAL AND DEMOCRACY", *PAKISTAN TIMES* (Lahore), 20 April 1958, p. 8.

910.   **HASHMI, Yousouf Abbas**, "IQBAL'S CONCEPTION OF STATE", *VOICE OF ISLAM*, March 1959-30 April 1959, pp. 251-57.

911.   **HASIENA, Shaikh**, "THE CONCEPT OF THE PERFECT MAN IN IQBAL", *PAKISTAN QUARTERLY* 4, no. 1 (1954).

912.   **HASRAT, Muhammad Nawaz**, "IQBAL'S CONCEPTION OF PERSONALITY AND MODERN PSYCHOLOGY", University of the Punjab, Dept. Philosophy, 1965. 76 pp.
Promoters: Qazi Muhammad Aslam, K.G. Sadiq, and C.A. Qadir.
Contents: Part I - (1) Introduction, (2) The beginning of modern psychology, (3) Revolt against atomism; Part II - (4) Some leading theories of personality, (5) Psychoanalytic theories of personality, (6) Roger's Self theory and Murphy's biosocial theory, (7) Iqbal and

personality theory.

913. **HASSAN, Parveen Feroze**, mon., *THE POLITICAL PHILOSOPHY OF IQBAL*, Lahore: Publishers United Ltd, 1970. xxii+426 pp.
Originally a Doctoral Thesis; cf. HASAN, Parveen Feroze.
A well-documented study of the politically charged elements in Iqbal's philosophy. Following an elaborate introduction on the life and works of Iqbal, the author first sets out to examine to what extent some Western and Muslim thinkers and philosophies have had an impact on the philosophical outline of Iqbal's work: Plato, Aristotle, Dante, Goethe, Nietzsche and Bergson on the one hand - Ibn Arabi, Rumi, Al-Jili and Shaikh Ahmad Sirhindi on the other. Then follow analyses of Iqbal's concepts of *Hakimiyat* (the Sovereignty of Allah), the Prophet as the Ideal Leader, *ijtihad* (independent reasoning), *khudi* (the Self), *momin* (the Perfect Man), and *millat* (society). All aspects are presented from quotations from Iqbal's works, and attention is focused on their political significance. The second part of the book is devoted to some of the broader political implications of Iqbal's thought: the question of nationalism, Muslim universalism, islam vs. communism, islam vs. the Western concept of democracy. Each of these topics is gradually narrowed down, from their universal definitions, via the muslim concept of them, to the Iqbal viewpoint.
Finally, the author presents a series of case-studies in applied Iqbal political thinking, and more in particular of Iqbal's role in the genesis of Pakistan. The main aim of the author is to present Iqbal as having laid down a coherent political philosophy, based primarily on Quranic elements, and enriched by a distinct stamp of his own genius. 'From Quranic thought', the author states, 'Iqbal cleared the debris to rediscover the sterling principles, whose inherent worth could revitalise all aspects of Muslim life.'
The book contains an elaborate bibliography and an index.

914. **HASSAN, Riffat**, "THE DEVELOPMENT OF POLITICAL PHILOSOPHY", *IQBAL: POET-PHILOSOPHER OF PAKISTAN*, Hafeez MALIK (ed.), New York: Columbia UP, 1971, pp. 136-38.

915. ———, "GOD AND THE UNIVERSE IN IQBAL'S PHILOSOPHY", *IQBAL REVIEW* 28, no. 1: April-June (1987): pp. 9-26.

916. ———, "'IBLIS' IN IQBAL'S PHILOSOPHY", *IQBAL REVIEW* 25, no. 3: October (1984): pp. 25-45.

917. ———, comp., *AN IQBAL PRIMER: AN INTRODUCTION TO IQBAL'S PHILOSOPHY*, Lahore: Aziz Publishers, 1979. 269 pp.

This 'Primer' gives a systematic description and analysis of the major works of Iqbal, and includes quotations in Persian and Urdu.

918.   ———, "IQBAL'S ANALYSIS OF VARIOUS TIME-CONCEPTS AND HIS OWN VIEW OF TIME", *IQBAL REVIEW* 25, no. 1: April (1984): pp. 21-46.

919.   ———, "IQBAL'S IDEAL PERSON AND RUMI'S INFLUENCE", *IQBAL REVIEW* 24, no. 3: October (1983): pp. 119-26.
Comparison of Rumi's *mard-i haqq* and Iqbal's *mard-i mo'min* as opposed to Nietzsche's Übermensch.

920.   ———, "IQBAL'S PHILOSOPHY OF ART", *IQBAL REVIEW* 26, no. 3: October-November-December (1985): pp. 19-46.

921.   ———, "IQBAL'S VIEW OF PRAYER", *IQBAL REVIEW* 28, no. 3: October-December (1987): pp. 61-75.

922.   ———, "THE MEANING AND ROLE OF INTUITION IN IQBAL'S PHILOSOPHY", *IQBAL REVIEW* 27, no. 1: April-May-June (1985): pp. 67-99.

923.   ———, mon., *THE SWORD AND THE SCEPTRE: A COLLECTION OF WRITINGS ON IQBAL, DEALING MAINLY WITH HIS LIFE AND POETICAL WORKS*, Lahore: Iqbal Academy, 1977.
A collection of 36 articles by 29 authors from various countries (UK, Germany, Italym Czechoslovakia, Canada, Pakistan and India); all articles were originally published between 1920 and 1967.

924.   **HATEM, Mohammad Abdul Kader**, "ADDRESS, IQBAL DAY IN CAIRO", *IQBAL REVIEW* 8, no. 1: April (1967): pp. 91-93.

925.   **HAUSER, Walter**, "HAFEEZ MALIK, Ed., "Iqbal: Poet-Philosopher of Pakistan" (Book Review)", *AMERICAN HISTORICAL REVIEW* 80, no. 2: April (1975): pp. 470.

926.   **HAYAT K. SIAL**, "MESSAGE AND PHILOSOPHY", *CIVIL AND MILITARY GAZETTE* (Lahore), 21 April 1960, p. 4.

927.   **HAYIT BAYMIRZA**, mon., *MUHAMMAD IQBAL UND DIE WELT DES ISLAM*, Köln, 1956. 22 pp.
Variant name: Bayminza.

G.

928. **HAYWOOD, John A.**, "THE WISDOM OF MUHAMMAD IQBAL - SOME CONSIDERATIONS OF FORM AND CONTENT", *IQBAL REVIEW* 9, no. 1: April (1968): pp. 22-33.

929. **HERMANSEN, Marcia**, "'IQBAL: LIFE, ART, AND THOUGHT', LEONARD LIBRANDE AND NUZRAT YAR KHAN, EDITORS (Book Review)", *STUDIES IN RELIGION / SCIENCES RELIGIEUSES* 9, no. 4 (1980): pp. 478. Canadian Journal of Theology.
E or F [?].

930. **HILAL, Abdul Aleem**, *SOCIAL PHILOSOPHY OF SIR MUHAMMAD IQBAL: A CRITICAL STUDY*, Delhi: Adam Publishers & Distributors, 1995

931. **HOBOHM, M. A. H.**, "MOHAMMAD IQBAL AND GERMANY (A CORRESPONDENCE OF THE HEART)", *IQBAL REVIEW* 30-31, no. 3: October and 1: April (1989-1990): pp. 95-104.

932. **HOBOHM, Muhammad Aman**, "IQBAL'S CONTRIBUTION TO THE REAWAKENING OF THE MUSLIM WORLD", *IQBAL REVIEW* 30, no. 1: April-June (1989): pp. 55-62.

933. **HOLROYDE, Peggy & Mohammed IQBAL & Dharam Kumar YOHRA**, mon., *EAST COMES TO WEST: A BACKGROUND TO SOME ASIAN FAITHS*, London: Community Relations Commission, n.d. 88 pp.

934. **HOLST, Arthur Carl**, "TOWARD A DEFINITION OF A TRANSCULTURAL STATE: A STUDY OF EASTERN AND WESTERN IDEAS, ESPECIALLY IN THE WRITINGS OF MUHAMMAD IQBAL AND WALT WHITMAN", *DISSERTATIONS ABSTRACTS INTERNATIONAL* (Ann Arbor) 40, (1980): pp. 5083A. Dissertation Abstract.

935. **HORANI, Jamil-ur-Rehman**, "IQBAL - THE PROBLEM OF POETIC BELIEF", *IQBAL REVIEW* (Karachi) 4, no. 1: April (1964): pp. 23-47.

936. **HOSEINI, Ashraf**, "METAPHYSICS OF IQBAL AND DANTE", *IQBAL* 30, no. 1: January (1983): pp. 85-93.
Analysis of Mars in Iqbal's astronomical scheme, which is taken over from Dante. A folder

(extra, numberless page) contains comparative schemes of Mt. Purgatory, the path of the Sun and the Zodiac.

937. **HOSSFELD, Paul**, "GOTT, WELT UND MENSCH AUS DER PHILOSOPHISCHEN SICHT VON SIR MUHAMMAD IQBAL", *ZEITSCHRIFT FÜR MISSIONSWISSENSCHAFT UND RELIGIONSWISSEN-SCHAFT* (Münster, Westfalen) 64, no. 1 (1980): pp. 39-50.

938. **HOUBEN, J. J.**, "(THE) INDIVIDUAL IN DEMOCRACY AND IQBAL'S CONCEPTION OF KHUDI", *PAKISTAN QUARTERLY* 4, no. 1: Spring (1954): pp. 18-21, 63, 67.
Also in *CRESCENT AND GREEN*, London: Cassell & Co., 1955, pp. 142-161.

939. **HURI, Sofi**, tr. E/T, *ISLAM DA DINI DEFKURUN YEVIDU TESDKULU* (THE RECONSTRUCTON OF RELIGIOUS THOUGHT IN ISLAM), Istanbul, 1964.
Turkish translation of (I) THE RECONSTRUCTION OF RELIGIOUS THOUGHT IN ISLAM.
T.

940. **HUSAIN, Abadul**, "IMPACT OF IQBAL ON BENGALI THOUGHT", *IQBAL REVIEW* (Karachi) [vol. ?], no. [?]: April (1966).

941. **HUSAIN, Altaf**, tr. P/E, *THE COMPLAINT AND THE ANSWER, BEING ALLAMA SIR MUHAMMAD IQBAL'S SHIKWAH & JAWAB-I-SHIKWAH, DONE/RENDERED INTO ENGLISH VERSE*, Lahore: Shaikh Muhammad Ashraf, 1948. xiv+39 or 72 pp. [?].
English verse translation of (I) SHIKWA and (I) JAWAB-I-SHIKWA from BANG-I-DARA, with an introduction by the translator, and a glossary.

942. **HUSAIN, Anwar**, "IQBAL IN EAST PAKISTAN", *PAKISTAN TIMES*, 24 June 1966, p. 2.

943. **HUSAIN, B. S. RAZA**, "DIAGNOSIS OF NATION. IQBAL AND AKBAR SUPPORT EACH OTHER", *THE TIMES OF KARACHI*, 21 April 1954.

944. **HUSAIN, Farouk**, "SCIENTIFIC INTERPRETATION OF IQBAL", *DAWN*, 15 April 1960.

945. **HUSAIN, Karrar**, "IQBAL: HISTORICAL PERSPECTIVE AND MESSAGE", *DAWN*

(Karachi), 9 November 1977.

946. **HUSAIN, M.**, "THE POET WAS A WORLD CITIZEN", *PAKISTAN TIMES*, 21 April 1950, p. 6.
Special Suppl.

947. **HUSAIN, Mahmud**, mon., *EDUCATIONAL IDEAS OF IQBAL (TEXT OF PRESIDENTIAL ADDRESS AT THE IQBAL DAY MEETING HELD AT KARACHI ON APRIL 21 1961, UNDER THE AUSPICES OF THE IQBAL ACADEMY, KARACHI)*, Dacca, 1961.
Variant name: HUSSAIN.

948. **HUSAIN, Murtaza**, "IQBAL'S PHILOSOPHY OF KHUDI", *DAWN* (Karachi), 9 November 1986.

949. ———, "IQBAL'S POETRY OF DYNAMISM AND HOPE", *MORNING NEWS* (Karachi), 9 November 1979.

950. ———, "OPTIMISM KEYNOTE OF IQBAL'S POETRY", *MORNING NEWS* (Karachi), 21 April 1981.

951. **HUSAIN, Riaz**, "IQBAL-JINNAH COLLABORATION: PAKISTAN DEMAND AT THE ROUND-TABLE CONFERENCE, 1930-31", *IQBAL* (Lahore) 30, no. 3-4: July-October (1983): pp. 81-87.

952. **HUSAIN, S. Sajjad**, "IQBAL AND WORDSWORTH", *IQBAL REVIEW* 24, no. 1: April (1983): pp. 21-23.

953. **HUSAIN, Sayyid Badshah**, mon., *IQBAL'S PLAGIARISM*, Karachi, 1951.
A reply to Dr. Khalifa Abdul Hakim's ardent attack on Iqbal and his supposed plagiarism of Rumi and others.

954. **HUSAIN, Syed Sajjad**, "IQBAL IN MUSLIM BENGAL", *IQBAL* 37, no. 1-2 (1990): pp. 1-8.

955. **HUSAINI, Kalimullah**, "IQBAL'S GULSHAN-E-RAZ-E-JADID AND BANDAGI NAMAH, BY BASHIR AHMED DAR", *ISLAMIC CULTURE* 43, no. 2 (1969).

956. **HUSSAIN, Afzal**, "MY PRECEPTOR", *PAKISTAN TIMES*, 21 April 1961, p. 4.

957. **HUSSAIN, Altaf**, "ALLAMA IQBAL: THE POET OF THE EAST", *ILLUSTRATED WEEKLY OF PAKISTAN*, 25 April 1954, pp. 29-30.
Iqbal Day address at the Leiden University, Holland, 1953.

958. ———, mon., *IQBAL DAY 1953 IN THE NETHERLANDS*, Leiden: E.J. Brill, 1954. 19 pp.
Speech by Altaf Hussain.

959. ———, "SPEECH, IQBAL DAY AT THE LEIDEN UNIVERSITY, NETHERLANDS", *IQBAL REVIEW* 8, no. 1: April (1967): pp. 67-73.

960. **HUSSAIN, Arif**, "IQBAL AND CASELY HAYFORD: A PHASE IN AFRO-ASIAN PHILOSOPHY", *IBADAN REVIEW* (Ibadan, Nigeria) 29, (1971): pp. 45-52.

961. ———, "POET'S POLITICAL PHILOSOPHY", *TIMES OF KARACHI*, 21 April 1956, p. 5.

962. **HUSSAIN, Iqbal**, "STUDY OF IQBAL'S POETRY", *HINDUSTAN REVIEW* 75, no. [?]: October-November (1942): pp. 143-52 / 207-209.

963. **HUSSAIN, Massood**, "MUHAMMAD IQBAL, PHILOSOPHE-POÈTE", University of Paris, 1953.
A PhD-thesis.
F.

964. **HUSSAIN, Mumtaz**, "IQBAL: A BIOGRAPHICAL SKETCH", *DAWN* (Karachi), 21 April 1948, p. 10.
Variant name: HASAN, Mumtaz.

965. ———, "THE POET AS A WORLD CITIZEN", *THE PAKISTAN TIMES* (Lahore), 21 April 1950, p. 6.

966. **HUSSAIN, Muzaffar**, "ALLAMA ON PROBLEMS OF POVERTY", *PAKISTAN TIMES*, 21 April 1974, p. 2.

967. ———, "IQBAL'S THOUGHT ON ECONOMIC DEVELOPMENT", *IQBAL REVIEW*

24, no. 3: October (1983): pp. 55-65.

968.   ———, "THE KEY POINT IN IQBAL'S EDUCATIONAL PHILOSOPHY", *IQBAL REVIEW* 23, no. 3: October (1982): pp. 65-72.
Short pamphlet on an educational programme, centred on Iqbal's *education is the training of human will*. Re-issued in [Various authors], *SELECTIONS FROM THE IQBAL REVIEW*, ed. Waheed Qureshi, Lahore, 1983. pp. 365-372.

969.   **HUSSAIN, Riaz**, "AMERICAN, WEST EUROPEAN AND SOVIET ATTITUDES TO IQBAL", *IQBAL REVIEW* 26, no. 3: October-November-December (1985): pp. 97-112.

970.   ———, "THE EVOLUTION OF IQBAL'S POETIC THOUGHT - A MYTH EXPLODED", *IQBAL REVIEW* 18, no. 1: April (1977): pp. 19-22.
Rebuttal of the myth that Iqbal was a "nationalist poet of the secular Congress brand", whose Islamic political engagement grew out of a sudden metamorphosis of his thought in the closing years of his life.

971.   ———, mon., *IQBAL: AN INTERNATIONAL MISSIONARY OF ISLAM*, Lahore: Iqbal Academy, 1983. vi+92 pp.
Includes 8 pages of plates, an index and a bibliography (pp. 81-82). Also published by South Asia Books (Columbia, U.S.A.) and by Anmol Publications (New Delhi, 1993).

972.   ———, "IQBAL AND CONTEMPORARY FOREIGN AFFAIRS", *IQBAL* 24, no. 4: October (1977): pp. 117-23.

973.   ———, "IQBAL AND JAWAHARLAL NEHRU", *IQBAL REVIEW* 18, no. 4: January (1978): pp. 143-47.

974.   ———, mon., *IQBAL: POET AND POLITICS*, New Delhi: Uppal Publishing House, n.d. viii+160 pp.

975.   ———, "IQBAL'S PARLEYS WITH A BRITISH ECONOMIST", *IQBAL REVIEW* 30-31, no. 3: October and 1: April (1989-1990): pp. 83-94.
A verbatim English translation of the Press Report of Iqbal's parleys with Prof. Stanley Webb, published in Pasis Akhbar, Lahore of 13 March 1912.

976.   ———, "IQBAL'S RELATIONS WITH THE BRITISH IMPERIAL POWER", *IQBAL REVIEW* 19, no. 3: October (1978): pp. 55-58.

977.   ———, "JINNAH CALLS ON IQBAL AND LEAGUE BECOMES A MASS MOVEMENT", *THE PAKISTAN TIMES* (Rawalpindi), 23 December 1983.

978.   ———, mon., *THE POLITICS OF IQBAL: A STUDY OF HIS POLITICAL THOUGHTS AND ACTION*, Lahore: Islamic Book Service, 1977. 159 pp.
       E.

979.   ———, "PUNJAB IN IQBAL'S LIFE-TIME", *IQBAL REVIEW* 24, no. 3: October (1983): pp. 127-36.
       Survey of the social, political and economic conditions in the Punjab between 1901 and 1938, and Iqbal's reaction to these.

980.   ———, "REVIVAL OF PUNJAB MUSLIM LEAGUE, JINNAH-IQBAL COLLABORATION", *IQBAL REVIEW* 28, no. 3: October-December (1987): pp. 91-99.

981.   ———, "SOME UNREALISED DREAMS OF IQBAL", *IQBAL REVIEW* 20, no. 3: October (1979): pp. 45-47.
       The unrealised dreams of Iqbal concern (1) the formation of Muslim educational and cultural Youth Leagues, (2) the establishing of a chair for Islamic research on modern lines in the Islamia College, Lahore, and (3) the establishing of an Institute of Pharmacy to teach the *hakim*s the improved methods of preparing medecines, which are however no copies of the Western system of medicine.

982.   ———, "TWO RARE DOCUMENTS OF IQBALIAT", *IQBAL REVIEW* 25, no. 1: April (1984): pp. 63-75.

983.   **HUSSAIN, S. Liaquat**, "WRONG APPRECIATION OF IQBAL", *CIVIL AND MILITARY GAZETTE* (Lahore), 21 April 1953, p. 4.

984.   **HUSSAIN, Syed Murtza**, "(A) CLEAR CONTACT WITH REALITY", *MORNING NEWS*, 9 November 1975, p. 4.

985.   ———, "IQBAL AND THE DOCTRINE OF KHUDI", *DAWN*, 21 April 1972, pp. 6, 9.

986.   ———, "IQBAL VISUALISATION OF MURDIMOMIN", *DAWN*, 21 April 1971, p. 5.

987.   **HUSSAIN, Syed Sajjad**, "UNDERSTANDING OF IQBAL", *IQBAL: A CRITICAL STUDY*, Misbah-ul-Haq SIDDIQUI (ed.), Lahore: Farhan Publishers, 1977, pp. 123-27.
       General appraisal of Iqbal, from a non-Urdu and non-Persian speaking Pakistani.

Article taken from *THE CIVIL AND MILITARY GAZETTE*, 14 August 1963.

988. **HUSSAIN, Taha**, "ABUL ALA AL-MUARRI AND ALLAMA IQBAL", *THE PAKISTAN TIMES* (Rawalpindi), 2 December 1977.

989. **HUSSAINI, I.**, mon., *POET'S VISION & MAGIC OF WORDS: MUHAMMAD IQBAL*, Chicago: Kazi Publications, 1985. 145 pp.

990. **HYDER, Ruhafza**, "IQBAL'S MESSAGE", *THE MUSLIM* (Islamabad), 9 November 1982.

991. **HYDER, S.**, *PROGRESS OF PAKISTAN*, Lahore: Lion Press, 1947. Cf. esp. pp. 8, 24, 35.

992. **HYDER, Syed Akbar**, "COMBATTING COLONIALISM: THE URDU RESISTANCE POETRY OF MUHAMMAD IQBAL AND AKBAR ALLAHABADI", *SAGAR* 2, no. 2: April (1996).

993. **IBN AFAQ**, "UNIVERSE AND MAN", *TIMES OF KARACHI*, 21 April 1956, p. 3.

994. **IBRAHIM, A. M. M.**, "IQBAL'S CONCEPTION OF SHAHADAT", *ISLAMIC LITERATURE* (Lahore) 7, no. 9: September (1955): pp. 19-22.

995. ———, "IQBAL'S CONCEPTION OF THE ISLAMIC STATE", *ISLAMIC LITERATURE (Lahore)* 7, no. 1-2: January-February (1955): pp. 143-52.

996. ———, "IQBAL'S CONCEPTION OF TIME", *ISLAMIC LITERATURE* [vol. ?], no. [?]: October (1956): pp. 27-36.

997. ———, "IQBAL'S PHILOSOPHY OF LAW", *ISLAMIC LITERATURE* 7, no. 7: July (1955): pp. 21-30.

998. ———, "IQBAL'S PHILOSOPHY OF LOVE", *ISLAMIC LITERATURE* (Lahore) 3, no. 7: July (1955): pp. 21-30.

999. **IBRAHIM, Mir**, "ALLAMA IQBAL AND JAVID NAMA", *THE PAKISTAN TIMES* (Lahore), 21 April 1992.

1000. ———, "ALLAMA IQBAL AND TIPU SULTAN", *THE PAKISTAN TIMES* (Lahore), 14 April 1992.

1001. **IDRIS, Najmi S. M.**, "THE IDEAL MAN OF IQBAL", *OASIS*, April 1950, pp. 20-25.

1002. **IKBAL, Muchammad**, mon., *IZBRANNOE* (SELECTED OPERA), Moskva: Nauka, 1981.
Russian translation of selected Persian and Urdu works by Iqbal.
R.

1003. **IKRAM, S. M.**, mon., *MODERN MUSLIM INDIA AND THE BIRTH OF PAKISTAN, 1858-1951*, Lahore: Institute of Islamic Culture, 1977.
Published earlier in Karachi: Sheikh Muhammad Ashraf, 1970. xiv+506 pp.; of which see esp. pp. 54, 63, 68, 70*f.*, 93, 131*f.*, 148, 160-181, 191, 207, 213*f.*, 231, 240-247, 251-256, 340, 355*f.*, 359, 468.

1004. **IKRAMULLAH, Begum Sha'ista**, "IQBAL: HIS ART AND THOUGHT", *MORNING NEWS* (Karachi), 21 April 1960.
A review of the Oxford edition of S.A. Vahid's *IQBAL: HIS ART AND THOUGHT* (1959) - qv.

1005. **ILYAS AHMAD**, "ALLAMA IQBAL ON LIBERTY", *VOICE OF ISLAM*, March 1959-30 April 1959, pp. 258-61.

1006. **ILYAS MASOOD**, "(A) BOY'S IMPRESSIONS OF THE POET", *PAKISTAN TIMES*, 21 April 1961, p. 5.

1007. **IMTIAZ, Mohammad**, "IQBAL'S MURSHID RUMI", *PAKISTAN TIMES*, 21 April 1965, p. 7.

1008. **INAMUL HAQ**, "IQBAL AND ENGLISH POETS", *JOURNAL OF THE RESEARCH SOCIETY OF PAKISTAN* 21, no. 2: April (1984): pp. 1-30.

1009. ———, "WHITMAN, MAYAKOVSKY AND IQBAL", *IQBAL REVIEW* 33, no. 1: April (1992): pp. 123-37.
On Walt Whitman, Mayakovsky and Iqbal as three poets with a message.

1010. **INAYAT, Fauzia**, "TRIBUTES TO ALLAMA IQBAL: IQBAL, AN INSTITUTION",

THE MUSLIM (Islamabad), 20 April 1984.

1011. **INAYAT ULLAH**, "DR. HAMEEDULLAH, IQBAL AND IJTIHAD IN PAKISTAN", *THE NATION* (Lahore), 14 May 1992.

1012. **INAYATULLAH**, mon., *IQBAL'S RELEVANCE TODAY*, Lahore: Pakistan Academy for Administrative Training, n.d.

1013. **Indian Arts and Letters** (Editorial), "FIFTEENTH ANNIVERSARY OF THE POET OF IQBAL", *INDIAN ARTS AND LETTERS* 27, (1953): pp. 25-32.
Editorial note.

1014. **IONOVA, A.**, "MUHAMMAD IQBAL AND SOCIAL THOUGHT IN SOUTH-EAST ASIA", *THE WORK OF MUHAMMAD IQBAL: ARTICLES BY SOVIET SCHOLARS*, Abdur Rauf MALIK (ed.), Lahore: People's Publishing House, 1983, pp. 85-97.

IQBAL (ed.), see **editor** (no. 702).

1015. **IQBAL**, "ON THE BASIS OF NATIONALISM", *DAWN* (Karachi), 21 April 1952, p. 6.

1016. **IQBAL, A.**, "IQBAL AND WESTERN POETS", *ISLAMIC REVIEW AND ARAB AFFAIRS* 55, no. [?]: June (1967): pp. 12.

1017. ————, "IQBAL AS A POET", *ISLAMIC REVIEW AND ARAB AFFAIRS* 57, no. [?]: June (1969): pp. 17, 18.

1018. ————, "IQBAL AS POLITICIAN", *PAKISTAN TIMES*, 18 March 1967, pp. 6, 7.

1019. ————, "IQBAL'S ROLE IN PAKISTAN CRUSADE, FIRST VOICE RAISED FOR MUSLIM LEAGUE", *PAKISTAN TIMES*, 12 March 1967, p. 12.

1020. **Iqbal Academy**, "THE DECADE OF PROGRESS (1958-1968)", *IQBAL REVIEW* 9, no. 3: October (1969): pp. 1-46.
Contents: Introduction, Aims and Objects, Iqbal material, Iqbal Days, Library, Iqbal in East Pakistan, Translations of Iqbal's works, R.C.D. and Iqbal Academy, Publications, Foreign visits to the Academy, Grant-in-Aid and sale of books, and two Appendices, (1) list of publications, (2) new programme of work.

1021. ———, comp., *IQBAL DAY SPEECHES AND ARTICLES: IN MEMORIAM*, Vol. 2, Karachi: The Academy, 1968. 65 pp.

1022. **Iqbal Academy (Hyderabad)**, ed., *THREE ARTICLES OF IQBAL*, Muhammad IQBAL (mon.), Hyderabad: Iqbal Academy, n.d. 30 pp.
Reprint of three articles published by Iqbal in *INDIAN ANTIQUARY OF BOMBAY* (Sept. 1900) - and later in *THE ISLAMIC REVIEW* (May 1959, Woking, London)-, *ISLAMIC CULTURE* (April 1929, Hyderabad) and *ISLAMIC CULTURE* (October 1928, Hyderabad) respectively: (I) IQBAL ON THE DOCTRINE OF ABSOLUTE UNITY AS EXPOUNDED BY ABDUL KARIM AL-JILANI, (II) A PLEA FOR THE DEEPER STUDY OF THE MUSLIM SCIENTISTS, and (III) KHUSHHAL KHAN KHATTACK, THE AFGHAN WARRIOR-POET.

1023. **IQBAL, Aftab**, "ADDRESS, IQBAL DAY AT KARACHI", *IQBAL REVIEW* 10, no. 1: April (1969): pp. 1-9.

1024. ———, "AS HIS SON SEES HIM", *PAKISTAN TIMES*, 21 April 1969, pp. 1, 2.

1025. ———, "GREATNESS OF IQBAL", *MORNING NEWS*, 24 April 1966, p. 1.

1026. ———, "IQBAL'S MESSAGE TO MANKIND", *PAKISTAN TIMES*, 21 April 1968, p. 1.

1027. ———, "IQBAL'S MESSAGE TO MANKIND", *IQBAL: A CRITICAL STUDY*, Misbah-ul-Haq SIDDIQUI (ed.), Lahore: Farhan Publishers, 1977, pp. 26-27.
A short article celebrating the 30th anniversary of the death of Muhammad Iqbal, sub-titled 'A Son's Tribute to Father'. Published also in *THE PAKISTAN TIMES*, 21 April 1961, p. 4.

1028. ———, "IQBAL WAS BORN AHEAD OF HIS TIME", *IQBAL: A CRITICAL STUDY*, Misbah-ul-Haq SIDDIQUI (ed.), Lahore: Farhan Publishers, 1977, pp. 28-30. General hommage to Muhammad Iqbal. Obviously an obituary. Published also in *THE PAKISTAN TIMES*, 21 April 1966, pp. 1-2.

1029. **IQBAL, Afzal**, "IF IQBAL HAD BEEN HERE TODAY", *THE CIVIL AND MILITARY GAZETTE* (Lahore), 18 April 1948.

1030. ———, "IMPACT OF RUMI ON IQBAL", *THE MUSLIM* (Islamabad), 21 April 1980.

1031. ———, "IQBAL: THE GERMAN CONNECTION", *THE MUSLIM* (Islamabad), 21

April 1981.

1032. ———, "JALALUDDIN RUMI'S IMPACT ON IQBAL", *JOURNAL OF SOUTH ASIAN AND MIDDLE EASTERN STUDIES* 1, no. 2 (1977): pp. 33-40.

1033. ———, "JALALUDIN RUMI'S IMPACT OF IQBAL'S PHILOSOPHY", *THE PAKISTAN TIMES* (Rawalpindi / Lahore), 9 November 1978.

1034. ———, "RUMI AND IQBAL", *PAKISTAN STANDARD*, 21 April 1955.

1035. ———, "RUMI AND IQBAL", *PAKISTAN PHILOSOPHICAL JOURNAL* 1, no. 4: April (1958): pp. 63-72.

1036. **IQBAL, 'Allama Muhammad**, mon., *CALL FROM THE MINARET; A MUSLIM FAMILY IN BRITAIN*, Sevenoaks: Hodder and Stoughton, 1980.
On the social life of the Muslim diaspora - aimed at use in schools. Including a short biographical survey (pp. 50-52).

1037. ———, *THE DEVELOPMENT OF METAPHYSICS IN PERSIA: A CONTRIBUTION TO THE HISTORY OF MUSLIM PHILOSOPHY*, 3rd ed., Lahore: Bazm-i-Iqbal, 1964. xii+149+viii pp. or xiii+195 pp. [?].
Originally a Ph.D. Thesis, Munich (Cambridge 1908); first publication in 1908 (Cambridge UP / London: Luzacs).

1038. ———, *DIE ENTWICKLUNG DER METAPHYSIK IN PERSIEN*, 1982

1039. ———, "DIVINE RIGHT TO RULE", *THE LIGHT* (Lahore), 30 August 1928.

1040. ———, "DOCTRINE OF ABSOLUTE UNITY AS EXPLAINED BY 'ABDUL KARIM AL-JILANI", *INDIAN ANTIQUARY* (Bombay), 29 September 1900, pp. 237-46. Reprinted in *ISLAMIC REVIEW*, May 1959.

1041. ———, "FACSIMILE OF ALLAMA IQBAL'S LETTER ", *SADIQNAMA*, Nazeer Ali SHAH (ed.), Lahore: Maktab-i-Jadeed, 1959, pp. 47.

1042. ———, "FOREWORD", *SELECTED MASTER-PAINTINGS OF M.A. RAHMAN CHUGHTAY*, Muraqqa-yi CHUGHTAY (mon.), Lahore, 1928.

1043. ———, "FOREWORD", *A HISTORY OF PERSIAN NAVIGATION*, Hadi HASAN (mon.), London: Metheun, 1928.

1044. ———, "FOREWORD", *AFGHANISTAN - A BRIEF SURVEY*, Jamal-ud-din & AZIZ Muhammad Abdul AHMAD (mon.), London: Longmans Green, 1936, pp. v-x [sic].

1045. ———, "IN DEFENSE OF 'ASRAR-I-KHUDI' (IQBAL'S LETTER TO DR. NICHOLSON)", *DAWN* (Karachi), 21 April 1949, p. 4.

1046. ———, "INNER SYNTHESIS OF LIFE", *INDIAN REVIEW* (Madras) 27, (1926): pp. 2.

1047. ———, "INVOCATION (TRANSLATION OF FIRST 25 PAGES OF 'JAVED NAMAH'), TRANSLATED BY PROF. MAHMUD AHMAD", *ISLAMIC CULTURE* 22, no. 4 (1948): pp. 343-54.

1048. ———, "IQBAL ON THE BASIS OF NATIONALISM", *DAWN*, 21 April 1952, p. 6.
Condensed from the presidential address delivered at the annual session of All India Muslim League at Allahabad, 29 December 1930.

1049. ———, "IQBAL ON THE DOCTRINE OF ABSOLUTE UNITY AS EXPOUNDED BY ABDUL KARIM AL-JILANI, A PLEA FOR DEEPER STUDY OF THE MUSLIM SCIENTISTS, and KHUSHHAL KHAN KHATTACK, THE AFGHAN WARRIOR-POET", *IQBAL REVIEW* (Hyderabad) 1, no. [?]: July-October (1978): pp. 1-30.
Reprint of three articles by Iqbal, which were first published in (1) *INDIAN ANTIQUARY OF BOMBAY*, September 1900; and *THE ISLAMIC REVIEW* (Woking / London), May 1959; (2) *ISLAMIC CULTURE* (Hyderabad), April 1929; (3) *ISLAMIC CULTURE* (Hyderabad), October 1928, respectively.

1050. ———, "IQBAL'S LETTER TO THE QUAID", *PAKISTAN TIMES*, 23 March 1977, p. 3.

1051. ———, "IQBAL TO NEHRU", *IQBAL* 16, no. 3: January (1968): pp. 68.
Statement on the political future of India, issued on 6 December 1933.

1052. ———, "IS RELIGION POSSIBLE?", *PROCEEDINGS OF THE ARISTOTELIAN SOCIETY*, London, 1932-1933.
Included as the last chapter, lecture VII (pp. 171-188), of the Oxford UP edition of Iqbal's lectures on "The Reconstruction of Religious Thought in Islam", London, 1934.

1053. ———, "ISLAM AND AHMADISM", *ISLAM* 1, no. 16: 22 January (1936): pp. 1-47.

1054. ———, *ISLAM AND AHMADISM*, Javid IQBAL (ed.), Lucknow: Academy of Islamic Research and Publications, 1974. 31 or 47 pp.
This essay was originally published in *THE STATESMAN*, 1935, and appeared also in *ISLAM*, 22 January 1936. Published as a monograph firstly in Lahore: Iqbal Academy, 1945; thereafter re-issued by Shaikh Muhammad Ashraf (Lahore 1976).

1055. ———, mon., *ISLAM AND AHMADISM, WITH REPLY TO THE QUESTIONS RAISED BY PANDAT JAWAHAR LAL NEHRU*, Lahore: Anjuman-i-Khuddam-ud-Din, 1936. 97 pp.
Cf, pp. 1-47 on Iqbal and Qadianism.

1056. ———, "ISLAM AND KHILAFAT", *SOCIOLOGICAL REVIEW* (London) [vol. ?], (1908).
An Urdu translation of this article appeared in Lahore (1923), by Ch. Muhammad Husain, and was reprinted in *IQBAL* (Lahore) 4, no. 2 (1956).

1057. ———, "ISLAM AND KHILAFAT", *SOCIOLOGICAL REVIEW* [vol. ?], (1908).

1058. ———, "ISLAM AS A MORAL AND POLITICAL IDEAL", *THE OBSERVER* (Lahore), 14 April 1909.
This essay was reprinted in the *HINUSTAN REVIEW* 20 (1909), and re-issued as a pamphlet with critical remarks by Hafiz Ghulam Sarwar (Lahore, 1910) - qv. Also published as *ISLAM AS AN ETHICAL AND POLITICAL IDEAL*, Lahore: Islamic Book Service,1977.

1059. ———, "ISLAM AS A MORAL AND POLITICAL IDEAL", *HINDUSTAN REVIEW* 35, no. 3 (1936): pp. 81-120.
Extracts quoted from this article by Pandit Hari Kishan Kaul in the *CENSUS OF INDIA, 1911*, vol. 14, Punjab, pp. 164 *f.*

1060. ———, "ISLAM AS A POLITICAL IDEAL", *IQBAL* 16, no. 3: January (1968): pp. 80.
Re-issue of an extract from the *HINDUSTAN REVIEW*, December 1909.

1061. ———, "KHUSHHAL KHAN KHATAK: THE AFGHAN WARRIOR POET", *ISLAMIC CULTURE* (Hyderabad) 2, no. 4 (1928): pp. 485-94.

1062. ———, "KHUSHHAL KHAN KHATTAK", *ISLAMIC CULTURE* 2, no. 4 (1928): pp.

485-94.

1063. ———, "LETTER TO DR. NICHOLSON, 24th January 1927", *DAWN* (Karachi), 21 April 1949.
A letter to Dr. Nicholson dd. 24 January 1927.

1064. ———, mon., *LETTER TO PANDIT JAWAHAR LALL NEHRU*, Bombay: Asia Publishing House, 1960.
In bunch of letters, pp. 187-188.

1065. ———, "LETTER WRITTEN BY DR. SIR MUHAMMAD IQBAL TO THE AUTHOR", *OASIS* (Bahawalpur) 3, no. [?]: April (1941).

1066. ———, *LETTERS OF IQBAL TO JINNAH*, M. A. JINNAH (ed.), Lahore: Shaikh Muhammad Ashraf, 1963. 32 pp.
Allama Iqbal's views on the political future of Muslim India.

1067. ———, "McTAGGART'S PHILOSOPHY", *INDIAN ARTS AND LETTERS* 6, no. 1 or 11 (1932): pp. 25-31.
Published simultaneously in *MUSLIM REVIVAL* 1, no. 3: September (1932), pp. 226-234; and reproduced in *TRUTH* (Lahore), July 1937; as well as in Shamloo's *SPEECHES AND STATEMENTS OF IQBAL*, Lahore, 1945 - qv.

1068. ———, "McTAGGART'S PHILOSOPHY", *MUSLIM REVIVAL* 1, no. 3: September (1932): pp. 226-34.

1069. ———, *THE MUSLIM COMMUNITY - A SOCIOLOGICAL STUDY*, Lahore: Bazm-e-Iqbal, 1994. 33 pp.
English text with Urdu translation.

1070. ———, "THE MUSLIM COMMUNITY, A SOCIOLOGICAL STUDY", *IQBAL* 42, no. 1 (1995): pp. 33-76-34.
Introduction, pp. 35-42; Urdu text, pp. 43-62; English text, pp. 76-63.

1071. ———, "MUSLIM DEMOCRACY", *The New Era* (Allahabad) [vol. ?], (1916).

1072. ———, "MUSLIMS DEMAND", *MANCHESTER GUARDIAN*, 30 December [n.d. ?].

A summary of Iqbal's address to the Muslim League Session at Allahabad.

1073. ———, "(THE) NEW MOON (A POEM BY IQBAL)", *LIVING AGE* (Boston) [vol. ?], no. [?]: February (1922): pp. 306.

1074. ———, "NEW YEARS MESSAGE (1938)", *TRUTH* (Lahore), 11 January 1938. Originally in Urdu.

1075. ———, "NOTES ON MUSLIM DEMOCRACY", *THE NEW ERA* (Allahabad) [vol. ?], (1916).

1076. ———, "NOTES ON MUSLIM DEMOCRACY", *NEW ERA* [vol. ?], (1916).

1077. ———, "ON CORPOREAL RESURRECTION AFTER DEATH", *MUSLIM REVIVAL* (Lahore) [vol. ?], no. [?]: September (1932).
Reprinted in *THE CIVIL AND MILITARY GAZETTE*, 20 April 1952 or 1962 [?], p. 3. Iqbal Day Supplement.

1078. ———, "OUR PROPHET'S CRITICISM OF CONTEMPORARY ARABIC POETRY", *THE NEW ERA* (Allahabad), 28 July 1915/1917 [?].

1079. ———, "A PASSAGE FROM IQBAL // IQBAL SPEAKS: // WORDS FROM IQBAL", *IQBAL* 16, no. 3: January (1968): pp. 26, 48, 58.
New Year Message (1 January 1938) on the tyranny of imperialism behind the progress in knowledge and scientific developments of the modern age.

1080. ———, "THE PERSIAN MOVEMENT IN GERMAN LITERATURE", *PAKISTAN QUARTERLY* 6, no. 4 (1956): pp. 35-36.

1081. ———, "PLAN FOR DEEPER STUDY OF THE MUSLIM SCIENTISTS", *ISLAMIC CULTURE* [vol. ?], no. [?]: April (1929): pp. 201-9.

1082. ———, "A PLEA FOR DEEPER STUDY OF THE MUSLIM SCIENTISTS", *ISLAMIC CULTURE* (Hyderabad) 3, no. 2 (1929): pp. 201-9.

1083. ———, "POLITICAL THOUGHT IN ISLAM", *HINDUSTAN REVIEW* 22-23, no. [?]: December and January (1910/1911): pp. 527-33 and 22-26 resp.
Variant date: December 1960/1961.   Presidential

address to the All India Muslim League, Allahabad Session, December 1930; published seperately by Bazm-i-Iqbal, Lahore 1989. Also published in *SOCIOLOGICAL REVIEW* (UK) 1, 1908, pp. 249 *ff.*

1084. ———, "PRESIDENTIAL ADDRESS, ALL INDIA MUSLIM CONFERENCE", *MUSLIM REVIVAL* [vol. ?], no. [?]: March (n.d. [?]): pp. 58-59.

1085. ———, "PROLOGUE TO IQBAL'S 'ASRAR-I-KHUDI', TRANSLATED BY HADI HUSAIN", *IQBAL REVIEW* 14, no. 3: October (1973): pp. 1-8.

1086. ———, mon., *RECONSTRUCTION DEL PENSIAMENTE RELIGIOSO EN EL ISLAM*, Lahore: Iqbal Academy, 1989.
Italian translation of (I) THE RECONSTRUCTION OF RELIGIOUS THOUGHT IN ISLAM.
I.

1087. ———, mon., *THE RECONSTRUCTION OF RELIGIOUS THOUGHT IN ISLAM*, London: Oxford UP, 1934. 192 pp.
Lahore [Muhammad Ashraf] 1930, 1934, 1960, 1962.
Re-issue of the (I) SIX LECTURES etc, with an added 7th chapter ("IS RELIGION POSSIBLE?"), originally published by Proc. of the Aristotelian Society, London 1932-33 - qv.).
This book was re-issued by Shaikh Muhammad Ashraf (Lahore, 1975, 1980 and 1982), and once more by the same publisher under the editorship of M. Saeed Sheikh (Lahore, 1986 and 1989. viii+206 pp.), with annotations by the latter. The 1960 issue contains vi+205 pp.

1088. ———, mon., *RELIGION AND AHMADISM*, Lahore: Shaikh Muhammad Ashraf, 1980

1089. ———, "SELECTIONS FROM IQBAL'S POEMS", *ISLAMIC REVIEW* [vol. ?], no. [?]: September (1957): pp. 27.

1090. ———, "SELF IN THE LIGHT OF RELATIVITY", *THE CRESCENT* (Lahore) [vol. ?], (1925).
This article was reprinted in B.A. Dar's *A STUDY IN IQBAL'S PHILOSOPHY*, Lahore, 1944 - qv.

1091. ———, mon., *SIX LECTURES ON THE RECONSTRUCTION OF RELIGIOUS THOUGHT IN ISLAM*, Lahore: Kapur Art Printing Press, 1930. 249 pp.

2nd edition with additional last chapter issued as *RECONSTRUCTION OF RELIGIOUS THOUGHT IN ISLAM*, London: Oxford UP, 1934.

1092. ———, "SOME STUDY NOTES", *MUSLIM REVIVAL* 1, no. 3: September (1932): pp. 217-20.
Urdu translation by Sadiq Hasan in the monthly *HUMAYUN*, April 1950, pp. 264-266.

1093. ———, "SOME THOUGHTS ON ISLAMIC STUDIES", *IQBAL REVIEW* 3, no. 3: October (1962): pp. 1-5.
Iqbal's letter dd. 4 June 1925, addressed to Sahibzada Aftab Ahmed Khan, copied from the records of the Muslim University Aligarh and published through the courtesy of Dr. S.M. Yousuf, Head of the Department of Arabic, University of Karachi. An Urdu translation of this letter was already published in *IQBAL NAMAH*.

1094. ———, mon., *URDU COURSE*, Hakim Muhammad SHUJA (mon.), Lahore, 1924

1095. ———, mon., *WAY OF THE MUSLIM*, Chester Springs, U.S.A.: Dufour Editions Inc., 1983

1096. **IQBAL, Javed**, "THE INDIVIDUAL AND THE COMMUNITY", *THE PAKISTAN TIMES* (Rawalpindi), 21 April 1983.

1097. **IQBAL, Javid**, "DEVELOPMENT OF MUSLIM POLITICAL PHILOSOPHY IN THE INDO-PAKISTAN SUB-CONTINENT", Cambridge University, 1960. Ph.D. dissertation.

1098. ———, "HE WAS MY FATHER", *DAWN* (Karachi), 21 April 1949, p. 3.
Also published in the *ILLUSTRATED WEEKLY OF PAKISTAN*, 16 April 1950 or 1960 [?], p. 23.

1099. ———, mon., *IDEOLOGY OF PAKISTAN*, Karachi: Ferozsons, 1971. 178 pp. Cf. esp. pp. 12-156.

1100. ———, "THE IMAGE OF TURKEY AND TURKISH DEMOCRACY IN IQBAL'S THOUGHT AND HIS CONCEPT OF A MODERN ISLAMIC STATE", *IQBAL REVIEW* 28, no. 3: October-December (1987): pp. 25-39.

1101. ———, "INFLUENCE OF THE MATHNAVI ON MUSLIM THOUGHT IN SOUTH ASIA", *IQBAL REVIEW* 31, no. 3: October (1990): pp. 1*ff.*

Address at the Second International Mevlana Rumi Congress Held at Seljuk University Konya. The central idea of this address is exemplified in extracts of Iqbal's poem "Sage Rumi and Indian Disciple".

1102. ———, "INTRODUCTION TO THE STUDY OF IQBAL", *IQBAL, THE POET OF TOMORROW*, Khawaja Abdur RAHIM (ed.), Lahore: Abdul Hameed Khan at Ferozsons Ltd., n.d., pp. 1-20.
This paper (in fact only pp. 5-20) was, as indicated in the footnote on p. 5, meant for a foreign audience and was read in October 1966.

1103. ———, "IQBAL AND NIETZSCHE", *MUHAMMAD IQBAL*, Various authors (mon.), Karachi: German-Pakistan Forum, 1960.

1104. ———, "IQBAL AS A FATHER", *PAKISTAN QUARTERLY* [vol. ?], no. [?] Supplement (1960).

1105. ———, "IQBAL: MY FATHER", *IQBAL: POET-PHILOSOPHER OF PAKISTAN*, Hafeez MALIK (ed.), New York: Columbia UP, 1971, pp. 56-65.

1106. ———, "IQBAL'S CONCEPT OF IJTIHAD", *THE CIVIL AND MILITARY GAZETTE* (Lahore), 21 April 1948, p. 4.

1107. ———, "IQBAL'S CONTRIBUTION TO LIBERALISM IN MODERN ISLAM", *IQBAL REVIEW* 1, no. 3: October (1960): pp. 17-20.
Short note, in which Iqbal is presented as *the last of the great 'liberal' reformers*, having created a 'liberalism', blended with the *conservatism* of Sayyid Ahmad Khan, the *radicalism* of Muhammad Shibli, and the *Pan-Islamism* of Jamal-al-Din Afghani. Published also (without reference to the Iqbal Review-issue) in Khawaja Abdur RAHIM (ed.), *IQBAL, THE POET OF TOMORROW*, Lahore: Abdul Hameed Khan at Ferozsons Ltd., n.d., pp. 213[215]-219, where, in the footnote on p. 215, this paper is identified as having been read as an address on 21 April 1957.   Re-issued   in   [Various authors], *SELECTIONS FROM THE IQBAL REVIEW*, ed. Waheed Qureshi, Lahore, 1983, pp. 119-122.

1108. ———, "IQBAL'S VIEWS ON THE MATERIAL AND SPIRITUAL FUTURE OF HUMANITY", *IQBAL REVIEW* 32, no. 3: October (1991): pp. 1-17.
The survival of humanity depends, so the author concludes (p. 17), on man's respect for his fellow-men and for religions other than his own.

1109. ———, "PLACE OF MORALITY IN IQBAL'S METAPHYSICS", *PAKISTAN TIMES* (Lahore), 21 April 1949, pp. 6, 7.

1110. ———, ed., *STRAY REFLECTIONS: A NOTEBOOK OF ALLAMA IQBAL*, Muhammad IQBAL (mon.), Lahore: Shaikh Ghulam Ali and Sons, 1961. xxxi+161 pp.
A collection of notes and quotations, written down by Muhammad Iqbal in a notebook from 27 April 1910, and containing 'odd jottings based on his impressions of the books he was reading at that time, his thoughts and feelings about the environment in which he lived, and reminiscences of his student days'. From Iqbal's titlepage, it appears that the original title was to be 'Stray Thoughts' - the word is barred and substitued by 'Reflections'. The book contains the germs of many of the major ideas which were developed and elaborated later in both Iqbal's poetical and his philosophical works. The collection contains an elaborate introduction by Javid Iqbal, 13 reproductions of pages from the original (I) notebook in Iqbal's handwriting (in English), and an index.
A revised edition, including facsimiles, was published in Lahore: Iqbal Academy Pakistan, 1992, 252 pp.

1111. **IQBAL, Mahmood**, "THE CRITERIA OF PROGRESS", *IQBAL* 20, no. 1: July-October (1972): pp. 41-48.

1112. **IQBAL, Muhammad**, "ELEGIAC NOTE IN IQBAL'S POETRY", *IQBAL REVIEW* 19, no. 3: October (1978): pp. 11-33.

1113. ———, *IQBAL 'IN QUOTES'*, Sharif BAQA (ed.), London: Race Relations Unit / Walthamstow Town Hall, 1993. 84 pp.

1114. ———, "IQBAL'S IDEA OF PAKISTAN", *MORNING NEWS* (Karachi), 23 March 1957, p. 10.

1115. ———, "IQBAL'S WARNING AGAINST ATHEISTIC MATERIALISM", *THE CIVIL AND MILITARY GAZETTE* (Lahore), 21 April 1956, p. 3.
Extracts from Iqbal's presidential address at the session of the All India Muslim Conference held at Lahore, 21-22 March 1932.

1116. ———, "IQBAL, THE POET OF NATURE", *IQBAL REVIEW* 18, no. 4: January (1978): pp. 195-214.

1117. **IQBAL, N.**, "IQBAL AND THE WEST", *PERSPECTIVE* 3, no. [?]: April (1970): pp.

21-24.

IQBAL REVIEW (red.), see **redaction** (nos. 1893-1896).

1118. **IQBAL, S. M.**, "IQBAL ON THE DOCTRINE OF ABSOLUTE UNITY", *ISLAMIC REVIEW AND ARAB AFFAIRS* 47, no. [?]: May (1959): pp. 7-12.

1119. **IRFANI, Suroosh**, "AN EXAMPLE OF THE PROPHET'S "PBUH" METHODOLOGY FOR SOCIAL CHANGE IN THE WORKS OF IQBAL", *THE MUSLIM* (Islamabad), 21 April 1983.

1120. ———, "IQBAL AND DYNAMISM OF QURAN", *THE MUSLIM* (Islamabad), 9 November 1983.

1121. ———, "IQBAL AND TRANSPERSONAL PSYCHOLOGY", *THE MUSLIM* (Islamabad), 21 April 1982.

1122. ———, "THE REDISCOVERY OF IQBAL", *THE MUSLIM* (Islamabad), 21 April 1981.

1123. **IRSHAD, Nasreen**, "MESSAGE AND CALIBRE OF HAFIZ AND IQBAL", *IQBAL* 40, no. 3 (1993): pp. 19-30.

1124. **ISHAQ, Khalid**, "THREE GREAT THINKERS (GHAZALI, WILLIAM JAMES, AND IQBAL)", *PAKISTAN QUARTERLY* 3, no. 1 (1953): pp. 24-28.

1125. **ISHAQUE, Khalid**, "IQBAL AND THE MODERN MAN", *IQBAL REVIEW* 15, no. 3: October (1974): pp. 12-21.
On the sick state of modern society, and the remedy Iqbal sought in Islam.

1126. **ISHAQUE, Khalid M.**, "IQBAL AND THE PRINCIPLES OF IJTIHAD", *THE FRONTIER POST* (Peshawar), 9 November 1986.

1127. **ISHRAT, Waheed**, "IQBAL AND COMMUNISM", *IQBAL REVIEW* 32, no. 3: October (1991): pp. 105-22.
Translated into English by M.A.K. Khalil.
Iqbal pointed out that both capitalism and communism are harmful, and that Islam only is the correct system.

1128. ———, "IQBAL AND DEMOCRACY", *IQBAL REVIEW* 34 and 35, no. 3: October and 1: April (1993-1994): pp. 69-104 and 19-60 resp.
On Iqbal's criticism of democracy (that it needs the creation of special circumstances, and that it reveals some basic defects), which, if corrective measures for its defects were adopted, became even acceptible to him. In conclusion suggestions with reference to Pakistan's special conditions and problems are made how Iqbal's "spiritual democracy" may find roots in the country (Part II, pp. 45-48).

1129. ———, "IQBAL'S PHILOSOPHY OF REVOLUTION", *IQBAL REVIEW* 36, no. 3: October (1995): pp. 25-48.
English translation by M.A.K. KHALIL.
A condensed version of this paper was published in the Iqbal Number of the monthly *SHA'ER* (Bombay), 1989; and in the monthly *THE CRESCENT*, as well as in the Persian *IQBALIAT* 5 (1990) and the daily *MASHRIQ*, 9 November 1990. This paper was also read in the "Iqbal Forum International", "Halqah-i-Iqbal", "Islamic Philosophical Association", and "Wasa Staff Training Institute", Samanabad, Lahore, on 5 September 1990, 24 October 1990, 14 November 1990, and 1 November 1990, respectively.

1130. ———, "THE ORIGINS AND SOURCES OF IQBAL'S PHILOSOPHY", *IQBAL REVIEW* 31, no. 3: October (1990): pp. 25-72.
This paper was first presented on 1 November 1987, during the Iqbal week celebrations at the Govt. Foreman Christian College, Lahore. It was published in *IQBALIAT* 28, no. 4: January-March (1988), pp. 393-424. The present translation into English is provided by M.A.K. Khalil.

1131. ———, "RECONSTRUCTION OF ISLAMIC THOUGHT, REVIEW ARTICLE", *IQBAL REVIEW* 37, no. 3: October (1996): pp. 111-21.
Translated by M.A.K. KHALIL.
Special issue on the Reconstruction of Religious Thought in Islam.

1132. **ISLAM, Amin-ul**, "IQBAL'S PHILOSOPHY, A MESSAGE OF LIBERTY", *PAKISTAN OBSERVER*, 14 August 1966, p. 9.

1133. **ISLAM AYAN, Syed Zia-ul**, "IQBAL'S CONCEPT OF ISHQ", *IQBAL: A CRITICAL STUDY*, Misbah-ul-Haq SIDDIQUI (ed.), Lahore: Farhan Publishers, 1977, pp. 37-46.
On '*Ishq* (love), with quotations from Iqbal's works, both in the original and in English translation.

1134. **ISLAM AYAN, Syed Ziaul**, "IQBAL'S CONCEPT OF ISHQ", *PAKISTAN TIMES*, 21

April 1967, pp. 1-4.

1135. **ISLAM, Jinnah-ul**, "IQBAL, IRAN AND REVOLUTION", *THE MUSLIM* (Islamabad), 21 April 1983.

1136. **ISLAM, Muhammad Ziaul**, "IQBAL INTERNATIONALISM AND HUMANISM", *PAKISTAN TIMES*, 21 April 1969, p. 3.

1137. ————, ed., *IQBAL STUDIES*, Karachi: Bazm-i-Iqbal, 1950/1951/1959. 34/91 pp. A collection of three essays under the editorship of Muhammad Ziaul Islam: (1) S.A. Vahid, IQBAL AS A LYRICAL POET; (2) Raziuddin Siddiqi, IQBAL AND THE PROBLEM OF FREE WILL; and (3) Mumtaz Hasan, IQBAL, A RECOLLECTION. *Description under the respective authors.*

1138. **Islam** (red.), "SIR MUHAMMAD IQBAL'S STATEMENT", *ISLAM* 1, no. 17: 7 February (1936): pp. 1-12. Comments on Iqbal's statement on Islam and Ahmadism published in *ISLAM*.

1139. **ISLAM, Zia-ul**, *GLIMPSES OF MODERN URDU LITERATURE*, Allahabad: Kitabistan, 1945. Cf. esp. pp. 23-25, 127-128.

1140. **ISLAM, Ziaul**, "GROWTH OF MUSLIM POLITICS IN INDIA: INFLUENCE OF IQBAL AND JINNAH", *THE CIVIL AND MILITARY GAZETTE* (Lahore), 13 September 1953, pp. 2, 4.

1141. ————, "IQBAL'S TOUR OF THE MUSLIM WORLD", *PAKISTAN CALLING* 6, no. 8 (1952): pp. 10-11.

1142. **IZHARUL HAQ, S. M.**, "IQBAL'S ROLE IN REAWAKENING THE MUSLIMS", *THE PAKISTAN TIMES* (Lahore), 9 November 1992.

1143. **IZHARUL, S. M.**, "ALLAMA IQBAL AS A POLITICAL THINKER", *THE PAKISTAN TIMES* (Rawalpindi), 21 April 1984.

1144. **JAFFERY, Abbas Ali**, "IQBAL'S CONCEPT OF THE 'PERFECT MAN'", *THE MUSLIM* (Islamabad), 9 November 1979.

1145. **JAFRI, Ali Sardar**, "IQBAL: POET OF THE EAST", *ILLUSTRATED WEEKLY OF INDIA* 90, no. 17: 27 April (1969): pp. 30-33.

1146. **JAFRI, Ali Sardar & K. S. DUGGAL**, eds., *IQBAL COMMEMORATIVE VOLUME*, New Delhi: All India Iqbal Centenary Celebrations Committee, 1977. 318 pp.
Contents:
I: Introduction (K.S. Duggal), Opening Speech (Ali Sardar JAFRI), Inaugural Address (Umashankar Joshi), and Iqbal, a Tribute (Fida Husain);
II: Iqbal's Relevance to the Present-Day World: Persian Writings of Iqbal (G.R. SABRI TABRIZI), Iqbal as Prophet of Change: the Message of the East (V.G. KIERNAN), Iqbal: a Universal Poet (Mulk Raj ANAND), Iqbal and Germany, Germany and Iqbal (Annemarie SCHIMMEL), Iqbal, Islam and the Modern Age (Jagan Nath AZAD), A Study of the Concepts of Transformation, Leadership and Freedom in the Political Philosophy of Iqbal (S. Alam KHUNDMIRI), Existentialist Elements in Iqbal's Thought (Waheed AKHTAR), A Critical Appraisal of Iqbal's "Reconstruction of Religious Thought in Islam" (Asghar Ali ENGINEER), Iqbal and the Price of Philosopher's Stone (Waris ALAVI), Iqbal and Social Justice (L.R. GORDON-POLONSKAYA), Nature in Iqbal's Poetry (Zahida ZAIDI), Research into Iqbal's Life and Works in the Soviet Union (A.S. SUKHOCHEV), Iqbal: "Sirrul-Firaq" (Zoe ANSARI), The Concept of Love in Iqbal's Poetry (Prabhakar MACHWE), The Ideal Man of the Orient in Iqbal's Poetry (M.A. Eslami NADUSHAN), Kashmir and Kashmiris in Iqbal's Verse (P.N. PUSHP), The Sound Structure of Iqbal's Urdu Poetry (Gopi Chand NARANG), Chughtai and Iqbal (Arif Rahman CHUGHTAI);
III: Amir Khusrau and Iqbal (Syed Sabahuddin Abdur RAHMAN), Iqbal and Milton (V.G. KIERNAN), Iqbal and Goethe (Annemarie SCHIMMEL), Iqbal and Wordsworth (V.G. KIERNAN), Mohammad Iqbal - Classic of World Literature (Y. CHELYSHEV), Browning and Iqbal (Ish KUMAR), Iqbal and Tagore (Tara Charan RASTOGI), Mohammad Iqbal and Pablo Neruda (Jan MAREK), Iqbal, Nirala and Dinkar (Prabhakar MACHWE).
Includes 4 leaves of plates, and bibliographical references.

1147. **JAFRI, Fareed S.**, mon., *THE LIBERATION OF ISLAM*, Karachi: Civil and Military Gazette Press, 1952. 61 pp.
Cf. esp. pp. 2-4, 39-48.

1148. ———, *SPIRIT OF PAKISTAN*, Karachi: Ansari Publications / Ansari Publishing House, 1951. 151 pp.
See esp. pp. 13, 17, 27-43, 103-120; including his paper: IQBAL AND THE CONCEPTION OF PAKISTAN, pp. 13, 16.

1149. **JAFRI, Farid S.**, "HAD IQBAL LIVED TODAY WHAT MESSAGE WOULD HE

HAD GIVEN TO HIS NATION", *ILLUSTRATED WEEKLY OF PAKISTAN* 9, no. 39 (1950): pp. 18-19.

1150. ———, "INSPIRATION FROM IQBAL", *MORNING NEWS*, 23 April 1967, p. 17.

1151. ———, "IQBAL'S ISLAMIC STATE", *ILLUSTRATED WEEKLY OF PAKISTAN* 3, no. 3: 22 April (1951): pp. 9-10.

1152. ———, "IQBAL'S REVOLUTION OF ISLAMIC POLICY", *TIMES OF KARACHI*, 21 April 1954.
Special Suppl.

1153. ———, "THE MAN WHO CONCEIVED PAKISTAN: MUHAMMAD IQBAL", *THE CIVIL AND MILITARY GAZETTE* (Lahore), 21 April 1951, pp. 2, 3.

1154. ———, "MUHAMMAD IQBAL (1873-1938): THE MAN WHO CONCEIVED PAKISTAN", *ISLAMIC REVIEW* 37, no. 4 (1949): pp. 8-13.

1155. **JAFRI, Hasan Abid**, "SOME ASPECTS OF IQBAL", *ILLUSTRATED WEEKLY OF PAKISTAN*, 16 April 1950, p. 30.
Iqbal Number.

1156. **JAFRI, S. Hadi Husain**, "IQBAL AND THE WEST", *MORNING NEWS*, 14 August 1957.

1157. **JAFRI, Syed Rais Ahmad**, comp., *RARE DOCUMENTS*, Lahore: Muhammad Ali Academy, 1967. 313 pp.
Includes a.o. Iqbal-Presidential addresses (pp. 5-42).

1158. **JALALI, Sayyid Hamid**, *'ALLAMA IQBAL KI IZDIVAJI ZINDAGI*, Dihli: Ejukeshnal Pablishing Haus, 1990. 175 pp.
Urdu, with some passages in English. On the family life of Iqbal.

1159. **JAMAL-UD-DIN, Master**, "IQBAL ON ISLAMIC JURISPRUDENCE", *PAKISTAN TIMES*, 21 April 1966, p. 3.

1160. **JAMALI, Tufail A.**, "POETIC GENIUS OF ALLAMA IQBAL", *TIMES OF KARACHI*,

21 April 1954.

1161. **JAMES, B. Prior**, "IQBAL'S VIEW OF 'ISLAMIC NATIONALISM' IN *JAVED NAMAH*", *IQBAL* 19, no. 1: July (1971): pp. 20-40.

1162. **JAMI, Majeed**, "A COMPARATIVE STUDY OF IQBAL AND SHAWQI", *IQBAL REVIEW* 30-31, no. 3: October and 1: April (1989-1990): pp. 151-57.

1163. ———, "IQBAL AND 'ARSHI", *IQBAL REVIEW* 37, no. 1: April (1996): pp. 61-69. On the friendship between the like-minded contemporary poets and writers, Iqbal and Arshi.

1164. **JAMIL, K. M.**, "DR. IQBAL ON EDUCATION", *PAKISTAN OBSERVER*, 2 May 1959.

1165. **JAVID, Khadim Ali**, "IQBALIAT, INDEX 1992", *IQBAL REVIEW* 35, no. 1: October (1994): pp. 79-83.

1166. ———, "SOME REFLECTIONS ON THE CLASSIFICATION SYSTEM FOR IQBAL'S STUDIES", *IQBAL REVIEW* 30-31, no. 3: October and 1: April (1989-1990): pp. 229-35.

1167. **JEFFERY, Arthur**, "IL MODERNISMO MUSULMANO DELL INDIANO 'SIR' MOHAMMAD IQBAL", *ORIENTE MODERNO* (Roma) 14, (1934): pp. 505-13. Review of Iqbal's THE RECONSTRUCTION OF RELIGIOUS THOUGHT IN ISLAM. I.

1168. **JHA, A.**, mon., *IQBAL'S LIGHT VERSE*, Allahabad, n.d.

1169. **JILANI, Asghar Ghulam**, "IQBAL ON THE DECLINE OF THE WEST", *THE PAKISTAN TIMES* (Rawalpindi), 8 November 1985.

1170. **JILANI, Ghulam**, "IQBAL AS A REFORMER", *IQBAL REVIEW* 1, no. 3: October (1960): pp. 5-16.

1171. ———, mon., *SOME THOUGHTS ON IQBAL*, Karachi: Iqbal Academy, 1960

1172. ———, "SOME THOUGHTS ON IQBAL (TEXT OF A PAPER READ ON THE OCCASION OF IQBAL DAY CELEBRATIONS ORGANIZED BY THE IQBAL

ACADEMY, KARACHI, APRIL 21ST 1960)", *VOICE OF ISLAM* (Karachi) 7, no. 9: June and 10: July (1960): pp. 378-83 and 419-424 resp.

1173. **JINNAH, M. A.**, ed./intr., *LETTERS OF IQBAL TO JINNAH: A COLLECTION CONVEYING HIS VIEWS ON THE POLITICAL FUTURE OF MUSLIM INDIA*, Lahore: Sheikh Muhammad Ashraf, 1965. 32 pp.

1174. ———, "MESSAGE", *OASIS* (Bahawalpur), April 1941, p. 88.
Iqbal Day message.

1175. ———, "MESSAGE ON THE OCCASION OF CELEBRATION OF IQBAL DAY AT LAHORE, 9th December, 1944", *SOME RECENT SPEECHES AND WRITINGS OF MR. JINNAH*, J. D. AHMAD (ed.), Lahore: Muhammad Ashraf, 1947, Vol. 2, pp. 231-32.

1176. **JINNAH, Muhammad Ali**, mon., *QUAID-E-AZAM JINNAH'S CORRESPONDENCE*, Syed Sharifuddin PIRZADA (ed.), 3rd rev. enl. ed., Karachi: East and West Publishing, 1977. xxiv+424 pp.
Cf. esp. pp. 35, 138-142, 386.

1177. **JINNAH, Muhammad Ali QUAID-I-AZAM**, "IQBAL'S VISION AND QUAID'S ACHIEVEMENT. PAKISTAN MIGHT GIVE A LEAD FOR A HUMANISTIC INTERNATIONAL SOCIETY", *PAKISTAN TIMES*, 20 March 1977, p. 1.
Iqbal Day speech of Quaid-i-Azam M.A. Jinnah (25 March 1940).

1178. **JONES, H.**, "M. IQBAL. MESSAGE DE L'ORIENT (Book Review)", *REVUE D'ESTHÉTIQUE* 10, (1957): pp. 466.

1179. **JORDAN, W. M.**, "IQBAL'S MYSTIC INSIGHT", *PAKISTAN REVIEW* 9, no. [?]: August (1961): pp. 37-39.
Variant: August 1960, pp. 7, 8.

1180. **JORDAN, William**, "POETRY OF IQBAL", *PANORAMA* [vol. ?], no. [?]: June (1962): pp. 16, 17.

1181. **JUDD, Walter H.**, "SPEECH, IQBAL DAY IN WASHINGTON", *IQBAL REVIEW* 8, no. 1: April (1967): pp. 60-64.

1182. **JULLNDHRI, Rashid A.**, "DR. SIR MUHAMMAD IQBAL, QUAID-E-AZAM

MUHAMMAD ALI JINNAH AND KASHMIR", *IQBAL* 41, no. 1 (1994): pp. 1-9.

1183. **JUSTYN'SKI, Janusz**, "NARÓD I PAŃSTWO W DOKTRYNIE INDYJSKIEH REPREZENTANTÓW ODRODZENIA MUZULMAŃSKIEGO [The Nation and the State in the Doctrine of Indian Representatives of the Muslim Revival]", *CZASOPISMO PRAWNO-HISTORYCZNE* (Poland) 35, no. 1 (1983): pp. 119-34.
The author examines the role of four prominent Indian muslims: Abdul LATIF, Sayyid AHMAD KHAN, Muhammad Ali JINNAH, and Muhammad IQBAL.
Pol.

1184. **KAAF, Jeem pseud.**, "IQBAL'S MASJID-I-QURTABA", *PAKISTAN REVIEW* 2, no. 4: April (1956): pp. 37-39, 46.

1185. **KABIR, Q. A.**, "FRENZY'S DRIVE", *IQBAL REVIEW* 18, no. 4: January (1978): pp. 215-19.
English translation of one of Iqbal's poems in BAL-I JIBRIL.

1186. ———, tr. P/E, *GIFT OF HIJAZ* (ARMAGHAN-I-HIJAZ), Lahore: Iqbal Academy, 1983. vi+157 pp.
Versified English rendering in iambic pentagon meter, with examples of catalectic and tetrametric styles as well.

1187. ———, "IQBAL'S QUATRAINS IN ARMUGHAN-I HIJAZ", *IQBAL REVIEW* 16, no. 3: October (1975): pp. 63-67.
English translation of the quatrains.

1188. **KABIR, Qazi Abdul**, "SONG OF STARS (IN TETRAMETRIC HEXASTICH)", *IQBAL* 24, no. 4: October (1977): pp. 125*ff*.
English translation of Iqbal's poem SAROD-I ANJUM, from KULLIYAT-I IQBAL (Persian), PAYAM-I MASHRIQ (p. 98), with original Persian text and some explanatory notes.

1189. ———, "TRANSLATION OF THE POEMS FROM IQBAL'S BAL-I-JIBRAIL", *PAKISTAN REVIEW* 14, no. 4 (1966): pp. 24-25.
English translation of two poems from (I) BAL-I-JIBRIL.

1190. **KADIR, Kazi A.**, "SCIENCE AND ITS PHILOSOPHY", *THE PAKISTAN TIMES* (Rawalpindi), 9 November 1977.

1191. **KAHLE, P. E.**, "ADDRESS TO THE OPENING SESSION OF THE PAKISTAN HISTORY CONFERENCE, KARACHI, 1956 (EXTRACT)", *MUHAMMAD IQBAL - POET AND PHILOSOPHER, A COLLECTION OF TRANSLATIONS, ESSAYS AND OTHER ARTICLES, PRESENTED BY THE PAKISTAN-GERMAN FORUM*, Karachi: Din Mohammad Press, 1960.

1192. **KALBAN, J. N.**, "IQBAL: POET AND ENIGMA OF HIS AGE", *THE TIMES OF INDIA* (Delhi), 19 March 1961.

1193. **KALEEM, Siddiq**, "THE TONE AND TEMPER OF IQBAL'S POETRY", *PAKISTAN: A CULTURAL SPECTRUM*, Siddiq KALEEM (mon.), Lahore: Arsalan Publications, 1973, pp. 176-79.

1194. **KALIA, H. C.**, "IQBAL: SCHOLAR-POET OF EMINENCE", *THE TIMES OF INDIA* (Delhi), 19 March 1961.
Variant date: 24 April 1955.

1195. **KALIM, A.**, "IQBAL'S CONCEPT OF MUSLIM REVIVAL", *INDO-IRANICA* (Dordrecht, NL) 45, no. 1-4 (1992): pp. 18-26.

1196. **KAMAL, A. A.**, "IQBAL AND THE IDEAL PERSONALITY", *THE PAKISTAN TIMES* (Lahore), 20 May 1962, p. 4.

1197. **KAMAL, Muhammad Hanif**, "IQBAL POETIC ACHIEVEMENTS", *PAKISTAN QUARTERLY* 11, no. [?]: Spring (1967): pp. 30-36.

1198. **KAMAL, R.**, "IQBAL'S CONCEPT OF MAN", *ISLAMIC CULTURE* (Hyderabad) 37, no. 1: January (1963): pp. 30-48.

1199. **KAMALI, A. H.**, "CONCEPTUAL MODEL OF THE ASRAR-O-RUMUZ AND IQBAL'S MONADOLOGY", *IQBAL REVIEW* 11, no. 1: April (1970): pp. 59-72.
A far-reaching philosophical analysis of (I) ASRAR-I-KHUDI and (I) RUMUZ-I-BEKHUDI (together labeled as Iqbal's *mathnavi period*, according to the use of rhyming *doha*'s in both these poetical works), in the light of the so-called *philosophies of Cosmic Sway,* Iqbal's rejoinders in reply to polemics started by many of Iqbal's contemporary Indian mystics, his drawing on Shaikh Ahmad Sirhindi for defending his position, and the evolution of Iqbal's thought towards the SIX LECTURES (1929) and JAVID NAMAH (1934), *both of which,* the author states, *are written and composed definitely mostly beyond the metaphysical categories of the Mathnavi.* Conclusion is that *Iqbal was finally*

not a philosopher of Cosmic sway. Iqbal took time to develop his own model, and came out of their influence - and all of his deductions and conclusions have to be reinterpreted in terms of his own ontology and monadology.
Re-issued in [Various authors], *SELECTIONS FROM THE IQBAL REVIEW*, ed. Waheed Qureshi, Lahore, 1983, pp. 87-100.

1200. ———, "THE HERITAGE OF ISLAMIC THOUGHT", *IQBAL: POET-PHILOSOPHER OF PAKISTAN*, Hafeez MALIK (ed.), New Delhi / New York: Columbia UP, 1971.

1201. ———, "NATURE OF EXPERIENCE IN THE PHILOSOPHY OF SELF", *IQBAL REVIEW* 1, no. 3: October (1960): pp. 41-57.

1202. ———, "THE PHILOSOPHY OF SELF AND HISTORICISM", *IQBAL REVIEW* [vol. ?], no. [?]: July (1961).

1203. **KAMALI, Abdul Hameed**, mon., *POLITICAL PHILOSOPHY IN ISLAM*, Vol. 3, Karachi: Iqbal Academy Pakistan, 1971. 135 pp.
Iqbal's political and social views: pp. 115-134.

1204. **KAMALI, Rahimuddin**, "IQBAL'S THEORY OF ETHICS, BY PROF. SAYEED AHMED RAFIQUE", *ISLAMIC CULTURE* 36, no. 4 (1962).

1205. **KAMPFFMEYER, G.**, "THE RECONSTRUCTION OF RELIGIOUS THOUGHT IN ISLAM", *DIE WELT DES ISLAMS* (Leiden) 15, (1933): pp. 122-24. Review of Iqbal's THE RECONSTRUCTION OF RELIGIOUS THOUGHT IN ISLAM. G.

1206. **KAMRAN, Gilani**, "IQBAL - A VIEW OF POLITICO-CULTURAL PERSPECTIVE", *IQBAL REVIEW* 19, no. 3: October (1978): pp. 35-40.
An address presented at the Eastern Washington State University, Cheney, Washington, and at Duke University, Durham, N.C., in February 1978. In the perspective suggested by Iqbal's politico-cultural thinking the human ego has a definite political and cultural destiny which anticipates its fulfilment in the ever-shifting geo-historical situations of the modern world (p. 40).
Re-issued in [Various authors], *SELECTIONS FROM THE IQBAL REVIEW*, ed. Waheed Qureshi, Lahore, 1983, pp.183-188.

1207. ———, "IQBAL AND THE IDEA OF MUSLIM CULTURE", *IQBAL* 36, no. 2 (1989):

pp. 10-15.

1208. ———, "IQBAL'S JAVID NAMA", *IQBAL REVIEW* 25, no. 1: April (1984): pp. 59-92.

1209. **KARANDIKAR, M. A.**, mon., *ISLAM IN INDIA'S TRANSITION TO MODERNITY*, Karachi: Eastern Pubishers, 1968. 414 pp.
Iqbal's political and social views: pp. 162, 184, 186, 188, 220-224, 347, 368.

1210. **KARIM, A. H.**, "THE NATURE OF EXPERIENCE IN THE PHILOSOPHY OF THE SELF", *IQBAL REVIEW* 1, no. 3: October (1960): pp. 41-57.

1211. ———, "SCIENTIFIC EXPOSITION OF IQBAL", *DAWN* (Karachi), 5/12 April 1960. A reply to Dr. Muhammad Raffiuddin's letter on the same subject in *DAWN*, 12 April 1960.

1212. **KARIMUDDIN, S.**, "IQBAL - THE STAR OF THE EAST", *PAKISTAN REVIEW* 15, no. 4 (1967): pp. 34.

1213. **KASHYAP, Subhash**, "SIR MOHAMMAD IQBAL AND FRIEDRICH NIETZSCHE", *ISLAMIC QUARTERLY* 2, no. 3: October (1955): pp. 175.

1214. **KAUSAR, Zeenath**, *ISLAM AND NATIONALISM: AN ANALYSIS OF THE VIEWS OF AZAD, IQBAL AND MAUDUDI*, [place ?]: A.S. Noordeen, 1994

1215. **KAYSHYAP, Subhash**, "SIR MUHAMMAD IQBAL AND FRIEDRICH NIETZSCHE", *ISLAMIC QUARTERLY* (London) 2/3, no. 1: October/April (1955): pp. 175-94.
Variant name: KASHIAB.

1216. **KAZI, I.**, mon., *IQBAL DAY ADDRESS, APRIL 1958*, Karachi: Iqbal Academy, 1959. 14 pp.

1217. **KAZI, I. I.**, mon., *CASUAL PEEPS AT SOPHIA*, 2nd ed., Hyderabad: Sindhi Adabi Board, 1977. 194 pp.
Iqbal and the philosophy of Islam: pp. 47-62.

1218. **KAZIMI**, "IQBAL'S REVOLT", *IQBAL* (Lahore) 3, no. 1: July (1954): pp. 87-113.
Variant name: KAZ(I)MI, K.

A short account of Iqbal's inspiring treatment of certain traditional conceptions.

1219. **KAZMI, K.**, "FLAWS IN IQBAL'S CONCEPT OF SELF", *PHULELI* 56-57, (1956): pp. 40-44.

1220. ———, "IQBAL AS REPRESENTATIVE OF THE EAST", *PAKISTAN REVIEW* (Lahore) 1, no. 9 (1953): pp. 14, 19, 25.

1221. **KAZMI, Latif Hussain**, "IQBAL'S CONCEPTION OF HUMAN EXISTENCE", *IQBAL REVIEW* 37, no. 1: April (1996): pp. 77-92.

1222. **KERR, David A.**, "MUHAMMAD IQBAL ON RELIGION", *IQBAL REVIEW / IQBALIAT* (Lahore) 29, no. 3: October-December (1988): pp. 47-78.
A paper, combining the substance of two lectures by Prof. Kerr (Director and Professor of Islamic Studies, McDonald Centre for Islam and Christian-Muslim Relations, Hartford Seminary, Connecticut, U.S.A.), one at Coventry for the Iqbal Academy (U.K.) in June 1987, and the other on the occasion of the "Iqbal and Mysticism" seminar at the University of Birmingham on November 7th 1987.
Iqbal is presented as "a man of our time", having renewed the essential messages of Islam, and brought them into place within our modern society. The essence of Iqbal's modernism is however combined with a strong attachment within the Sufi tradition. The paper concludes with Iqbal's invitation to a novel interfaith dialogue, stressing his warnings to Muslims as well as his challenge to Christianity. *I find that* [both Muslims and Christians], says Kerr, *are talking a common theological language,* [and since] *Iqbal addressed himself to Muslims with the intellectual context of his deep personal dialogue with western thought,* [we should] *continue to honour his memory by addressing ourselves to the contemporary world of East and West alike - within our collective experience of Muslim-Christian dialogue.*
This paper was also published as a pamphlet (International Centre for Islamic Studies, London, 1988), with a short editorial note.

1223. ———, "MUHAMMAD IQBAL'S THOUGHTS ON RELIGION: REFLECTIONS ON THE SPIRIT OF CHRISTIAN-MUSLIM DIALOGUE", *ISLAMOCHRISTIANA* (Roma) 41, no. 15 (1989): pp. 321.

1224. **KHALID, Abdul Aziz**, "IQBAL: AN ASSESSMENT", *OUTLOOK* (Karachi) 2, no. 1: March (1953): pp. 7, 13, 31.

1225. **KHALID, Detlev**, "AHMAD AMIN AND MUHAMMAD IQBAL", *IQBAL REVIEW* 12,

no. 1: April (1971): pp. 39-68.
Ahmad Amin (1872-1954), the Egyptian historian who demanded the adoption of Western sciences into the Islamic culture, admired Iqbal and Amir Ali as outstanding examples of these ideas. His dependence on Iqbal's thought was, however, not overtly admitted (he mentions Iqbal only once), for to the Arab world Iqbal was a little-known outsider.

1226. ———, "DIE STELLUNG IQBALS IN DER MUSLIMISCHEN GEISTESGESCHICHTE", *MUHAMMAD IQBAL UND DIE DREI REICHE DES GEISTES*, Wolfgang KOEHLER (ed.), Hamburg: Deutsch-Pakistanisches Forum, 1977, pp. 119-48.
Followed by an English summary: IQBAL AND HIS POSITION IN THE HISTORY OF MUSLIM THOUGHT, pp. 149-152.
G-E.

1227. **KHALIL, M. A. K.**, "THE HIMAL(A)YAS (TRANSLATION)", *IQBAL REVIEW* 33, no. 1: April (1992): pp. 1-8.
English translation of the opening poem of Iqbal's BANG-I DARA, "The Clarion Call", with an introduction and explanatory notes.

1228. ———, "THE RISE OF ISLAM", *IQBAL REVIEW* 28, no. 3: October-December (1987): pp. 1-13.
English translation of Iqbal's poem "TULU-E-ISLAM".

1229. **KHALIL, Mohammad Fauzi Hassan**, "IQBAL, THE RENOVATOR OF THE MUSLIM WORLD", *IQBAL, THE POET OF TOMORROW*, Khawaja Abdur RAHIM (ed.), Lahore: Abdul Hameed Khan at Ferozsons Ltd., n.d., pp. 269[271]-273.
This paper focuses on Iqbal as *a thinker who devoted his life to the guidance of others* (p. 271). The environment and circumstances explain his initial tendency towards Indian nationalist struggle, apparently aiming at the liberation of India from the foreign yoke, until, in Europe, his eyes were opened to the fact *that Europe, in her glorious age of renaissance and before that, had vastly borrowed from the light of Islam, and that if the darkening future of mankind was ever to receive illumination, it could only do so by re-exposing itself to the real light of Islam* (p. 272). The author even identifies the awakened poet-philosopher with Pakistan, even though he, unfortunately, never *beheld the rising banner of crescent and star over the Shahi Mosque of Lahore* (p. 273).

1230. **KHALIQ, Abdul**, "IQBAL ON OBSERVATION OF NATURE AND GOD-KNOWLEDGE", *IQBAL REVIEW* 20, no. 3: October (1979): pp. 1-9.

1231. ———, "IQBAL'S CONCEPT OF THE LIFE HEREAFTER", *IQBAL REVIEW* 37, no.

3: October (1996): pp. 35-47.
Special issue on the Reconstruction of Religious Thought in Islam.

1232. ———, "IQBAL'S CONCEPT OF THE PERFECT MAN", *IQBAL REVIEW* 25, no. 1: April (1984): pp. 47-57.

1233. ———, "IQBAL'S DOCTRINE OF EGOS AND THE LEIBNIZIAN MONADS", *IQBAL REVIEW* 36, no. 1: April (1995): pp. 1-19.
Both Leibniz and Iqbal are generally believed to have preferred theism (creativeness), rather than pantheism (emanationism).

1234. ———, *IQBAL STUDIES AND THE JOURNAL OF PHILOSOPHY CONGRESS*, Lahore: Bazm-e-Iqbal, 1993. 232 pp.

1235. ———, "RECONSTRUCTION OF ISLAMIC THOUGHT FROM SIR SAYYID AHMAD KHAN TO IQBAL", *IQBAL REVIEW* 36, no. 3: October (1995): pp. 1-7.

1236. **KHALIQUE, M.**, "WORDSWORTH AND IQBAL", *DAWN* (Karachi), 14 May 1950, p. 15.

1237. **KHAMENAI, Syed Ali**, "IQBAL - THE SHINING STAR OF THE EAST", *IQBAL REVIEW* 30-31, no. 3: October and 1: April (1989-1990): pp. 1-47.
English translation by M.A.K. KHALIL of an address delivered at the World Congress for Commemoration of the 108th Birth Anniversary of Allama Muhammad Iqbal.

1238. **KHAN, A. A.**, "IQBAL'S EDUCATIONAL OUTLOOK AND THOUGHT", *JOURNAL OF THE PAKISTAN HISTORICAL SOCIETY* 32, no. 2 (1984): pp. 97-113.
Iqbal regarded individuality as developing through constant struggle against internal and external disruptive forces; education should reconcile the material and spiritual and strive for a unity of emotions between the individual and the community. Intellect, intuition, and creative evolution are to be expressed through the social code of Islam, based on loyalty to God and to mankind's ideal nature, and on freedom, equality and human brotherhood.

1239. **KHAN, A. Ali**, mon., *IQBAL: HIS POETRY AND MESSAGE*, Lahore, 1931

1240. **KHAN, A'alia Sohail**, "YEATS AND IQBAL", *IQBAL* 42, no. 4 (1995): pp. 39-50 or 55-66 [?].

1241. **KHAN, Aalia Sohail**, "GLORIFICATION OF THE PAST IN IQBAL'S POETRY",

IQBAL 43, no. 1 (1996): pp. 1-22.
As a conclusion (p. 19), the author puts forward that *Iqbal's view of history is "both creative and conservative". The conservative element means an adherence to the positive values of the past, whereas the dynamic-creative element requires expunging the dead traditions, and making an incessant pursuit of new positive goals.*

1242. ———, "IQBAL AND DEMOCRACY", *IQBAL* 43, no. 2 (1996): pp. 3-10.

1243. ———, "ISLAM: A RELIGION OF PEACE AND TOLERANCE", *IQBAL REVIEW* 37, no. 1: April (1996): pp. 71-76.

1244. ———, "LANDSCAPE IN IQBAL'S POETRY", *IQBAL REVIEW* 38, no. 1: April (1997): pp. 39-48.

1245. ———, "A NATION AND ITS CULTURE", *IQBAL* 44, no. 3-4 (1997): pp. 155-62.

1246. **KHAN, Abdul Hamid**, "IS IQBAL [A] 'PAROCHIAL' POET? HE DISCOVERED INADEQUACY OF REGIONAL PATRIOTISM", *THE CIVIL AND MILITARY GAZETTE* (Lahore), 21 April 1961, pp. 1, 2.

1247. **KHAN, Abdul Waheed**, "THE GENIUS WHO DIED", *PAKISTAN TIMES*, 21 April 1967.

1248. ———, mon., *INDIA WINS FREEDOM. THE OTHER SIDE*, Karachi: Pakistan Educational Publishers, 1961. 405 pp.
See pp. 17-120 on Iqbal.

1249. **KHAN, Abdur Raoof**, "CONTRIBUTION OF IQBAL TO THE ADVANCEMENT OF MUSLIM THOUGHT", University of the Punjab, 44 pp.
M.A. Political Science.
Contents: (1) The sources of Iqbal's thought, (2) Iqbal and the Reconstruction of Religious Thought, (3) Iqbal, nationalism and Western democracy, (4) Iqbal and socialism, and (5) Conclusion.

1250. **KHAN, Aftab Ahmad**, "IQBAL'S VIEWS ON TIME AND SPACE", *EDUCATION RESEARCH BULLETIN* [vol. ?], no. [?]: December (1977): pp. 39-46.

1251. **KHAN, Ahmad Nabi**, "THE HOUSE WHERE THE POET WAS BORN", *THE*

PAKISTAN TIMES (Rawalpindi), 21 April 1979.

1252. **KHAN, Alia Sohail**, "RECOVERY OF THE LAND IN IQBAL'S POETRY", *IQBAL* 42, no. 3 (1995): pp. 29-35.

1253. **KHAN, Amanullah**, "ISLAMIC CONCEPTION OF THE BROTHERHOOD OF MAN", *IQBAL* 24, no. 4: October (1977): pp. 129-34.

1254. **KHAN, Asif Iqbal**, "IQBAL ON ISLAMIC CULTURE", *PAKISTAN TIMES*, 8 July 1977, p. 1.

1255. ———, "IQBAL ON THE FUNCTION OF ART", *CONTRIBUTIONS TO IQBAL' THOUGHT*, Mohammed MARUF (ed.), Lahore: Islamic Book Service, 1977, pp. 126-41.

1256. ———, "IQBAL'S CONCEPT OF THE SELF (A PHILOSOPHICAL ANALYSIS)", *IQBAL REVIEW* 24, no. 3: October (1983): pp. 81-88.
Criticism of Iqbal's restricted treatment of personal identity.

1257. ———, "IQBAL'S INFLUENCE ON QUAID-I-AZAM", *PAKISTAN TIMES*, 12 and 19 August 1977, p. 1 and 1.
Two parts.

1258. ———, "JAMES AND IQBAL (A NEW APPROACH TO PSYCHOLOGY OF RELIGION)", *IQBAL REVIEW* 37, no. 3: October (1996): pp. 73-87.
Special issue on the Reconstruction of Religious Thought in Islam.
Comparison of Iqbal's approach to interpret religious phenomena by employing psychological instruments of explanation and understanding with that of James and that of transpersonal psychology (A. Maslow).

1259. ———, "THE PROBLEM OF METHOD IN IQBAL'S THOUGHT", *IQBAL REVIEW* 35, no. 1: April (1994): pp. 1-18.
On Iqbal's attempt to reconcile the distinct (Western philosophical) systems of idealism, rationalism and empiricism both at the metaphysical and the epistemological levels. The conclusion is that *while as a philosopher he considers himself du[l]y bound to exercise logical rigour and methodical coherence in his thought, his humanistic/pragmatic enterprise refuses to accept the logical limits of such an exercise* (p. 16-17).

1260. ———, "THE PROBLEM OF PERSONAL IDENTITY IN LIFE AFTER DEATH", *IQBAL REVIEW* 29, no. 1: April (1988): pp. 17-31.

Essay on the basic *non-testibility in principle* of the concept of *life after death* and Iqbal's failing quest to put revelation to the test of reason. Like other Muslim rationalists, the author states, Iqbal, *in his application of intellectual and pragmatic tests to religious assertions, has done little more than to point out different meanings attached to religious concepts*, and the author is glad to note that Iqbal *appears to have realised the impossibility of his position, and in his later works laid greater stress on the non-rational character of religion.*

1261. ———, "RELIGION AS A PROGRESSIVE FORCE IN IQBAL'S THOUGHT", *PAKISTAN TIMES*, 8 and 15 May 1977, pp. 1, and 2.
Two parts.

1262. ———, mon., *SOME ASPECTS OF IQBAL'S THOUGHTS*, Chicago: Kazi Publications, 1996. 100 pp.
Earlier published in Lahore: Islamic Book Service, 1977, 102 pp.

1263. ———, "WAS IQBAL AN EPISTEMOLOGIST?", *IQBAL REVIEW* 30, no. 1: April-June (1989): pp. 63-84.

1264. **KHAN, Hameedullah**, "GHALIB, THE PREDECESSOR OF IQBAL", *IQBAL* (Lahore) 36, no. 3 (1989): pp. 1-9.
While Ghalib sings melodious and rapturous songs, Iqbal seems to be brandishing a sword and challenging the evil forces of life. One is a singer, and the other is a crusader (p. 9).

1265. **KHAN, M. H.**, "DEMOCRACY IS A SYSTEM OF A GOVERNMENT IN WHICH MEN ARE COUNTED NOT WEIGHED", *THE CIVIL AND MILITARY GAZETTE* (Lahore), 21 April 1955, p. 1.

1266. **KHAN, Mohammad Raza**, mon., *WHAT PRICE FREEDOM: A HISTORICAL SURVEY OF THE POLITICAL TRENDS AND CONDITIONS LEADING TO INDEPENDENCE AND THE BIRTH OF PAKISTAN AND AFTER*, Karachi: Indus, 1977

1267. **KHAN, Muhammad Jahangir**, "APPOINTMENT TO AND RESIGNATION FROM GOVERNMENT SERVICE OF SHEIKH MUHAMMAD IQBAL", *JOURNAL OF THE RESEARCH SOCIETY OF PAKISTAN* 14, no. 4: October (1977): pp. 1-22.

1268. **KHAN, Muhammad Tufail**, "AN INTERPRETATION OF IQBAL'S CONCEPT OF MUSLIM EDUCATION", University of the Punjab, Dept.: Institute of Education and

Research, n.d.

1269. **KHAN, Muhammad Yaqub**, "IQBAL AS I KNEW HIM", *THE CIVIL AND MILITARY GAZETTE* (Lahore), 21 April 1950, p. 3.
Variant date: 1955.

1270. **KHAN, Mumtaz Ahmad**, "THE CHINESE EVALUATION OF IQBAL", *THE NEWS* (Islamabad / Lahore), 21 April 1992.

1271. ———, "(POET OF THE EAST) THROUGH CHINESE EYES", *THE MUSLIM* (Islamabad), 21 April 1980.
Published earlier in *THE PAKISTAN TIMES*, 21 April 1966, p. 5; and also in *DAWN*, 21 April 1974, p. 2 or 4 [?].

1272. **KHAN, Mumtaz Ahmed**, "IQBAL THROUGH THE CHINESE EYES", *THE PAKISTAN TIMES* (Rawalpindi), 8 November 1981.

1273. **KHAN, N. A.**, "TAGORE AND IQBAL", *INDO-IRANICA* 14, no. 3: September (1961): pp. 44-56.

1274. **KHAN, Nawab Zulfiqar Ali**, mon., *A VOICE FROM THE EAST: THE POETRY OF IQBAL*, Umrao SINGH (intr.), Karachi: Iqbal Academy, 1966. viii+42 pp.
Re-issue of the first ever book on Iqbal, published in his lifetime. Foreword by Umrao Singh, including translation of selected poems by Sir Joginder Singh. The book includes 6 chapters: (1) The Period of Decadence, (2) The Dawn of Indian Renaissance, (3) Iqbal's Early Days, (4) His Studies in Europe, (5) Selections from His Poems, and (6) His Great Work.
The book was further re-issued several times, a.o. by Aziz Publications (Lahore 1977, 104 pp.).

1275. **KHAN, Nazir Ahmad**, "COMMONWEALTH OF MUSLIM NATIONS", *PAKISTAN TIMES*, 21 April 1961, p. 1.

1276. ———, "A COMMONWEALTH OF MUSLIM NATIONS", *IQBAL REVIEW* 13, no. 1: April (1972): pp. 71-79.

1277. **KHAN, Niaz Ahmad**, "THE POET OF THE EAST", *CHIRAG-I RAHGUZAR* [vol. ?], no. [?]: December and [?]: 1 January (1977-1978).

The Muslim Institute, Allama Iqbal Birth Centenary Committee (Calcutta).

1278. **KHAN, Niaz Muhammad**, "JAVEED NAMA IN IQBAL'S OWN WORDS", *IQBAL: A CRITICAL STUDY*, Misbah-ul-Haq SIDDIQUI (ed.), Lahore: Farhan Publishers, 1977, pp. 102-6.
A biographical incident about Iqbal in London (1931), and his own description of the contents and the meaning of *JAVID NAMAH*.
Article taken from *THE CIVIL AND MILITARY GAZETTE*, Iqbal Day Supplement 1963. Originally published in *MORNING NEWS*, 1944.

1279. **KHAN, Rafiq**, "IQBAL'S VIEW OF CHANGE AND PROGRESS", *THE PAKISTAN TIMES* (Rawalpindi), 21 April 1979.

1280. **KHAN, Rahim Bux**, mon., *DYNAMISM, AN ELABORATION*, Karachi: Trade and Industry Publications, 1977. 75 pp.
Book dedicated to Iqbal's philosophical "Secret of the Self" theory, and his relation with the young people.

1281. **KHAN, Sa'adat Ali**, "A NOTE ON IQBAL", *INDIAN ART(S) AND LETTERS* (London) (NS) 17, no. 1: 17 November (1943): pp. 71-73.

1282. **KHAN, Saadat Ali**, "SICILY", *POETRY* 93, no. 4 (1959): pp. 233-34.
English translation of a poem.

1283. **KHAN, Shafiq Ali**, "IQBAL AS A VITALIST", *EDUCATION RESEARCH BULLETIN* [vol. ?], no. [?]: December (1977): pp. 11-18.

1284. **KHAN, Shafique Ali**, "IQBAL AND JINNAH", *JOURNAL OF THE PAKISTAN HISTORICAL SOCIETY* 39, no. 4: October (1991): pp. 315-41.
A comparative study of their views on Islamic state, polity and economy.

1285. ———, mon., *IQBAL'S CONCEPT OF SEPARATE NORTH-WEST MUSLIM STATE: A CRITIQUE OF HIS ALLAHABAD ADDRESS OF 1930*, Karachi: Markez-e-Shaoor-o-Adab, 1987. 140 pp.
Includes an index and a bibliography.

1286. ———, mon., *TWO NATION THEORY AS A CONCEPT, STRATEGY AND IDEOLOGY*, Hyderabad: Markaz-i-Shaoor-o-Adab, 1973. 976 pp.
Re-issued in Karachi: Royal Book, 1985. On Iqbal's political views in relation to Pakistan,

see pp. 613-633.

1287. **KHAN, Zulfiqar Ali**, mon., *A VOICE FROM THE EAST, OR THE POETRY OF IQBAL*, Umrao SINGH (forword), Lahore: The Mercantile (Electric?) Press, 1922. vi+47 pp.
The first ever book on Iqbal, appeared during his lifetime. New Impression in Karachi: Iqbal Academy (Pakistan), 1966, with an Introduction by B.A. DAR.

1288. **KHATANA, Manzoor H.**, *IQBAL AND FOUNDATIONS OF PAKISTANI NATIONALISM 1857-1947*, Lahore: Mustafa Waheed / Shirkat Printing Press, 1992
Chapters: I. The Political Environment on the Eve of Iqbal's Birth, II. Iqbal's Formative Years, III. The European Influence on Iqbal, IV. Iqbal's Political Philosophies, V. Political Activism of Indian Muslims, VI. The Concept of the Muslim State.

1289. **KHATOON, Jameela**, "IQBAL'S THEORY OF KNOWLEDGE", *IQBAL REVIEW* 1, no. 1: April (1960): pp. 91-104.
Iqbal's theory of knowledge is presented as an endeavour to provide man a clue to the Ultime Reality which, according to Iqbal, *can be known, grasped and comprehended not only in its partial and fragmentary aspect, but also in its completeness.* Iqbal's theory thus promises both direct evidence and indirect experience of God or Reality, the former by intuition or immediate experience, and the latter by reflective thought. In this, the author states, *Iqbal cannot be classed under any of the three schools of philosophical thought - empiricist, rationalist or institutionist.* Rather, he feels that the ontological problem needs to be approached from all angles, whether scientific or religious, and *the great merit and virtue of his theory lies in the fact that he does not adopt and exalt any one method at the cost of the others.*
Re-issued in [Various authors], *SELECTIONS FROM THE IQBAL REVIEW*, ed. Waheed Qureshi, Lahore, 1983, pp. 43-56.

1290. **KHATOON, Jamila**, "IQBAL'S PERFECT MAN", *IQBAL* (Lahore) 1, no. 1: July (1952): pp. 57-64.
Reproduced in SHEIKH, M. Saeed (ed.), *STUDIES IN IQBAL'S THOUGHT AND ART*, Lahore, 1972, pp. 125-132.

1291. ————, mon., *THE PLACE OF GOD, MAN AND UNIVERSE IN THE PHILOSOPHIC SYSTEM OF IQBAL*, 3rd ed., Karachi or Lahore [?]: Iqbal Academy Pakistan, 1997. xviii+184 pp.
Originally published in 1963, and re-issued in 1977.
Contents: (I) The Knowledge of God with Special Reference to the Sources of Knowledge, (II) God: Proofs of His existence, (III) God: His Essence and Attributes, (IV) Creation, (V) Matter, Space and Time, (VI) Man: The Finite Self, (VII) Freedom of Will,

(VIII) The Problem of Immortality.

Iqbal is neither an empiricist, a rationalist nor an intuitionalist, but all three combined in an organic whole. Starting with the intuition of the Self, one rises to the intuition of the Ultimate Reality (viz. Being: permanent, personal and eternal). Being, then, is correlative with Becoming, and Becoming is to God as Behaviour is to man. Men and Universe are related to God as the created to the Creator.

1292. **KHATOON, Saeeda**, "IQBAL AND THEORY OF KNOWLEDGE", *THE PAKISTAN TIMES* (Rawalpindi), 21 April 1982.

1293. ———, "SELF OR EGO IN IQBAL'S PHILOSOPHY", *THE PAKISTAN TIMES* (Rawalpindi), 9 November 1983.

1294. **KHATTAK, Yousuf**, "IQBAL'S JOURNEY TO PAKISTAN", *IQBAL REVIEW* 15, no. 1: April (1974): pp. 13-20.
Text of a lecture, read in a meeting held under the auspices of the Iqbal Academy, Karachi, on the occasion of the 36th Death Anniversary of Allama Iqbal, April 21st 1974, offering a brief survey of Iqbal's developing political thought and his ideas on nationhood, leading towards the creation of Pakistan.

1295. **KHAWAR, Rafique**, "IQBAL: A RE-EXAMINATION, HIS THOUGHTS", *ILLUSTRATED WEEKLY OF PAKISTAN* 5, no. 28: 26 April (1952): pp. 12-33.

1296. **KHAYAL, Taj Muhammad**, ed., *IQBAL AS A THINKER - EIGHT ESSAYS BY EMINENT SCHOLARS*, various authors (mon.), Lahore: Sheikh Muhammad Ashraf, 1944. 304 pp.
A collection of essays on the philosophy of IQBAL; *detailed description under 'Various authors'*.
Reprinted in Lahore: Sheikh Muhammad Ashraf, 1973.

1297. ———, ed., *IQBAL AS A THINKER - EIGHT ESSAYS BY EMINENT SCHOLARS*, various authors (mon.), 3rd ed., Lahore, 1960. 304 pp.
A collection of eight essays on various aspects of Iqbal as a philosopher, and particularly on Iqbal as a muslim thinker. The publishers approached Taj Muhammad Khayal as an editor, and although Khayal was responsible for the choice of the 8 contributions, he left the project prior to publication. The book was later published with just a short prefatory note by the publishers.
Contributors are: (1) Dr. M. Razi-ud-Din Siddiqi (IQBAL'S CONCEPTION OF TIME AND SPACE), (2) K.G. Saiyidain (PROGRESSIVE TRENDS IN IQBAL'S THOUGHT), (3) M.M. Sharif (IQBAL'S CONCEPTION OF GOD), (4) Dr. Khalifa Abdul Hakim

(RUMI, NIETZSCHE AND IQBAL), (5) Fazlur-Rahman (IQBAL AND MYSTICISM), (6) Dr. M. Aziz Ahmad (IQBAL'S POLITICAL THEORY), (7) Kalim-ud-Din Ahmad (IQBAL'S CONCEPTION OF ART), and (8) Fayyaz Mahmood (IQBAL'S ATTITUDE TOWARDS GOD). *All of these articles are described under their respective authors - qv.*

Re-issued by Kazi Publications (Chicago, n.d.).

1298. ———, "IQBAL'S CONCEPTION OF SATAN AND HIS PLACE IN IDEAL SOCIETY", *IQBAL* (Lahore) 2, no. 1: July (1953): pp. 1-17. Published also in Khawaja Abdur RAHIM (ed.), *IQBAL, POET OF TOMORROW*, Lahore: Abdul Hameed Khan at Ferozsons Ltd., n.d., pp. 221[223]-239. This paper was originally read at Iqbal Day on 21 April 1952, and its author holds that, according to Iqbal, Good and Evil are not absolute qualities of reality, but facts of human life. *The distinction of good and evil appears merely in the process of struggle and growth* [...], in which struggle *power is the standard of value but power is not, for Iqbal, merely brute force or physical power. It springs from a full growth of human personality and, in this growth, mental and moral elements are equally [e]ssential and important* (p. 239). The author concludes that Iqbal's approach of the problem is thus *purely scientific* (ibid.).

1299. ———, "IQBAL'S CONCEPTION OF STATE", *IQBAL* [vol. ?], no. [?]: July (1953): pp. 1-17.

1300. **KHERNAN, V. G.**, "IQBAL AS PROPHET OF CHANGE", *THE ILLUSTRATED WEEKLY OF INDIA* (Bombay), 30 October 1977.

1301. **KHOKHAR, Masood-ul-Hasan**, "A LIFE, GENIUS AND INSPIRATION", *THE NATION* (Lahore), 9 November 1986.
Iqbal Day Supplement.

1302. **KHOKHAR, Muhammad Sulaiman**, "IQBAL AS A POLITICAL THINKER", University of the Punjab, Dept. of Political Science, n.d. 41 pp.
Contents: (1) Life and works, (2) Sources of Iqbal's inspirations, (3) Iqbal and his missions, (4) Ideal society, (5) Perfect man, (6) Iqbal's thought governmental forum, (7) Religion and politics, (8) Democracy, (9) Iqbal and nationality, (10) Commonwealth of Muslim nations, (11) Socialism and capitalism, and (12) Last words.

1303. **KHORASANEE, Amin**, "A GHAZAL OF IQBAL", *IQBAL REVIEW* 9, no. 1: April (1968): pp. 76-79 [sic in "contents"] / 66 [in volume].

1304. **KHUNDMIRI, Alam**, "IQBAL AND THE REVALUATION OF MAN", *POETRY AND RENAISSANCE: KUMARAM ASAN BIRTH CENTENARY VOLUME*, M. GOVINDAN (ed.), Madras: Sameeksha, 1974, pp. 107-14.

1305. **KHUNDMIRI, Alam S.**, "THE POLITICAL PHILOSOPHY OF IQBAL", *NEW QUEST* (Bombay) 8, (1978): pp. 117-24.
Previously published under the full title of "A STUDY OF THE CONCEPTS OF TRANSFORMATION, LEADERSHIP AND FREEDOM IN THE POLITICAL PHILOSOPHY OF IQBAL", in Ali Sardar JAFRI and K.S. DUGGAL (eds.), *IQBAL COMMEMORATIVE VOLUME*, New Delhi: All India Iqbal Centenary Celebrations Committtee, 1977, pp. 93-102.

1306. **KHUNDMIRI, S. Alam**, "CONCEPTION OF TIME", *IQBAL: POET-PHILOSOPHER OF PAKISTAN*, Hafeez MALIK (ed.), New Delhi / New York: Columbia UP, 1971.

1307. **KHURSHID, Abdul Salam**, "IQBAL AND PAKISTAN", *THE PAKISTAN TIMES* (Rawalpindi), 9 November 1982.

1308. **KHURSHID, Abdusalam**, "IQBAL'S OBSERVATIONS ON MUSLIM NATIONHOOD", *BALUCHISTAN TIMES* (Quetta), 9 November 1979.
Previously published in *THE PAKISTAN TIMES*, 5 June 1977, p. 1.

1309. **KHURSHID, Alam**, "THE VISION OF A UTOPIA IN JAVED NAMA", *IQBAL: A CRITICAL STUDY*, Misbah-ul-Haq SIDDIQUI (ed.), Lahore: Farhan Publishers, 1977, pp. 51-57.
Short analysis of Iqbal's *utopia*, as presented in JAVID NAMAH, which, according to the author, *is not a poet's fantasy, but a realisable goal*. Originally published in *THE CIVIL AND MILITARY GAZETTE*, 21 April 1962, pp. 2-4.

1310. ———, "ZINDA ROOD ON MARS, IQBAL'S UTOPIA", *THE CIVIL AND MILITARY GAZETTE* (Lahore), 21 April 1960, p. 3.

1311. **KIDWAI, Abdur Raheem**, "MALIK, G.R., THE BLOODY HORIZON: A STUDY OF IQBAL'S RESPONSE TO THE WEST", *THE MUSLIM WORLD* 15, no. 2 (1995): pp. 19.

1312. ———, "RASTOGI, T.C., WESTERN INFLUENCE ON IQBAL", *THE MUSLIM WORLD BOOK REVIEW* 15, no. 2 (1995): pp. 19-21.

1313. **KIDWAI, Saleem**, "IQBAL - PHILOSOPHIC POET", *INDIAN LITERATURE* (New Delhi) 18, no. 3: July-September (1975): pp. 71-82.

1314. **KIERNAN, V. G.**, "IQBAL AND MILTON", *IQBAL COMMEMORATIVE VOLUME*, Ali Sardar JAFRI & K.S. DUGGAL (eds.), New Delhi: All India Iqbal Centenary Celebrations Committee, 1977, pp. 231-41.

1315. ———, "IQBAL AND WORDSWORTH", *IQBAL COMMEMORATIVE VOLUME*, Ali Sardar JAFRI & K.S. DUGGAL (eds.), New Delhi: All India Iqbal Centenary Celebrations Committee, 1977, pp. 254-66.

1316. ———, "IQBAL AS A PROPHET OF CHANGE: THE MESSAGE OF THE EAST", *IQBAL, COMMEMORATIVE VOLUME*, Ali Sardar JAFRI & K.S. DUGGAL (eds.), New Delhi: All India Iqbal Centenary Celebrations Committee, 1977, pp. 43-53.
This article deals with Iqbal's PAYAM-I MASHRIQ, which is *a collection of detached pieces or sequences, combining a loose unity of theme with the freedom of the short poem* (p. 43). Much of it is criticism, even denunciation, of Europe, and *frequently Iqbal may seem to be urging us to action with only an indefinite indication of its motive, as if action were an end in itself* (p. 53). However, *the thought is always with him of the contrast between man's physical frailty and grandeur of spirit, between the handful of dust and the limitless desire*, but attention should be paid to the last lines of his Message from the East, which are *a call [...] to throw off the chains of the past, not to imitate but to create* (p. 53).

1317. **KIERNAN, Victor G.**, "THE MOSQUE OF CORDOVA", *PAKISTAN QUARTERLY* (Karachi) 2, no. 3 (1952).
English translation of (I) MASJID-I-QURTUBAH.

1318. ———, "ODE", *THOUGHT* 8, no. 19 (1956): pp. 14.
English translation of a poem.

1319. ———, tr. U/E P/E, *POEMS FROM IQBAL*, H.D. TASEER & KHWAJA ABDUL HAMID (intr. and remarks, respectively), 1st ed., WISDOM OF THE EAST, London: John Murray, 1955. xxviii+112.
Revised edition of op.cit., Bombay (Kutub Publishers) 1947, being a selection of verses translated into English from: BANG-I-DARA (The Call of the Road), BAL-I-JIBRIL (Gabriel's Wing), ZARB-I-KALIM (The Rod of Moses), ARMAGHAN-I-HEJAZ (The Gift of Hejaz), and PYAM-I-MASHRIQ (The Message of the East).

Later editions have 133 pp.

1320. ——, tr. U/E, *POEMS FROM IQBAL, TRANSLATED FROM URDU*, M.D. TASEER (intr.), Bombay: Kutub Publishers, 1974. 134 pp.
English translation of selected Urdu poems, with an introduction by M.D. TASEER.

1321. ——, "THREE POEMS FROM IQBAL", *INDO-ASIAN CULTURE* 2, (1953-1954).
Three poems from Kiernan's collection *POEMS FROM IQBAL*, Bombay, 1947).

1322. **KIFAIT, Ali Mian**, "IQBAL'S DOCTRINE OF KHUDI", *PAKISTAN TIMES*, 18 January 1963, p. 1.

1323. **KOEHLER, Wolfgang**, ed., *MUHAMMAD IQBAL AND THE THREE REALMS OF THE SPIRIT* (MUHAMMAD IQBAL UND DIE DREI REICHE DES GEISTES), Schriftenreihe Des Deutsch-Pakistanisches Forum 3, Hamburg: German-Pakistan Forum / Deutsch-Pakistanisches Forum, 1977.
Articles in German with a brief summary in English:
Annemarie Schimmel, IQBAL, LEBEN UND WERK / IQBAL, HIS LIFE AND WORK, SUMMARY
- GERMANY AND IQBAL / IQBAL UND DEUTSCHLAND, KURZFASSUNG
Hans-Hasso von Veltheim-Ostrau (+), LETZTE BEGEGNUNG MIT IQBAL
Syed Nazir Niazi (+), CONVERSATIONS WITH IQBAL / GESPRACHE MIT IQBAL, KURZFASSUNG
Johannes W. Fuck (+), IQBAL UND DER INDO-MUSLIMISCHE MODERNISMUS
Annemarie Schimmel, IQBAL IN THE CONTEXT OF INDO-MUSLIM MYSTICAL REFORM MOVEMENTS / IQBAL IM ZUSAMMENHANG MIT INDO-MUSLIMISCHEN MYSTISCHEN REFORMBEWEGUNGEN, KURZFASSUNG
Detlev Khalid, DIE STELLUNG IQBALS IN DER MUSLIMISCHEN GEISTESGESCHICHTE / IQBAL AND HIS POSITION IN THE HISTORY OF MUSLIM THOUGHT, SUMMARY
Annemarie Schimmel, OST-WESTLICHE DICHTUNG / EAST-WESTERN POETRY, SUMMARY
- DIE GESTALT DES SATAN IN THE WORK OF MUHAMMAD IQBAL
- THE FIGURE OF SATAN IN THE WORK OF MUHAMMAD IQBAL, SUMMARY
Munir D. Ahmed, IQBAL ALS POLITISCHER DENKER - IQBAL AND HIS POLITICAL PHILOSOPHY, SUMMARY
Mumtaz Haan (+), A NATION IS BORN
- GEBURT EINER NATION, KURZFASSUNG.
E-G.

1324. **KOSTYUK, R.**, mon., *PAKISTAN, PHILOSOPHY AND SOCIOLOGY*, M. T. STEPANYANTS (tr. R/E), Lahore: Peoples Publishing House, 1972. 150 pp. Essays on Iqbal and nationalism, Pakistan, poetry, philosophy, Sufism/Mysticism, Nietzsche, Islamic philosophy, etc.

1325. **KRISHNIAH, S.**, "THE SPIRIT OF IQBAL", *THOUGHT* 6, no. 33: 14 August (1954): pp. 10-11.

1326. **KRITZECK, James**, mon., *MODERN ISLAMIC LITERATURE*, New York: Holt Rinehardt and Winston, 1970. 310 pp. See pp. 69-73 on Iqbal's philosophy (Secret of Self theory), and pp. 170-190 on Iqbal and religion.

1327. **KULHAN, J. N.**, "IQBAL: POET AND ENIGMA OF HIS AGE", *TIMES OF INDIA*, 19 March 1961.

1328. **KUMAR, Ish**, "BROWNING AND IQBAL", *PANJAB UNIVERSITY RESEARCH BULLETIN, ARTS* (Chandigarh) 7, no. 1 (1976): pp. 17-30.

1329. ———, "BROWNING AND IQBAL", *IQBAL COMMEMORATIVE VOLUME*, Ali Sardar JAFRI & K.S. DUGGAL (eds.), New Delhi: All India Iqbal Centenary Celebrations Committee, 1977, pp. 281-93.

1330. ———, mon., *GHALIB AND IQBAL*, Chandigarh: Publication Bureau / Panjab University, 1988

1331. ———, "ROBERT BROWNING AND ALLAMA IQBAL", *THE PAKISTAN TIMES* (Rawalpindi), 2 December 1977.

1332. **LALL, Inder Jit**, "MUHAMMAD IQBAL: A POET OF STRESS AND STRUGGLE", *THE STATESMAN*, 22 April 1967, p. 6:4.

1333. ———, "MUHAMMAD IQBAL - STAR OF THE EAST", *THOUGHT* 25, no. 16: 21 April (1973): pp. 19-20.

1334. **LAMB, Christopher**, "IQBAL AND INTERFAITH DIALOGUE", *IQBAL REVIEW* 29, no. 3: October (1988): pp. 115-19. Short thought about Iqbal and his place and value in the context of interfaith dialogue, delivered at a one day Seminar on Iqbal and Mysticism (University of Birmingham, 7

November 1987).

1335. **LARI, Kishwar Jamal**, "IQBAL ON THE NATURE OF PROPHECY", University of the Punjab, Dept. Philosophy, 1970. ix+124 pp.
Promoter: 'Abdul Khaliq.
Contents: (1) Introduction, (2) Orthodox concept of prophecy, (3) The concept of prophecy in Muslim philosophy, (4) Iqbal on the nature of prophecy, and (5) Conclusion, with (6) Summary.

1336. **LEHMANN, Fritz**, "IQBAL, JINNAH, AND PAKISTAN. THE VISION AND THE REALITY. EDITED BY C.M. NAIM (Book Review)", *PACIFIC AFFAIRS* 54, no. 3: Fall (1981): pp. 545.

1337. **M.M.S.**, "IQBAL: HIS ART AND THOUGHT, BY SYED ABDUL VAHID", *IQBAL* 12, no. 1: July (1963): pp. 84-85.
Review of the first edition published in England, for which the author, Syed Abdul Vahid, added two extra chapters and performed extensive revisions.

1338. **MA'RUF, Mohammed**, mon., *IQBAL AND HIS CONTEMPORARY WESTERN RELIGIOUS THOUGHT*, Lahore: Iqbal Academy, 1987. ix+312 pp.
Variant name: RAUF, M.
Topics dealt with include: Iqbal and Idealist traditions (Hegelianism, Absolutism, English theologians, American Absolutism, and personal idealism, Ch. 1-2); Philosophies of spirit (Ch. 3); Neo-Kantian philosophy (Ch. 4); Naturalism (Ch. 5-6); Pragmatism (Ch. 7); Philosophy of history (Ch. 8); New Realism (Ch. 9); and Sociological Philosophies (Ch. 10).

1339. **MA'RUF, Muhammad**, "IQBAL'S PHILOSOPHY OF KNOWLEDGE, A CRITICAL APPROACH TO IQBAL'S POSITION ON RELIGIOUS EXPERIENCE AS A SOURCE OF KNOWLEDGE", University of the Punjab, Dept. of Philosophy, 1968. vii+355 pp.
Ph.D. dissertation; Promoter: K.G. Sadiq.
Contents: Part I - (1) Introduction, (2) Naturalistic theories of religion, (3) Psychoanalysis and religion, (4) Psychoanalysis and religion (continued), (5) Proofs for religion, (6) Verification of religious experience; Part II - (1) The nature of religious experience, (2) The characteristics of religious experience, (3) The cognitive value of religious experience, (4) Concluding remarks; Appendices - (A) Iqbal's view of divine knowledge, (B) Russell's critique of religion.

1340. ———, "JAVID NAMA: A STUDY OF WORLD CIVILIZATION", *IQBAL REVIEW*

26, no. 3: October-November-December (1985): pp. 123-28.

1341. **MACHAVE, Prabhakar**, "CONCEPT OF MAN IN IQBAL", *MULTI-DISCIPLINARY APPROACH TO IQBAL*, IQBAL CENTENARY SYMPOSIUM (New Delhi), n.d..

1342. **MACHWE, Prabhakar**, "THE CONCEPT OF LOVE IN IQBAL'S POETRY", *IQBAL COMMEMORATIVE VOLUME*, Ali Sardar JAFRI & K.S. DUGGAL (eds.), New Delhi: All India Iqbal Centenary Celebrations Committee, 1977, pp. 182-90.

1343. ———, "IQBAL, NIRALA AND DINKAR", *IQBAL COMMEMORATIVE VOLUME*, Ali Sardar JAFRI & K.S. DUGGAL (eds.), New Delhi: All India Iqbal Centenary Celebrations Committee, 1977, pp. 309-18.

1344. **MAHDIHASSAN, S.**, "CHINESE ALCHEMY AND A FEW OF ITS TERMS AS USED BY IQBAL", *IQBAL REVIEW* 18, no. 1: April (1977): pp. 55-65.
Attempt to trace the technical terms *sufi*, *dervish* and *qalandar* to Chinese.

1345. ———, "IQBAL", *IQBAL REVIEW* 10, no. 1: April (1977): pp. 55-65.

1346. **MAHMOOD, Fayyaz**, "IQBAL'S ATTITUDE TOWARDS GOD", *IQBAL AS A THINKER - EIGHT ESSAYS BY EMINENT SCHOLARS*, Taj Muhammad KHAYAL (ed.), Lahore: Shaikh Muhammad Ashraf, 1944, pp. 269-82.
Essay on Iqbal's developing attitude towards God, as expressed in his poetical work (with references to Wordsworth and Tagore), and culminating in the statement: *In the development of 'khudi' lies the secret of Godhead.*
Includes quotes and citations from different poems. Reprinted (under the name of Sayyad Fayyaz MAHMOOD) in Khawaja Abdur RAHIM (ed.), *IQBAL, THE POET OF TOMORROW*, Lahore: Abdul Hameed Khan at Ferozsons Ltd., n.d., pp. 185[187]-199.

1347. **MAHMOUD, Abdul Qader**, "MOHAMMAD IQBAL AND MODERN RELIGIOUS THOUGHT", *IQBAL REVIEW* 8, no. 1: April (1967): pp. 109-18.
This article appeared in *AL-FIKR AL-MAASAR* (Contemporary Thought), a journal published by the U.A.R. Ministry of Culture and National Guidance, "on the occasion of the anniversary of the poet of humanity and philosopher of Islam". The English rendering was supplied by the Pakistan Embassy, Cairo.
Part of the contributions included in the IQBAL DAY IN CAIRO section.

1348. **MAHMUD, Ali**, mon., *NATION AND NATIONALITY*, Lahore: Student Services, 1976. 112 pp.

On Iqbal and Pan-Islamism, pp. 17-38; further also pp. 42, 100.

1349. **MAHMUD, Brelvi**, "NAZM-I-IQBAL", *OUR PAKISTAN*, Brelvi MAHMUD (mon. [?]), Lahore: Ferozsons, 1949, pp. 145.

1350. **MAHMUD, F. S.**, "THE MAN OF ACTION IN IQBAL'S POETRY", *IQBAL* 15, no. 1: July (1966): pp. 47-55.
Reproduced in SHEIKH, M. Saeed, *STUDIES IN IQBAL'S THOUGHT AND ART*, Lahore, 1972, pp. 133-143.

1351. **MAHROOF, M. M. M.**, "SIR SYED AHMAD KHAN AND IQBAL IN SRI LANKA", *IQBAL REVIEW* 34, no. 1: April (1993): pp. 1-19.
On Iqbal's and Syed Ahmad Khan's important influence in the intellectual history of the Muslims of Sri Lanka.

1352. **MAITRE, L.-C.**, *MOHAMMAD IQBAL*, Paris: Éditions Pierre Seghers, 1964.
Introduction with a selection of verses translated into French.
F.

1353. **MAITRE, Luce-Claude**, mon., *INTRODUCTION À LA PENSÉE D'IQBAL*, Collection "Autour Du Monde", Paris: Pierre Seghers, 1955. 93 pp.
English translation by M.A.M. DAR, Karachi 1961.
F.

1354. ———, mon., *INTRODUCTION TO THE THOUGHT OF IQBAL* (INTRODUCTION À LA PENSÉE D'IQBAL), Mulla Abdul Majeed DAR (tr. F/E), Karachi: Iqbal Academy / Feroz-sons, 1961/1962. 53 pp.
English translation of Maitre's INTRODUCTION À LA PENSÉE D'IQBAL (Paris, 1955) - qv.
Re-issued in Chicago: Kazi Publications, 1996, 55 pp.

1355. ———, "IQBAL: A GREAT HUMANIST", *IQBAL REVIEW* 2, no. 1: April (1961): pp. 22-34.

1356. ———, "THE PERSONALITY OF IQBAL'S MAN", *THE NATION* (Lahore), 9 November 1986.
Iqbal Day Supplement.

1357. ———, "UN GRAND HUMANISTE ORIENTAL, MOHAMMAD IQBAL", *ORIENT*

13, no. 1 (1960).
Translated as IQBAL, A GREAT HUMANIST, in *IQBAL REVIEW*, April 1961.
F.

1358. **MAJEED, Javed**, "PUTTING GOD IN HIS PLACE: BRADLEY, McTAGGART, AND MUHAMMAD IQBAL", *JOURNAL OF ISLAMIC STUDIES* 4, no. 2: July (1993): pp. 208-36.

1359. **MAJEED, Tariq**, "IQBAL'S PERCEPTION OF WORLD EVENTS", *THE PAKISTAN TIMES* (Islamabad / Lahore), 9 November 1986.

1360. **MAJID, A.**, "IQBAL: THE POET AND PHILOSOPHER", *PAKISTAN TIMES*, 1948, pp. 33-35.

1361. **MAJID, Abdul**, "IQBAL: DESTINY'S OWN CONFIDENT", *PAKISTAN TIMES*, 21 April 1966, p. 4.

1362. **MAJID, M. A.**, "ANECDOTES PERTAINING TO ALLAMA IQBAL", *PAKISTAN REVIEW* 14, no. 4: April (1966): pp. 13-15.

1363. ———, "IQBAL AND GIRAMI - ANECDOTES", *PAKISTAN REVIEW* 15, no. 4: April (1967): pp. 30-31.

1364. ———, "RANDOM RECITALS FROM IQBAL", *PAKISTAN REVIEW* 14, no. 4: April (1966): pp. 20-21.

1365. **MALAK, Shamim**, ed., *IQBAL SHINASI AIR MAHMAL*, Lahore: Bazm-i-Iqbal, 1988. 112+48 pp.
Essays on Iqbal, both in English and in Urdu (Urdu title page).

1366. **MALIK, Abdur Rauf**, ed., *THE WORK OF MUHAMMAD IQBAL: ARTICLES BY SOVIET SCHOLARS*, Lahore: People's Publishing House, 1983. 235 pp.
Table of Contents:
N. PRIGARINA, *The Ethic and the Poetic in Iqbal*, pp. 1-20; Y. CHELYSHEV, *Muhammad Iqbal - A World Class*, pp. 21-31; F. ROZOVSKY, *Muhammad Iqbal's Poem* The Con[...]nt of the Fellow Believers, pp. 32-46; S. PULATOVA, Book of Servitude *and Iqbal's View* [...]rt, pp. 47-63; L. POLONSKAYA, *Iqbal on the Revolution*, pp. 64-84; A. IONOVA, *Muhammad Iqbal and Social thought in South-East Asia*, pp. 85-97; I. ZOTOVA, *Interpretation of the Sufi Theme of 'Journey' in M. Iqbal's* Mathnawi The New

Garden of Mystery, pp. 98-117; M. STEPANYANTS, *The Concept of the Perfect Man in the Work of Jalal ad-Din Rumi and Muhammad Iqbal*, pp. 118-137; S. SHUKUROV, *Bedil and Iqbal*, pp. 138-152; A. GAFAROV, *Muhammad Iqbal and Persian=Language Poets in India and Pakistan*, pp. 153-165; A. SUVOROVA, *Iqbal's* Javid-nama *and Dante*, pp. 166-183; A. SUKHOTCHEV, *Nazir Ahmad and Muhammad Iqbal*, pp. 184-199; L. VASILYEVA, *Altaf Hussain Hali - Muhammad Iqbal's Predecessor*, pp. 200-218; A. SUKHOTCHEV, *Muhammad Iqbal as Seen by Progressive Writers in India and Pakistan*, pp. 219-235.

1367. **MALIK, Fateh Muhammad**, *IQBAL: THOUGHT AND PRAXIS*, Lahore: Bazm-i-Iqbal. 52 pp.
Reviewed by Mumtaz AHMAD in *IQBAL REVIEW* 28, no. 3: October-December (1987), pp. 113-114.

1368. **MALIK, G. R.**, "D.J. MATTHEWS, IQBAL: A SELECTION OF URDU VERSE", *THE MUSLIM WORLD BOOK REVIEW* 17, no. 4 (1997): pp. 48-49.

1369. ———, "THE NATURE OF EGO", *IQBAL REVIEW* (Karachi) 5, no. 3: October (1964): pp. 45-60.

1370. **MALIK, Ghulam Rasool**, mon., *IQBAL AND THE ENGLISH ROMANTICS*, New Delhi: Atlantic Publishers & Distributors Peacock Books, 1988. vi+165 pp.
A revision of the author's Ph.D.-thesis (University of Kashmir), including a chapter on 'The Poet as a Revolutionary'.

1371. **MALIK, Hafeez**, "AN APPRECIATION OF GURU NANAK IN IQBAL'S POETRY", *STUDIES IN ISLAM* (Delhi) 5, no. [?]: July (1968): pp. 146-60.

1372. ———, "THE IMPACT OF ECOLOGY ON IQBAL'S THOUGHT", *IQBAL REVIEW* (Karachi) 9, no. 3: October (1968): pp. 47-67.

1373. ———, ed., *IQBAL, POET-PHILOSOPHER OF PAKISTAN*, Various authors (mon.), Studies in Oriental Culture 7, New York / London: Columbia UP, 1971. xviii+441 pp.
An interesting study, with a bibliography (pp. 416-429) and the following contributions:
HAFEEZ MALIK & Lynda P. MALIK, The Life of the Poet-Philosopher
MUHAMMAD DAUD RAHBAR, Glimpses of the Man
JAVID IQBAL, Iqbal: my Father
HAFEEZ MALIK, The Man of Thought and the Man of Action
L.R. GORDON-POLONSKAYA, Ideology of Muslim Nationalism

RIFFAT HASSAN, The Development of Political Philosophy
Jan MAREK, Perceptions of International Politics
Freeland ABBOTT, View of Democracy and the West
B.A. DAR, Inspiration from the West
A.H. KAMALI, The Heritage of Islamic Thought
S. ALAM KHUNDMIRI, Conception of Time
N.P. ANIKEYEV, The Doctrine of Personality
ABU SAYEED NUR-UD-DIN, Attitude toward Sufism
M.T. STEPANYANTS, The Demise of Fatalism
A. SCHIMMEL, Mystic Impact of Hallaj
HADI HUSSAIN, Conception of Poetry and the Poet
S.A. VAHID, Iqbal and Western Poets
(Appendix:) Letters of Iqbal to Jinnah.

1374. ———, "IQBAL'S CONCEPTION OF EGO", *THE MUSLIM WORLD* (Hartford) 60, no. 2: April (1970): pp. 160-169.

1375. ———, "THE MAN OF THOUGHT AND THE MAN OF ACTION", *IQBAL: POET-PHILOSOPHER OF PAKISTAN*, Hafeez MALIK (ed.), New York: Columbia UP, 1971, pp. 69-107.

1376. ———, mon., *MOSLEM NATIONALISM IN INDIA AND PAKISTAN*, Washington: Public Affairs Press, 1962. vi+355 pp.
See esp. pp. 120, 136, 217, 239-245, 253, and pp. 227*f.* (on Iqbal and Pan-Islamism).

1377. **MALIK, Hafeez & Lynda P. MALIK**, "THE LIFE OF THE POET-PHILOSOPHER", *IQBAL: POET-PHILOSOPHER OF PAKISTAN*, Hafeez MALIK (ed.), New York / London: Columbia UP, 1971, pp. 3-35.

1378. **MALIK, Mohammad**, "IQBAL'S CONCEPT OF PAKISTAN", *THE PAKISTAN TIMES* (Rawalpindi), 9 November 1977.

1379. ———, "IQBAL'S ROLE IN MUSLIM REAWAKENING ", *THE NEWS* (Islamabad), 9 November 1993.

1380. **MALIK, Mohammad Jafar**, "IQBAL'S LECTURES - OBSCURITY CHARGE UNFOUNDED", *THE PAKISTAN TIMES* (Rawalpindi), 2 December 1977.

1381. ———, "IQBAL'S PHILOSOPHY OF SELF-DETERMINISM VERSUS GENETICS",

THE PAKISTAN TIMES (Rawalpindi), 21 April 1986.

1382. ————, "IQBAL'S POETIC THOUGHT IN THE LIGHT OF HIS LECTURES", *THE MUSLIM* (Islamabad), 9 November 1979.

1383. ————, "IQBAL'S THOUGHT ON RELIGIOUS EXPERIENCE", *THE MUSLIM*, 16 May 1980.

1384. **MALIK, Muhammad**, "ROLE OF MUHAMMAD IQBAL IN MUSLIM REAWAKENING", *ISLAM, POLTICS AND SOCIETY IN SOUTH ASIA*, Andre WINK (ed.), New Delhi, 1991.
Article on the nature and extent of Iqbal's influence and prestige in the contemporary Muslim world, with particular reference to his role in the renaissance of Muslim thought.

1385. **MALIK, Muhammad 'Aslam**, "IQBAL'S PERFECTIONISM", University of the Punjab, Dept. Philosophy, 1963. iv+38 pp.
Promoter: K.G. Sadiq.

1386. **MALIK, Muzaffar Hasan**, "BACKGROUND AND SIGNIFICANCE OF 'ALLAMAH'S PRESIDENTIAL ADDRESS OF 1930 ALLAHABAD SESSION OF THE MUSLIM LEAGUE", *IQBAL* (Lahore) 32, no. 3: July (1985): pp. 45-49.

1387. **MALIK, Nadeem Shafiq**, mon., *IQBAL AND THE ENGLISH PRESS OF PAKISTAN 1948-1971: A CHRONOLOGICAL LIST*, Lahore: Iqbal Academy, 1996. 47 pp.

1388. **MALLIK, Gurdial**, "THE POET IQBAL-INDIAN", *ARYAN PATH* 17, no. 4: April (1946): pp. 127.

1389. **MANAN, Syed Abdul**, mon., *IQBAL'S EDUCATIONAL PHILOSOPHY*, Dacca: Iqbal Academy, 1958

1390. **MANJU, M.**, *IQBAL*, Delhi: Azad Kitab Ghar, 1955.
Language unknown.

1391. **MANSHARDT, Clifford**, "IQBAL AND DEWEY", *THE CIVIL AND MILITARY GAZETTE* (Lahore), 21 April 1961, p. 4.

1392. **MANSURI, Syed Muhammad**, "SPEECH ON IQBAL", *IQBAL REVIEW* 9, no. 1: April

(1968): pp. 57-61.

1393. **MARCUS, Margaret**, "IQBAL: THE POET OF ISLAM", *VOICE OF ISLAM* (Karachi) 9, no. 7: April (1961): pp. 327-36.

1394. **MAREK, J.**, "MOHAMMED IQBAL, 'RECONSTRUIRE LA PENSÉE RELIGIEUSE DE L'ISLAM' (Book Review)", *ARCHIV ORIENTÁLNÍ* 25, no. 2 (1957): pp. 310-311.

1395. ———, "MUHAMMAD IQBALS SOZIALE IDEEN", *IQBAL UND EUROPA - VIER VORTRAGE*, J. C. BURGEL (ed.), Bern: P.Lang, 1980.
G.

1396. ———, tr. P/Cz, *POSELSTVI Z VYCHODU*, Praha: Ceskoslovenske Akademie Ved, 1960. 45 pp.
Czech translation of selected poems from (I) PAYAM-I-MASHRIQ, with illustrations. Further information (Series ?): Mala kniznice Orientu, Nakladatelstvi. Cz.

1397. **MAREK, Jan**, "THE DATE OF MUHAMMAD IQBAL'S BIRTH", *ARCHIV ORIENTÁLNÍ* (Nakladatelstvi Ceskoslovenske Akademie, Praha) 26, no. 4 (1958): pp. 617-20.

1398. ———, "MOHAMMAD IQBAL AND PABLO NERUDA", *IQBAL COMMEMORATIVE VOLUME*, Ali Sardar JAFRI & K.S. DUGGAL (eds.), New Delhi: All India Iqbal Centenary Celebrations Committee, 1977, pp. 301-8.

1399. ———, "MUHAMMAD IQBAL AND PABLO NERUDA", *THE PAKISTAN TIMES* (Rawalpindi), 2 December 1977.

1400. ———, "PERCEPTIONS OF INTERNATIONAL POLITICS", *IQBAL: POET-PHILOSOPHER OF PAKISTAN*, Hafeez MALIK (ed.), New Delhi / New York: Columbia UP, 1971.

1401. ———, mon., *PO SLEDAM SULTANOV I RADZHEJ* (In the Footsteps of Sultans and Rajas), Moskva: Nauka, 1987. 256 pp.
Translation from Czech into Russian.
R.

1402. ———, "SOCIALIST IDEAS IN THE POETRY OF MUHAMMAD IQBAL", *STUDIES*

IN ISLAM (New Delhi) 5, no. 2-3: April-July (1968): pp. 167-79.
Iqbal number.

1403. **MARICAR, N. M. S.**, "IQBAL: THE MUSLIM INTERNATIONAL POET", *ISLAMIC REVIEW AND ARAB AFFAIRS* 50, no. [?]: April (1962): pp. 28-31.

1404. **MARUF, Mohammad**, mon./ed., *CONTRIBUTIONS TO IQBAL'S THOUGHT*, Lahore: Islamic Book Service, 1977. xv+148 pp.

1405. ———, "IQBAL AS A POET", *IQBAL* 35, no. 1-2 (1988): pp. 1-11.
On the universal aspect of Iqbal's poetry.

1406. ———, mon., *IQBAL'S PHILOSOPHY OF RELIGION - A STUDY IN THE COGNITIVE VALUE OF RELIGIOUS EXPERIENCE*, Lahore: Islamic Book Service, 1977. 267 pp.
A study, dealing primarily with the concept of *religious experience as a source of knowledge*. To Iqbal, the author states, *religion is not merely a body of dogmas or rituals, but rather a form of experience which ensures a grasp of nothing short of a direct and immediate illumination of the very core of Reality*. The aim of the book is to reply, by way of an analysis of Iqbal's *grasping Reality through religious experience*, to the loss of prestige that both religion and metaphysics reportedly suffer from the scientific advancement in this Scientific Era of Mankind. The first part of the book deals with some of the various polemics which have been hurled on religion during the course of the last two centuries, from the naturalist standpoint, from psychoanalysis (Freud, Young), from medical materialism (Huxley), and from linguistics and philology (Russell). An appendix to these chapters contains a brief treatment of Bertrand Russell's critique of religion. The second and concluding part deals with the nature, characteristics and cognitive value of religious experience, and in particular with Iqbal's original addenda to this idea, i.e. (1) the distinction between prophetic and mystic consciousness, (2) the Quranic importance of other levels of experience, as subservient to the spiritual uplift of man, (3) the denial of the merger of the individual self into the Infinite Self of God as a condition for the attainment of religious knowledge (a concept taken from Sufism), and (4) the importance of thought in the attainment of religious knowledge. Appended to this, is a brief treatment of Iqbal's *View of Divine Knowledge*, in which the main discussion centres round the possibility or impossibility of God's fore-knowledge of particular events, and Iqbal's denial of any pre-destined events, in view of a God who can only know *potentialities* and/or *possibilities* - leaving room for man's freedom and creativity to act.
Includes a short bibliography, and an index.
Re-issued by Kazi Publications (Chicago, n.d.).

1407. **MARUF, Mohammed**, "DANA-I RAZ - BIOGRAPHY OF DR MUHAMMAD IQBAL

(URDU), COMPILED BY SYED NAZIR NIAZI, LAHORE: IQBAL ACADEMY PAKISTAN, 1979, 452 pp., foreword/review by DR MUHAMMAD BAQIR", *IQBAL REVIEW* 22, no. 1: April (1981): pp. 84-88.
Review.

1408. ———, "IQBAL ON DEMOCRACY", *IQBAL REVIEW* 18, no. 1: April (1977): pp. 67-76.
Short essay on Iqbal's interpretation of *Islamic democrary* vs. the Western type of democracy, which is based on a quantitative approach. The *Islamic democracy* on the other hand, is a *spiritual democracy*, built on a fundamental *Tawhid*-basis. Re-issued in [Various authors], *SELECTIONS FROM THE IQBAL REVIEW*, ed. Waheed Qureshi, Lahore 1983, pp. 215-224.

1409. ———, "IQBAL'S CONCEPT OF GOD: AN APPRAISAL", *RELIGIOUS STUDIES* (London) 19, no. 3 (1983): pp. 375.

1410. ———, "IQBAL'S THEORY OF INTELLECT", *IQBAL* 25, no. 3: July (1978): pp. 35-43.
Keeping in mind Iqbal's distinction between various senses of intellect, three kinds of reason/intellect can be distinguished: pure reason, practical reason, and divine intellect (*'aql-i burhani*).

1411. ———, "JAVID NAMA: A STUDY OF WORLD CIVILIZATIONS", *IQBAL REVIEW* 26, no. 3: October-November-December (1985): pp. 123-28.

1412. ———, "METAPHYSICAL IMPLICATIONS OF IQBAL'S EPISTEMIC VIEWS", *IQBAL REVIEW* 20, no. 3: October (1979): pp. 31-43.

1413. ———, "THE SPHERE OF MARS IN IQBAL'S 'JAVID NAMA'", *IQBAL* (Lahore) 36, no. 3 (1989): pp. 10-16.
Paper presented to the Second Allama Iqbal International Conference held in Lahore. Reprinted in *IQBAL REVIEW*, October-December 1985, pp. 123-28.

1414. **MARUF, Muhammad**, "IQBAL AND OUR PRESENT POLITICAL SITUATION", *THE PAKISTAN TIMES* (Rawalpindi), 9 November 1978.

1415. ———, "IQBAL, KANT, McTAGGART AND WARD", *IQBAL REVIEW* 24, no. 3: October (1983): pp. 67-79.

1416. ———, "IQBAL ON GOD'S KNOWLEDGE", *IQBAL* (Lahore) 22, no. 3: July (1975): pp. 55-60.
Reprinted in MARUF, M. (ed.), *CONTRIBUTIONS TO IQBAL'S THOUGHT*, Lahore: Islamic Book Service, 1977, pp. 17-25.

1417. ———, "IQBAL'S ANALYSIS OF RELIGIOUS KNOWLEDGE", *THE PAKISTAN TIMES* (Rawalpindi), 21 April 1980.

1418. ———, "IQBAL'S CRITICISM OF NIETZSCHE", *IQBAL REVIEW* 23, no. 3: October (1982): pp. 37-44.

1419. ———, "IQBAL'S EPISTEMIC VIEWS", *IQBAL REVIEW* 37, no. 3: October (1997): pp. 49-57.
Special issue on the Reconstruction of Religious Thought in Islam.

1420. ———, "IQBAL'S THEORY OF KNOWLEDGE", *IQBAL* 36, no. 2 (1989): pp. 1-9.

1421. ———, "IQBAL - THE UNIVERSALLY ACCLAIMED GENIUS", *THE PAKISTAN TIMES* (Rawalpindi), 9 November 1979.

1422. ———, "ISLAMIC THEORY OF KNOWLEDGE", *IQBAL REVIEW* 37, no. 1: April (1996): pp. 93-100.
The author explicitly bases his study on the Qur'an and Hadith, and includes some references to Iqbal, *who is considered a great interpreter of the Qur'an* (p. 99).

1423. ———, "A REPLY TO SOME CRITICS OF IQBAL", *IQBAL REVIEW* 36, no. 3: October (1995): pp. 117-25.
Reply to Ishrat Hasan Enver's "TESTING IQBAL'S PHILOSOPHICAL TEST OF THE REVELATIONS OF THE RELIGIOUS EXPERIENCE", in *IQBAL* 41, no. 3: July (1994), a reply to which had already appeared in *IQBALIAT*, July 1994.

1424. **MARUF, Muhammad & Latif Ahmad SHERWANI** , "RUMI'S IMPACT ON IQBAL'S RELIGIOUS THOUGHT by Dr. Nazir Qaiser", *IQBAL* 40, no. 4 (1993): pp. 97-102.

1425. **MARYAM JAMEELAH**, ed., *ISLAM IN THEORY AND PRACTICE*, 2nd ed., Lahore: Mohammad Yusuf Khan, 1973. 422 pp.
Iqbal messages: pp. 246-259.

1426. **MASHOOR, S. M. E.**, mon., *MUSLIM HEROES OF THE TWENTIETH CENTURY*, Lahore: Shaikh Muhammad Ashraf, 1978

1427. **MASOOD, M. Ilyas**, "HE PRAYED IN THIS MOSQUE", *THE CIVIL AND MILITARY GAZETTE* (Lahore), 21 April 1962, p. 3*ff.*

1428. **MASSE, Henri**, "ÉTUDE SUR IQBAL", *BULLETIN OF THE PAKISTAN EMBASSY* (Paris) 2, no. 8: 20 April (1954).
F.

1429. **MASUD, Jawed**, "HUSSAIN AND IQBAL'S MARD-I-MOMIN", *DAWN*, 21 April 1967, p. 9.

1430. **MASUD, Khawaja**, "ALLAMA IQBAL: HUMANIST PAR EXCELLENCE", *DAILY NEWS* (Islamabad), 9 November 1983.
Published also in *THE MUSLIM*, 21 April 1984.

1431. ————, "IQBAL ON LENIN", *THE MUSLIM* (Islamabad), 22 April 1984.

1432. ————, "IQBAL'S MESSAGE: CREATIVITY IS THE SUPREME GOAL", *THE MUSLIM* (Islamabad), 9 November 1984.

1433. ————, "IQBAL'S MESSAGE: RECTIVITY IN THE SUPREME GOOD", *THE MUSLIM* (Islamabad), 21 April 1982.

1434. ————, "IQBAL'S MISSION: DESTRUCTION OF FALSE GODS", *THE MUSLIM* (Islamabad), 21 April 1983.

1435. ————, "IQBAL THE ICONOCLAST", *THE MUSLIM* (Islamabad), 9 November 1985.

1436. **MASUD, Khwaja**, "IQBAL'S MESSAGE - CREATE A NEW WORLD", *THE MUSLIM* (Islamabad), 21 April 1986.

1437. ————, "IRANIAN REVOLUTION AND IQBAL", *THE MUSLIM* (Islamabad), 21 April 1980.

1438. **MASUD, Mohammad Khalid**, "IQBAL", *IQBAL REVIEW* 16, no. 1: April (1975): pp.

66-70.

1439. **MASUD, Muhammad K. & M. Mumtaz LIAQAT**, eds., *IQBAL THROUGHT WESTERN EYES*, Eliot (USA): Apt Books (Sterling Publishers Pvt Ltd), 1993. 320 pp.

1440. **MASUD, Muhammad Khalid**, "IQBAL'S LECTURE ON IJTIHAD", *IQBAL REVIEW* 19, no. 3: October (1978): pp. 1-9.
The *Lecture on Ijtihad* constitutes the sixth chapter in Iqbal's RECONSTRUCTION OF RELIGIOUS THOUGHT IN ISLAM, and was propably delivered at Hyderabad University, 1930, although there is only one indirect reference to this effect. This article starts with a discussion of the defintion given by Iqbal to the term *Ijtihad*, which according to the author was not the conventional one, but was rather inclined towards *a principle of movement in Islam*, which was subject to *relapse* causing momentaneous *immobility*, and then sets forth to provide a detailed exegesis of the lecture and the circumstances under which it was (or was never) delivered.
Re-issued in [Various authors], *SELECTIONS FROM THE IQBAL REVIEW*, ed. Waheen Qureshi, Lahore, 1983, pp. 109-117.

1441. ———, "MOHAMMAD IQBAL", *IQBAL REVIEW* 8, no. 1: April (1967): pp. 94-97.

1442. **MASUD, Muhammad Khalil**, mon., *IQBAL'S RECONSTRUCTION OF IJTIHAD*, Lahore: Iqbal Academy Pakistan, 1939.
Also published in Islamabad: Islamic Research Institute, 1995.
Contents: (1) the doctrine of Ijtihad, (2) development of the doctrine of Ijtihad in the sub-continent, (3) semantic development of the concept of Ijtihad, (4) Iqbal's lecture on Ijtihad, (5) dynamism vs. mechanism is Islam: Iqbal's reconstruction of the definition of Ijtihad, (6) law, state and 'Ulama': Iqbal's reconstruction of Ijma', (7) justice, law and reform: Iqbal's reconstruction of Qiyas, and (8) an analytical review of the criticism of Iqbal's lecture.

1443. **MATSIR, Mohammad**, "IQBAL DAY IN INDONESIA - SPEECH", *IQBAL REVIEW* 8, no. 1: April (1967): pp. 34-40.

1444. **MATTHEWS, D. J.**, tr. U/E, *IQBAL - A SELECTION OF THE URDU VERSE, TEXT AND TRANSLATION*, London: School of Oriental and African Studies, 1993. x+289 pp.
An English rendering of (44) selected Urdu poems, facing the original text, namely: Zuhd o Rindi, Tilfl-e Shirxwar, Tarana-e Hindi, Naya Shivala, Dagh, Kinara-e Ravi, Ek Sham, Siqilliya, Tarana-e Milli, Shikva, Valida Marhuma ki yad men, Khizr-e Rah, and Tulu'-e Islam (from BANG-E DARA); Ghazal no. 16(i), 2(ii), 4(ii), 7(ii), 15(ii), Masjid-e Qurtuba, Lenin, Saqinama, Javed ke Nam, Panjab ke Dahqan se, and Panjab ke Pirzadon se (from BAL-E JIBRAIL); La ilah ill' Allah, 'Ilm o 'Ishq, Tauhid, Hindi Musalman, Jihad,

Afrangzada, Taqdir, Aqvam-e Mashriq, Talib-e 'Ilm, Madrasa, Mard-e Firang, Parda, Azadi-e Nisvan, Pairis ki Masjid, Karl Marks ki Avaz, Manasab, Yurap aur Yahud, Bolshevik Rus, Jami'at-e Aqvam aur Mashriq, and Mussolini (from ZARB-E KALIM). Apart from a commentary, the book is completed by useful appendices : (1) Prosody, Metre and Genres of Verse, (2) Iqbal's Persian, (3) Index of proper names and technical terms, (4) Bibliography; and a Vocabulary of words which would normally be unknown to someone with a knowledge of basic modern Urdu. Also published by South Asia Books (Columbia, USA).

1445. ———, mon., *IQBAL AND HIS AGE*, 1994 or 1995 [?].

1446. **MAY, Harry S.**, "MARTIN BUBER AND MOHAMMED IQBAL: TWO POETS OF EAST AND WEST", *JUDAISM: A QUARTERLY JOURNAL OF JEWISH LIFE AND THOUGHT* (New York) 18, no. 2: Spring (1969): pp. 177-87.

1447. **MAY, L. S.**, "IQBAL AND HIS PHILOSOPHY", *IQBAL* [vol. ?], no. [?]: January (1958).
A general introduction into Iqbal's philosophy; reproduced in SHEIKH, M. Saeed (ed.): *STUDIES IN IQBAL'S THOUGHT AND ART*, Lahore: Bazm-i-Iqbal, 1972, pp. 1-30.

1448. ———, "IQBAL'S DOCTRINE OF KHUDI", *IQBAL* 18, no. 3: January-March (1971): pp. 55-64.

1449. ———, "IQBAL'S SOCIO-ECONOMIC REFORM IDEAS AND IDEALS", *IQBAL* 24, no. 4: October (1977): pp. 9-44.

1450. ———, "IQBAL, THE HUMANIST. IN MEMORIAM", *IQBAL REVIEW* 18, no. 4: January (1978): pp. 15-23.

1451. ———, "THE SCIENTIFIC FOUNDATION OF DR MUHAMMAD IQBAL'S DOCTRINE OF CHANGE", *IQBAL* (Lahore) 24, no. 1: January (1977): pp. 1-40.

1452. ———, "A UNIQUE ASPECT OF IQBAL'S EVOLUTION THEORY", *IQBAL REVIEW* (Karachi) 16, no. 3: October (1975): pp. 26-31.
From the anthropological side of his evolution theory Iqbal appears anti-Darwinian in sofar as the latter's materialist and non-spiritual theories are concerned.

1453. **MAY, Lini S.**, mon., *THE EVOLUTION OF INDO-MUSLIM THOUGHT AFTER 1857*, Lahore: Sh. Muhammad Ashraf, 1970. vii+488 pp.

On Iqbal, see pp. 213-231.

1454. ———, "IQBAL", *IQBAL* 6, no. 3: January (1958): pp. 28-60.

1455. ———, mon., *IQBAL: HIS LIFE AND TIMES*, Lahore: Shaikh Muhammad Ashraf, 1974. iv+347 pp.
Two parts: (I) The Life and Times of Iqbal, and (II) Iqbal's Views on Life and Man, in which Iqbal is presented as a modernist and liberal reformist; the book further includes an index and a bibliography.

1456. **McCARTHY, Edward**, "IQBAL AS A POET AND PHILOSOPHER", *IQBAL REVIEW* 2, no. 3: October (1961): pp. 18-23.
Short essay, awarded with a prize by the Pakistan Embassy of Khartoum. Re-issued in [Various authors], *SELECTIONS FROM THE IQBAL REVIEW*, ed. Waheed Qureshi, Lahore, 1983, pp. 280-285.

1457. **McD., S.**, "IQBAL, Muhammad", *THE NEW ENCYCLOPAEDIA BRITANNICA*, 15th ed., Chicago: Encyclopaedia Britannica, 1974, Vol. 9, pp. 820-821.

1458. **McDONOUGH, Sheila**, mon., *THE AUTHORITY OF THE PAST: A STUDY OF THREE MUSLIM MODERNISTS*, Studies in Religion 1, Chambersburg, Pa.: American Academy of Religion, 1970. 56 pp.
A comparative study of Muhammad Iqbal, Ghulam Ahmad Parviz and Sayyid Ahmad Khan.

1459. ———, "THE MOSQUE OF CORDOVA: VISION OR PERISH", *IQBAL REVIEW* 8, no. 1: April (1967): pp. 46-51.
Iqbal Day in Washington, address.

1460. **MEENAI, S. A.**, "IQBAL'S LETTERS TO RAGHIB", *DAWN* (Karachi), 9 November 1984.

1461. **MEER, Hamid**, "EAGLES OF IQBAL", *THE MUSLIM* (Islamabad), 9 November 1984.

1462. **MEMON, Muhammad Umar**, "MALIK, (Ed.), "IQBAL: POET-PHILOSOPHER OF PAKISTAN" (Book Review)", *JOURNAL OF ASIAN STUDIES* 31, no. 4: August (1972): pp. 982.

1463. **MENON. K.P.S.**, "THE MESSAGE OF IQBAL", *INDIAN REVIEW* 26, (1925): pp. 506-

9.
Variant : monograph of the same title published in Madras, 1979.

1464. **METZEMAEKERS, L. A. V. M. & VOETEN Bert**, tr. P/D, *DE ROEP VAN DE KARAVAN: MOEHAMMED IQBAL, DICHTER VAN PAKISTAN*, BEGUM LIAQUAT ALI KHAN (intr.), 's Gravenhage, 1956.
Dutch translation of selected poems.
D.

1465. **MEYEROVITCH, Eva**, "IQBAL, POÈTE ET PHILOSOPHE", *BULLETIN OF THE PAKISTAN EMBASSY* 2, no. 8: 20 April (1954).
Published also in ÉGLISE VIVANTE 6 (n.d.), p. 218.
F.

1466. ———, tr. E/F, *RECONSTRUIRE LA PENSÉE RELIGIEUSE DE L'ISLAM* (THE RECONSTRUCTION OF RELIGIOUS THOUGHT IN ISLAM), L. MASSIGNON (intr.), Paris: Éditions Adrien Maisonneuve, 1955.
French translation of (I) THE RECONSTRUCTION OF RELIGIOUS THOUGHT IN ISLAM, with an introduction by L. Massignon. An English translation of Massignon's Introduction is published as a part of S.A. Vahid's *GLIMPSES OF IQBAL*, Karachi, 1974 - qv.
F.

1467. **MEYEROVITCH, Eva & Mohammad ACHENA**, tr. P/F, *MESSAGE DE L'ORIENT* (PAYAM-I-MASHRIQ), Muhammad IQBAL (mon.), Collection Unesco D'Oeuvres Représentatives / Traductions De Textes Persans Publiées Sous Le Patronage De L'Association Guillaume Budé, Paris: Les Belles Lettres, 1956. 194 pp.
French prose translation of (I) PAYAM-I-MASHRIQ.
F.

1468. **MEYEROVITCH, Eva & Mohammad MOKRI**, tr. P/F, *LE LIVRE DE L'ÉTERNITE* (JAVID-NAMAH), Muhammad IQBAL (mon.), Collection Spiritualités Vivantes, Série Islam / Collection Unesco D'Oeuvres Représentatives, Série Persane, Paris: Éditions Albin Michel, 1962. 178 pp.
French prose translation of (I) JAVID-NAMAH.
F.

1469. **MINAI, I. A.**, "IQBAL: THE REALIST", *ILLUSTRATED WEEKLY OF PAKISTAN*, 18

June 1950, pp. 9-27.

1470. **MIR, Abdul Aziz**, "GUIDE, FRIEND, AND PHILOSOPHY", *THE MUSLIM* (Islamabad), 21 April 1980.

1471. ———, "IQBAL AND KASHMIR", *THE PAKISTAN TIMES* (Rawalpindi), 21 April 1981.

1472. ———, "IQBAL'S CONTRIBUTION TO KASHMIR AWAKENING", *THE PAKISTAN TIMES* (Lahore), 9 November 1992.

1473. ———, "THE POET AND KASHMIR", *PAKISTAN TIMES*, 21 April 1961, p. 6.

1474. ———, "THE POET AND KASHMIR", *IQBAL: A CRITICAL STUDY*, Misbah-ul-Haq SIDDIQUI (ed.), Lahore: Farhan Publishers, 1977, pp. 1-8.
On Iqbal's devotion to the land of his birth, his visit to Kashmir, and his involvement with the *All-India Kashmir Committee* (1931).

1475. **MIR, Muhammad Safdar**, mon., *IQBAL THE PROGRESSIVE*, Lahore: Book Traders, 1990

1476. **MIR, Mustansir**, "TRANSLATIONS FROM IQBAL: SOLITUDE, THE POET, THE NIGHT AND THE POET, THE HOURI AND THE POET", *IQBAL REVIEW* 36, no. 1: April (1995): pp. 21*ff.*
Annotated translation into English by M. Mir of Iqbal's poems "Solitude" (TANHAI, from PAYAM-I MASHRIQ), "The Poet" and "The Night and the Poet" (from BANG-I DARA), and "The Houri and the Poet" (from PAYAM-I MASHRIQ).

1477. ———, "TRANSLATIONS FROM IQBAL: THE SAGES, MUSLIM", *IQBAL REVIEW* 36, no. 3: October (1995): pp. 69-80.
In "the Sages" a study is presented of three verses by Iqbal on Locke, Kant, and Bergson: PAYAM-I MASHRIQ; in "Muslim" (a poem from BANG-I DARA) is discussed the future as seen in the mirror of the past.

1478. ———, "WORDPLAY AND IRONY IN IQBAL'S POETRY", *JOURNAL OF ISLAMIC STUDIES* 3, no. 1: January (1992): pp. 72-93.

1479. **MIR, Safdar**, "SUFISM AS METAPHYSICS OF ISLAM", *THE MUSLIM* (Islamabad),

21 April 1980.

1480. **MIRSHAKAR, M.**, tr./intr., *IKBOL SH'ERHO*, Stalinabad, 1958.
Tadjik translation of selected poems, with an introduction.
Tadj.

1481. **MIRZA, Anis**, "AGHA'S DOCUMENTARY OF IDEAS OF IQBAL", *DAWN* (Karachi), 21 April 1981.

1482. **MIRZA, Jalaluddin**, "SOME REMINISCENCES", *PAKISTAN TIMES* (Lahore), 21 April 1956, p. 6.

1483. **MIRZA, Manzoor**, "SOCIO-ECONOMIC IMPLICATIONS OF KHUDI", *THE PAKISTAN TIMES* (Rawalpindi / Lahore), 9 November 1985.

1484. **MIRZA, Muhammad Munawwar**, "UMMAH VS. NATIONALISM", *THE PAKISTAN TIMES* (Rawalpindi / Lahore), 9 November 1985.

1485. **MIRZA, Munawwar Muhammed**, mon., *IQBAL AND QURANIC WISDOM*, New Delhi, 1987

1486. **MISRA, Gopal Chandra**, "A COMPARATIVE STUDY OF GOPABANDHU AND IQBAL", *INDIAN LITERATURE* (New Delhi) 22, no. 1 (1979): pp. 122-35.

1487. **MOGHNI, Abdul**, mon., *IQBAL THE POET*, Lahore: Bazm-i-Iqbal, 1992

1488. **MOHAMMAD, A. Ali**, "IQBAL'S CONCEPT OF WORSHIP", *THE PAKISTAN TIMES* (Rawalpindi), 21 April 1985.

1489. **MOHAMMAD, Ali**, "IQBAL: A HERO AMONG PHILOSOPHERS", *THE PAKISTAN TIMES* (Rawalpindi), 9 November 1984.

1490. **MOHAMMAD ALI** (Prime Minister), "WHAT THEN IS TO BE DONE BY MUSLIMS, IQBAL GAVE YOU THE RIGHT ANSWER", *TIMES OF KARACHI*, 21 April 1956, p. 2.

1491. **MOHAMMAD, Anwar Ali**, "IQBAL'S RELIGIOSE IDEEN", University of Marburg, 1954.

Ph.D. diss.

1492. **MOHAMMAD IQBAL, M. A.**, "DOCTRINE OF ABSOLUTE UNITY", *THE CIVIL AND MILITARY GAZETTE* (Lahore), 21 April 1960, p. 1.
Iqbal Day Suppl.

1493. **MOHAMMAD JAFAR, Malik**, "CONCEPT OF RELIGIOUS EXPERIENCE", *THE MUSLIM* (Islamabad), 21 April 1980.

1494. ———, "THE FALL OF MAN: IQBAL'S VIEW OF THE LEGEND", *PAKISTAN TIMES*, 21 April 1975.

1495. ———, "A FOREWORD TO IQBAL'S METAPHYSICS", *PAKISTAN TIMES*, 17 August 1977, p. 4.

1496. ———, "IQBAL ON RELIGIOUS EXPERIENCE", *PAKISTAN TIMES*, 9 and 30 September 1977, pp. 2, and 1 resp.
Two parts.

1497. **MOHAMMAD NASIR**, "IQBAL DID NOT WANT PAKISTAN TO BE A THEOCRATIC STATE", *THE CIVIL AND MILITARY GAZETTE* (Lahore), 26 July 1953, pp. 1-8.

1498. ———, "IQBAL WAS AGAINST THEOCRACY", *THE CIVIL AND MILITARY GAZETTE* (Lahore), 21 April 1954.

1499. **MOHAMMAD RIAZ**, "IQBAL'S IDEA OF TAUHID", *IQBAL* 21, no. 1: January-March (1974): pp. 41-50.

1500. **MOHAMMAD SAID, Hakim**, ed., *MAIN CURRENTS OF CONTEMPORARY THOUGHT IN PAKISTAN, DISCOURSES DELIVERED AT SHAM-I-HAMDARD: Vol. I (1965-1969), Vol. II (1970-1972)*, Vol. 1-2, Karachi: Hamdard Academy, 1973. 572 pp. and 496 pp. resp.
Vol. I: Iqbal as a lawyer, pp. 43, 49; Iqbal poetry, pp. 64; Iqbal dreams, p. 113; Iqbal and Pakistan, p. 121; Iqbal and nationalism, pp. 124, 224; Iqbal as thinker of Pakistan, p. 332; Iqbal as poet, pp. 332, 367, 369, 490; Iqbal and philosophy of Islam, pp. 372-373, etc.
Vol. II: Iqbal addresses, essays and lectures, pp. 180; Iqbal and nationalism, pp. 195-196, 304, 308, 315, 322, 350, 353, 356; Iqbal Day, p. 365; about Iqbal, p. 383; Iqbal and Pan-

Islamism, p. 385; Iqbal as poet, p. 386; Iqbal and Western poets, pp. 388-389, etc.

1501. **MOHAN, Ramesh**, "IQBAL AS POET AND PHILOSOPHER", *IQBAL REVIEW* (Hyderabad) 1, no. [?]: July-October (1978): pp. 31-36.
Text of the speech delivered by Prof. Ramesh Mohan, Director of Central Institute of English & Foreign Languages, Hyderabad, on the occasion of Inaugural function of Iqbal Centenary Celebrations held on 9th November 1977, at Exhibition Grounds, Hyderabad.

1502. **MOIZUDDIN, M.**, "FACETS OF IQBAL'S CONCEPT OF NATIONALISM", *IQBAL REVIEW* (Karachi) 16, no. 3: October (1975): pp. 18-25.
Iqbal's concept of nationalism is not only a blue-print for the national integration of Pakistan, but also a message for Islamic brotherhood.

1503. ———, "IQBAL AND HUSAIN'S MARTYRDOM", *THE PAKISTAN TIMES* (Rawalpindi), 8 November 1981.

1504. ———, "IQBAL AND ISLAMIC SOCIAL JUSTICE", *THE PAKISTAN TIMES* (Rawalpindi), 9 November 1984.

1505. ———, "IQBAL AND MUSLIM UNITY", *DAWN*, 11 November 1975, p. 7.
Also in *THE PAKISTAN TIMES*, 30 January 1977.

1506. ———, "IQBAL AND MUSLIM UNIVERSALISM", *THE PAKISTAN TIMES* (Rawalpindi), 21 April 1981.
Reprinted in *THE PAKISTAN TIMES* (Rawalpindi), 9 November 1983.

1507. ———, "IQBAL AND QUAID-I-AZAM", *IQBAL REVIEW* 17, no. 3: October (1976): pp. 65-74.

1508. ———, "IQBAL AND THE QUAID-I-AZAM - THE SEER AND THE REALIST", *PAPERS PRESENTED AT THE INTERNATIONAL CONGRESS ON QUAID-I-AZAM (19-25 DECEMBER 1976) (4 Vols.)*, Various authors (mon.), Islamabad: Quaid-i-Azam University, 1976, pp. 105-15 (vol. 2).
Short essay on the Quaid and Iqbal, *two great personalities with different psyches, diametrically opposite in views, and unlike in approach to life (...) but having become so close to achieve a common goal, that their ideas and ideals became absolutely identical*; mainly with reference to Iqbal's *Allahabad Address*.
Also published in *IQBAL REVIEW* 18, no. 4: January (1978), pp. 133-141.

1509. ——, "IQBAL, MUSLIM UNITY AND SUMMIT CONFERENCE", *IQBAL REVIEW* 16, no. 1: April (1975): pp. 1-5.

1510. ——, "IQBAL'S AND QUAID-I-AZAM'S ROLES IN ACHIEVEMENT OF PAKISTAN", *DAWN* (Karachi), 9 November 1977.

1511. ——, "IQBAL'S CONCEPTION OF HISTORY", *IQBAL REVIEW* 21, no. 3: October (1980): pp. 21-25.
Published also in *THE PAKISTAN TIMES*, 21 April 1980.

1512. ——, "IQBAL'S MESSAGE TO THE WEST", *THE PAKISTAN TIMES* (Rawalpindi), 9 November 1977.
Reprinted in *THE PAKISTAN TIMES*, 21 April 1983.

1513. **MOIZUDDIN, Muhammad**, mon., *ALLAMA IQBAL*, Lahore: Iqbal Academy, 1981. 193 pp.

1514. ——, "IQBAL AND MAN'S ROLE IN THE WORLD", *THE PAKISTAN TIMES* (Rawalpindi), 21 April 1984.

1515. ——, mon., *THE WORLD OF IQBAL: A COLLECTION OF PAPERS BY DR. M. MOIZUDDIN*, Mohammad Ashraf DAR (ed.), Lahore: Iqbal Academy, 1982. 132 pp.

1516. **MONNOT, M.**, "IQBAL, M. "LA MÉTAPHYSIQUE EN PERSE" (Book Review)", *REVUE DE L'HISTOIRE DES RELIGIONS* 199, (1982): pp. 207-8.
F.

1517. **MOOKARJEE, H. C.**, "(THE) POETICAL WORLD OF IQBAL", *TIMES OF KARACHI*, 15 May 1955.
Text of the speech delivered on Iqbal Day (21 April 1955) at the Pakistan Deputy High Commission, Calcutta.

1518. **MOOSVI, Z. H.**, "IQBAL AND THE ARAB WORLD", *ILLUSTRATED WEEKLY OF PAKISTAN* 4, no. [?]: 20 April (1952): pp. 32-34.

1519. **MOREAU, Talaat**, "ELEMENTARY IMAGERY IN THE POETRY OF ELIOT AND IQBAL: A BACHELARDIAN APPROACH", Catholic University of America, 1991.

1520. **MORTAZAVI, Djamchid & Eva VITRAY-MEYEROVITCH**, tr. P/F, *LES SECRETS DU SOI, SUIVI PAR LES MYSTÈRES DU NON-MOI* (ASRAR-I-KHUDI and RUMUZ-I-BEKHUDI), Muhammad IQBAL (mon.), Spiritualités Vivantes, Série Islam, ed. Marc DE SMEDT, Paris: Editions Albin Michel, 1989. 181 pp.
French verse translation of (I) ASRAR-I-KHUDI and (I) RUMUZ-I-BEKHUDI, with a short introduction by Eva de Vitray-Meyerovitch.
F.

1521. **MUHAMMAB IQBAL**, "IQBAL'S CONCEPT OF AGRO-FISCAL SET UP", *PAKISTAN TIMES*, 29 July 1977, p. 1.

1522. **MUHAMMAD ALI, Choudhri**, mon., *IQBAL'S VISION OF ISLAM'S INTERNATIONAL MISSION IN THE INDUSTRIAL ERA*, Lahore: Dept. of Islamiyat, Punajb University, 1952. 27 pp.
A paper read on Iqbal Day, 21 April 1952, in the Punjab University, Senate Hall, Lahore.

1523. **MUHAMMAD ALI, Maulana**, mon., *THE AHMADIYYAH MOVEMENT*, Lahore: Ahmadiyyah Anjuman Ishaat Islam, 1973. xv+382 pp.
On Iqbal and Qadianism, and Iqbal speeches and statements, pp. 346-368.

1524. **MUHAMMAD AYUB (President of Pakistan)**, "MESSAGE ON IQBAL DAY", *DAWN*, 22 April 1960.

1525. **MUHAMMAD, Jan**, "IMPORTANCE OF ALLAMAH IQBAL'S WORK IN THE PROPAGATION OF ISLAM IN THE WESTERN WORLD", *IQBAL REVIEW* 22, no. 3: October (1981): pp. 43-52.
Paper read on the 1981 Anniversary of Iqbal's death (21 April).

1526. **MUHAMMAD, K.**, "MESSAGE OF IQBAL", *UNIVERSITY ORIENTAL COLLEGE MAGAZINE* (Trivandrum) 2, no. 4 (1946).

1527. **MUHAR, P. S.**, "POLITICAL PHILOSOPHY OF SIR MUHAMMAD IQBAL", *INDIAN JOURNAL OF POLITICAL SCIENCE* (Aligarh) 18, no. 3-4: July-December (1957): pp. 175-90.

1528. **MUNADI, Sayyid Azeemuddin**, tr., *PAYAM-E-MASHRIQ*, Karachi: Iqbal Academy, n.d.

1529. ———, tr., *ZABOOR-I-AJAM*, Karachi: Iqbal Academy, 1960

1530. **MUNAWWAR, Mohammad**, "IQBAL AND MAN'S SELF-EVASION", *THE PAKISTAN TIMES* (Rawalpindi), 21 April 1984.

1531. ———, ed., *IQBAL CENTENARY PAPERS - PRESENTED AT THE INTERNATIONAL CONGRESS ON ALLAMA MUHAMMAD IQBAL 2-8 DECEMBER 1977*, Lahore: University of Punjab, Department of Iqbal Studies, 1977. 2 vols.
Variant date: 1982.

1532. ———, "IQBAL ON DEVELOPMENT OF PERSONALITY", *IQBAL REVIEW* 32, no. 3: October (1991): pp. 63-85.
Paper delivered at the Military Staff and Command College, Quetta, May 1989.

1533. **MUNAWWAR, Muhammad**, "ALLAMA IQBAL AND THE YOUNG GENERATION", *IQBAL REVIEW* 27, no. 1: April-September (1986): pp. 63-80.

1534. ———, "ALLAMA IQBAL - REFUSING TO BE CALLED A POET", *IQBAL REVIEW* 29, no. 1: April (1988): pp. 209-35.
Essay explaining Iqbal's well-known refusal to be called *[just] a poet*, with biographical anecdotes and quotes from different works of Iqbal's.

1535. ———, "ALLAMA IQBAL'S LIFE AND ACHIEVEMENTS", *THE PAKISTAN TIMES* (Rawalpindi), 9 November 1983.

1536. ———, "ALLAMA IQBAL'S TEST OF FAITH", *THE PAKISTAN TIMES* (Rawalpindi), 8 November 1981.

1537. ———, "A DIALOGUE IN PARADISE", *PAKISTAN REVIEW* 14, no. 4: April (1966): pp. 22-25.

1538. ———, mon., *DIMENSIONS OF IQBAL*, Lahore: Iqbal Academy, 1986.
Reprint available in 1996.

1539. ———, mon., *DIMENSIONS OF PAKISTAN MOVEMENT*, Lahore: Institute of Islamic Culture, 1987

1540. ———, "HARMONY IN IQBAL'S THOUGHT", *IQBAL* 18, no. 1: July (1969): pp. 46-53.
Iqbal's idea of balance or harmony is no other than that of compulsion accepted by the

component parts of an organic whole (p. 52).

1541. ———, "IQBAL: A PREACHER OF PURPOSEFUL LIFE", *THE PAKISTAN TIMES* (Rawalpindi), 9 November 1984.

1542. ———, mon., *IQBAL AND QURANIC WISDOM*, A. K. BROHI (intr.), 1st ed., Lahore: Iqbal Academy, 1981. 156 pp.
A collection of 9 essays by Prof. Munawwar, presented and introduced by K.A. Brohi:
(1) HARMONY IN IQBAL'S THOUGHT: On order and harmony in Quranic philosophy and Iqbal's works. 'Harmony', says Munawwar, 'with its implied dialectical bipolarity of the opposites, seems to be the very quintessence of Iqbal's thought.
(2) IQBAL'S IDEA OF FAQR: The authors differentiates between two different concepts of Quranic *faqr* (poverty), the first being a *state of destitution* (in which sense the Quranic utterance of the Prophet's: *Poverty borders on infidelity*), and the second being *faqr* by choice, or a deliberate attitude of detachment. In Iqbal's work, it is the second *faqr* that we come across. 'Iqbal ranks the men of *faqr* far higher than the *Mullas* (theologians) and the *Sufis* (theosophists), for the true *faqirs* are men of vision and light, who open our eyes to new possibilities of human experience and new dimensions of human existence'.
(3) IQBAL ON QURANIC CONCEPT OF HISTORY: From Toynbee's concept of history, the author comes to the Quranic view of *tarikh*, in which the historian, by the act of writing history, himself becomes part of history. 'For Iqbal', he concludes, 'the whole history of mankind is a perpetual strife between soul and matter, wherein *Islam* symbolises all that is good for man, i.e. the soul-dominion'.
(4) IQBAL ON LIFE AFTER DEATH: Following a brief account of the treatment of death, after-life and resurrection in some of the main religious traditions (Egypt, Hinduism, Buddhism), different aspects of after-life in Muslim belief are discussed: resurrection, immortality, Day of Judgment and others, and exemplified by quotes from Iqbal's works, and in particular from BANG-I-DARA.
(5) IQBAL'S IDEA OF TAQDIR (DESTINY): An explanation of Iqbal's criticism of the traditional concept of *taqdir* (destiny, predestination), 'a notion current among almost all religious communities'. Iqbal warns the public against apparent fatalism, and has shown that '*taqdir* means that an infinite number of possibilities and destinies exist, and we should choose our destinies sincerely and create in ourselves capabilities which our chosen destiny demands.'
(6) IQBAL ON ADVANCEMENT SANS MORALS: On Iqbal's criticism of socio-political advancement without moral implications, and the necessary factor of *idealism* in social reforms.
(7) IQBAL AND REALISATION OF SELF: On the realisation of *khudi* (Self) within the guidance of the Divine Law. 'Without the Divine Law, man cannot grow into a self-conscious and well-balanced whole'.
(8) IQBAL ON MAN'S QUEST FOR THE OBJECT WORTHY OF HUMAN

WORSHIP: A short explanation of man's eternal feeling that he lacks something within him without which he is not complete, and his quest for the fulfillment of this defect.
(9) IQBAL ON MAN'S ACCOUNTABILITY: How, according to Iqbal, man is always free to accept or reject the one perfect code offered by the Quran, and this freedom of choice, along with the accountability for the choice made, is essential for the unification of all human beings.
With an index.
The introduction by A.K.Brohi is not included in the first edition (Iqbal Academy, 1981), but appears in editions by Islamic Book Foundation (Lahore 1981) and Noor Publishing House (New Delhi 1987). The 2nd edition was published in 1985, the 3rd one in 1992.

1543. ———, "IQBAL AND THE WORDS OF THE QUR'AN", *IQBAL REVIEW* 26, no. 3: October-November-December (1985): pp. 83-88.

1544. ———, "IQBAL AND THE WORLD OF QUR'AN", *IQBAL REVIEW* 25, no. 1: April (1984): pp. 77-101.

1545. ———, "IQBAL - EPOCH-MAKING POET-PHILOSOPHER", *IQBAL REVIEW* 25, no. 3: October (1984): pp. 107-27.

1546. ———, "IQBAL - MAN OF FAITH AND VISION", *IQBAL REVIEW* 23, no. 3: October (1982): pp. 1-33.

1547. ———, "IQBAL ON ADVANCEMENT WITHOUT MORALS", *THE PAKISTAN TIMES* (Rawallpindi), 21 April 1981.

1548. ———, "IQBAL ON BELIEF IN TAWHID FOR GROWTH OF SELF", *IQBAL* 36, no. 1 (1989): pp. 1-15.

1549. ———, "IQBAL ON FINALITY OF PROPHETHOOD", *IQBAL* (Lahore) 29, no. 3-4: July-October (1982): pp. 1-15.

1550. ———, "IQBAL ON MAN'S METAPHORICAL DEATH", *IQBAL REVIEW* 24, no. 3: October (1983): pp. 99-118.

1551. ———, "IQBAL ON MAN'S RESPECT FOR MAN", *THE PAKISTAN TIMES* (Rawalpindi), 21 April 1982.

1552. ———, "IQBAL ON MAN'S SEARCH FOR SELF", *THE PAKISTAN TIMES*

(Rawalpindi), 21 April 1983.

1553. ———, "IQBAL ON QUR'ANIC CONCEPT OF HISTORY", *IQBAL REVIEW* 20, no.
3: October (1979): pp. 11-30.
Short essay on Iqbal as an advocate for historic research and studies in history, with
reference to the traditional Muslim historians and their views on Quranic historical
concepts.
Re-issued in [Various authors], *SELECTIONS FROM THE IQBAL REVIEW*, ed. Waheed
Qureshi, Lahore, 1983, pp. 381-400.

1554. ———, "IQBAL'S HOPES FOR UMMAH'S FUTURE", *THE PAKISTAN TIMES*
(Rawalpindi), 9 November 1982.

1555. ———, "IQBAL'S IDEA OF DEMOCRACY", *IQBAL REVIEW* 27, no. 1: April-May-
June (1985): pp. 101-18.

1556. ———, "IQBAL'S IDEA OF FAQR", *IQBAL* 19, no. 3: January (1972): pp. 68-81.

1557. ———, mon., *IQBAL, THE POET-PHILOSOPHER OF ISLAM*, Khalid M. ISHAQUE
(intr.), Lahore: Iqbal Academy Pakistan, 1985. 182 pp.
A collection of 7 essays on different aspects of Iqbal's concepts and use of quranic
elements in his thought and works, and a interview.
This book offers critical studies of Iqbal from purely Islamic (and Arabic) viewpoints.
(1) IMPACT OF ARABIC LITERATURE ON IQBAL'S POETRY: The author analyses
the Arabic element in the poems of Iqbal, and the impact of Arabic literature on his works
and thoughts in general. After all, it is said, 'Iqbal himself vehemently claimed that the spirit
of his poetry and thought was Arabic, rather than Indian or Persian.' The aim of this article
is clearly to de-Indianise Iqbal, and bring him back to realm of a pure Arabic tradition.
(2) PROPHET IBRAHIM AS A SYMBOL IN IQBAL'S POETRY: A scrupulous analysis
of the quranic episodes on Ibrahim, and how Iqbal has treated these as symbols in his
works. In particular, Ibrahim's gradual *insight* into the oneness of God, and the dilemma on
occasion of the offering of Isma'il's life are being discussed.
(3) IQBAL - MAN OF FAITH AND VISION: Quotes from Iqbal's poetry illustrate his
deep faith in islam, his realisation that the Muslim *Ummah* in his days was seriously being
put to test, and his vision and hope for a restoration of *Ummah*, also on a political level,
with the genesis of Pakistan as an independent nation.
(4) IQBAL ON *UMMAH*'S BRIGHT FUTURE: An argument against interpreting the
concept of *Ummah* as mere *nationalism* in Western terms. *Ummah*, according to Iqbal,
must be seen quite differently, i.e. as a feeling of being united by *religion*, rather than by
race, tongue or territory. Iqbal prophesised and saw a renaissance of *Ummah*, and

proclaimed it to be a guarantee for a *bright future*.

(5) IQBAL ON MAN'S RESPECT FOR MAN: A portrait of the *tragedy of the modern world* ('vast learning arising out of its principles of observation and discovery, but without any sympathy and understanding of the needs of human beings') reflects Iqbal's dual view on modern society, i.e. admiration for science and philosophy on the hand, and great disappointment in moral and ethical standards on the other. A renewal of man's link with God, and a re-establishment of the Path of the Prophet are affered as a way out of this 'tragedy'.

(6) IQBAL ON FINALITY OF PROPHETHOOD: A short exposition of Iqbal's stands on the definite oneness of God and the finality of prophethood, brings the author to Iqbals' New-Year Day message, issued on All-India Radio, january 1st 1938. This message is a kind of an Iqbal Testament, epitomising what Iqbal thought of man's development in respect to science and other fields of knowledge, without due reference to human values. Similarly, it contains his views on all sorts of 'isms' of his day, and the cruelties perpetrated in their name, the cure being man's respect for man. The text of Iqbal's message is reproduced in full.

(7) IQBAL ON KNOWLEDGE VIS-A-VIS EDUCATION: Another essay on Iqbal's dual feelings towards the development of knowledge and the lack of moral and ethical values therein. 'The separation of heart and intellect', says the author, 'is typically Western, and can be answered by a renaissance of Islam.'

Followed by an interview with Hafeez Sahib (born 1900, author of *SHAHNAMAH-I ISLAM* and of Pakistan's national anthem) discussing his meetings with Iqbal. This interview was originally published in Urdu, in the weekly *CHATAN* (Iqbal Number 1963), entitled "ABUL ATHAR IQBAL KE HUDUR MEM", and was translated into English by R.A. Khan.

With a bibliography and an index.

1558. ———, "MAN'S QUEST FOR THE SUPERIOR", *THE PAKISTAN TIMES* (Rawalpindi), 21 April 1980.

1559. ———, "PROCEEDINGS OF A ONE DAY SEMINAR HELD IN THE UNIVERSITY OF BIRMINGHAM, UNDER THE AUSPICES OF IQBAL ACADEMY (U.K.) ON IQBAL AND MYSTICISM", *IQBAL REVIEW / IQBALIAT* (Lahore) 29, no. 3: October-December (1988).

A special issue of the *IQBAL REVIEW*, edited by Muhammad MUNAWWAR, assisted by Muhammad Suheyl UMAR (assoc.ed.), Waheed ISJRAT (assoc.ed.), Ahmad JAVID (asst.) and M. Ashgar NIAZI (asst.), with contributions by several authors, an introduction (pages 3-9) and an afterword (pages 121-126).

Contributions (*abstract* qv, except articels marked *,which do not directly deal with M. Iqbal):

(1) S.A. Durrani: IQBAL AND MYSTICISM (Opening adress),

(2) Dr. Muhammad Ajmal: IQBAL AND MYSTICISM,
(3) Bishop Michael J.Nazir Ali: IQBAL AND RUMI,
(4) Dr. David Kerr: MUHAMMAD IQBAL ON RELIGION,
(5) Dr. Khalid Alavi: IQBAL AND SUFISM,
(6) * Dr. Erica Hunter: ISAAC OF NINEVEH: THE PERSIAN MYSTIC,
(7) * Revd. Peter Berry: CHRISTIAN MYSTICAL TRADITION,
(8) A.B.A. Bawhab: HENRI BERGSON AND IQBAL,
(9) Christopher Lamb: IQBAL AND INTERFAITH DIALOGUE,
(10) * H.E. Shahayar Khan: IQBAL AND MYSTICISM (Closing Adress).

1560. ———, "PROPHET IBRAHIM AS A SYMBOL IN IQBAL'S POETRY", *PAKISTAN REVIEW* (Lahore) 19, no. 4 (1971): pp. 4-7.
Special Iqbal Number.

1561. ———, "THE QURAN AND MAN'S SPIRITUAL EVOLUTION", *IQBAL REVIEW* 33, no. 3: October (1992): pp. 1-16.
On the Quranic concept of brotherhood and Iqbal's "spiritual democracy".

1562. **MURSHAD** (Justice), "IQBAL BROUGHT ABOUT MORAL, INTELLECTUAL REVOLUTION AMONG MUSLIMS", *MORNING NEWS*, 22 April 1966, p. 12.

1563. **MURSHED, Syed Mahbub**, "IQBAL, SOME ANNIVERSARY MUSINGS", *IQBAL: A CRITICAL STUDY*, Misbah-ul-Haq SIDDIQUI (ed.), Lahore: Farhan Publishers, 1977, pp. 58-66.
An Iqbal Day Address by the former Chief of Justice in East Pakistan (year unknown).

1564. **MURSHEED, S. M.**, "ALLAMA IQBAL", *PAKISTAN REVIEW* 14, no. 8: August (1966): pp. 6-7.

1565. **MURSHID, S. M.**, "ADDRESS, IQBAL DAY AT LAHORE", *IQBAL REVIEW* 8, no. 1: April (1967): pp. 1-12.

1566. ———, "THE PEBBLED SHORE", *IQBAL, THE POET OF TOMORROW*, Khawaja Abdur RAHIM (ed.), Lahore: Abdul Hameed Khan at Ferozsons Ltd., n.d., pp. 127[131]-145.
Paper read as presidential address on 21 April 1966; divided into seven sections, entitled (I) The Golden Links, (II) The Pebbled Shore, (III) Lyric Poems, (IV) His Philosophy, (V) Political Thought, (VI) The Man, and (VII) And the Bells Toll.

1567. **MURSHID, S. M. Justice**, "IQBAL DAY AT LAHORE - ADDRESS", *IQBAL REVIEW* 8, no. 1: April (1967): pp. 1-12.

1568. **MURTADAWI, Jamshid**, ed., *LES SECRETS DU SOI* (ASRAR-I KHUDI), Muhammad IQBAL (mon.), [place ?], 1989
F.

1569. **MUSTAFA, A. T. M.**, "IQBAL'S INTERPRETATION OF LIFE", *IQBAL: A CRITICAL STUDY*, Misbah-ul-Haq SIDDIQUI (ed.), Lahore: Farhan Publishers, 1977, pp. 87-101.
A short survey of Iqbal's view on the concept of Life, an entity *with a meaning and a purpose, which he discovered in the system of values, in the regulative principles of life, and in the institutional doctrines of a self-compact, self-contained monistic philosophy: Islam.*
Article taken from *THE PAKISTAN TIMES*, Iqbal Day Supplement 1964.

1570. ———, "THE NATURE OF ULTIMATE REALITY AND TAUHID AS A PRINCIPLE OF INTEGRATION", *IQBAL, THE POET OF TOMORROW*, Khawaja Abdur RAHIM (ed.), Lahore: Abdul Hameed Khan at Ferozsons Ltd., n.d., pp. 77[81]-91.
Paper read as presidential address on 21 April 1963, on the scientific and philosophical background of *the painful opposition between the meaning and purpose of life and the spiritual and moral bankruptcy that plague the whole human scene* [and] *has the tragic effect of depriving man's efforts of organic wholeness and spiritual and moral vitality* (p. 90). To this problem the author concludes (p. 91): *The voice of the Philosopher-Poet of the twentieth Century may yet prove to be the clarion call [...] for the rediscovery of the meaning and purpose of life - the clarion call of Islam -* [which] *may yet be the voice of hope for mankind.*

1571. **MUSTAFA, Ghulam**, mon., *KALAM-E-IQBAL*, Dacca: Iqbal Academy, 1957

1572. **MUSTAFA, Kavi Ghulam**, "THE IDEA OF GOD AND UNIVERSE IN TAGORE AND IQBAL", *IQBAL REVIEW* 1, no. 3: October (1960): pp. 26-34.
Whereas the terminus station of Rabindranath Tagore's journey of life is God, that of Iqbal is Eternity (p. 34).

1573. ———, "IQBAL AND RABINDRA NATH TAGORE", *IQBAL, THE POET OF TOMORROW*, Khawaja Abdur RAHIM (ed.), Lahore: Abdul Hameed Khan at Ferozsons Ltd., n.d., pp. 251[253]-260.
According to the footnote on p. 253, the author, who is regarded as the leader of the group of Bengali poets who have been deeply influenced by the philosophy and religious ardour of Iqbal, read this paper on 21 April 1963 at Lahore.

The paper deals with the conception of life as revealed in the poetry of Iqbal and Tagore. The latter was, of course, inspired by the teachings of the Vedanta or Upanishads, and his conception of life was, accordingly, *perfectly in tune with the Pantheistic Idealism of Plato* (p. 253), *bordering, at places, on Paganism* (p. 258). On the other hand, *against this Idealistic-Pantheistic-Vedantic-Sufistic background of under-estimation of life, Iqbal boldly proclaims the individuality and immortality of the Soul and its never-ending progress and development in our after-life* (p. 258). In conclusion, *Rabindranath's view of life is [...] out-dated or medieval in character. To Iqbal man is the viceregent of God, and he will abide forever with God; but to Rabindranath man is a sad weary pilgrim bound for the valley of eternal death* (p. 260).

1574. ———, "IQBAL ON THE CONCEPT OF IDEAL STATE", *IQBAL REVIEW* 3, no. 1: April (1962): pp. 17-24.
On the failure of Capitalism, Socialism, Communism, etc. to unite the world, and the answer to this ideal provided by Islam as maintained by Iqbal.

1575. ———, "IQBAL: THE PHILOSOPHER POET", *IQBAL REVIEW* 1, no. 1: April (1960): pp. 43-53.
The author emphasizes the overriding importance of Iqbal as a poet, as against his philosophical activity.

1576. **MUTAHHARI, Murtaza**, mon., *IQBAL: MANIFESTATION OF THE ISLAMIC SPIRIT*, Laleh BAKHTIAR (tr. P/E), Chicago: Abjad Book Designers & Builders, 1993. 130 pp. Translated from Persian.

1577. **MUZAFFAR ALI, Syed**, "ISHFAQ INITIATES A NEW DEBATE ON IQBAL", *IQBAL* 39-40, no. 1: October and 4: January (1992-1993): pp. 97-100.

1578. **NADUSHAN, M. A. Eslami**, "THE IDEAL MAN OF THE ORIENT IN IQBAL'S POETRY", *IQBAL COMMEMORATIVE VOLUME*, Ali Sardar JAFRI & K.S. DUGGAL (eds.), New Delhi: All India Iqbal Centenary Celebrations Committee, 1977, pp. 191-93.
On fervour and self-realisation as the two factors of Iqbal's poetic thinking about the ideal man.

1579. **NADWI, Abul Hassan Ali**, mon., *BUYUK ISLAM SAIRI DR. MUHAMMAD IKBAL, YAZAN EBU'L-HASAN EL-NEDEVI, TERCUME VE TAHSIYE EDEN ALI ULVI KURUCU* (GLORY OF IQBAL - NUQUSH-I-IQBAL), Ali Ulvi KURUCU (tr. U/T or E/T), Ankara, 1957.
Turkish translation of Nadwi's classic *GLORY OF IQBAL* - qv.

T.

1580. ———, mon., *GLORY OF IQBAL - NUQUSH-I-IQBAL* (NUQUSH-I-IQBAL), Muhammad Asif KIDWAI (tr. U/E), 3rd ed., Lucknow: Academy of Islamic Research & Publications, 1973. 220 pp.
Variant name: NADVI, Syed Abul Hasan Ali.
Reprinted in Lahore: Progressive Books, 1977; Luknow: Islamic Research and Publications, 1979; and London: Kazi Publications, 1981.

1581. **NAFICY, Said**, "MYSTICISM IN IQBAL'S POETRY", *IQBAL REVIEW* 1, no. 1: April (1960): pp. 5-9.

1582. **NAIM, C. M.**, "A BIBLIOGRAPHY OF ENGLISH SOURCES FOR THE URDU LANGUAGE AND LITERATURE", *LITERATURE EAST AND WEST* 7, no. 1: Spring (1963): pp. 10-18.

1583. ———, ed., *IQBAL, JINNAH AND PAKISTAN: THE VISION AND REALITY*, Manzooruddin AHMED (co-ed.), Foreign and Comparative Studies, South Asian Series 5, Syracuse, New York: Maxwell Scholl of Citizenship and Public Affairs (Syracuse University), 1979. 214 pp.
A collection of papers presented at a conference organized by the Muslim Studies Subcommittee of the Committee on Southern Asian Studies, University of Chicago, April 1977. Includes bibliographical references. Re-issued by Vanguard (Lahore, 1984).

1584. ———, "THE 'PSEUDO-DRAMATIC' POEMS OF IQBAL", *IQBAL REVIEW* 20, no. 1: April (1979): pp. 1-12.
The author feels a lack of writings on the aesthetic values of Iqbal's poems, whereas as a writer *on* aesthetics Iqbal has been given due credit. In this short essay Naim prefers not to deal with Iqbal's *ghazal's* or conventional lyrics, but rather with his *nazm*-literature. In labeling these poems *pseudo-dramatic* the author wishes to emphasise the fact that they are *devoid of bare narrative - as is proper for true drama - and yet they lack genuine action*. He further subdivides the poems into three categories, viz. (1) *poems of disputation*, (2) *poems of inquiry*, and (3) *poems of witnessing*. Includes English renderings   of   selected   poems.
Reprinted from *JOURNAL OF SOUTH ASIAN AND MIDDLE EASTERN STUDIES* 1, no. 2 (1977), pp. 58-67. Re-issued in [Various authors], *SELECTIONS FROM THE IQBAL REVIEW*, ed. Waheed Qureshi, Lahore, 1983, pp. 467-478.

1585. **NAIM, Muhammad**, "IQBAL WAS AGAINST THEOCRACY", *THE CIVIL AND*

MILITARY GAZETTE (Lahore), 21 April 1954, pp. 1, 2.

1586. **NAIM-UR-REHMAN**, "ASRAR-I-KHUDI OR THE SECRETS OF THE SELF", *INDIAN REVIEW* (Madras) 22, (1921): pp. 156-58.
Variant name: RAHMAN, M.N.

1587. **NAIMUDDIN, Sayyid**, "THE CONCEPT OF LOVE IN RUMI AND IQBAL", *ISLAMIC CULTURE* 42, no. 4: October (1968): pp. 6-7 or 185-210 [?].

1588. ———, "EVIL AND FREE WILL IN RUMI AND IQBAL", *ISLAMIC CULTURE* 46, no. 3: July (1972): pp. 227-34.

1589. ———, "THE IDEAL MAN IN RUMI AND IQBAL", *ISLAMIC CULTURE* 45, no. 2: April (1971): pp. 81-94.

1590. **NALLINO, Maria**, "RECENTE ECO INDO-PERSIANA DELLA *DIVINA COMMEDIA*: MOHAMMAD IQBAL", *ORIENTE MODERNO* (Roma) 12, (1932): pp. 210-223.
Variant name: VALLINO, M.; variant page(s): 610-622.
Translation of an article published in the *MUSLIM REVIEW* (Lahore) 1, June (1932), pp. 183-200.

1591. **NAMAZI, M. M.**, mon., *IQBAL*, Calcutta, 1962

1592. **NAMUS, M. Shuja**, mon., *A DISCUSSION ON IQBAL'S PHILOSOPHY OF LIFE*, Lahore: Lion Press, 1948. v+163/164 pp.
A general introduction on Iqbal's place in Muslim literature and thought, in which he is placed within the threesome *Ghalib, Hali, Iqbal* as *those responsible for moulding into shape the poetic thought of Muslim India as we find it today*, is followed by an analysis of first ASRAR-I-KHUDI, and then RUMUZ-I-BEKHUDI, with quotations from both works and their English equivalents. From there, the author tries to define Iqbal's concepts of *khudi* and *bekhudi*, and then broadens these within the framework of Quranic spirituality.
The book closes with a discussion on the *factors which develop a Free Nation*, and with this provides the (newly created) state of Pakistan with a general outline on its way to *developed nationhood*.
Dr. Shuja Namus was a personal acquaintance of Iqbal's; she figures on one of both photographs included (1932), the other one shows Iqbal saying prayers at the Cordoba Mosque; also included are facsimiles of two handwritten letters by Iqbal to the author.
Parts of this book originally appeared in *THE OASIS* (Bahawalpur, Sadiq Egerton

College), Iqbal Number, April (1941), pp. 1-87.
Variant name: NAMUS, M.A.

1593. **NAMUS, Muhammad Shuja**, "ANALYSIS OF PHILOSOPHY", *OASIS* (Bahawalpur),
April 1941, pp. 865-67.

1594. **NANDY, B. C.**, "IQBAL'S HUMANISM", *IQBAL REVIEW* 4, no. 1: April (1963): pp.
32-34.

1595. **NAQVI, S. A.**, "CONCEPT OF ART IN IQBAL", *PAKISTAN REVIEW* 19, no. 4 (1971):
pp. 31-34.
Special Iqbal Number.

1596. ———, "IQBAL AS A FULL-BLOODED OPTIMIST", *PAKISTAN REVIEW* (Lahore)
15, no. 4 (1967): pp. 32-34.

1597. **NAQVI, S. A. H.**, "THE CONCEPT OF IQBAL'S ART", *PERSPECTIVE* 4, no. 10:
April (1971): pp. 23-26.

1598. **NAQVI, S. H.**, "ALLAMA IQBAL", *ILLUSTRATED WEEKLY OF PAKISTAN*, 22 April
1951, p. 23.

1599. **NAQVI, Tahir Hussain**, "IQBAL AND THE MUSLIM COMMUNITY", *THE MUSLIM*
(Islamabad), 20 April 1984.

1600. **NARANG, Gopi Chand**, "THE SOUND STRUCTURE OF IQBAL'S URDU
POETRY", *IQBAL COMMEMORATIVE VOLUME* , Ali Sardar JAFRI and K.S.
DUGGAL (eds.), New Delhi: All India Iqbal Centenary Celebrations Committee, 1977, pp.
202-6.
Analysis of the sound structure of Iqbal's poetic art, *through which, coupled with some
other features, he casts a spell, and which, because of the high degree of his inspiration
and his special semantic urge, has acquired a mysteriously unique quality* (p. 202).

1601. ———, "SOUND STRUCTURE OF IQBAL'S URDU POETRY", *THE PAKISTAN
TIMES* (Rawalpindi / Lahore), 9 November 1977.

1602. **NASEEMA, Tahira**, "THE METAPHYSICAL CONCEPT OF EVOLUTION IN
MISKAWAIH, RUMI AND IQBAL", University of the Punjab, Dept. of Philosophy,
1967. vi+128 pp.

Variant name: NASREEN, Tahira.
M.A. Philosophy; promoter: K.G. Sadiq. Contents: (1) Introduction, (2) What is evolution, (3) Ibn-i-Miskawaih, (4) Jalal-ud-Din Rumi, (5) Dr. Muhammad Iqbal, and Conclusion.

1603. **NASIM, K. B.**, "IQBAL: A FASCINATION WITH IRAN", *THE FRONTIER POST* (Peshawar), 6 May 1988.

1604. **NASIR, Muhammad**, "IQBAL ON THE SEPARATION OF RELIGION AND STATE", *ISLAMIC REVIEW* 12, no. 7 (1953): pp. 5-8.

1605. **NASREEN, 'Azra**, "IQBAL'S DEFENCE OF RELIGION", University of the Punjab, Dept. of Philosophy, 1968. vi+95 pp.
Contents: (1) Introduction, (2) Iqbal's concept of religion, (3) Modern challenges, and (4) Iqbal's defence of religion.
Promoters: C.A. Qadir, K.G. Sadiq, and Abdul Khaliq.

1606. **NATH, Kidar**, "POET-PHILOSOPHER WHO STIRRED RESURGENT INDIA", *THE TIMES OF INDIA* (Bombay), 22 April 1962, p. 8.
Two letters criticising the article by G.R. Kanwal and S. Iqbal Mehdi (in *THE TIMES OF INDIA*, 27 May 1962, p. 8).

1607. **NATSIR, Muhammad**, "SPEECH, IQBAL DAY IN INDONESIA", *IQBAL REVIEW* 8, no. 1: October (1967): pp. 34-40.

1608. **NAZIR ALI, Michael J.**, "IQBAL AND RUMI", *IQBAL REVIEW / IQBALIAT* (Lahore) 29, no. 3: October-December (1988): pp. 31-46.
Text of a lecture delivered at the one day Seminar on Iqbal and Mysticism (University of Birmingham, 7 November 1987), on the influence of Islamic philosophical and theological traditions on Iqbal, viz. (1) formal theology or *Kalam*, (2) Arabic and Persian *Dar-ul-Islam* philosophy, and (3) *Tassawuf* or mysticism, in the works of a.o. Rumi, Hallaj, Al-Jili, Wahid Mahmud and Al-Ghazzali.

1609. **NAZIR, M.**, "THE IMPACT OF RUMI UPON THE RELIGIOUS THOUGHT OF IQBAL", University of the Punjab, 475 pp.
Ph.D. dissertation; promoter: C.A. Qadir.
Contents: Introduction; *Part I, Religious life - Psychological aspect*: (1) The human Self, (2) The destiny of the Self, (3) Values, (4) Disvalues; *Part II, Religious life - Metaphysical aspect*: (1) Stages of religious life, (2) Religious symbolism, (3) The physical world, (4) God; *Part III, Religious life - The apex*: (1) The perfect man, (2) Muhammad - the most

perfect man; Conclusion, and Short Abstract.

1610. **NAZIR, Muhammad Aslam**, "BERGSON AND IQBAL", University of the Punjab, 111 pp.
M.A. Philosophy; promoter: K.G. Sadiq.
Contents: Introduction, (1) Evolution, (2) Time, (3) Intuition, (4) Ideal man; Conclusion and Abstract.

1611. **NAZIR, Muhammad 'Aslam**, "IQBAL AND BERGSON", University of the Punjab, Dept. Philosophy, 1959. ix+111 pp.
Promoter: K.G. Sadiq.

1612. **NEHRU, Jawaharlal**, "A REPLY TO SIR MUHAMMAD IQBAL", *RECENT ESSAYS AND WRITINGS*, Jawaharlal NEHRU (mon.), Allahabad: Kitabistan, 1934, pp. 60-69.

1613. **NELSON, Richard L.**, "HAFEEZ MALIK, IQBAL: POET-PHILOSOPHER OF PAKISTAN (Book Review)", *PHILOSOPHY EAST AND WEST* 22, no. 4: October (1972): pp. 479.

1614. **NEUFELDT, Ronald W.**, "ISLAM AND INDIA: THE VIEWS OF MUHAMMAD IQBAL", *MUSLIM WORLD* 71, no. 3-4: July-October (1981): pp. 178-91.
Variant name: NEWFELDT.
Hitherto Iqbal's views on India and Hinduism have been neglected in favour of his consideration of the West and because of the emergence of Pakistan. The examination of his writings do not substantiate the view that Iqbal was anti-Hindu and antinationalistic.

1615. **NIAZ, A. Q.**, tr., *IQBAL'S JAVID NAMA*, Muhammad IQBAL (mon.), Lahore: Iqbal Academy, 1984.
Versified translation of (I) JAVID NAMAH.

1616. ———, tr. U/E, *IQBAL'S KHIZR-E-RAAH, TRANSLATED INTO ENGLISH*, IQBAL (mon.), Lahore: Friends in Counsel, 1952. 40 pp.

1617. ———, tr. E, *IQBAL'S SUPERMAN*, Muhammad IQBAL (mon.), Lahore: Ferozsons, 1960. 122 pp.
Variant names: NIAZ, Safee A. and NAIB, A.Q.
English translation of six of Iqbal's poems.

1618. ———, tr., *KHIZR-I-RAAH: PRESENTATION IN ENGLISH*, Muhammad IQBAL

(mon.), Lahore: Friends in Council Publishers, 1952. 40 pp.
English translation of (I) KHIZR-I RAH.

1619. **NIAZ, M. H.**, "IQBAL AND THE DYNAMISM OF ACTION", *DAWN*, 21 April 1973, p. 3.

1620. **NIAZI, Kausar**, mon., *IQBAL AND THE THIRD WORLD*, Lahore: Shaikh Muhammad Ashraf, 1977. 40 pp.
A short treatise on Iqbal's opinions about developing countries.
Re-issued by Kazi Publications (Chicago 1988).

1621. **NIAZI, Shaheer**, "DIOTIMA, TAHIRA AND IQBAL", *IQBAL REVIEW* 15, no. 3: October (1974): pp. 22-29.
On Iqbal's verses referring to the Qurratul-Ain Tahira of Iran and the Diotima of Greece, whom he regarded as the symbols of evil and wisdom respectively (while the name of Sharafun-Nisa figures as a symbol of piety).

1622. ———, "IQBAL AND OUTER SPACE", *IQBAL REVIEW* 23, no. 3: October (1982): pp. 45-64.
An analysis of Iqbal's portrayal of Martians in JAVED NAMAH (with an elaborate prose translation) brings the author to the questions (1) whether or not extra-terrestial life is possible, (2) and if there is, whether or not extra-terrestials have ever visited Earth, (3) and if not, whether or not such an event would be possible. The author concludes with the statement that *we have no alternative but to regard Iqbal's work as a science-fiction at the moment, which may prove its own worth along with the scientific progress and shocking discoveries in the future.*
Re-issued in [Various authors], *SELECTIONS FROM THE IQBAL REVIEW*, ed. Waheed Qureshi, Lahore, 1983, pp. 499-518.

1623. ———, "IQBAL ON MARX", *IQBAL REVIEW* 24, no. 3: October (1983): pp. 35-43.

1624. **NIAZI, Syed Nazir**, "CONVERSATION WITH IQBAL", *MUHAMMAD IQBAL - POET AND PHILOSOPHER, A COLLECTION OF TRANSLATIONS, ESSAYS AND OTHER ARTICLES, PRESENTED BY THE PAKISTAN-GERMAN FORUM*, Karachi: Din Mohammad Press / German-Pakistan Forum, 1960.

1625. ———, "CONVERSATIONS WITH IQBAL", *MUHAMMAD IQBAL UND DIE DREI REICHE DES GEISTES*, Wolfgang KOEHLER (ed.), Hamburg: Deutsch-Pakistanisches Forum, 1977, pp. 67-76.

German summary: GESPRÄCHE MIT IQBAL, pp. 77-78.
E-G.

1626. ———, mon., *IQBAL ON NIETZSCHE*, Karachi: Iqbal Academy, [n.d.].
Based on Iqbal's notes on the German philosopher; it contradicts the presumed inspiration of Iqbal from Nietzsche.

1627. ———, mon., *TALKS WITH IQBAL*, Karachi: Iqbal Academy, n.d.
A collection of the author's talks with Iqbal, covering various subjects in the social, political and religious sphere.

1628. **NICHOLSON, R. A.**, "IQBAL'S MESSAGE OF THE EAST", *ISLAMICA* (Leipzig) 1, no. 1 (1925): pp. 112-24.
Re-issued in *CRESCENT* (Islamia College Magazine, Lahore) 20, no. (8)1: March-April (1926), pp. 9-18; and *IQBAL REVIEW* 13, no. 3: October (1972), pp. 6-16.

1629. ———, "THE SECRETS OF THE SELF: A MUSLEM POET'S INTERPRETATION OF VITALISM", *THE QUEST* (London) 11, no. 4: July (1920): pp. 433-50.
Also in RIFFAT HASSAN, ed., *THE SWORD AND THE SCEPTRE*, Lahore: Iqbal Academy, 1977.

1630. ———, tr. P/E, *SECRETS OF THE SELF: A PHILOSOPHICAL POEM* (ASRAR-I-KHUDI), London: MacMillan, 1920. 147 pp.
English verse translation of (I) ASRAR-I-KHUDI, with an introduction and notes; including Iqbal's Foreword to *Muraqqa-i-Chughtai* (1928), Note sent to R.A. Nicholson. Also published in Lahore: Sh. Mohammad Ashraf, 1944, 1950, 1955, 1960, 1961, 1964, 1975.

1631. ———, tr. P/E, *SECRETS OF THE SELF (ASRAR-I-KHUDI): A PHILOSOPHICAL POEM BY MUHAMMAD IQBAL, TRANSLATED INTO ENGLISH WITH INTRODUCTION AND NOTES* (ASRAR-I-KHUDI), Lahore: Farhan Publishers, 1977. xx+87 pp.
Revised edition of Nicholson's English verse translation of (I) ASRAR-I-KUDI, first published by MacMillan (London, 1920) - qv. The 1944 issue contains xxxi+148 pp. and was published at Lahore: Sheikh Muhammad Ashraf.

1632. ———, "SUMMARY OF THE PAPER ON THE *ASRAR-I-KHUDI*", *JOURNAL OF THE ROYAL ASIATIC SOCIETY* 1920, no. [?]: January: pp. 142-43.

1633. **NICHOLSON, Reynold Alleyne**, mon., *STUDIES IN ISLAMIC MYSTICISM*, Lahore: Hijra, 1983

1634. **NICHOLSON, Reynold & Zulfiqar KHAN**, mon./tr. P/E/tr. U/E, *VOICE FROM THE EAST: A COMMENTARY ON SOME POEMS OF IQBAL*, Lahore: Iqbal Academy, 1982. Translation of selected poems from Persian and Urdu, with commentaries.

1635. **NIYAZI, Ghani**, "DISSERVICE TO IQBAL", *DAWN*, 7 January 1960.

1636. **NIZAM-UD-DIN, Khwaja**, "THE POETIC NOTE-BOOK OF MULLAZADE ZAIGHAM OF LAULAB", *IQBAL* 22, no. 1: January (1975): pp. 71-78. An English rendering of the last portion of Iqbal's ARMUGHAN-I HIJAZ.

1637. **NIZAMI, K. A.**, "THREE UNPUBLISHED LETTERS OF IQBAL", *STUDIES IN ISLAM* 5, no. 2-3: April-July (1968): pp. 188-92. English translation of (I) 3 original letters.

1638. **NIZAMUDDIN, Kh.**, "TO GOD", *IQBAL* 24, no. 1: January (1977): pp. 77-88. English rendering of the first part of ARMUGHAN-I HIJAZ, entitled HUDUR-I HAQQ ("In the Presence of God"), which contains about forty-one *ruba'iyat*, divided into eleven sections, each of which has a different number of quatrains addressed to God.

1639. **NIZAMUDDUN, Khwajah**, "FOR THE COMPANIONS OF THE WAY", *IQBAL REVIEW* 17, no. 1: April (1976): pp. 57-65. English rendering of the last Persian part of ARMUGHAN-I HIJAZ.

1640. **NN**, "ALLAMA MOHAMMAD IQBAL (1877-1938)", *FIRST IQBAL CENTENARY - INTERNATIONAL CONGRESS, UNIVERSITY OF THE PUNJAB, Lahore, December 2nd-8th 1977 (Leaflet)*, Lahore: University of the Punjab, 1977, pp. 1-4. General introduction.

1641. **NOMAN, Muhammad**, mon., *OUR STRUGGLE*, Karachi: Pakistan Publications, 1954. Contains the paper "DR. MUHAMMAD IQBAL", pp. 44-45; photo and brief bibliography; as well as "IQBAL: PRESIDENTIAL ADDRESS", pp. 1-18, and "IQBAL: LETTERS TO JINNAH", pp. 19-32.

1642. **NOMANI, Abdul Qadeer**, "CLASSICAL THOUGHT, THE QURAN, AND IQBAL", *THE PAKISTAN TIMES* (RAWALPINDI), 21 April 1982.

1643. ———, "FAMILY BACKGROUND AND EARLY LIFE", *THE PAKISTAN TIMES* (Rawalpindi), 9 November 1982.

1644. ———, "IQBAL ON NATIONALISM", *THE PAKISTAN TIMES* (Rawalpindi), 21 April 1983.

1645. ———, "IQBAL ON NATURE OF INDIAN POLITY", *THE PAKISTAN TIMES* (Rawalpindi), 9 November 1984.

1646. ———, "IQBAL'S ROLE IN PAKISTAN MOVEMENT", *THE PAKISTAN TIMES* (Rawalpindi), 8 November 1981.

1647. ———, "IQBAL'S THEORY OF KNOWLEDGE", *THE PAKISTAN TIMES* (Rawalpindi), 9 November 1983.

1648. ———, "QUAID-I-AZAM AND ALLAMA IQBAL", *THE PAKISTAN TIMES* (Rawalpindi), 21 April 1985.

1649. **NORDGULEN, George**, "THEISTIC ONTOLOGY IN RADHAKRISHNAN AND IQBAL", *IQBAL REVIEW* 25, no. 3: October (1984): pp. 51-65.

1650. **NORTHROP, S. C.**, "IQBAL THROUGH U.S. EYES", *DAWN* (Karachi), 11 May 1952, sec. Magazine Section, p. 12.
Also published as a chapter in the author's book *WORLD AND U.S. FOREIGN POLICY*, New York: Macmillan, [n.d.].

1651. **NUR AHMAD, Syed**, "ALLAHABAD ADDRESS IN HISTORICAL PERSPECTIVE", *PAKISTAN TIMES*, 21 April 1969, pp. 1-2.

1652. ———, "WHEN ALLAMA AND QUAID WERE IN OPPOSITE CAMP", *PAKISTAN TIMES*, 21 April 1968, p. 4.

1653. **NUR-UD-DIN, Abu Sayeed**, "ATTITUDE TOWARDS SUFISM", *IQBAL: POET-PHILOSOPHER OF PAKISTAN*, Hafeez MALIK (ed.), New York / London: Columbia UP, 1971, pp. 287-300 [?].

1654. **NUR-UN-NABI, Chowdhri**, "IQBAL'S INDIVIDUALISM", *PAKISTAN OBSERVER*,

26 April and 10 May 1959.

1655. **NURADDIN, Amira**, tr., *GEMS OF IQBAL*, Baghdad, n.d.
English translation of selected poems.

1656. **NURUDDIN, Abu Sayeed**, mon., *ALLAMA IQBAL'S ATTITUDE TOWARDS SUFISM AND HIS UNIQUE PHILOSOPHY OF KHUDI-SELF*, [place ?]: Baitul Mukarram / Iqbal Foundation Bangladesh, 1978

1657. **Oasis** (red.), "ASRAR-I-KHUDI", *OASIS* (Bahawalpur), [?], pp. 25-48.

1658. ———, "EDITORIAL NOTE", *OASIS* (Bahawalpur), April 1941, pp. 91-105.

1659. ———, "IQBAL'S PHILOSOPHY OF LIFE", *OASIS* (Bahawalpur), April 1941, pp. 1-10.

1660. ———, "IQBAL'S PLACE IN SPACE", *OASIS* (Bahawalpur), April 1941, pp. 11-24.

1661. ———, "RAMUZ-I-BEKHUDI", *OASIS* (Bahawalpur), April 1941, pp. 49-64.

1662. **OMAR, Ahmad Khalid**, "IQBAL'S PRACTICAL IDEAL", *THE CIVIL AND MILITARY GAZETTE* (Lahore), 21 April 1951, p. 6.

1663. **OWAIS, S. M.**, "THE GUIDE OF THE AGE", *IQBAL REVIEW* (Karachi) 16, no. 3: October (1975): pp. 61-62.
Translation of a poem from ZABUR-I 'AJAM.

1664. **Pakistan, Department of Libraries**, *EXHIBITION OF BOOKS ON ALLAMA MOHAMMAD IQBAL, 7-9 NOVEMBER 1977*, Karachi, 1977. 30 pp.
List of direct books on display.

1665. **Pakistan - German Forum**, comp., *MOHAMMAD IQBAL - POET AND PHILOSOPHER, A COLLECTION OF TRANSLATIONS, ESSAYS AND OTHER ARTICLES, PRESENTED BY THE PAKISTAN-GERMAN FORUM*, Karachi: Din Mohammad Press, 1960. iii+142+iii pp.
Anthology with Iqbal's original text (Preface to the PAYAM-I MASHRIQ; Goethe; The Fragrance of the Rose; Science and Love; Life; The Tulip; Appearance of Iblis, the Prince of Schismatics; The Lamentation of Iblis; Beyond the Spheres; An Evening; Sicily; March

1907; Lament of the Bird in the Cage) and translations into English and German by Mumtaz HASAN, Annemarie SCHIMMEL, Otto von GLASENAPP, and including also "The Ascension of the Poet" by A. SCHIMMEL, "The Song of Tahira" by Tahira QURRAT-UL-AIN, "Iqbal and Nietzsche" by Javid IQBAL, "The Idea of Prayer in the Thought of Iqbal" by A. SCHIMMEL, an extract from "Tagebücher aus Asien" by Hans-Otto von VELTHEIM OSTRAU, an extract from "Address to the Opening Session of the Pakistan History Conference, Karachi, 1956" by P.E. KAHLE, "Mohammad Iqbal and German Thought" and "Iqbal and Hallaj" by A. SCHIMMEL, "Conversation with Iqbal" by Syed Nazir NIAZI, and "A Day in the Life of Muhammad Iqbal" by Mumtaz HASAN.

1666. **Pakistan Historical Society,** *A HISTORY OF THE FREEDOM MOVEMENT*, Karachi: The Society, 1957. 630 pp., 601+2 pp. and 553 pp. resp.
Three vols.: I (1707-1831), II (1831-1905), III (1906-1936), of which see esp. the latter.

1667. **Pakistan Times** (red.), "PLEA FOR RENDERING IQBAL IN BENGAL. BIRTH ANNIVERSARY MEETING", *PAKISTAN TIMES*, 2 February 1962.
Report of a Public Meeting held at Lahore on February 22, 1962; STAFF REPORTER'S REPORT.

1668. **PANDE, B. N.,** ed., *A CENTENARY HISTORY OF THE INDIAN NATIONAL CONGRESS, 1885-1985*, New Delhi: All India Congress Committee / Vikas Publ. House, 1985

1669. **Panorama** (red.), "PRESIDENT EISENHOWER LANDS CONTRIBUTION OF POET IQBAL", *PANORAMA* [vol. ?], no. [?]: May (1959): pp. 3.
Summary of President Eisenhower's tribute to Iqbal, read at a gathering at the Islamic Centre, Wahington, in commemoration of the poet's death.

1670. **PARET, R.,** "IQBAL, M.: RECONSTRUIRE LA PENSÉE RELIGIEUSE DE L'ISLAM (Book Review)", *ORIENTALISTISCHE LITERATURZEITUNG* 52, (1957): pp. 528.
F [?].

1671. ———, "IQBAL, Moh.: THE RECONSTRUCTION OF RELIGIOUS THOUGHT IN ISLAM (Book Review)", *ORIENTALISTISCHE LITERATUR-ZEITUNG* (Leipzig) 38, (1935): pp. 531.

1672. **PARVEZ,** "IQBAL: THE INTERPRETER OF ISLAMIC IDEALS", *DAWN* (Karachi), 21 April 1948, p. 9.

1673. **PAUS, Ansgar**, "MUHAMMAD IQBAL: EIN MODERNER MUSLIMISCHER RELIGIONSPHILOSOPH UND DAS PROBLEM DER RELIGIOSEN ERFAHRUNG", *SALZBURGER JAHRBUCH FÜR PHILOSOPHIE* (Salzburg) 35, (1990): pp. 49-73.
Treatise on Iqbal's religious thought within the context of Indian sub-continent's Islam, with emphasis on Iqbal's conceptions of the Self and the Absolute Ego, from within the religious and/or mystical experience.
G.

1674. **PEARSON, M. N.**, "MALIK (Ed.): "Iqbal. Poet-Philosopher of Pakistan" (Book Review)", *JOURNAL OF THE AMERICAN ORIENTAL SOCIETY* 93, no. 2: April-June (1973): pp. 250.

1675. **PICKTHALL, Muhammad Marmaduke**, "(REVIEW OF) SIR MUHAMMAD IQBAL'S LECTURES", *ISLAMIC CULTURE* (Hyderabad) 5, no. 4: October (1931): pp. 677-83.

1676. **Pictorial** (red.), "IQBAL: POET AND POLITICIAN", *PICTORIAL (WEEKLY)* 6, no. 11: 21 April (1961): pp. 1-2.

1677. **PIQUARD, Brigitte**, tr., *IQBAL - (LE) POÈTE DE L'ISLAM*, Sharif AL-MUJAHID (mon.), BROCHURE SERIES, ed. Muhammad SUHEYL UMAR 2, Lahore: Iqbal Academy Pakistan, 1991 or 1993 [?]. 75 pp.
A French rendering of Sharif Al-Mujahid's classic *THE POET OF THE EAST - THE STORY OF MUHAMMAD IQBAL*, Lahore / London: Oxford UP, 1961 (qv.), with an introduction and notes by the translator.
F.

1678. **PIRZADA, Abdul Hafeez**, "IQBAL AND QUAID-I-AZAM", *IQBAL REVIEW* 17, no. 3: October (1976): pp. 1-4.

1679. **PIRZADA, S. A. A.**, "IQBAL'S CONCEPT OF SELF", *PAKISTAN REVIEW* 14, no. 4: April (1966): pp. 10-12.

1680. **PIRZADA, Syed Sharifuddin**, mon., *EVOLUTION OF PAKISTAN*, Lahore: All-Pakistan Legal Decisions, 1963. ii+309 pp.
On Iqbal, see pp. 19*f*., 59, 121-130, 148, 257, 266, 276.

1681. ———, ed., *FOUNDATIONS OF PAKISTAN. ALL-INDIA MUSLIM LEAGUE DOCUMENTS, 1906-1947*, Vol. 2 (1924-1947), Karachi: National Publishing House,

1970. 636 pp.
Includes Iqbal - Presidential addresses, pp. 151-171; general, p. 206; and poetry, pp. 444*ff.*

1682. **POLONSKAYA, L.**, "IQBAL ON THE REVOLUTION", *THE WORK OF MUHAMMAD IQBAL: ARTICLES BY SOVIET SCHOLARS*, Abdur Rauf MALIK (ed.), Lahore: People's Publishing House, 1983, pp. 64-84.

1683. **POLONSKAYA, L. R.**, tr./intr., *[THE RING OF THE CARAVAN BELL]*, Moscow, 1964.
Russian translation of selected poems, with an introduction by Polonskaya.
R.

1684. **POLONSKAYA, Madam L. R. Gordon**, "MUHAMMAD IQBAL'S SOCIAL THOUGHT", *IQBAL REVIEW* 10, no. 3: October (1969): pp. 9-15.

1685. **PRIGARINA, Nataliya I.**, "THE ETHIC AND THE POETIC IN IQBAL", *THE WORK OF MUHAMMAD IQBAL: ARTICLES BY SOVIET SCHOLARS*, Abdur Rauf MALIK (ed.), Lahore: People's Publishing House, 1983, pp. 1-20.

1686. ———, "GHALIB I IQBAL. POPYTKA SRAVNITELNOGO IZUCHENIYA STILYA [AN ESSAY OF COMPARATIVE STUDY OF GHALIB AND IQBAL'S STYLE]", *MIRZA GHALIB - VELIKIY POET VOSTOKA*, Moscow, 1972, pp. 199-224.
R.

1687. ———, "GORST' PRAHA, ZHIVOYE SERDZE [A HANDFUL OF DUST, LIVING HEART]", *IZBRANNOYE MUHAMADA IQBALA [THE BOOK OF TRANSLATIONS OF IQBAL'S POETRY]*, Moscow, 1981, pp. 5-24.
The rest of the book (216 pp.) presents the edition, line by line translation and commentary to Iqbal's poetry.
R.

1688. ———, "GUMANIZM V FILOSOFSKOY LIRIKE IQBALA [HUMANISM IN PHILOSOPHICAL LYRICS OF IQBAL IN 20TH (PAYAM-I MASHRIQ)]", *NARODY ASII I AFRIKI* 5, (1965): pp. 95-107.
R.

1689. ———, "'ISTILAHAT ASH-SHUARA V POESII MUHAMMADA IQBALA ['ISTILAHAT ASH-SHUARA' IN THE POETRY OF MUHAMMAD IQBAL]", *TEORETICHESKIYE PROBLEMY VOSTOCHNYH LITERATUR*, Moscow, 1969, pp.

166-73.
R.

1690. ———, "MELODY OF JOY AND SORROW", *PROBLEMS OF MODERN INDIAN LITERATURE*, Calcutta: Statistical Publishing Society, 1974, pp. 160-166.

1691. ———, "MUHAMMAD IQBAL: AN INTRODUCTION TO *THE SECRETS OF THE SELF*", *IQBAL REVIEW* 7, no. 3: October (1966): pp. 1-17.
An English translation (tr. Edward K. Kolbenev) of Prigarina's introduction into the philosophy of (I) ASRAR-I-KHUDI, which appeared in Russian (MUHAMMAD IQBAL. VSTUPLENIYE V POEMU *TAINY LICHNOSTY*) in *KRATKIYE SOOBSHCHENIYA INSTITUTA NARODOV AZZI* [Brief Proceedings of the Institute of the Peoples of Asia, Moscow], 1964, pp. 80-93. This translation was later re-issued in [Various authors], *SELECTIONS FROM THE IQBAL REVIEW*, ed. Waheed Qureshi, Lahore, 1983, pp. 239-255, with a basic bibliography of Iqbal in the Russian language.

1692. ———, "MUHAMMAD IQBAL ARTICLES 1916-'17", *PHILOSOPHSKIYE ASPECTY SOUFISMA*, M. STEPANIANZ (ed.), Moscow, 1987, pp. 176-89.
Foreword, translation and commentary of Iqbal's articles.
R.

1693. ———, "[MUHAMMAD IQBAL: INTRODUCTION TO *THE SECRET OF THE SELF*]", *KRATKIYE SOOBSHCHENIYA INSTITUTA NARODOV AZII* (Moscow) 80, (1964).
An introduction into the philosophy of (I) ASRAR-I-KHUDI.
R.

1694. ———, "NEKOTORYE ASPEKTY FILOSOFSKOY LIRIKI MUHAMMADA IQBALA V NACHALE 20-H GODOV [SOME ASPECTS OF PHILOSOPHICAL LYRICS OF MUHAMMAD IQBAL IN THE BEGINNING OF THE 20TH CENTURY]", 1967.
English summary of Ph.D. thesis on pp. 1-22.
E-R.

1695. ———, "THE PERFECT MAN IN IQBAL'S POETRY AND MUSLIM TRADITION", *PROCEEDINGS OF THE THIRTY-FIRST INTERNATIONAL CONGRESS OF HUMAN SCIENCES IN ASIA AND NORTH AFRICA (Tokyo - Kyoto, 1983)*, p. 556, Tokyo: 1984.

1696. ———, "PERFECT MAN - SIGN OF REVOLUTION", *VIEWPOINT* (Lahore) 3, no. 39:

May (1978).

1697. ——, mon., *POÈZIJA MUCHAMMADA IKBALA (1900-1924 Gg.)* (THE POETRY OF MUHAMMAD IQBAL), Moskva: Nauka, 1972. 194 pp.
R.

1698. ——, *POETIKA TVORCHESTVA MUHAMMADA IQBALA [THE POETICS OF MUHAMMAD IQBAL'S WORK]*, Moscow, 1978. 232 pp.

1699. ——, "[WHILE READING IQBAL]", *ASIYA Y AFRICA SEGODNYA* 6, (1963). Article on the occasion of the 25th death anniversary of Muhammad Iqbal.
R.

1700. **PRIGARINA, Natliya I.**, "THE ETHIC AND POETIC IN IQBAL", *THE WORK OF MUHAMMAD IQBAL. ARTICLES BY SOVIET SCHOLARS*, Abdur Rauf MALIK (ed.), Lahore, 1983, pp. 1-20.

1701. ——, "GHALIB AND IQBAL. A COMPARATIVE STUDY", *SOVIET REVIEW* (New Delhi) 7, no. 16 (1966): pp. 41-50.

1702. ——, "NEKOTORYE ASPECTY OBRAZA 'SOVERSHENNOGO CHELOVEKA' V SVETE MUSULMANSKOY TRADIZII [SOME ASPECTS OF THE IMAGE OF IQBAL'S PERFECT MAN IN THE LIGHT OF MUSLIM TRADITION]", *HUDOJESTVENNYE TRADIZYY LITERATUR VOSTOKA [COLLECTION OF ARTICLES]*, Moscow, 1985, pp. 172-99.
R.

1703. ——, "OZHIZNI I TVORCHEST VE M. IQBALA [ON THE LIFE AND POETRY OF M. IQBAL]", *TVORCHESTVO MUHAMMADA IQBALA [A COLLECTION OF ARTICLES OF SOVIET AND OTHER SCHOLARS]*, Moscow, 1982, pp. 3-23.
R.

1704. ——, "PREDISLOVIYE IQBALA K MATHNAVI 'TAINSTVA LICHNOSTI' [PROSE FOREWORD OF IQBAL TO THE MATHNAVI 'THE SECRETS OF THE SELF']", *LITERATURY INDII - [A COLLECTION OF ARTICLES]*, Moscow, 1988, pp. 155-77.
Translation from Urdu of Iqbal's foreword to his ASRAR-I KHUDI.
R.

1705. **PRIOR, James B.**, "IQBAL'S VIEW OF 'ISLAMIC NATIONALISM' IN JAVIDNAMEH", *IQBAL* 19, no. 1: July-September (1971): pp. 20-60.

1706. **PRITCHETT, Frances W.**, comp., *URDU LITERATURE: A BIBLIOGRPHY OF ENGLISH LANGUAGE SOURCES*, New Delhi: Manohar, 1979

1707. **PULATOVA, S.**, "*BOOK OF SERVITUDE* AND IQBAL'S VIEW [...]RT", *THE WORK OF MUHAMMAD IQBAL: ARTICLES BY SOVIET SCHOLARS*, Abdur Rauf MALIK (ed.), Lahore: People's Publishing House, 1983, pp. 47-63.

1708. **PUN, Balraj**, "PERSPECTIVES - AZAD AND IQBAL: A COMPARATIVE STUDY", *ECONOMIC AND POLITICAL WEEKLY: A SAMEEKSHA TRUST PUBLICATION* 31, no. 10 (1996): pp. 591-95.

1709. **PURI, Balarj**, "AZAD AND IQBAL: A COMPARATIVE STUDY", *ISLAM AND THE MODERN AGE* (New Delhi) 22, no. 1 (1992): pp. 75-90.

1710. **PUSHP, P. N.**, "KASHMIR AND KASHMIRIS IN IQBAL'S VERSE", *IQBAL COMMEMORATIVE VOLUME*, Ali Sardar JAFRI & K.S. DUGGAL (eds.), New Delhi: All India Iqbal Centenary Celebrations Committee, 1977, pp. 194-201.
Iqbal was aware and proud of Kashmir as the homeland of his ancestors, and in his poetry *we find Iqbal deeply concerned with the future of Kashmir, and despite his emphasis on pan-Islamic perspective [...] he reserved a special corner of concern for the Kashmiris* (p. 201).

1711. **QABIR, Q. A.**, tr., *ARMUGHAN-I-HIJAZ*, Lahore: Iqbal Academy, 1983. A versified translation of (I) ARMUGHAN-I-HIJAZ.

1712. **QADEER, Fazl**, "PLANNER OF PAKISTAN", *THE PAKISTAN TIMES* (Rawalpindi), 9 November 1982.

1713. **QADIR, Abdul**, "DR. SIR MUHAMMAD IQBAL - THE GREAT POET OF ISLAM, 1873-1938", *GREAT MEN OF INDIA*, L. F. RUSHBROOK WILLIAM (ed.), Bombay: Home Library Club, 1939, pp. 562-71.
Re-issued by Sang-e-Meel Publications (Lahore 1975).

1714. ———, "THE INFLUENCE OF IQBAL ON URDU LITERATURE", *IQBAL* 19, no. 1: July-September (1971): pp. 1-7.

1715. ———, "IQBAL: PATRIOT, POET AND PHILOSOPHER", *THE ILLUSTRATED WEEKLY OF PAKISTAN* 4, no. 29: 20 April (1952): pp. 32-34.

1716. ———, "MESSAGE", *OASIS*, April 1941, p. 89.

1717. ———, "PERSIAN POEMS OF IQBAL", *PANJAB UNIVERSITY UNION MAGAZINE* (Lahore) 1, no. 1: February (1931).
Paper originally delivered at a meeting of the Punjab Literary League in 1930, but not included in that collection. Reprinted in *IQBAL REVIEW* October 1982, pp. 96-108, with an introduction by Afzal Haq QARSHI (pp. 95*f.*), discussion and Chairman's remarks (pp. 108*f.*).

1718. ———, "THE PRINCIPAL THEMES IN IQBAL'S POETRY", *MODERN INDIA AND THE WEST: MUSLIM CULTURE AND RELIGIOUS THOUGHT*, L. S. S. O'MALLEY (ed.), London: Oxford UP, 1941, pp. 530-532.

1719. ———, "THE SEER AND THE MYSTIC", *PAKISTAN TIMES*, 21 April 1950, pp. 5, 7, 8.

1720. **QADIR, C. A.**, "GULSHAN-I-RAZ AND GULSHAN-I-RAZ-I-JADID (THE NATURE AND ROLE OF REASON)", *IQBAL REVIEW* 24, no. 3: October (1983): pp. 15-33 or 45-53 [?].
Shabistari's GULSHAN-I-RAZ and Iqbal's GULSHAN-I-RAZ-I-JADID.

1721. ———, "MYSTICISM IN MODERN CONTEXT", *IQBAL REVIEW* [vol. ?], no. [?]: April (1981): pp. 55-79.

1722. ———, ed., *THE WORLD OF PHILOSOPHY*, Lahore: The Sharif Presentation Volume Committee, 1965. xx+367 pp.
Cf. pp. 63, 76, 156, 161*f.*, 174*f.*, 192, 194*f.*, 200-202, 204, 225, 227, 266, 272, 276.

1723. **QADIR EL-GAYLANI, Syed Abdul**, "IQBAL GREAT ADVOCATE OF MUSLIM UNITY: POETRY A GUIDING LINE", *DAWN*, 21 April 1971, p. 5.

1724. **QADIR, Qazi A.**, "PHYSICAL WORLD AND THE PRINCIPLE OF COSMIC DYNAMICS", *IQBAL REVIEW* 2, no. 1: April (1961): pp. 45-50.

1725. **QADIR, Sheikh Abdul**, mon., *IQBAL - THE GREAT POET OF ISLAM*, Muhammad Hanif SHAHID (ed.), Lahore: Sang-e-Meel Publications, 1975/1986. 160 pp.

A collection of nine articles by Shaikh Abdul Qadir, a contemporary and intimate friend of Iqbal since as early as 1898, and editor of the literary journal MAKHZAN, in which Iqbal's early Urdu poems were published. The first article presents a general introduction to the life and works of Iqbal. Two contributions are more-or-less *In Memoriam*s, and were clearly written shortly after Iqbal's death. In Article no. 4 Iqbal is highlighted as a poet-philosopher and a seer, in no. 5 as a patriot, in no. 6 as a mystic (THE SEER AND THE MYSTIC is Qadir's last and hitherto unpublished article in the English language). Further contributions are an essay on Iqbal's influence on modern Urdu literature, an analysis of Iqbal's views on the modernisation of society and civilisation, and a paper on the Urdu poem IBLIS KI MAJLIS-I-SHURA, traditionally rendered as *The Devil's Conference*. The book concludes with a letter dd. 5 May 1938 from Qadir to Aftad Iqbal on the occasion of the death of his father, an elementary bibliography, and an index. With a preface from the editor and a foreword by Javid Iqbal.

1726. **QADRI, Asadul**, "IQBAL'S CONTRIBUTION TO SCIENCE", *DAWN*, 21 April 1966, pp. 5-10.

1727. **QADRI, K. H.**, "FAIZ AND IQBAL", *PAKISTAN TIMES*, 15 July 1973, p. 2.

1728. **QADRI, Noor Ahmad**, "IQBAL IN BAHASA INDONESIA", *INDONESIA TODAY* 3, no. 2: March-April (1970): pp. 20-30.
Journal issued by the Press and Public Relations Department, Embassy of the Republic of Indonesia, Karachi.

1729. **QAISER, Nazir**, "AN ANALYSIS OF WESTERN SOURCES OF IQBAL'S PHILOSOPHY", *THE NATION* (Islamabad / Lahore), 9 November 1992.

1730. ———, *A CRITIQUE OF WESTERN PSYCHOLOGY AND PSYCHOTHERAPY AND IQBAL'S APPROACH*, Lahore: Iqbal Academy Pakistan, 1994. 239 pp.

1731. ———, "HIS CONCEPTION, OF ANNIHILATION", *THE PAKISTAN TIMES* (Rawalpindi), 21 April 1979.

1732. ———, "IQBAL AND MONTESSORI: TWO SEERS OF HUMAN DESTINY", *THE PAKISTAN TIMES* (Rawalpindi), 21 April 1980.

1733. ———, "IQBAL AND PSYCHO-ANALYSIS", *THE PAKISTAN TIMES* (Rawalpindi), 8 November 1981.

1734. ———, "IQBAL'S PHILOSOPHY OF FAQR", *THE PAKISTAN TIMES* (Rawalpindi), 21 April 1984.

1735. ———, "IQBAL'S PURPOSIVE ACTIVISM AND LOGOTHERAPY", *THE NATION* (Islamabad / Lahore), 21 April 1992.

1736. ———, "LIFE AFTER DEATH: IQBAL AND RUMI", *THE PAKISTAN TIMES* (Rawalpindi), 21 April 1983.

1737. ———, "LIMITATIONS OF SCIENTIFIC PSYCHOLOGY AND IQBAL", *THE PAKISTAN TIMES* (Rawalpindi), 9 November 1982.

1738. ———, "MASLOW AND IQBAL", *THE PAKISTAN TIMES* (Rawalpindi), 21 April 1982.

1739. ———, "PERFECT MAN AS VISUALISED BY RUMI AND IQBAL", *THE PAKISTAN TIMES* (Rawalpindi), 9 November 1977.

1740. ———, "PSYCHOTHERAPEUTIC ASPECTS OF IQBAL'S THOUGHT", *THE PAKISTAN TIMES* (Lahore), 9 November 1978.

1741. ———, "RUMI AND IQBAL: RELIGIOUS EXPERIENCE", *THE PAKISTAN TIMES* (Rawalpindi), 21 April 1981.

1742. ———, "RUMI'S IMPACT ON IQBAL'S CONCEPT OF UNIVERSE", *THE PAKISTAN TIMES* (Rawalpindi / Lahore), 9 November 1985.

1743. ———, mon., *RUMI'S IMPACT ON IQBAL'S RELIGIOUS THOUGHT*, London: Iqbal Academy Pakistan, 1989

1744. ———, "THE SOURCES OF IQBAL'S THOUGHT", *PAKISTAN TIMES*, 29 May 1977, p. 1.

1745. ———, "VOLUNTARISM OF SCHOPENHAUER AND IQBAL", *IQBAL* 25, no. 3: July (1978): pp. 25-33.
Although Schopenhauer's voluntarism is negative in Nature and basically differs from that of Iqbal, both are upholders of action and struggle.

1746. ———, "WAS IQBAL A PANTHEIST?", *IQBAL REVIEW* 24, no. 3: October (1983): pp. 45-53.
This paper admits Iqbal to have been a pantheist during his stay in England (1905-1908), but holds that afterwards the poet-philosopher changed his position (cf. the letter by McTaggart), under the influence of Rumi's MATHNAWI.

1747. ———, "WAS IQBAL A PANTHEIST?", *THE PAKISTAN TIMES* (Rawalpindi), 9 November 1983.

1748. ———, "WAS IQBAL INFLUENCED BY JAMES WARD?", *THE PAKISTAN TIMES* (Rawalpindi), 9 November 1979.

1749. ———, "WHY IQBAL REGARDED RUMI AS GUIDE", *THE PAKISTAN TIMES* (Rawalpindi), 21 April 1985.

1750. **QAISER, Shahzad**, "A CRITICAL STUDY OF ASH'ARISM WITH REFERENCE TO IQBAL AND SCHUON", *IQBAL REVIEW* 27, no. 1: April-September (1986): pp. 7-20.

1751. ———, "IQBAL AND KHAWAJA GHULAM FARID ON MAN-GOD POLARITY", *IQBAL REVIEW* 37, no. 1: April (1996): pp. 17-44.

1752. ———, "IQBAL'S ANALYSIS OF MUSLIM CULTURE - A CRITICAL STUDY", *IQBAL REVIEW* 26, no. 3: October-November-December (1985): pp. 111-22.

1753. **QAMAR, M. H.**, "IQBAL'S POETRY", *THE PAKISTAN TIMES* (Lahore), 17 January 1992.

1754. **QAMARUDDIN KHAN**, "RELIGIOUS THOUGHT OF IQBAL", *PAKISTAN TIMES*, 21 April 1961, p. 3.

1755. **QARSHI, Afzal Haq**, "INDEX OF ARTICLES AND REVIEWS PUBLISHED IN THE *IQBAL REVIEW* (1960-1983)", *IQBAL REVIEW* 25, no. 3: October (1984): pp. 129-52. Cf. esp. pp. 138-140, on Muhammad Iqbal.

1756. ———, "INTRODUCTION, PERSIAN POEMS OF IQBAL", *IQBAL REVIEW* 23, no. 2: October (1982): pp. 95-96.

1757. ———, "A RARE WRITING OF IQBAL", *IQBAL REVIEW* 24, no. 1: April (1983): pp.

39-42.

Reprint of Iqbal's article STRAY THOUGHTS, in *THE NEW ORIENT* 1, no. 6-8: June-August (1925), which is not included in the following anthologies: VAHID, Syed Abdul, *THOUGHTS AND REFLECTIONS OF IQBAL*, Lahore, 1964; DAR, B.A., *LETTERS AND WRITINGS OF IQBAL*, Karachi, 1967; RAZZAQI, Shahid Hussain, *DISCOURSES OF IQBAL*, Lahore, 1979; SHAHEEM, Rahim Bakhsh, *MEMENTOS OF IQBAL*, Lahore, n.d.; SHERWANI, Latif Ahmed, *SPEECHES, WRITINGS AND STATEMENTS OF IQBAL*, Lahore, 1977. This article is also not found in Iqbal's STRAY THOUGHTS edited by Javed IQBAL (Lahore, 1961). It presents 10 "STRAY THOUGHTS" concerning religion, philosophy (comparative / self / knowledge).

1758. **QASIMI, Ahmad Nadim**, "LYRICS OF IQBAL", *PAKISTAN TIMES*, 21 April 1952, p. 6.

1759. **QAVI AHMAD, Saiyid**, "IQBAL'S PHILOSOPHY OF EGO", *EDUCATION RESEARCH BULLETIN* [vol. ?], no. [?]: December (1977).

1760. **QAYUM, Abdul**, "IS RELIGION POSSIBLE?", *IQBAL* (Lahore) 23, no. 3: July (1976): pp. 59-78.

1761. **QAYYUM, Abdul**, "THE NATURALISM OF IQBAL", *IQBAL REVIEW* 32, no. 3: October (1991): pp. 45-61.

1762. **QAZI, Allama I. I.**, "THE CONCEPTION OF ISLAMIC POETRY", *IQBAL REVIEW* 1, no. 1: April (1960): pp. 10-19.

1763. **QUADIRI, M. A.**, "THE POET OF HUMANISM", *THE MUSLIM* (Islamabad), 21 April 1981.

1764. **QUADRI, Maulana Asadul**, "IQBAL - THE POLITICAL VISIONARY", *THE PAKISTAN TIMES* (Rawalpindi), 21 April 1980.

1765. **QUARONI, Pietro**, "UN POETA DIFFICILE", *CORRIERE DELLA SERA* (Milano), 11 February 1956.
Reprinted in *IL MONDO DI UN AMBASCIATORE*, Milano: Ferro Edizioni, 1965, pp. 106-112.
I.

1766. **QUDDUSI, Irshadul Haq**, "IQBAL AND HIS ROLE IN CREATION OF PAKISTAN",

MORNING NEWS (Karachi), 9 November 1979.

1767. **QURAISHI, Muhammad Abdulla**, "THE MEANING OF REVELATION", *IQBAL REVIEW* 3, no. 3: October (1962): pp. 11-16.
On the mutual friendship and respect of Iqbal and Sir Ross Masud, and Dr. Zahir-ud-Din Ahmad Aljamaee's remarks on the poetry Iqbal wrote in the house of his friend in Bhopal.

1768. **QURAISHI, Muhammad Abdullah**, "IQBAL AND THE JOURNAL TAREEQAT", *IQBAL REVIEW* [vol. ?], no. [?] (1961).

1769. ———, "IQBAL IN THE WITNESS BOX", *IQBAL REVIEW* 2, no. 1: April (1961): pp. 35-44.
Short article on the disturbances in Kashmir (1931) and the ill-reputed court case against the poet Shaikh Ghulam Mustafa, editor of the monthly *FIRDAUS* and the weekly *AKA BAKA*, who had been identified by a Hindu shopkeeper as the man who had beaten him. In order to prove the innocence of the accused, many prominent Muslims, among whom Muhammad Iqbal, offered to give evidence before the court. The article contains Iqbal's statement before the court, as well the original Urdu poem (with English translation) of Maulana Zafar Ali Khan, published on the front page of *ZAMINDAR* on the occasion of the dismissal of the case.
Re-issued in [Various authors], *SELECTIONS FROM THE IQBAL REVIEW*, ed. Waheed Qureshi, Lahore, 1983, pp. 521-530.

1770. **QURAT-UL-AIN, Tahira**, "THE SONG OF TAHIRA", *MUHAMMAD IQBAL: POET AND PHILOSOPHER, A COLLECTION OF TRANSLATIONS, ESSAYS AND OTHER ARTICLES, PRESENTED BY THE PAKISTAN-GERMAN FORUM*, Karachi: Din Mohammad Press, 1960.

1771. **QURESHI, A. H.**, *A CRITICAL STUDY OF ALLUSIONS IN IQBAL'S POETRY.*
Book in the press in 1996.

1772. **QURESHI, Ahmad Hasan**, "TENNYSON AND IQBAL, A STUDY IN AFFINITIES", *IQBAL REVIEW* 18, no. 4: January (1978): pp. 89-125.

1773. **QURESHI, Altaf Hussain**, "IQBAL'S POLITICAL CONCEPTION OF SOCIETY", *OASIS* (Bahawalpur), April 1941, pp. 141-42.

1774. **QURESHI, Anwar Iqbal**, "IQBAL: THE GREAT POET OF THE EAST", *DAWN*, 21

April 1971, p. 7.

1775. **QURESHI, H. K.**, "IQBAL: AN INTERPRETER OF ISLAM", *IQBAL REVIEW* 21, no. 3: October (1980): pp. 9-19.

1776. **QURESHI, Muhammad Abdullah**, "SOME ASPECTS OF IQBAL'S BIOGRAPHY", *IQBAL* 7, no. 1: July (1958): pp. 63-71.

1777. **QURESHI, Saleem M. M.**, "PAKISTANI NATIONALISM RECONSIDERED", *PACIFFIC AFFAIRS* (Canada) 45, no. 4 (1972): pp. 556-72.

1778. **QURESHI, Waheed**, "IQBAL AND THE CONCEPT OF MUSLIM NATIONALISM", *THE PAKISTAN TIMES* (Rawalpindi), 21 April 1980.

1779. ———, ed./comp., *SELECTIONS FROM THE IQBAL REVIEW*, various authors (ed.), Lahore: Iqbal Academy, 1983. 541 pp.
A selection of 35 articles from the *IQBAL REVIEW*, published by the Iqbal Academy (Lahore) as a quarterly journal from April 1960 onwards; two issues a year in English, and two in Urdu. A very short foreword by the editor provides no clues as to the choice of the selected articles. Contributions (*abstract of each article is given under the respective author*):
(1) Dr. M. Rafiuddin: IQBAL'S CONCEPT OF EVOLUTION,
(2) Naeem Ahmad: IQBAL'S CONCEPT OF ETERNITY,
(3) Jameela Khatoon: IQBAL'S THEORY OF KNOWLEDGE,
(4) Absar Ahmad: THE HEGELIAN KEY TO UNDERSTANDING IQBAL,
(5) Manzoor Ahmad: METAPHYSICS OF PERSIA AND IQBAL,
(6) A.H. Kamali: CONCEPTUAL MODEL OF THE ASRAR-O-RUMUZ & IQBAL'S MONADOLOGY,
(7) Mohammad Taqi: DYNAMIC CONCEPTION OF THE WEST AND THE PHILOSOPHY OF SELF,
(8) Khalid Masud: IQBAL'S LECTURE ON IJTIHAD,
(9) Javid Iqbal: IQBAL'S CONTRIBUTION TO LIBERALISM IN MODERN ISLAM,
(10) S.M. Yousuf: A STUDY OF IQBAL'S VIEW ON IJMA,
(11) Manzooruddin Ahmad: IQBAL'S THEORY OF MUSLIM COMMUNITY AND ISLAMIC UNIVERSALISM,
(12) Khurshid Ahmad: IQBAL AND RECONSTRUCTION OF ISLAMIC LAW,
(13) Gilani Kamran: IQBAL - A VIEW OF POLITICO-CULTURAL PERSPECTIVE,
(14) S. Qudratullah Fatimi: ISLAMIC UNIVERSALISM AND TERRITORIAL NATIONALISM IN IQBAL'S THOUGHT,
(15) Mohammad Maruf: IQBAL ON DEMOCRACY,

(16) Kh. Amjad Saeed: ECONOMIC PHILOSOPHY OF IQBAL,

(17) N.I. Pragarina: MOHAMMAD IQBAL: INTRODUCTION TO THE SECRET OF THE SELF,

(18) Robert Whittemore: IQBAL'S PANENTHEISM,

(19) R. Haree: IQBAL: A REFORMER OF ISLAMIC PHILOSOPHY,

(20) Edward McCarthy: IQBAL AS A POET AND PHILSOPHER,

(21) A. Bausani (English translation by R.A. Butler): SATAN IN IQBAL'S PHILOSOPHICAL AND POETICAL WORKS,

(22) M.T. Stepanyants: PROBLEM OF ETHICS IN MOHAMMAD IQBAL'S PHILOSOPHY,

(23) Mumtaz Hasan: IQBAL AS A SEER,

(24) Muzaffar Hussain: THE KEY POINT IN IQBAL'S EDUCATIONAL PHILOSOPHY,

(25) M.M. Sharif: IQBAL ON THE NATURE OF TIME,

(26) Muhammad Munawwar: IQBAL ON QURANIC CONCEPT OF HISTORY,

(27) M. Usman Ramz: IQBAL'S PHILOSOPHY OF HISTORY,

(28) Reyazur Rehman: IQBAL'S EMPHASIS ON THE STUDY OF HISTORY,

(29) Rayazul Hasan: IQBAL'S TULIP OF SINAI,

(30) S.M. Abdullah: THE NATURE OF DANTE'S INFLUENCE ON IQBAL,

(31) C.M. Naim: THE PSEUDO-DRAMATIC POEMS OF IQBAL,

(32) K.A. Rashid: RECENT ADVANCES IN SCIENCE AND IQBAL'S CONCEPT OF LIFE AND DEATH,

(33) Shaheer Niazi: IQBAL AND OUTER SPACE,

(34) M. Abdullah Qureshi: IQBAL IN THE WITNESS BOX,

(35) Q.M. Aslam: IQBAL AT A COLLEGE RECEPTION IN LAHORE.

1780. **QURESHI, Zafar Ali**, "WHAT NATIONS OF THE EAST SHOULD DO", *PAKISTAN TIMES* (Lahore), 21 April 1961, p. 4.

1781. **QURRATULAIN HYDER**, "AN ASPECT OF IQBAL'S PHILOSOPHY", *MEHMIL* 4, no. 1: November (1942).

1782. ———, "BROUGHT AN AWAKENING", *DAWN* (Karachi), 21 April 1952, p. 6.

1783. ———, "DR. IQBAL", *THE CIVIL AND MILITARY GAZETTE* (Lahore), 21 April 1952.

1784. **RÜSTAU, Hiltrud**, "PHILOSOPHISCHE REFLEXIONEN DES NATIONALEN IN INDIEN IN DER ERSTEN ETAPPE DER ALLGEMEINEN KRISE UND DIE WELTANSCHAULICHE BEGRÜNDUNG DES NATIONALISMUS", *WISSENSCHAFTLICHE ZEITSCHRIFT DER HUMBOLDT-UNIVERSITÄT ZU*

BERLIN. GESELLSCHAFTSWISSENSCHAFT-LICHE REIHE [East Germany] 32, no. 6 (1983): pp. 663-68.
Comparison of Tagore's and Iqbal's impressions of the nationalist movement in India, the influence on it of the Russian Revolution, and the beginnings of socialism. G.

1785. **RADHAKRISHNAN, S.**, "IQBAL DAY MUSHA'IRA", *OCCASIONAL SPEECHES AND WRITINGS*, New Delhi, 1957, Vol. 2nd series.

1786. **RAFI, M. A.**, "IQBAL - THE SEER AND THE GUIDE", *DAWN* (Karachi), 9 November 1977.

1787. **RAFI-UD-DIN, Muhammad**, "IQBAL'S CONTRIBUTION TO KNOWLEDGE", *PAKISTAN TIMES*, 21 April 1962, p. 1.

1788. ———, "IQBAL WAS AGAINST GODLESS SCIENCE", *PAKISTAN TIMES*, 21 April 1971, p. 4.
Variant title and date: IQBAL'S WAR AGAINST GODLESS SCIENCE, in *THE PAKISTAN TIMES*, 21 April 1967, p. 5.

1789. ———, "NEED FOR SCIENTIFIC EXPOSITION OF IQBAL", *PAKISTAN TIMES* (Lahore), 21 April 1960, p. 7.

1790. **RAFIQ, Said Ahmad**, "POLITICAL PHILOSOPHY OF IQBAL", *IQBAL REVIEW* 29, no. 1: April (1988): pp. 57-71.
Notes on the history of Muslim intellectualism, on Iqbal's emphasis on the inseperability of Islam and politics, and on Iqbal's role in the development of the two-nation theory and the genesis of Pakistan.

1791. **RAFIQUE AFZAL, M.**, mon., *MALIK BARKAT ALI, HIS LIFE AND WRITINGS*, Lahore: Research Society of Pakistan, 1969. 378 pp.
Iqbal as politician, pp. 1-266.

1792. **RAFIQUE, M.**, "THE PROBLEM OF SUFFERING IN IQBAL'S PHILOSOPHY", *STUDIES IN ISLAM* 5, no. 2-3: April (1968): pp. 114-19.

1793. ———, mon., *SRI AUROBINDO AND IQBAL. A COMPARATIVE STUDY OF THEIR PHILOSOPHY*, Ishrat Hasan ENVER (foreword), 1st ed., Aligarh: Aligarh Muslim University, 1974. 213 pp.

Originally presented as the author's Ph.D. thesis, Aligarh (Faculty of Arts Publication). Contents: (I) Biographical Facts & the Historical Background, (II) Sources of Knowledge, (III) Metaphysical Foundations, (IV) The Ideal of Human Life. Including an index and a bibliography.

1794. **RAFIQUE, Syed Ahmed**, mon., *IQBAL'S THEORY OF ETHICS*, Lahore: Institute of Islamic Culture, n.d.

1795. **RAFIUDDIN HASHMI**, "IQBAL, ISLAMIC RESURGENCE AND THE MUSLIM WORLD", *IQBAL* 43, no. 2: April (1996): pp. 11-22.

1796. **RAFIUDDIN, Mohammad**, "IQBAL'S CONCEPT OF EVOLUTION", *IQBAL REVIEW* 1, no. 1: April (1960): pp. 20-42.
An analysis of Iqbal's evolutionist ideas, set against their Darwinian background, and the question whether or not the concept of evolution is teleologically conditioned. Includes a quote from Iqbal's (WHITHER CIVILISATION?).
Re-issued in [Various authors], *SELECTIONS FROM THE IQBAL REVIEW*, ed. Waheed Qureshi, Lahore, 1983, pp. 1-23.

1797. ———, "IQBAL'S IDEA OF THE SELF", *IQBAL* (Lahore) 1, no. 3: January (1953): pp. 1-28.
Reproduced in *IQBAL REVIEW* 4, no. 3: October (1963), pp. 1-31; and in SHEIKH, M. Saeed (ed.): *STUDIES IN IQBAL'S THOUGHT AND ART*, Lahore 1972, pp. 75-106.

1798. ———, "IQBAL'S WAR AGAINST GODLESS SCIENCE", *PAKISTAN TIMES*, 21 April 1967, p. 5.

1799. ———, "THE PHILOSOPHY OF IQBAL, ITS NATURE AND IMPORTANCE", *IQBAL REVIEW* 2, no. 3: October (1961): pp. 86-129.

1800. ———, "REALITY OF THE UNIVERSE AND MAN", *IQBAL REVIEW* [vol. ?], no. [?]: January (1961).

1801. **RAGHIB, Ahsan**, "THE MECHANISM OF AIWAN AND DIWAN FOR IQBALIAN STATE", *ISLAMIC LITERATURE* [vol. ?], no. [?]: January-February (1955).

1802. **RAHANVEE, Shabbir Awan**, "IQBAL: GREAT THINKER OF THE EAST", *THE CIVIL AND MILITARY GAZETTE* (Lahore), 21 April 1956, p. 4.

1803. **RAHBAR, Ali-Reza & Annemarie SCHIMMEL**, tr., *MUHAMMAD IQBAL, DIE ENTWICKLUNG DER METAPHYSIK IN PERSIEN* (THE DEVELOPMENT OF METAPHYSICS IN PERSIA), Muhammad IQBAL (mon.), AUSGEWAHLTE SCHRIFTENREIHE 1, Bonn: Hafiz-Verlagsgesellschaft mbH, Co Iranzamin KG, 1982. 85 pp.
Contents: Introduction by A. SCHIMMEL; translation of IQBAL's Inaugural Dissertation (THE DEVELOPMENT OF METAPHYSICS IN PERSIA); and Nachwort by A. SCHIMMEL; followed by an Index of proper names.
G.

1804. **RAHBAR, D.**, "REVIEW OF 'STRAY REFLECTIONS'", *THE MUSLIM WORLD* (Hartford) 5, no. 3: July (1963).

1805. **RAHBAR, Daud**, "IQBAL'S PLACE IN AMERICAN LETTERS", *IQBAL* 17, no. 1: July (1968): pp. 87-92.
Paper read at the American Cultural Centre, Lahore, during the programme entitled "A Tribute to Iqbal" on 18 April 1968. (1) Iqbal's memory lives on in United States, (2) The study of Iqbal at American academic centres.

1806. **RAHBAR, Muhammad Daud**, "GLIMPSES OF THE MAN", *IQBAL: POET-PHILOSOPHER OF PAKISTAN*, Hafeez MALIK (ed.), New York / London: Columbia UP, 1971, pp. 36-55.

1807. **RAHIM, Habibeh**, "PERFECTION MANIFESTED: 'ALI IBN ABI TALIB'S IMAGE IN CLASSICAL PERSIAN AND MODERN INDIAN MUSLIM POETRY", 1990.
A comparison of the treatment of the first Imam 'Ali ibn Abi Talib in classical Iranian literature and in the works of a.o. Muhammad Iqbal.

1808. **RAHIM, Khawaja Abdur**, ed., *IQBAL, THE POET OF TOMORROW*, Lahore: Markaziyya Majlis-i-Iqbal / Abdul Hameed Khan at Ferozsons Ltd., 1980. xxi+273 pp.
Contents:
Khawaja Abdur RAHIM, Foreword; List of Members of the Executive Committee of the Markaziyya Majlis-i-Iqbal; Extract of Speech delivered by Quaid-i-Azam Mohammad Ali Jinnah at Iqbal Day, March 25, 1940; Message of Quaid-i-Azam Mohammad Ali Jinnah on Iqbal Day, 1944; and Javid IQBAL, Introduction to the Study of Iqbal.
Part I (containing in chronological order the presidential and inaugural addresses delivered at Iqbal Day sessions organized by the Markaziyya Majlis-i-Iqbal, the Central Iqbal Committee, in Lahore):
Raziuddin SIDDIQI, Iqbal's Conception of Time and Space
A.K. BROHI, Iqbal's Concept of an Islamic State

Justice Anwarul HAQ, Iqbal's Conception of the Human Ego
A.T.M. MUSTAFA, Nature of Ultimate Reality
Justice A.R. CORNELIUS, Ideological Foundation for Democracy in Islam
Justice S.A. RAHMAN, Iqbal, the Apostle of Muslim Renaissance
Justice Hamoodur RAHMAN, Kingdom of God on Earth
Justice Syed Mahbub MURSHID, The Pebbled Shore
Justice Hamoodur RAHMAN, Iqbal's Ideal
Part II:
Annemarie SCHIMMEL, The Idea of Prayer in the Thought of Iqbal
Sayyad Fayyaz MAHMOOD, Iqbal's Attitude towards God
Syed Abdul VAHID, Iqbal as a Seer
Javid IQBAL, Iqbal's Contribution to Liberalism in Modern Islam
Taj Mohammad KHAYAL, Iqbal's Conception of Satan and his place in Ideal Society
A.K.M. Kabir CHAUDRY, Some Aspects of Iqbal's Poetry
Kavi Ghulam MUSTAFA, Iqbal and Rabindra Nath Tagore
Syed Ali AHSAN, The Problem of Translating Iqbal in Bengali
Mohammad Fauzi Hassan KHALIL, Iqbal, the Renovator of the Muslim World.

1809. **RAHIM, Maulana Abdul**, mon., *THE POLITICAL THOUGHT OF IQBAL*, Dacca / Karachi: Bengali Academy / Iqbal Academy, 1967

1810. **RAHMAN, Abdur**, "IQBAL'S PHILOSOPHY OF THE SELF", *IQBAL* 2, no. 2: July (1953): pp. 35-45.
Reproduced in SHEIKH, M. Saeed (ed.), *STUDIES IN IQBAL'S THOUGHT AND ART*, Lahore, 1972, pp. 64-74.

1811. ———, "LOVE AND HUMAN SOCIETY", *PAKISTAN TIMES*, 15 April 1966, pp. 1, 2.

1812. **RAHMAN, F.**, "IQBAL'S IDEA OF THE MUSLIM", *ISLAMIC REVIEW AND ARAB AFFAIRS* 58, no. [?]: May (1970): pp. 38-40.

1813. **RAHMAN, Fazlur**, "IQBAL AND MODERN MUSLIM THOUGHT", *IQBAL* [vol. ?], no. [?]: January (1955).
Reproduced in SHEIKH, M. Saeed (ed.), *STUDIES IN IQBAL'S THOUGHT AND ART*, Lahore, 1972. pp. 38-51.

1814. ———, "IQBAL AND MYSTICISM", *IQBAL AS A THINKER - EIGHT ESSAYS BY EMINENT SCHOLARS*, Taj Muhammad KHAYAL (ed.), Lahore: Shaikh Muhammad Ashraf, 1944.
An analysis of Iqbal's views on mysticism and the mystical experience, and the influence of

the two major Muslim mystics Ibn-al-'Arabi and Abdul Karim Ibrahim al-Jili.

1815. ———, "IQBAL'S IDEA OF PROGRESS", *IQBAL REVIEW* 4, no. 1: April (1963): pp. 1-4.

1816. ———, "MODERN MUSLIM THOUGHT", *THE MUSLIM WORLD* 5, no. 1 (1955). Previously published in: *IQBAL* 3, no. 3 (1955), pp. 26-38.

1817. ———, "MUHAMMAD IQBAL AND ATATURK'S REFORMS", *JOURNAL OF NEAR EASTERN STUDIES* (Chicago) 43, no. 2: April (1984): pp. 157-62.
On Iqbal's treatment of the political and sociological reforms of Kemal Ataturk.

1818. ———, "SOME ASPECTS OF IQBAL'S POLITICAL THOUGHT", *STUDIES IN ISLAM* 5, no. 2-3: April-July (1968): pp. 161-66.

1819. **RAHMAN, Justice Hamoodur**, "IQBAL'S IDEAL", *IQBAL, THE POET OF TOMORROW*, Khawaja Abdur RAHIM (ed.), Lahore: Abdul Hameed Khan at Ferozsons Ltd., n.d., pp. 147[149]-152.
Paper read as presidential address on 23 April 1967, on Iqbal's *profound and transcendental thoughts*, which, according to the author (p. 149), *are not often understood even by those who claim to be well-versed in the languages in which he expressed his thoughts*.

1820. ———, "KINGDOM OF GOD ON EARTH", *IQBAL, THE POET OF TOMORROW*, Khawaja Abdur RAHIM (ed.), Lahore: Abdul Hameed Khan at Ferozsons Ltd., n.d., pp. 119[123]-125.
Paper read as presidential address on Iqbal Day on 21 April 1965, maintaining that Iqbal's Islamic idealism was not restricted to the birth of Pakistan, but was instead *to reawaken the Muslim nation and to inspire it to reconstruct its "world of sin and misery into a veritable paradise" by returning to the path of* Tauhid *and* Tasdiq (p. 123), which leads man to become a *mard-i-momin*.

1821. **RAHMAN, Justice S. A.**, "IQBAL, THE APOSTLE OF MUSLIM RENAISSANCE", *IQBAL, THE POET OF TOMORROW*, Khawaja Abdur RAHIM (ed.), Lahore: Abdul Hameed Khan at Ferozsons Ltd., n.d., pp. 109[113]-117.
Iqbal's ideal of humanity is reflected in his conception of the Perfect Man, who is clearly distinct from Nietzsche's *a-moral, power-drunk superman whose eternal recurrence is guaranteed by the blind forces of nature* (p. 116); instead, Iqbal's Perfect Man embodies the ideal self (*khudi*), in which the importance of love (*ishq*) and *faqr* (the idealistic

Activist's detachment from the consequences of his action) surpass that of intellect (*aql*). Through ranking Iqbal in the category of distinguished literary artists as Goethe and Rumi, the "apostle of Muslim Renaissance" *bridged the traditional gulf between East and West* (p. 117).

1822. **RAHMAN KHAN, Abdur**, "SPEECH - IQBAL DAY IN WEST GERMANY", *IQBAL REVIEW* 10, no. 1: April (1969): pp. 11.

1823. **RAHMAN KHAN, K. B. Abdur**, "THE POET AND THE MAN AS I REMEMBER HIM", *THE PAKISTAN TIMES* (Rawalpindi), 9 November 1977.

1824. **RAHMAN, Mahmudur**, "ALLAMA IQBAL AS A POET FOR THE CHILD", *DAWN* (Karachi), 9 November 1977.

1825. **RAHMAN, Mizanur**, "IQBAL'S POLITICAL IDEALS", *PAKISTAN TODAY* 2, no. 5 (1949): pp. 229-32.

1826. **RAHMAN, Muhammad Khalilur**, "IQBAL AND NATIONALISM", *PAKISTAN REVIEW* 2, no. 4 (1954): pp. 27-30.

1827. **RAHMAN, Mustazid Wali al**, "IQBAL'S DOCTRINE OF DESTINY", *ISLAMIC CULTURE* (Hyderabad) 13, no. 2: April (1939): pp. 150-175.
Variant name: Wali-ur-REHMAN.

1828. **RAHMAN, Reyazur**, "IQBAL'S CONCEPT OF POWER", *IQBAL REVIEW* 15, no. 3: October (1974): pp. 44-56.
Comparison of the philosophy of Iqbal with that of Nietzsche and Fascism with regard to power, and Iqbal's contribution to international peace. As a conclusion it is argued that *a person with self control will obey the law out of his own conviction and not under coercion* (p. 56). Through his theory of *khudi* Iqbal aims at transforming the barbarian man into a civilized member of society.

1829. ———, "IQBAL'S EMPHASIS ON THE STUDY OF HISTORY", *IQBAL REVIEW* 21, no. 1: April (1980): pp. 61-68.
Short essay on Iqbal's philospohical evolution, from a vehement discouragment of the study of history, towards his emphasising the importance of historical studies. The turning point in this evolution is considered to be the poem MARCH 1907 from BANG-I-DARA.
Re-issued in [Various authors], *SELECTIONS FROM THE IQBAL REVIEW*, ed. Waheed

Qureshi, Lahore, 1983, pp. 443-450.

1830. **RAHMAN, S. A.**, "THE CONCEPT OF LAW IN ISLAM", *IQBAL REVIEW* 24, no. 3: October (1983): pp. 1-7.

1831. ———, "THE IMMORTAL IQBAL", *DAWN* (Karachi), 9 November 1993.

1832. ———, mon., *IQBAL AND MUSLIM RENAISSANCE*, Sheema MAJEED (ed.), Lahore: Bazm-i-Iqbal, 1991

1833. ———, mon., *IQBAL AND SOCIALISM, WITH PRESIDENTIAL REMARKS BY A.K. BROHI AND INTRODUCTION BY HAKIM MOHAMMAD SAID - PROCEEDINGS OF SHAM-I-HAMDARD HELD AT LAHORE, 2 MAY 1974*, Hakim Mohammad SAID (intr.), Karachi: Hamdard National Foundation, 1974. 64 pp.

1834. ———, "IQBAL ON MAN'S PLACE IN THE UNIVERSE", *IQBAL* (Lahore) 21, no. 3: July-September (1974): pp. 1-17.
Paper read at an Iqbal Day Function at the American Center, Lahore, on 19 April 1974.

1835. **RAHMAN, S. M.**, "IQBAL'S CONCEPT OF MENTAL HEALTH", *IQBAL REVIEW* 21, no. 3: October (1980): pp. 1-8.

1836. **RAHMAN, Shaikh Abdur**, mon., *IQBAL AND SOCIALISM*, Karachi: Hamdard National Foundation / Hamdard Academy, 1974. 64 pp.

1837. **RAHMAN, Syed Abdul**, "IDEOLOGICAL ORIENTATION OF IQBAL'S DEMAND FOR PAKISTAN", *IQBAL REVIEW* 20, no. 3: October (1979): pp. 61-74.

1838. ———, "IQBAL'S CONCEPT OF SOVEREIGNTY AND LEGISLATION", *DER ISLAM* (Berlin) 25, no. 1 (1986): pp. 45-58.

1839. **RAHMAN, Syed Sabahuddin Abdur**, "AMIR KHUSRAU AND IQBAL", *IQBAL COMMEMORATIVE VOLUME*, Ali Sardar JAFRI & K.S. DUGGAL (eds.), New Delhi: All India Iqbal Centenary Celebrations Committee, 1977, pp. 219-30.

1840. **RAHMAN, T. Abdur**, mon., *THE GUIDE - IQBAL'S KHIZR-E-RAAH*, Lahore: Pan-Islamic Publications, 1965

1841. **RAHMANI, Saleh**, "IQBAL'S PHILOSOPHY OF LIFE", *OASIS*, 1941, pp. 127-28.

1842. **RAHMATULLAH, S.**, "ART IN IQBAL'S POETRY", *ILLUSTRATED WEEKLY OF PAKISTAN*, 21 April 1957, p. 32.

1843. ———, "BANG-I-DARA AND ITS MESSAGE", *THE PAKISTAN TIMES* (Rawalpindi), 9 November 1982.

1844. ———, "IMAGERY IN IQBAL", *IQBAL REVIEW* (Karachi) 16, no. 1: April (1975): pp. 6-13.

1845. ———, "IQBAL'S CLARION CALL TO CARAVAN", *MORNING NEWS* (Karachi), 8 November 1981.

1846. **RAHMATULLAH, Shahabuddin**, mon., *ART IN URDU POETRY, WITH TWENTY-TWO ILLUSTRATIONS*, Rajshahi: [author's private publ.], 1954. 120 pp. On Iqbal's poetry, pp. 81-108; biography, pp. 80-85; and philosophy, pp. 85-92.

1847. ———, "POETRY OF IQBAL", *ART IN URDU POETRY*, Shahabuddin RAHMATULLAH (Dacca: Pakistan Co-operative Book Society, 1954, pp. 80-108.

1848. **RAINA, Chaman Lal**, *IQBAL AND THE INDIAN HERITAGE*, Chichester / New York: Wiley, 1988/1996

1849. **RAJA, Mushtaq Ahmad**, "IQBAL'S CONTRIBUTION TOWARDS THE CREATION OF PAKISTAN", University of the Punjab, 41 pp.
M.A. Political Science; Promoter: Shaukat Ali. Contents: (1) Iqbal and modern nationalism, (2) Iqbal's concept of millat, (3) The events leading to the demand of separate state, (4) He finds a leader, and Conclusion.

1850. **RAJU, P. T.**, "THE IDEALISM OF SIR MUHAMMAD IQBAL", *VISHVABHARATI QUARTERLY* (NS) 6, no. 2: August-October (1940).

1851. ———, "IDEALISM OF SIR MUHAMMAD IQBAL", *IDEALISTIC THOUGHTS OF INDIA*, P. T. RAJU (mon.), London: Allen and Unwin, 1953, pp. 383-94.

1852. **RAM GOPAL**, mon., *INDIAN MUSLIMS, A POLITICAL HISTORY (1858-1947)*, Lahore: Book Traders, 1976. x+351 pp.

On Iqbal, pp. 117*f.*, 230, 369*f.*; on Iqbal and the Unionist Party, pp. 245*f.*, 279-286, 304*f.*, 322.

1853. **RAMPOLA DEL TINDARO**, "'SICILIA' DI M. IQBAL", *L'OSSERVATORE ROMANO* (Rome), 3 August 1941.
I.

1854. **RAMZ, Mohammad Usman**, "IQBAL'S PHILOSOPHY OF HISTORY: AN ANALYSIS & COMPARISON", *IQBAL REVIEW* 4, no. 3: October (1963): pp. 48-87. Following treatment of the Iqbalian definition of *history*, its method and motifs, the author analyses the views of what he calls the *Universal Historians*, viz. Augustine, Ibn-e Khaldun, Kant, Hegel, Marx and Spengler, arriving at an insight into Iqbal's *philosophy of history*, drawn from elaborate quotes from Iqbal's works. Re-issued in [Various authors], *SELECTIONS FROM THE IQBAL REVIEW*, ed. Waheed Qureshi, Lahore, 1983, pp. 401-441.

1855. **RANDOT, Pierre**, "THE SPIRIT OF MOVEMENT IN THE HISTORY OF ISLAM", *VISION* 11, no. 2: May (1961): pp. 22-23.

1856. **RASCHID, M.**, "IQBAL - POET & THINKER", *IQBAL REVIEW* 8, no. 1: April (1967): pp. 124-33.
Iqbal Day at Karachi.

1857. **RASHID, A. N. M. Fazlur**, "IQBAL AS I HAVE SEEN HIM", *PAKISTAN REVIEW* (Lahore) 19, no. 4 (1971): pp. 29-30.
Special Iqbal Number.

1858. **RASHID, Ehsan**, "THE CONCEPT OF PAKISTAN IN THE LIGHT OF IQBAL'S ADDRESS AT ALLAHABAD", *IQBAL REVIEW* 24, no. 3: October (1983): pp. 9-14.
Iqbal Memorial Talk, 1977.

1859. **RASHID, K. A.**, "ALLAMA IQBAL AND HIS PHILOSOPHY OF SELF", *DAWN*, 21 April 1966, p. 5.

1860. ———, "IQBAL AND HIS PHILOSOPHY OF SELF", *IQBAL: A CRITICAL STUDY*, Misbah-ul-Haq SIDDIQUI (ed.), Lahore: Farhan Publishers, 1977, pp. 112-17. Short essay on Iqbal theory of *khudi* and its modern orientation, taken from *THE PAKISTAN TIMES*, 21 April 1963; published also in *DAWN*, 21 April 1966, p. 5.

1861. ———, "IQBAL AND MARTIN B[U]BER", *PAKISTAN TIMES*, 21 April 1967, p. 2.

1862. ———, "IQBAL AND THE VALUES OF LIFE", *DAWN*, 21 April 1968, p. 8.

1863. ———, "A NEW APPROACH TO IQBAL AND HIS THOUGHT", *PAKISTAN TIMES*, 21 April 1963, p. 3.

1864. ———, mon., *RE-EVALUATION OF ISLAMIC THOUGHT AND OTHER ESSAYS*, Lahore: Universal Books, 1975. xi+197 pp.
On Iqbal, see pp. 9, 17*f.*, 22*f.*, 34, 36, 39, 45, 47*f.*, 52, 54, 56, 78, 80, 88, 90*f.*, 94-96, 98, 101*f.*, 106*f.*, 111, 119, 134, 137, 158, 172, 188.

1865. ———, "SOLITUDE", *DAWN* (Karachi), 30 September 1962.
English translation of (I) TANHAI, from PAYAM-I-MASHRIQ (pp. 136-37); Published simultaneously in *THE PAKISTAN TIMES*, 30 September 1962; and re-issued in *IQBAL REVIEW* 8, no. 1: April (1967), p. 22.

1866. ———, "TWO PHILOSOPHERS COMPARED: IQBAL AND MARTIN B[U]BER", *DAWN*, 21 April 1967, p. 2.

1867. **RASHID, Khawaja Abdul**, "IQBAL AND OUSPENSKY", *PAKISTAN TIMES*, 21 April 1965, p. 2.

1868. ———, mon., *IQBAL, QURAN AND THE WESTERN WORLD*, Lahore: Progressive Books, 1978.
Including bibliographical references.

1869. **RASHID, Khwaja Abdur**, "HAS IQBAL'S THOUGHT BEEN DISTORTED ?", *IQBAL REVIEW* (Karachi) 16, no. 3: October (1975): pp. 45-54.
On Iqbal's arly apprciation of th non-Quranic influnc (through e.g. Manichaan, Zoroastrian, Vedantic and Buddhistic traditions) in non-Arab Muslim countries.

1870. ———, "IQBAL AND THE ROLE OF PHILOSOPHY IN RELIGION", *IQBAL REVIEW* 17, no. 1: April (1976): pp. 33-45.

1871. ———, "RECENT ADVANCES IN SCIENCE AND IQBAL'S CONCEPT OF LIFE AND DEATH", *IQBAL REVIEW* 18, no. 4: April (1978): pp. 71-88.
Short article, in which some of the Quranic concepts on reality are set against modern scientific findings, particularly in the fields of bio-chemistry and bio-physics. The author

deals with *The Vibration Theory of Creation*, the anatomy and functioning of the human brain and its mechanisms of communication, universal organisation, and the *time factor* (*Dahr* - eternal time of the noumenal world, vs. *'Asr* - serial time, vs. *Waqt* - physical time), and thus presents the physical universe from within a synthesis of scientific and Quranic insights.
Re-issued in [Various authors], *SELECTIONS FROM THE IQBAL REVIEW*, ed. Waheed Qureshi, Lahore, 1983, pp. 481-498.

1872. **RASHID, M. S.**, mon., *IQBAL'S CONCEPT OF GOD*, London: Kegan Paul International, 1981. xiv+124 pp.
Includes a bibliography (pp. 117-120) and an index.

1873. **RASHID, Q. M.**, "INDIVIDUAL AND SOCIETY: IQBAL'S CONCEPT", *THE DAWN* (Karachi), 14 August 1960.

1874. **RASHID, Syed Khalid**, "KAUSAR, Zeenath, ISLAM AND NATIONALISM: AN ANALYSIS OF THE VIEWS OF AZAD, IQBAL AND MAUDUDI", *THE MUSLIM WORLD BOOK REVIEW* 17, no. 1 (1996): pp. 16-17.

1875. **RASTOGI, T. C.**, mon., *IQBAL IN FINAL COUNTDOWN*, New Delhi: Omsons Publications, 1991. iii+123pp.
Includes bibliographic references.

1876. ————, "JAGGAN NATH AND IQBALEAN STUDIES", *IQBAL REVIEW* 26, no. 3: October-November-December (1985): pp. 103-10.
Includes a reproduction of Iqbal's letter to Tilok Chand Mahrum, dated 23 September 1915.

1877. ————, "ZINDA RUD IN JAVID NAMA - AN APPRAISAL IN THE PERSPECTIVE OF STREAM OF THOUGHT", *IQBAL REVIEW* 27, no. 1: April-September (1986): pp. 39-50.

1878. **RASTOGI, Tara Chand**, "IQBAL AND TAGORE", *IQBAL COMMEMORATIVE VOLUME*, Ali Sardar JAFRI and K.S. DUGGAL (eds.), New Delhi: All India Iqbal Centenary Celebrations Committee, 1977, pp. 294-300.

1879. **RASTOGI, Tara Charan**, mon., *WESTERN INFLUENCE IN IQBAL*, Columbia / New Delhi: South Asia Books / Ashish Publishing House, 1987. ix+282 pp.
An interesting study, which compares Iqbal with the following Western philosophical and

literary traditions: Kant, Leibniz, Fichte, Hegel, Schopenhauer, Nietzsche, Bergson, Marxism, William James, McTaggart, Whitehead, Einstein, James Ward, Dante, Milton, Goethe, Wordsworth, Browning, Gray, Shelley, Byron, Shaw, Rabindranath Tagore.

1880. **RASUL, Abdur**, "IQBAL AND THE RECONSTRUCTION OF MANKIND", *THE ISLAMIC LITERATURE* (Lahore) [vol. ?], no. [?]: May-July (1958): pp. 43-8.

1881. **RASUL, M. E.**, "REFLECTIONS ON THE THOUGHTS OF IQBAL", *PAKISTAN OBSERVER*, 21 April 1960.

1882. ———, "RUMI AND IQBAL", *ISLAMIC LITERATURE* (Lahore) no. April 1954 (1954): pp. 31-37.
variant name: RASUL, M.G.

1883. **RATTAN, Hans Raj**, "IQBAL: A GREAT ART CRITIC", *PIONEER*, 3 May 1959.

1884. **RAUF, Abdur**, "IQBAL AND THE IQBAL DAY", *PAKISTAN REVIEW* (Lahore) 19, no. 4 (1971): pp. 26-28.
Special Iqbal Number.

1885. ———, mon., *RENAISSANCE OF ISLAMIC CULTURE AND CIVILIZATION IN PAKISTAN*, Lahore: Sheikh Muhammad Ashraf, 1965. xix+320 pp.
Cf. esp. pp. 69, 90-94, 130, 241.

1886. **RAUF, Khawaja Nusrat**, "IQBAL'S IDEA OF WOMENHOOD", *PAKISTAN TIMES*, 21 April 1968, p. 3.

1887. **RAUF, Khwaja Nusrat**, "IQBAL'S IDEA OF WOMANHOOD", *IQBAL: A CRITICAL STUDY*, Misbah-ul-Haq SIDDIQUI (ed.), Lahore: Farhan Publishers, 1977, pp. 107-11.
An article on Iqbal's criticism of Western-style equality of gender, taken from *THE PAKISTAN TIMES*, 21 April 1968.

1888. **RAZA, S. Hashmi**, "SHAIR-I-MASHRIQ AND THE QUAID-I-AZAM", *DAWN* (Karachi), 21 April 1980.

1889. **RAZA, Syed Hashim**, "AN EVENING WITH ALLAMA IQBAL", *DAWN* (Karachi), 9 November 1977.

1890. ———, "THE PHILOSOPHER-POET OF ISLAM", *DAWN* (Karachi), 9 November 1978.

1891. **RAZWI, Shafqat**, "IQBAL, MAWLAWI SHAMSUDDIN AND THE NIZAM", *IQBAL* 41, no. 2 (1994): pp. 9-19.
Iqbal and Mian Fazal-i Hussain, Minister for Industries (of) Punjab, applied for monetary aid from the Nizam, Mir Osman Ali Khan of Hyderabad (Deccan), to Mawlawi Shamsuddin, Secretary of the Anjuman-i Himayat-u 'l-Islam in Lahore, and this application *contains a short history of the Anjuman and verses of the Allama in praise of the Nizam* (p. 9). Original Urdu text in Appendix, pp. 13-19.
Published earlier in the *JOURNAL OF THE PAKISTAN HISTORICAL SOCIETY* (Karachi) 41, no. 2 (1993), pp. 133-142.

1892. **RAZZAQI, Shahid Hussain**, ed., *DISCOURSES OF IQBAL*, Lahore: Shaikh Ghulam Ali & Sons, 1979. 288 pp.

1893. **red.** [?], "IQBAL DAY AT KARACHI", *IQBAL REVIEW* 10, no. 1: April (1969): pp. 1-9.
Reproduction of the inaugural address of Aftab Iqbal, son of Muhammad Iqbal and Bar-at-Law, at Hotel Intercontinental on 21 April 1968.

1894. ———, "IQBAL DAY IN GERMANY", *IQBAL REVIEW* 10, no. 1: April (1969): pp. 10-24.
Summary of the celebrations, including the speech by H.E. Mr. Abdur Rahman Khan; by Prime Minister Dr. Ludwig Huber, reporting on the unveiling of a Plaque commemorating Iqbal's stay in Heidelberg and the naming of a street on the bank of the Neckar in Heidelberg as *Iqbal Ufer*; completed with the English translation of the poems HEIDELBERG, AN EVENING, and Goethe's MAHOMET'S SONG.

1895. ———, "IQBAL DAY IN IRAN", *IQBAL REVIEW* 10, no. 1: April (1969): pp. 25-39.
Report based on Newsletter 2 of the Regional Cultural Institute of 15 June 1968. The message of the Shahanshah and a summary of the speech of Prof. Foruzanfar are reproduced in Persian.

1896. ———, "IQBAL DAY IN TUNISIA", *IQBAL REVIEW* 10, no. 1: April (1969): pp. 54-59.
This survey of Iqbal Day includes an article published in *AL-FIKR*, February 1969, by Prof. Raza b. Rajab.

1897. **REHMAN, Khalil-ur**, "IQBAL AND TERRITORIAL NATIONALISM", *THE CIVIL AND MILITARY GAZETTE* (Lahore), 21 April 1960, pp. 4-5.

1898. **REHMAN, Mizanur**, "IQBAL AND NAZRUL ISLAM", *DAWN*, 4 June 1951, p. 1.

1899. ———, "IQBAL AND NAZRUL ISLAM AT HOME AND ABROAD", *DAWN*, 27 October 1959.

1900. ———, "IQBAL IN EAST PAKISTAN", *PAKISTAN TIMES*, 20 May 1966, p. 2.

1901. **RIAZ, Ahmad**, ed., *IQBAL'S LETTERS TO QUAID-I-AZAM*, Lahore: Friends Educational Service, 1976. 68 pp.

1902. **RIAZ, M.**, "VIOLENT PROTESTS AGAINST THE WEST IN IQBAL'S LYRICAL POETRY", *IQBAL REVIEW* 30-31, no. 3: October and 1: April (1989-1990): pp. 105-28.

1903. **RIAZ, Mohammad**, "QUAID-I-AZAM'S AND IQBAL'S ROLE IN MUSLIM FREEDOM STRUGGLE", *DAWN* (Karachi), 21 April 1982.

1904. **RIAZ, Muhammad**, "ALLAMA IQBAL IN 50 VOLUMES OF THE 'ISLAMIC CULTURE'", *IQBAL REVIEW* 30, no. 1: April-June (1989): pp. 117-37.
Bibliography of studies on Iqbal in the *ISLAMIC CULTURE* (1928-1976) in which, unfortunately, no page ranges are indicated.

1905. ———, "ALLAMA IQBAL'S POETIC STYLE AND DICTION IN PERSIAN", *IQBAL REVIEW* 29, no. 1: April (1988): pp. 169-80.
A short paper, presented at an International Seminar on Iqbal at Aligarh Muslim University of India, February 1987, on the different traditional styles in Persian poetry, viz. (1) Khurasani (Turkistani, Azarbaijani), (2) Iraqi (Farsi), (3) Indian (Isfahani), and (4) a literary revivalism to the old styles of Khurasani and Iraqi. Iqbal is classified as an Iraqi-style poet, but, says the author, since *he had to add new words and meanings which do not correspond fully to the prevalent style*, he might as well be added to the list as a fifth category.

1906. ———, "ALLAMA IQBAL'S VIEWS ON CRITICAL AND CREATIVE THINKING", *IQBAL* (Lahore) 29, no. 3-4: July-October (1982): pp. 17-39.

1907. ———, "ALLAMA IQBAL'S VIEWS ON THE SIGNIFICANCE AND MANIFESTATION OF 'TAUHID'", *IQBAL* 30, no. 1: January (1983): pp. 25-37.

Analysis of the fundamental position of the belief in *tawhid* (unity of God) in Iqbal's vision of Islam.

1908. ———, "ARBERRY AND HIS TRANSLATION OF IQBAL WORKS", *IQBAL* (Lahore) 31, no. 1: January (1984): pp. 67-81.
Bio-bibliography of Arthur John ARBERRY, with special reference to his translations of Iqbal's works, and with a critical appraisal of the (partial) translations of THE TULIP OF SINAI, THE COMPLAINT AND ANSWER, PERSIAN PSALMS, THE MYSTERIES OF SELFLESSNESS, and JAVID NAMAH.

1909. ———, "A COMPARATIVE APPRAISAL OF IQBAL'S PERSIAN POETRY", *IQBAL REVIEW* 20, no. 1: April (1979): pp. 13-33.
Brief comparison of Iqbal's Persian poetry to that of Firdausi, Manuchihri, Nasir Khusrau, Mas'ud, Sana'i, Anwari, Khaqani, Nizami, 'Attar, Rumi, 'Iraqi, Sa'di, Qalandar, Khusrau, Hafiz, Jami, Faghani, Faidi, 'Urfi, Ghalib and others. In conclusion Iqbal's poetic art is nevertheless considered almost unprecedented and therefore deserves to be called Iqbal's own style.

1910. ———, "ESTIMATE OF IQBAL AS A PHILOSOPHER IN MAJID FAKHRY'S A HISTORY OF ISLAMIC PHILOSOPHY", *IQBAL REVIEW* 35, no. 3: October (1994): pp. 105-15.

1911. ———, "GLIMPSES OF IQBAL'S GENIUS IN THE *JAVID NAMAH*", *IQBAL REVIEW* 18, no. 4: January (1978): pp. 171-82.

1912. ———, "INFLUENCE OF BABA FAGHANI'S STYLE ON IQBAL", *JOURNAL OF THE PAKISTAN HISTORICAL SOCIETY* 16, no. [?]: October (1968): pp. 220-230.

1913. ———, "IQBAL-JINNAH CONCORD", *THE PAKISTAN TIMES* (Rawalpindi), 21 April 1982.

1914. ———, "IQBAL'S ENGLISH TRANSLATION OF HIS OWN PERSIAN COUPLETS", *IQBAL REVIEW / IQBALIAT* (Lahore) 27, no. 1: April-September (1986): pp. 177-84.

1915. ———, "IQBAL'S STUDIES IN PERSIAN - A NEW PERSPECTIVE", *IQBAL* 24, no. 4: October (1977): pp. 45-54.

1916. ———, "IQBAL'S VIEWS ON MUSLIM CULTURE", *THE PAKISTAN TIMES*

(Rawalpindi), 9 November 1982.

1917. ———, "REVIEW: Iqbal, Quran and the Western World by K.A. RASHID", *IQBAL REVIEW* 20, no. 1: April (1979): pp. 77-78.

1918. **RIZVI, J. H.**, "INTERNATIONALIST AND HUMANIST", *THE PAKISTAN TIMES* (Islamabad), 9 November 1987.

1919. ———, "IQBAL AS A POET", *PERSPECTIVE* 2, no. 10: April (1969): pp. 14-18.

1920. **RIZVI, Sajjad Baqar**, "IQBAL'S FIGHT AGAINST STAGNATION, STARVATION", *IQBAL* (Lahore) 36, no. 3 (1989): pp. 25-35.

1921. **RIZVI, Sajjad Baqir**, *ALLAMA IQBAL AND MY THOUGHTS*, Lahore: Iqbal Academy, 1994. 96 pp.
In Urdu and English.
U and E.

1922. **RIZVI, Shameem**, "NEW BOOKS ON IQBAL", *DAWN*, 30 April 1967, p. 16.

1923. **RIZVI, Syed Baqar**, "IQBAL'S FIGHT AGAINST STAGNATION & EXPLOITATION", *DAWN* (Karachi), 9 November 1977.

1924. **RIZVI, Syed Jamil Ahmad**, comp., *THESES ON IQBAL: A BIBLIOGRAPHICAL SURVEY OF THE THESES ON IQBAL SUBMITTED TO THE UNIVERSITY OF THE PUNJAB, LAHORE 1950-1976*, Lahore: Aziz Publishers, 1977. 148 pp.
Including 84 theses from the departments of Economics (1), History (1), Education and Research (5), Islamic Studies (4), Persian Studies (6), Philosophy (19), Political Science (2), and Urdu (46). Most theses are written in Urdu.

1925. **RIZWAN, Fauzia**, "IQBAL AND MUSLIM RENAISSANCE", *PAKISTAN TIMES*, 15 July 1977, p. 1.

1926. **ROCHER, Ludo**, "MUHAMMAD IQBAL: SYNTHESE VAN OOST EN WEST", *TIJDSCHRIFT VAN DE VRIJE UNIVERSITEIT VAN BRUSSEL* 5, (1963): pp. 193-203.
D.

1927. **ROFE, Hussain**, "THE SPIRITUAL MESSAGE OF IQBAL", *ISLAMIC LITERATURE*

(Lahore) [vol. ?], no. [?]: April (1953): pp. 23-25.

1928. **ROOMAN, M. Anwar**, "IQBAL - A HERO AND HIS HEROES", *IQBAL* 24, no. 4: October (1977): pp. 55-100.
Part I presents us with a short biography and the outlines of Iqbal's philosophy; Part II focuses on the 360 personalities Iqbal quoted in his works (205 in Persian, 155 in Urdu works, of which 84 are common to both).

1929. **ROOP, Krishna**, mon., *IQBAL*, Lahore: New India Publications, 1945. 38 pp.

1930. ———, "IQBAL, POET AND PREACHER", *MODERN TRENDS: A COLLECTION OF POEMS, SHORT STORIES, PLAYS, AND ARTICLES BY SOME EMINENT WRITERS IN THE PUNJAB*, V. P. VARMA (ed.), Lahore: New India Publications, 1944, pp. 34-44.
Published also in Misbah-ul-Haq SIDDIQUI (ed.), *IQBAL, A CRITICAL STUDY*, Lahore: Farhan Publications, 1977.

1931. ———, "IQBAL, POET AND PREACHER", *IQBAL: A CRITICAL STUDY*, Misbah-ul-Haq SIDDIQUI (ed.), Lahore: Farhan Publications, 1977.
In this article, the author treats Iqbal as a poet *pur sang*, and provides the reader with an elaborate apology to do so. *To enjoy poetry*, he says, [one must] *pursue poetry - not the subject matter, not the ideas, not the thoughts*. Just as one can appreciate the poetry of a decadent writer like for instance Baudelaire, one can overcome the *decadent preachings* of Iqbal, and still be fond of his poetical works. With elaborate quotations, both in the original and in English translation.
Originally published in V.P. VARMA (ed.), *MODERN TRENDS: A COLLECTION OF POEMS, SHORT STORIES, PLAYS, AND ARTICLES BY SOME EMINENT WRITERS IN THE PUNJAB*, Lahore: New India Publications, 1944, pp. 34-44.

1932. **ROSS, E. Denison**, "SIR MUHAMMAD IQBAL - OBITUARY NOTE", *URDU* (Hyderabad) 18, no. [?]: October (1938): pp. 737.
Iqbal Number. Re-issued in *URDU* 1944, p. 43.

1933. **ROTHENSTEIN, W.**, "IQBAL - A MEMORY", *SINCE FIFTY (MEN AND MEMORIES)*, W. ROTHENSTEIN (mon.), London, 1931-1939, Vol. 3, pp. 46-48.

1934. **ROY, N. B.**, "THE BACKGROUND OF IQBAL'S POETRY", *VISHVA-BHARATI QUARTERLY* (Shantiniketan) 20, no. 4: Spring (1955): pp. 321-31.
Variant date: 1920 (issue: September).

1935. **ROZOVSKY, F.**, "MUHAMMAD IQBAL'S POEM *THE CON[...]NT OF THE FELLOW BELIEVERS*", *THE WORK OF MUHAMMAD IQBAL: ARTICLES BY SOVIET SCHOLARS*, Abdur Rauf MALIK (ed.), Lahore: People's Publishing House, 1983, pp. 32-46.

1936. **RUDOLPH, Kurt**, "BÜRGEL, J.C. [Hrsg.]: IQBAL UND EUROPA (Book Review)", *ORIENTALISTISCHE LITERATURZEITUNG* 79, no. 6: November-Dezember (1984): pp. 576.
G.

1937. **S. A. R.**, "REVIEW ON *SECRETS OF EGO* BY A.R. TARIQ", *IQBAL REVIEW* 18, no. 1: April (1977): pp. 77-87.
Comparison of the translations of Iqbal's ASRAR-I KHUDI by Tariq and Nicholson.

1938. **S.N.Q.**, "EUROPEAN CRITICS HAIL FIRST HOOK IN FRENCH ON IQBAL", *DAWN*, 21 April 1956, p. 5.

1939. **SABIR, Muhammad**, "IQBAL, INDIVIDUAL AND MILLAT", *KHYBER MAIL* (Peshawar), 9 November 1986.

1940. **SABRI, Ehsan Qureshi**, "IQBAL'S HOME", *DAWN* (Karachi), 9 November 1985.

1941. **SABRI, G. R.**, "INDIVIDUAL AND SOCIETY IN IQBAL'S THINKING: THE CONCEPT OF SELF AND SELFLESSNESS", *IQBAL REVIEW* 18, no. 4: January (1978): pp. 1-14.

1942. **SADIQ, Khwaja Ghulam**, "IQBAL ON THE CONCEPT OF MORALITY", *IQBAL REVIEW* 10, no. 3: October (1967): pp. 45-54.

1943. **SADIQ, Muhammad**, "BORROWING(S) FROM ENGLISH", *THE CIVIL AND MILITARY GAZETTE* (Lahore), 21 April 1961, pp. 1, 2.

1944. ———, mon., *A HISTORY OF URDU LITERATURE*, Lahore: Oxford UP, 1964. ix+429 pp.
See esp. pp. 16, 155, 190, 228, 231, 242, 267, 311, 390, 392, 403, 406, 407; also pp. 357-391 (Biography); pp. 277, 228-231, 357-358, 369-372, 276, 328, 402-404 (Iqbal and Pan-Islamism); p. 360 (Iqbal's philosophy: Love theory); pp. 372-385 (Iqbal's poetry, history and criticism).

2nd ed. published in Delhi (Oxford UP), 1984, 652 pp.

1945. **SAEED, Khawaja Amjad**, "ECONOMIC PHILOSOPHY OF IQBAL", *IQBAL REVIEW* 23, no. 3: October (1982): pp. 73-83.
It is from a harsh *anti-imperialist* point of view that Iqbal (...*the first economist of the Indo-Pakistan subcontinent to raise his voice against the exploitation of Muslims by domestic and foreign classes controlling the means of production*) in 1903 came to his publication of 'ILM AL-IQTISAD, the first ever publication on economics in Urdu. Not only did Iqbal introduce an innovative economic vocabulary into the Urdu language, he also introduced the concept that *economic activity* and *human psychology* are interrelated, inasmuch that *"Poverty affects the Human Soul"*. Quoting elaborately from Iqbal's speeches and addresses on the subject, the author further analyses the economic genesis of the Pakistan Movement, and the important role of Iqbal's in the growth towards a *New Economic Order* in Pakistan.
Originally published in *IQBAL* 25, no. 1: January (1978), pp. 53-64; re-issued in [Various authors], *SELECTIONS FROM THE IQBAL REVIEW*, ed. Waheed Qureshi, Lahore, 1983, pp. 225-236.

1946. **SAEEDI, Ghulam Reza**, "IQBAL, THE POET OF ISLAM", *JOURNAL OF THE REGIONAL CULTURAL INSTITUTE (Iran)* 9, no. 1-2 (1977): pp. 13-26.

1947. **SAFDAR, 'Abdul Salam**, "IQBAL'S PSYCHOLOGY OF RELIGION", University of the Punjab, Dept. Philosophy, 1973. iv+90 pp.
Promoter: Naeem Ahmad.

1948. **SAFDAR BARLAS**, "HE LIVED WITH THE POET FOR FIFTY YEARS; AN INTERVIEW WITH ALI BUKSH", *ILLUSTRATED WEEKLY OF PAKISTAN*, 16 April 1950, p. 11.

1949. **SAFDAR MAHMOOD & JAVAID ZAFAR**, mon., *FOUNDERS OF PAKISTAN*, Lahore: Publishers United, 1968. x+249 pp.
Iqbal biography, pp. 154-186; Iqbal as politician, pp. 175-186.

1950. **SAHSARAMI, Kalim**, "IQBAL'S PHILOSOPHY OF MUSLIM RENAISSANCE", *ISLAMIC LITERATURE* 6, no. 4: April (1954): pp. 43-46 or 222-226 [?].

1951. **SAID, Yunus M.**, "IQBAL'S CONCEPTION OF SATAN", *IQBAL REVIEW* 3, no. 1: April (1962): pp. 48-57.

1952. **SAIYIDAIN, K. G.**, tr., *IQBAL'S POETRY*, Shayesta KHAN (comp.), Patna: Khuda Bakhsh Oriental Public Library, 1995. 34 pp.

1953. ———, mon., *IQBAL - THE MAN AND HIS MESSAGE*, London / Columbo, 1949/1953

1954. ———, "PROGRESSIVE TRENDS IN IQBAL'S THOUGHT", *IQBAL AS A THINKER - EIGHT ESSAYS BY EMINENT SCHOLARS*, Taj Muhammad KHAYAL (ed.), Lahore: Shaikh Muhammad Ashraf, 1944, pp. 39-96.
The author depicts a two-fold danger in marking Iqbal as a *progressive* thinker: on the one hand are 'his reactionary admirers, who themselves are entirely out of tune with the progressive forces and stand in the way of the creation of a new world, seeking, consciously or unconsciously, to conceal the fire and dynamism of his message for their own narrow ends'; and on the other hand there is a group of progressives and pseudo-progressives, who consider Iqbal's poetry as a *poetry of escape*, written by 'one who cannot come to grips with life'. In order to re-define Iqbal as a progressive thinker, and free him from being used by the above extremes, the author looks for a new definition of *progressivity*, both in traditional philosophy and in Islam, and in the varying concepts of politics (democracy) and idealism, and tries this definition out on several of Iqbal's poems. The article contains quotes of poems in Persian, with English verse translations.

1955. **SAIYIDAIN, Kh. Ghulam**, "IQBAL'S EDUCATIONAL PHILOSOPHY", *ISLAMIC CULTURE* 12, no. 1: January and 2: July (1938): pp. 33-40 and 334-351 resp.

1956. **SAIYIDAIN, Khwaja Ghulam**, mon., *IQBAL'S EDUCATIONAL PHILOSOPHY*, 3rd rev. ed., Lahore: Shaikh Muhammad Ashraf, 1965/1971. x+162 pp.
Appeared as an article in *ISLAMIC CULTURE* (Hyderabad) 12, no. 3: July (1938). Translated into Bengali by S.A. Mannan, and published by the Iqbal Academy (Karachi, 1960); once more re-issued by Shaikh Muhammad Ashraf (1971), and by Kazi Publications (n.d.). The 8th edition appeared in 1977.

1957. ———, "SOME SELECTED VERSES OF IQBAL", *IQBAL* 43, no. 2: April and 3: July (1996): pp. 23-61 and 37-75 resp.
Collection of translations by Saiyidain in various publications, compiled by Shayesta KHAN; with the original Urdu and Persian text compiled by Dr. Ghulam Hussain ZULFIQAR.

1958. **SAJID, Abdul Ahad**, "A FEW MOMENTS WITH IQBAL", *OASIS* (Bahawalpur), April 1941, pp. 143-47.

1959. **SAJJAD, Ahmad**, "CREATIVE WRITING AND ISLAMIC SOCIOLOGICAL CONSIDERATIONS (WITH SPECIAL REFERENCE TO IQBAL)", *IQBAL REVIEW* 30, no. 1: April-June (1989): pp. 85-99.

1960. **SAJJAD HAIDER**, "IQBAL AND HIS PHILOSOPHY", *IQBAL REVIEW* 9, no. 1: April (1968): pp. 1-17.

1961. **SAJJAD HYDER**, "ADDRESS, IQBAL DAY IN CAIRO", *IQBAL REVIEW* 8, no. 1: April (1967): pp. 99-103.

1962. **SALAHUDDIN, Ahmad**, "STING AND SMILE IN IQBAL", *THE CIVIL AND MILITARY GAZETTE* (Lahore), 21 April 1953, pp. 7, 8.

1963. **SALEEM SHEIKH, M.**, "IQBAL - A STUDY FROM HIS LETTERS", *THE CIVIL AND MILITARY GAZETTE* (Lahore), 23 April 1952, p. 4.

1964. **SALIERNO, Vito**, tr., *DUE POESIE DI IQBAL*, Karachi: Edizioni Il Gelsomino, 1964. 7 pp.
I.

1965. ———, "INCONTRO CON IQBAL", *MISSIONI* (Venezia) 66, no. 5: May (1960): pp. 18-21.
I.

1966. ———, "MUHAMMAD IQBAL", *CINZIA* (Firenze) 4, no. 5: May (1958): pp. 3-4.
I.

1967. ———, "MUHAMMAD IQBAL. L'ESSENZA DELLA BELLEZA", *POESIA* (Milano) 6, no. 66 (1993): pp. 49-54.
I.

1968. ———, "LA SICILIA ARABA NELL'OPERA POETICA DI MUHAMMAD IQBAL", *SIKELIA* (Palermo) 2, no. 4-5 (1992): pp. 17-18.
I.

1969. **SAMAN**, "IQBAL'S CONCEPTION OF THE FINE ART", *OASIS* (Bahawalpur), April 1941, pp. 133-34.

Variant name: SAMEN.

1970. **SARDAR, Muhammad**, "MESSAGE TO YOUTH", *PAKISTAN TIMES* (Lahore), 21 April 1953, p. 7.

1971. **SARWAR, Ghulam**, "IQBAL'S CONCEPT OF MUSLIM UMMAH", *IQBAL* (Lahore) 38-39, no. 4: October and 1: January (1991-1992): pp. 1-7.

1972. ————, "SOME ASPECTS OF IQBAL'S PHILOSOPHY", *S.P. SHAH: IN MEMORIAM VOLUME*, SHAH (ed.), Lucknow, 1941.

1973. **SARWAR, Hafiz Ghulam**, ed./intr., *ISLAM AS A MORAL AND POLITICAL IDEAL*, Allama Muhammad IQBAL (mon.), Lahore, 1910.
Re-issue of Iqbal's article in the *OBSERVER* (Lahore, 1909 - qv.), with critical remarks.

1974. **SATTAR, Sajidah Abdus**, mon., *DR. MOHAMMAD IQBAL - DICHTER EN DENKER, 1877-1938*, [place ?]: S.M. Latour Abdus-Sattar, 1987.
This booklet (in Dutch) contains a short biography, a survey of Iqbal's work, a selection from his writings, and a bibliography. This publication can be ordered at the Muslim Information Centre in The Hague, and at IQRA, Islamic and Pakistani Cultural Centre in Almere, Holland.

1975. **SCHAFER, Hermann**, "MUHAMMAD IQBAL: THE SPIRITUAL FATHER OF PAKISTAN", *IQBAL REVIEW* 21, no. 3: October (1980): pp. 27-29.

1976. **SCHIMMEL, A.**, "SOME THOUGHTS ABOUT FUTURE STUDIES OF IQBAL", *IQBAL* 24, no. 4: October (1977): pp. 1-8.
Topics for further research here suggested include Iqbal's connection with the Punjabi mystical tradition, Nietzsche, Jung and other philosophers.

1977. **SCHIMMEL, A. M.**, "BOOK REVIEW OF 'BAUSANI, A.: POESI DI MUHAMMAD IQBAL'", *DIE WELT DES ISLAMS* (Leiden) 5, (1958).

1978. **SCHIMMEL, Annemarie**, mon., *AS THROUGH A VEIL: MYSTICAL POETRY IN ISLAM*, New York: CUP, 1982

1979. ————, "THE ASCENSION OF THE POET", *MUHAMMAD IQBAL*, Various authors (mon.), Karachi: German Pakistan Forum, 1960.

1980. ———, tr. P/G, *BOTSCHAFT DES OSTENS (ALS ANTWORT AUF GOETHES WEST-ÖSTLICHEN DIVAN)* (PAYAM-I-MASHRIQ), Muhammad IQBAL (mon.), Wiesbaden: Otto Harrassowitz, 1963. 107 pp.
German verse translation of (I) PAYAM-I-MASHRIQ.
G.

1981. ———, tr. P/G, *BUCH DER EWIGKEIT* (JAVID NAMAH), München: Man Hueber Verlag, 1957.
German verse translation of (I) JAVID NAMAH.
G.

1982. ———, tr. P/T, *CAVIDNAME* (JAVID NAMAH), Allama Muhammad IQBAL (mon.), Ankara: Kultur Bakanligi, 1989.
Turkish prose translation of (I) JAVID NAMAH, with an extensive commentary.
T.

1983. ———, "CLASSICAL URDU LITERATURE FROM THE BEGINNING TO IQBAL", *A HISTORY OF INDIAN LITERATURE*, Jan GONDA (ed.), Wiesbaden: Otto Harrassowitz, 1975, Vol. III, pp. 126-261.
Including an extensive bibliographical apparatus on all periods covered.

1984. ———, "DIE GESTALT DES SATAN IN MUHAMMAD IQBALS WERK", *MUHAMMAD IQBAL UND DIE DREI REICHE DES GEISTES*, Wolfgang KOEHLER (ed.), Hamburg: Deutsch-Pakistanisches Forum, 1977, pp. 195-226.
Page numbers quoted here include the summary in English: THE FIGURE OF SATAN IN THE WORK OF MUHAMMAD IQBAL.

1985. ———, "EFFECTS OF WESTERN THOUGHT", *CIVIL AND MILITARY GAZETTE* (Lahore), 21 April 1961, p. iii / 1.
Iqbal Day Supplement.

1986. ———, "EINIGE BEMERKUNGEN ZU MUHAMMAD IQBAL'S GAVIDNAME", *DIE WELT DES ORIENTS* (1959).
G.

1987. ———, mon., *GABRIEL'S WING: A STUDY INTO THE RELIGIOUS IDEAS OF SIR MUHAMMAD IQBAL* (BAL-I JABRIL), Studies in the History of Religions 6, Leiden:

E.J.Brill, 1963. ix+428 pp.

Named after (I) BAL-I JIBRIL, a collection of Urdu poems published by Iqbal in 1936, this most exhaustive study of the religious philosophy of Iqbal explores the main themes of Iqbal's religious beliefs and thinking, according to the traditional, standard sets of Islamic faith. A broad outline of the historical background into which Iqbal came in this world, brings the reader to a brief discussion of Iqbal's biography, and a short glance at both the aesthetic and the religious sides of his poetic work.

The first part of the main body of the work is devoted to Iqbal's interpretation of the *Five Pillars of Faith* and Iqbal's handling of the concept of Holy War (*jihad*), viewed against Iqbal's well-known pacifism: (1) There is but one God, Muhammad is the Messenger of God; (2) Prayer (*salat, namaz*); (3) Fasting; (4) The Giving of Alms (*zakat*); and (5) the Pilgrimage to Mecca.

Secondly, Schimmel studies Iqbal's interpretation of the Essentials of Faith (*I believe in God, and in his Angels, and in his Books, and in his Messengers, and in the Last Day, and in the Predestination ...*), and the way in which Iqbal has incorporated all of these in his work and his philosophy.

The last part of the book contains a journey into the different philosophies which seem to have had an influence on Iqbal's thought, from both the East and the West - and, more in particular, a careful analysis of Iqbal's relation to the mystics in Islam, and mysticism as a form of religious experience in general. In her conclusion, Schimmel tries to counter-argue most of Iqbal's harsh critics and ill-users, and she presents Iqbal as a universal philosopher, with ideas obviously based in islamic tradition, but transcending towards a universal humanistic and religious level. *Although,* she says, *nobody will assert that Iqbal was a prophet (...) we may well admit that he has been touched by Gabriel's Wing.* With an extensive bibliography, and an index.

Reprinted by the Iqbal Academy Pakistan (Lahore 1989).

1988.   ———, "GERMANY AND IQBAL", *MUHAMMAD IQBAL UND DIE DREI REICHE DES GEISTES*, Wolfgang KOEHLER (ed.), Hamburg: Deutsch-Pakistanisches Forum, 1977, pp. 45-60.
German summary: IQBAL UND DEUTSCHLAND, pp. 61-62.
E-G.

1989.   ———, "THE IDEA OF PRAYER IN THE THOUGHT OF IQBAL", *MUSLIM WORLD (Hartford Seminary Quarterly)* 48, no. 3: July (1958): pp. 205-22.
This article was reprinted in [Various authors], *MOHAMMAD IQBAL*, Karachi: Pakistan-German Forum, 1960 - qv. Reprinted also in Khawaja Abdur RAHIM (ed.), *IQBAL, THE POET OF TOMORROW*, Lahore: Abdul Hameed Khan at Ferozsons Ltd., n.d., pp. 155[159]-183.

1990.   ———, "IKBAL, MUHAMMAD", *ENCYCLOPEDIA OF ISLAM*, Various authors (

Leiden: E.J. Brill, 1960-1971, Vol. 3, pp. 1057-59.

1991. ———, "IQBAL AND GERMANY, GERMANY AND IQBAL", *IQBAL, COMMEMORATIVE VOLUME*, Ali Sardar JAFRI & K.S. DUGGAL (eds.), New Delhi: All India Iqbal Centenary Celebrations Committee, 1977, pp. 68-72.
This paper deals with Iqbal as *the only Muslim poet who has succeeded in amalgamating Eastern and Western thought into a fascinating picture* (p. 68), and correctly identifies Germany as Iqbal's *spiritual home* in the Western World.

1992. ———, "IQBAL AND GOETHE", *IQBAL COMMEMORATIVE VOLUME*, Ali Sardar JAFRI & K.S. DUGGAL (eds.), New Delhi: All India Iqbal Centenary Celebrations Committee, 1977, pp. 242-53.

1993. ———, "IQBAL AND HALLAJ", *MUHAMMAD IQBAL*, Various authors (mon.), Karachi: German-Pakistan Forum, 1960.

1994. ———, "IQBAL GAVE NEW IDEALS TO HELPLESS MUSLIMS", *CIVIL AND MILITARY GAZETTE* (Lahore), 7 May 1960.
Text of a talk given at Munich on Iqbal Day.

1995. ———, "IQBAL: HIS ART AND THOUGHT (S.A. VAHID)", *ISLAMIC REVIEW* (Woking) 18, no. 3: March-April (1960): pp. 45-47.
A review of S.A. Vahid's *IQBAL: HIS ART AND THOUGHT*, London, 1969 - qv.

1996. ———, "IQBAL: IN FOREIGN COUNTRIES", *MORNING NEWS*, 22 April 1962, p. 7.

1997. ———, "IQBAL IN THE CONTEXT OF INDO-MUSLIM MYSTICAL REFORM", *MUHAMMAD IQBAL UND DIE DREI REICHE DES GEISTES*, Wolfgang KOEHLER (ed.), Hamburg: Deutsch-Pakistanisches Forum, 1977, pp. 97-114. Followed by a German summary: IQBAL IM ZUSAMMENHANG MIT INDO-MUSLIMISCHEN MYSTISCHEN REFORMBEWEGUNGEN, pp. 115-118. E-G.

1998. ———, "IQBAL, LEBEN UND WERK", *MUHAMMAD IQBAL UND DIE DREI REICHE DES GEISTES*, Wolfgang KOEHLER (ed.), Hamburg: Deutsch-Pakistanisches Forum, 1977, pp. 19-38.
Summary in English: IQBAL, HIS LIFE AND HIS WORK, pp. 39-44.

1999. ———, "IQBAL: LIFE AND WORKS", *THE NATION* (Lahore), 9 November 1986.

2000. ———, "IQBAL'S PERSIAN POETRY", *PERSIAN LITERATURE*, Ehsan YARSHATER (ed.), New York: Bibliotheca Persica / Persian Heritage Foundation, 1988. Columbia Lectures on Iranian Studies, Series No. 3.

2001. ———, "THE JAVIDNAME IN THE LIGHT OF THE COMPARATIVE HISTORY OF RELIGION", *PAKISTAN QUARTERLY* (Karachi) 6, no. 4: Winter (1956): pp. 29-32, 39.

2002. ———, "MUHAMMAD IQBAL", *PAKISTAN* 6, no. 9: 21 April (1960): pp. 1-4. PAKISTAN is a Bulletin of the Pakistan Embassy, Bonn.

2003. ———, "MUHAMMAD IQBAL (1873-1938)", *DIE WELT DES ISLAMS* (Leiden) 3-4, (1954): pp. 145-57.
G.

2004. ———, "MUHAMMAD IQBAL AND GERMAN THOUGHT", *MUHAMMAD IQBAL*, Various authors (mon.), Karachi: German-Pakistan Forum, 1960.

2005. ———, "MUHAMMAD IQBAL AS SEEN BY A EUROPEAN HISTORIAN OF RELIGION", *STUDIES IN ISLAM* 5, no. 2-3: April-July (1968): pp. 53-82.

2006. ———, "MUHAMMAD IQBAL - DER GEISTIGE VATER PAKISTANS", *IQBAL UND EUROPA - VIER VORTRAGE*, J. C. BURGEL (ed.), Bern: P. Lang, 1980.
G.

2007. ———, mon., *MUHAMMAD IQBAL - PROFETISCHE DICHTER EN FILOSOOF* (MUHAMMAD IQBAL - PROPHETISCHER POET UND PHILOSOPH), Winand M. CALLEWAERT (tr./intr.), Leuven: Peeters, 1990.
Dutch translation of a work by Annemarie Schimmel (*MUHAMMAD IQBAL - PROPHETISCHER POET UND PHILOSOPH*, Munchen, 1989 - qv.), with a short introduction by the translator.
D.

2008. ———, mon., *MUHAMMAD IQBAL - PROPHETISCHER POET UND PHILOSOPH*, Diederich's Gelbe Reihe 82, Munchen: Eugen Diederichs Verlag, 1989. 240 pp.
An introductory work into the life and works of Iqbal, made primarily for the general public. Following a more or less comprehensive biography, the author portrays Iqbal's conceptions of God, men and universe, as laid down in his poetic works. A short essay on Iqbal's political philosophy is followed by an analysis of Iqbal as a poet, including an elementary survey of his poetic output. A rather extensive analysis of (I) JAVID NAMAH

228

concludes the book.
Schimmel's work contains an elementary bibliography, and a series of indexes.
G.

2009. ———, "MUHAMMAD IQBAL: THE ASCENSION OF THE POET", *DIE WELT DES ISLAM* (Leiden) (NS) 3, (1954).

2010. ———, *MUHAMMAD IQBAL - ZWISCHEN POESIE, PHILOSOPHIE UND POLITIK*, 1997

2011. ———, "MYSTIC IMPACT OF HALLAJ", *IQBAL: POET-PHILOSOPHER OF PAKISTAN*, Hafeez MALIK (ed.), New Delhi / New York: Columbia UP, 1971.

2012. ———, mon., *MYSTICAL DIMENSIONS OF ISLAM*, Chapel Hill: University of North Carolina Press, 1975. 506 pp.
Iqbal philosophy, pp. 117, 204, 222; Iqbal-Sufism/Mysticism, pp. 22, 139, 160, 198, 200, 220, 227, 238, 263, 273, 306*f.*, 405*f.*; Iqbal and Eastern poets, pp. 155, 322*f.*, 327*f.*; also pp. 281, 406.

2013. ———, "THE ORIGIN AND EARLY DEVELOPMENT OF SUFISM", *JOURNAL OF P.H. SOCIETY* (1958).

2014. ———, "OST-WESTLICHE DICHTUNG", *MUHAMMAD IQBAL UND DIE DREI REICHE DES GEISTES*, Wolfgang KOEHLER (ed.), Hamburg: Deutsch-Pakistanisches Forum, 1977, pp. 153-88.
Followed by a summary in English: EAST-WESTERN POETRY, pp. 189-194.

2015. ———, tr. P-U-E/G, *PERSISCHER PSALTER*, Muhammad IQBAL (mon.), Koln: Verlag Jakob Hegner, 1968. 192 pp.
Contents: Vorwort; Der Klang der Karawanenglocke; Stray Reflections; Geheimnisse des Selbst und Mysterien der Selbstlosigkeit; Fruhe Aufsatze; Botschaft des Ostens; Persischer Psalter; Sechs Vorlesungen uber die Wiederherstellung des religiosen Denkens im Islam; Dschavidname - Buch der Ewigkeit; Die "Pakistan-Rede"; Gabriels Schwinge; Der Schlag Mosis; Neujahrsbotschaft 1938; Gabe der Hidschaz; with an appendix explaining names and terms, and a bibliography.
G.

2016. ———, "THE PROPHET MUHAMMAD IN MUHAMMAD IQBAL'S WORK", *AND MUHAMMAD IS HIS MESSENGER: THE VENERATION OF THE PROPHET IN*

ISLAMIC PIETY, Annemarie SCHIMMEL (mon.), Chapel Hill (North Carolina) - London: The University of North Carolina Press, 1985, pp. 239-56. Schimmel stresses the multifariousness of Iqbal, ranging from Islamic fundamentalism to the most recent Western scientific theories. In every aspect of Iqbal's work, however, she finds proof of a genuine piety towards the Prophet. In Iqbal, the image of the Prophet both stands for poetical, moral and philosophical inspiration, and as a political model for direct socio-political action and behaviour.

2017. ———, mon., *THE SECRETS OF CREATIVE LOVE, THE WORK OF MUHAMMAD IQBAL*, Sheikh Ahmed Zaki YAMANI (intr.), AL-FURQAN ISLAMIC HERITAGE FOUNDATION 29 (5th Public Lecture), London: The Royal Victoria and Albert Museum, 1998. 46 pp. + 48 pp.
Lecture at the Royal Victoria and Albert Museum, 11 November 1996, on the concept of creative love in Iqbal's work. The booklet is bilingual (English/Persian) and contains a bio-bibliography of the author in Persian.
E-P.

2018. ———, "SIR MUHAMMAD IQBAL - DICHTER UND REFORMER", *BUSTAN* (Wien) 8, (1967): pp. 3-8.
G.

2019. ———, "TIME AND ETERNITY IN MUHAMMAD IQBAL'S WORK", *PROCEEDINGS OF THE X. CONGRESS FOR THE HISTORY OF RELIGION*, Various authors (mon.), Marburg, 1962.

2020. ———, "WESTERN INFLUENCE ON IQBAL'S THOUGHT", *PAKISTAN TIMES* (Lahore), 21 April 1961, p. 10 .

2021. ———, "WESTERN INFLUENCE ON IQBAL'S THOUGHT", *IQBAL: A CRITICAL STUDY*, Misbah-ul-Haq SIDDIQUI (ed.), Lahore: Farhan Publishers, 1977, pp. 137-34 [?].
Short annotations on Iqbal being influenced by Hegelian thought, the Bergsonian idea of the *two levels of time*, Nietzsche and Milton, without in the process losing faith in the Quran. Paper originally delivered at the IXth International Congres for the History of Religion (Tokyo 1960), and published in the PROCEEDINGS.
Article taken from *THE CIVIL AND MILITARY GAZETTE*, 2 April 1962; variant: 21 April.

2022. ———, "THE WESTERN INFLUENCE ON SIR MUHAMMAD IQBAL'S THOUGHT", *PROCEEDINGS OF THE IX. INTERNATIONAL CONGRESS FOR THE*

HISTORY OF RELIGIONS, Various authors (mon.), Tokyo, 1960.
This article was reprinted in *THE CIVIL AND MILITARY GAZETTE* (Lahore), 21 April 1962), and translated into Urdu by Nuzhat Ara in *THAQAFAT* (Lahore), October 1961.

2023. ———, "WHERE EAST MEETS WEST", *PAKISTAN QUARTERLY* [vol. ?], no. [?]: 1 August (1951): pp. 18-20.

2024. ———, "ZUR ANTHROPOLOGIE DES ISLAM", *ANTHROPOLOGIE RELIGIEUSE* 2, (1955).
Suppl. Number.
G.

2025. **SCHIMMEL TARI, A.**, "A SELECTION FROM IQBAL'S POEMS (1873-1938)", *ISLAMIC REVIEW AND ARAB AFFAIRS* 45, no. [?]: September (1957): pp. 27.

2026. **SEN, S.**, "MUSLIM POLITICAL THOUGHT SINCE 1858", *INDIAN JOURNAL OF POLITICAL SCIENCE* 6, no. 2 (1944): pp. 97-108.
An essay on recent developments in Muslim political philosophy and their impact on modern history. On pages 103-104, Muhammad Iqbal is represented as one of the main modern muslim thinkers.

2027. **SHA'LAN, Ali Muhammad**, "A MOMENT ON IQBAL'S TOMB", *IQBAL REVIEW* 10, no. 1: April (1969): pp. 50-51.

2028. **SHADANI, Andalib**, "IQBAL'S CONCEPTION OF ART", *IQBAL* 19, no. 1: July-September (1971): pp. 8-19.

2029. **SHAFI, Ahmad**, "POET OF ISLAM - SIR MUHAMMAD IQBAL", *MODERN REVIEW* (Allahabad) 54, no. [?]: December (1933): pp. 619-24.
Variant place: Calcutta.

2030. **SHAFI, Mian Muhammad**, "AN IDEAL MASTER AND AN IDEAL SERVANT", *THE CIVIL AND MILITARY GAZETTE* (Lahore), 21 April 1954, p. i-iii.
Iqbal Day Supplement.

2031. ———, "THE LAST 24 HOURS OF IQBAL'S LIFE", *THE PAKISTAN TIMES* (Rawalpindi), 21 April 1981.

2032. ———, "THE LAST DAYS OF THE SAGE", *THE PAKISTAN TIMES* (Rawalpindi), 9

November 1977.

2033. **SHAFI, Muhammad**, "THE ALLAMA VISUALISED MUSLIM RENAISSANCE", *PAKISTAN TIMES*, 21 April 1952, p. 7.

2034. ———, "BIRTH OF A STANZA", *THE CIVIL AND MILITARY GAZETTE* (Lahore), 21 April 1961, p. 1.

2035. ———, "BOOKS THAT IQBAL PLANNED TO WRITE", *PAKISTAN TIMES* (Lahore), 21 April 1960, p. 7.

2036. ———, "IQBAL - A UNIQUE PHENOMENON", *THE PAKISTAN TIMES* (Rawalpindi), 8 November 1981.

2037. ———, "IQBAL AS A TENANT FOR 34 YEARS", *PAKISTAN TIMES* (Lahore), 21 April 1950, p. 7.

2038. ———, "IQBAL: MASTER AND AN IDEAL SERVANT", *THE CIVIL AND MILITARY GAZETTE* (Lahore), 21 April 1954.

2039. ———, "IQBAL'S CHILDHOOD", *PAKISTAN TIMES* (Lahore), 21 April 1949, p. 7.

2040. ———, "IQBAL'S CONCEPTION OF SOCIAL DEMOCRACY", *PAKISTAN TIMES* (Lahore), 21 April 1954, p. 5.
Special Suppl.

2041. ———, "IQBAL THROUGH HIS VALET'S EYES", *PAKISTAN TIMES*, 21 April 1948. Also published in *THE CIVIL AND MILITARY GAZETTE*, 21 April 1948, p. 5.

2042. ———, "JINNAH: IQBAL'S CORRESPONDENCE", *PAKISTAN TIMES*, 25 December 1955.

2043. ———, "LAST DAYS OF THE POET IQBAL", *THE CIVIL AND MILITARY GAZETTE* (Lahore), 21 April 1952, pp. 1, 4.

2044. ———, "LAST MOMENTS OF IQBAL", *ILLUSTRATED WEEKLY OF PAKISTAN*, 16 April 1926, p. 26.

2045. ———, "LIFE AT JAVID MANZIL", *THE CIVIL AND MILITARY GAZETTE* (Lahore), 21 April 1960, p. 2.

2046. ———, "POET'S VISITORS", *PAKISTAN TIMES* (Lahore), 21 April 1955, p. 5.

2047. **SHAFIQ BRELVI**, "UNPUBLISHED LETTERS OF IQBAL", *ILLUSTRATED WEEKLY OF PAKISTAN*, 16 April 1950, p. 3.
Iqbal Number.

2048. **SHAH, A. A.**, "BAL-I-JIBRIL: THIRTEEN GHAZALS", *IQBAL REVIEW* 11, no. 3: October (1970): pp. 1-16.
English translation of 13 Ghazals from Iqbal's BAL-I-JIBRIL.

2049. ———, "BEAUTY UNVEILED", *IQBAL* 13, no. 3: January (1965): pp. 29-30.
Translation of poem No. 7 from Part II of BAL-I JIBRIL.

2050. **SHAH, A. A**, "ENGLISH RENDERING OF GHAZALS IN *BAL-I-JIBRIL*", *IQBAL REVIEW* 16, no. 1: April (1975): pp. 14-20.
English translation of Ghazal (12-100), Bal-i-Jibril (pp. 42-43, pp. 43-44), and the poem PAN ISLAMISM.

2051. **SHAH, A. A.**, "ENGLISH TRANSLATION OF IQBAL'S POEMS", *IQBAL REVIEW* 10, no. 3: October (1969): pp. 8, 16, 24, 44.

2052. **SHAH, A. A. & Ameen KHORASANEE**, "IQBAL'S POEMS", *IQBAL REVIEW* 10, no. 1: April (1969): pp. 64-67.
English translation of Iqbal's poems SELF-AWARENESS and TRUE FAKR (from BAL-E JIBRIL, pp. 82-83, pp. 71-72) and an untitled poem faced by the original text.

2053. **SHAH, Syed Akbar Ali**, tr. U/E, *GABRIEL'S WING (BAL-I-GIBRIL): TRANSLATED INTO ENGLISH VERSE FROM THE URDU OF THE LATE DR. MUHAMMAD IQBAL*, Muhammad IQBAL (mon.), Islamabad: Modern Books Depot, 1979. v+162 pp.
With Foreword by Dr. Javid IQBAL.

2054. ———, tr. U/E, *ROD OF MOSES*, Lahore: Iqbal Academy, 1983. xix+170 pp.
A versified translation of (I) ZARB-I-KALIM.

2055. **SHAH, Syed Ghous Ali**, mon., *IQBAL: THE MEETING POINT OF THE EAST AND*

THE WEST: South Asia Institute, West Germany, 1987

2056. **SHAHAB, Rafiullah**, "ALLAMA IQBAL ON TASAWWUF", *THE PAKISTAN TIMES* (Rawalpindi), 9 November 1985.

2057. ———, "ALLAMA'S DEFENCE FOR SUFISM", *THE PAKISTAN TIMES* (Rawalpindi), 8 November 1981.

2058. **SHAHEED, M. Nawaz**, "DESTINY IN IQBAL", *OASIS* (Bahawalpur), April 1941, pp. 114-26.

2059. **SHAHEEN, A. R.**, "THE VERSATILITY OF IQBAL'S GENIUS", *DAWN* (Karachi), 9 November 1977.

2060. **SHAHEEN, Rahim Bakash**, "IQBAL'S CONCEPT OF STATE", *MORNING NEWS* (Karachi), 21 April 1981.

2061. **SHAHEEN, Rahim Bakhsh**, comp., *MEMENTOS OF IQBAL*, Lahore: All-Pakistan Islamic Education Congress, 1976. 130 pp.
Variant name: SHAHEEN, Rahim Bukhsh.
A collection of additional essays, statements and letters of Iqbal, along with a series of short articles about him, letters to him, etc. Included are also articles by Mohammad Afzal Hussain (MY PERCEPTOR), Mian Muhammad Shafi (LIFE AT JAVID MANZIL), Muhammad Baqir (EARLY CAREER OF ALLAMA IQBAL), and K.A. Rashid (NEW LIGHT ON THE EARLY LIFE OF IQBAL).
Very interesting are the CATALOGUE OF THE IQBAL COLLECTION OF BOOKS, reproduced at the end from *FARAN* (Islamia College, Lahore), June 1962, and the facsimile reproductions of Iqbal's handwriting in English.

2062. **SHAHEEN, Rahim Makhsah**, "IQBAL'S MESSAGE OF REAWAKENING", *THE NATION* (Islamabad), 9 November 1992.
Variant name: SHAHIN, Rahim Bakhsh; variant place of publ.: Lahore.

2063. **SHAHID, Mohammad Haneef**, "IQBAL AND THE SAUDI SCHOLARS", *IQBAL REVIEW* 29, no. 1: April 1988 (1988): pp. 157-67.
Survey of Saudi thinkers and authors, influenced by Muhammad Iqbal or any of the Arabic translations of his works.

2064. **SHAHID, Muhammad Hanif**, "ALLAMA IQBAL AND THE PUNJAB LEGISLATIVE

COUNCIL, BY MUHAMMAD HANIF SHAHID", *IQBAL* 39-40, no. 1: October and 4: January (1992-1993): pp. 75-94.
[Sic] Reference from IQBALIAT: Index 1992, p. 82.

2065. ———, "IQBAL AND THE ARABIC LANGUAGE", *JOURNAL OF THE RESEARCH SOCIETY OF PAKISTAN* 27, no. 2: April (1990): pp. 29-34.

2066. ———, mon., *TRIBUTES TO IQBAL*, Lahore: Sang-e-Meel, 1977. 335 pp.

2067. **SHAIKH, H.**, "IQBAL'S FLAMING PASSION", *DAWN*, 21 April 1957.

2068. **SHAIKH, Hasiena**, *THE CONCEPTION OF THE PERFECT MAN IN IQBAL*, Karachi: Iqbal Academy, n.d.

2069. **SHAKIR, Moin**, "SECULARISM AND IQBAL", *MAINSTREAM* 10, no. 8: 23 October (1971): pp. 24-26.

2070. **SHAMI, Parwaiz A.**, "RECALLING IQBAL", *MORNING NEWS*, 16 April 1961.

2071. **SHAMIM**, "LIFE OF THE POET", *ILLUSTRATED WEEKLY OF PAKISTAN*, 16 April 1950, p. 22.
Iqbal Number.

2072. **SHAMLOO, Latif Ahmad Sh.**, comp./ed., *SPEECHES AND STATEMENTS OF IQBAL*, Muhammad IQBAL (mon.), 2nd ed., Lahore: Al-Manar Academy, 1948. xii+239 pp.
This collection contains (a.o.): ISLAM AND AHMADISM (from *THE STATESMAN*, 1935), Iqbal's NEW YEAR MESSAGE 1938 (originally in Urdu - English translation in *THE TRUTH* (Lahore), 11 January 1938), Iqbal's PRESIDENTIAL ADRESS TO THE ALL INDIA MUSLIM LEAGUE - ALLAHABAD SESSION, December 1930 (originally published in Lahore, 1931), and McTAGGART'S PHILOSOPHY (from *INDIAN ART AND LETTERS*, 1932).

2073. **SHAMS MALIK**, "IQBAL'S POETRY IN PICTURES", *PAKISTAN TIMES* (Lahore), 21 April 1959, p. 3.

2074. **SHAMSI, Mohammad Ahmad**, "IQBAL AND THE QUR'AN", *IQBAL REVIEW* 22, no. 3: October (1981): pp. 19-32.

On the Quran as Iqbal's primary source of philosophical thought and poetic inspiration.

2075.   ———, "IQBAL AND THE WESTERN THOUGHT: A FEW PARALLELS", *IQBAL REVIEW* 21, no. 1: April (1980): pp. 47-60.

2076.   ———, "IQBAL'S ADAPTATION OF A MINOR POEM BY TENNYSON", *IQBAL REVIEW* 18, no. 4: January (1978): pp. 127-31.

2077.   **SHARIATI, Ali**, mon., *IQBAL: MANIFESTATION OF THE ISLAMIC SPIRIT*, Chicago: Kazi Publications, 1996. 130 pp.

2078.   **SHARIF-AL-MUJAHID**, mon., *ALLAMA IQBAL - POET-PHILOSOPHER OF THE EAST*, Karachi: Quaid-i-Azam Academy, 1986. 57 pp.
        A revised and partly rewritten edition of the children's classic, which first appeared as *THE POET OF THE EAST* in Lahore / London, 1961 - qv.

2079.   ———, mon., *ALLAMA IQBAL: POETA E FILOSOFO DO ORIENTE*, Anonym. (tr.), Lisboa, n.d. 43 pp.
        Portuguese translation of the classic children's book on Iqbal: Sharif-al-Mujahid's *THE POET OF THE EAST*, Lahore / London, 1961 - qv.
        Port.

2080.   **SHARIF AL-MUJAHID**, "IQBAL'S MESSAGE TO THE YOUTH", *ILLUSTRATED WEEKLY OF PAKISTAN*, 16 April 1950, p. 16.
        Iqbal Number. Probably reprinted in *THE UNIVERSAL MESSAGE* (Karachi), December 1991 - January 1992, pp. 31-33.

2081.   ———, "IQBAL'S PHILOSOPHY OF EDUCATION", *DAWN*, 19 February 1967.

2082.   **SHARIF-AL-MUJAHID**, "IQBAL'S ROLE IN THE FREEDOM STRUGGLE", *DAWN* (Karachi), 9 November 1977.

2083.   **SHARIF AL-MUJAHID**, "IQBAL'S ROLE LIKENED TO IBNE TIMIAS", *DAWN*, 27 April 1967, p. 8.

2084.   ———, "MUSLIM NATIONALISM: IQBAL' SYNTHESIS OF PAN-ISLAMISM AND NATIONALISM", *AMERICAN JOURNAL OF ISLAMIC SOCIAL SCIENCES* 2, no. 1

(1985): pp. 29-40.

2085. **SHARIF-AL-MUJAHID**, mon., *THE POET OF THE EAST: THE STORY OF MUHAMMAD IQBAL*, Lahore / London: Oxford UP, 1961/1963. 43 pp.
Small booklet, meant to introduce Muhammad Iqbal to students at the secondary school and college level (based on vocabulary from the Thorndike-Large List), and covering Iqbal's biography, an introductory survey of the development of his thought, an overview of his poetic achievements, and his role in the genesis of Pakistan. In 1986 re-issued by the Quaid-i-Azam Academy, Karachi, under the title *ALLAMA IQBAL - POET-PHILOSOPHER OF THE EAST.*

2086. **SHARIF, M. M.**, mon., *ABOUT IQBAL AND HIS THOUGHT*, 2nd ed., M.M. SHARIF - COLLECTED PAPERS 1, Lahore: Institute of Islamic Culture, 1976. 199 pp. / 119 pp.
A collection of six articles by a personal acquaintance of Iqbal's:
(1) MY CONTACT WITH IQBAL, recalling some anecdotes from the meetings between Iqbal and Sharif; (2) IQBAL'S CONCEPTION OF GOD, reportedly taken from the journal *ISLAMIC CULTURE*, also published in [Various authors], *IQBAL AS A THINKER - EIGHT ESSAYS BY EMINENT SCHOLARS*, Lahore 1944 (with numerous reprints) (*abstract* qv.); (3) AN UNFINISHED LETTER to Dr. Sacchidanand Sinha, dated August 26th 1947, in reply to Dr. Sinha's publication of IQBAL - HIS POETRY AND MESSAGE (Allahabad 1947 - qv.) - containing an extremely eloquent but at the same time severe and harsh rebuke of Dr. Sinha's criticism of Iqbal, and more in particular as to him being too hard on Plato and Hafiz, minor to Shelley as *the great poet of socialism*, and his choice to write in Persian as well as in Urdu (in reply to which Sharif stresses the difference between *Indo-Persian Language* and *Indo-Persian tradition*, and concludes that however much Iqbal chose to write in Persian, he nevertheless remained an *Indian* poet, a poet *of Islam*, true, but as much a poet of India, since *he has written more poems about Hindu India and Europe than any Hindu or European poet has ever written about the Muslim world.*), his belief that religion is more than just a personal affair (cf. correlation of *khudi* and *bekhudi*), and his personal interpretation of pantheist monotheism. Sharif then goes on to explain how and why, according to him, Iqbal was adverse to the idea of an Indian synthesis of Islam and Hinduism, and concludes by stating that Dr. Sinha *cannot have fully appreciated Iqbal's philosophical position, because it is totally different from the generally accepted Hindu point of view*; (4) WILLIAM JAMES AND IQBAL, a short article comparing Iqbal with his American contemporary James (1842-1910); (5) IQBAL'S THEORY OF BEAUTY, taken from the journal IQBAL (*abstract* qv.); (6) IQBAL'S THEORY OF ART, taken from the journal IQBAL (*abstract* qv.).
Re-issued by Kazi Publications (Chicago 1996).

2087. **SHARIF. M.M.**, "THE GENESIS OF IQBAL'S AESTHETICS", *IQBAL* (Lahore) 1, no.

1: July 1952 (1952): pp. 19-40.

2088. **SHARIF, M. M.**, "IQBAL ON THE NATURE OF TIME", *IQBAL REVIEW* 1, no. 3: October (1960): pp. 35-40.
Short essay on Iqbal's concept of *time*, with reference to the dictum of Heraclitus (*"relatity is ever changing and always in motion"*) and Bergson, and with a full quote of THE SONG OF TIME from PAYAM-I-MASHRIQ.
Re-issued in [Various authors], *SELECTIONS FROM THE IQBAL REVIEW*, ed. Waheed Qureshi, Lahore 1983, pp. 375-380.

2089. ———, "IQBAL'S CONCEPTION OF GOD", *IQBAL AS A THINKER - EIGHT ESSAYS BY EMINENT SCHOLARS*, Taj Muhammad KHAYAL (ed.), Lahore: Shaikh Muhammad Ashraf, 1944.
An analysis of Iqbal's changing conception of God, broadly through three different stages. In a first period (1901-1908) Iqbal's ideas are mainly derived from Platonic philosophy: He conceives God as an Eternal Beauty, 'existing in independence of, and prior to particulars - and yet being revealed in them all'. A second period (1908-1920) is the result of Iqbal's studies at Cambridge under McTaggart and James Ward, and his reading of Rumi, Nietzsche, MacDougall and Fichte. From this Iqbal's position tends towards a *vitalistic* position: God is no longer qualified as *Eternal Beauty*, but as the *Absolute Self*, as *Eternal Will* - and *beauty* is reduced to the position of an attribute of His, covering both the aesthetic and the moral values. Emphasis has shifted from *beauty* to *unity*. In a third period (1921-1938) Iqbal matures his ideas and arrives at a 'philosophy of change', in which the Absolute Ego is not static, but ' an absolutely free creative spirit.
This article reportedly first appeared in the journal *ISLAMIC CULTURE* 16, no. 3: July (1942), pp. 291-300; and is included in Sharif's own collection *ABOUT IQBAL AND HIS THOUGHT*, Lahore, 1964, 2nd ed 1976 - qv. Also published in Lahore, 1973.

2090. ———, "IQBAL'S THEORY OF ART", *IQBAL* (Lahore) 2, no. 3: January (1954): pp. 1-18.
Text of a lecture delivered in the Senate Hall of the University of Punjab (Lahore) under the auspices of the Bazm-i-Iqbal (date unknown).
The author traces the history of the great divide between *art for art's sake* and the functionalist movement, to which he proves Iqbal to belong. But apart from being a functionalist, Sharif states, Iqbal excels in his expressionism - albeit an expressionism which is only partly covered by Croce's definition, (1) *that art is an activity, completely autonomous, and free from all considerations of ethics* (point of view strongly opposed by Iqbal), (2) *that this activity is distinct from the activity of the intellect* (Iqbal agrees with Bergson rather than with Croce in taking *intuition* as a higher form of intellect, (3) *that it consists in the unfolding of the artist's personality* , and (4) *that the appreciation is the contemplator's re-living of the artist's experience*.

Includes quotes from Iqbal in the original, without English rendering.
Re-issued in Sharif's *ABOUT IQBAL AND HIS THOUGHT*, Lahore, 1964 (qv.).

2091. ———, "IQBAL'S THEORY OF BEAUTY", *IQBAL* [vol. ?], ([year ?]).
Text of a lecture delivered in the Senate Hall of the Univeresity of Punjab (Lahore), under the auspices of the Bazm-i-Iqbal (date unknown). A short survey of the aesthetics of Muslim Indian literature brings the author to an analysis of Iqbal's changing attitudes towards the concept of beauty, throughout his career. Periods more or less coincide with the periods defined in Sharif's article IQBAL'S CONCEPTION OF GOD (qv.). A first period, in which Iqbal is said to have been influenced by Neoplatonism and (British) romanticism, ends in 1908, when *Iqbal's stay in Europe and his visits to Spain and Italy brought before his mind the past glory of Islam - and made him deeply conscious of the dark and dismal state in which the Muslim world had fallen*, and he consequently came under the influence of a strongly Europe-oriented vitalism. Had *beauty* sofar been regarded as the creating factor of love, in a third and concluding period, from 1920 onwards, the process of creation is reversed. The essence of Reality is no longer *beauty*, but *love* or *the will of the ego*, and God, as the Supreme Ego, becomes the Ultimate Reality.
This article includes the text of BEAUTY, OBJECTIVE OR SUBJECTIVE? (part 3 from Sharif's *STUDIES IN AESTHETICS*, Lahore: Institute of Islamic Culture, 1964, pp. 166-211), as well as many quotations from the poetical works of Iqbal in the original (no English translation of the quotes is given).
Re-issued as part of Sharif's *ABOUT IQBAL AND HIS THOUGHT*, Lahore 1964 - qv.

2092. ———, "MY CONTACT WITH IQBAL", *PAKISTAN TIMES* (Lahore), 21 April 1959, p. 5.

2093. **SHARIF, Saad**, "IQBAL - AN APPRECIATION", *PAKISTAN REVIEW* 16, no. 5: May (1968): pp. 26-27.

2094. **SHARIF-UL-HASAN**, "IQBAL AND RUMI", *PAKISTAN TIMES*, 21 April 1964, p. 4.

2095. ———, "IQBAL'S AND RUMI'S CONCEPT OF SATAN", *PAKISTAN TIMES*, 26 August 1966, pp. 1, 2.

2096. **SHARMA, Mohan Lal**, "WHITMAN, TAGORE, IQBAL: WHITMANATED, UNDER-WHITMANATED, AND OVER-WHITMANATED SINGERS OF SELF", *WALT WHITMAN REVIEW* (Rochester, MI) 15, (1969): pp. 230-237.

2097. **SHAUKAT ALI**, "IQBAL AND CONTEMPORARY POLITICAL THOUGHT", *THE*

PAKISTAN TIMES (Lahore), 21 April 1952, p. 6.

2098. ———, "IQBAL AND HIS PHILOSOPHY OF EGO", *THE PAKISTAN TIMES* (Lahore), 21 April 1953, p. 6.

2099. ———, "IQBAL'S CRUSADE (IQBAL AND THE WOMEN OF ISLAM)", *THE CIVIL AND MILITARY GAZETTE* (Lahore), 21 April 1949.

2100. ———, "LETTERS TO ALLAMA", *PAKISTAN TIMES*, 21 April 1951, p. 5.

2101. **SHAUKAT ALI, K.**, "WHERE DID IQBAL LIVE? FROM SIALKOT TO THE MAZAR NEAR BADSHAHI MOSQUE", *PAKISTAN TIMES* (Lahore), 21 April 1954. Special Suppl.

2102. **SHAUKAT ALI, Parveen**, mon., *THE POLITICAL PHILOSOPHY OF IQBAL*, Lahore: United Publishers Ltd., 1978

2103. **SHEEN KAAF**, "IQBAL AND PUNJABI", *IQBAL: A CRITICAL STUDY*, Misbah-ul-Haq SIDDIQUI (ed.), Lahore: Farhan Publishers, 1977, pp. 144-49.
A short interview with Iqbal on the Panjabi language, taken from *THE CIVIL AND MILITARY GAZETTE*, 21 April 1963. It originally appeared in the Panjabi magazine *SARANG* in 1930, from which text Sheen Kaaf assumes that the (Hindu) editor of that magazine, Mr. L.S. Prasad, was the one who interviewed Iqbal on the matter. The interview was translated into Urdu by Maulana Hamid Ali Khan, and included in the book *ASAR-IQBAL* (Ghulam Dastgir Rashid, ed., Hyderabad, Deccan 1944).

2104. **SHEHAB, Rafi Ullah**, "ALLAMA IQBAL AND IJTEHAD", *THE PAKISTAN TIMES* (Rawalpindi), 8 November 1981.

2105. ———, "ALLAMA IQBAL AND MOHAMMAD BIN ABDUL WAHAAB", *THE PAKISTAN TIMES* (Rawalpindi), 9 November 1982.

2106. **SHEHAB, Rafiuddin**, "IQBAL'S CONCEPT OF MAN", *THE PAKISTAN TIMES* (Rawalpindi), 9 November 1984.

2107. **SHEHAB, Rafiullah**, "ALLAMA IQBAL AND IJTEHAD", *THE MUSLIM* (Islamabad), 9 November 1983.

2108. ———, "ALLAMA IQBAL AND ZIA GOKALP", *THE PAKISTAN TIMES* (Rawalpindi), 21 April 1986.

2109. ———, "IJTIHAD, IQBAL, RIBA", *THE FRONTIER POST* (Lahore), 13 February 1992.

2110. ———, "IQBAL AND IJTEHAD", *THE PAKISTAN TIMES* (Rawalpindi), 9 November 1983.

2111. ———, "IQBAL AND MADNI. WHY NATIONALIST MAULANAS LEFT THE QUAID", *PAKISTAN TIMES*, 13 January 1977, p. 1.

2112. ———, "IQBAL ON RECONSTRUCTION OF ISLAMIC LAW - A CRITICAL REAPPRAISAL", *THE PAKISTAN TIMES* (Rawalpindi), 21 April 1979.

2113. ———, "IQBAL ON RELIGIOUS EXPERIENCE", *THE PAKISTAN TIMES* (Rawalpindi), 21 April 1985.

2114. ———, "IQBAL'S CONCEPT OF MAN", *THE FRONTIER POST* (Lahore), 21 April 1992.

2115. ———, "IQBAL'S CONCEPT OF QURANIC KNOWLEDGE", *THE PAKISTAN TIMES* (Rawalpindi), 9 November 1986.

2116. ———, "RECONSTRUCTION OF ISLAMIC LAW AND IQBAL", *THE PAKISTAN TIMES* (Islamabad), 9 November 1987.

2117. **SHEIKH, Hasiena**, "IQBAL ON NATIONAL CHARACTER", *EVENING STAR*, 21 April 1962, p. 2.

2118. **SHEIKH, M. Saeed**, "ALLAMA IQBAL'S INTEREST IN THE SCIENCES", *IQBAL REVIEW* 30, no. 1: April-June (1989): pp. 29-43.

2119. ———, "IQBAL AS A MODERN INTERPRETER OF ISLAM", *IQBAL* 15, no. 3: January (1967): pp. 68-78.
An attempt to illustrate how Iqbal sought to reconstruct religious thought in Islam in terms of modern science and philosophy, and how this can be fully justified on basis of the teachings of the Quran and the Hadith.
Reproduced in SHEIKH, M. Saeed (ed.), *STUDIES IN IQBAL'S THOUGHT AND ART*,

Lahore, 1972, pp. 52-63.

2120. ———, "IQBAL'S MAIN RELIGIO-PHILOSOPHICAL DOCTRINES", *IQBAL* 16, no. 1: July (1967): pp. 67-72.
Reproduced in SHEIKH, M. Saeed (ed.), *STUDIES IN IQBAL'S THOUGHT AND ART*, Lahore, 1972, pp. 21-37.

2121. ———, "PHILOSOPHY OF MAN", *IQBAL REVIEW* 29, no. 1: April (1988): pp. 1-16.
An interesting article on the history of the *Philosophy of Man* (as opposed to the *Philosophies of God and Universe* - from Socrates and Aristotle onwards, leading towards a discussion on the *principle of accultration*, and a methodology for *transferring or transmitting the experiences of the great founders of human culture to the generality of mankind* (shared by Dilthey and Iqbal).
On the way, the statement in (I) THE RECONSTRUCTION OF RELIGIOUS THOUGHT IN ISLAM, that *No understanding of the Holy Book is possible until it is revealed to the believer just as it was revealed to the Prophet* , ascribed by Iqbal to *an unnamed Muslim Sufi*, is unmasked by the author as an authentic statement of Iqbal's himself.
Not only is the Allama the only Muslim thinker to have clearly enunciated the Diltheyian methodolgy, the author concludes, *but also the first to have practised it in his expositions of the many passages of the Quran.*

2122. ———, ed., *THE RECONSTRUCTION OF RELIGIOUS THOUGHT IN ISLAM*, Muhammad IQBAL (mon.), Lahore: Institute of Islamic Culture, 1986.
Reviewed by Arifa FARID in *IQBAL REVIEW* 28, no. 3: October-December (1987), pp. 131-135.

2123. **SHEIKH, Muhammad Saeed**, ed., *STUDIES IN IQBAL'S THOUGHT AND ART: SELECT ARTICLES FROM THE QUARTERLY "IQBAL"*, Lahore: Bazm-i-Iqbal, 1972. xii+518 pp.
A collection of 25 articles in English from IQBAL (the journal of the Bazm-i- Iqbal, Lahore).   Contributions:
(1) Dr L.S. May (IQBAL AND HIS PHILOSOPHY),
(2) M. Saeed Sheikh (also the editor of the volume)(IQBAL'S MAIN RELIGIO-PHILOSOPHICAL DOCTRINES),
(3) Dr Fazl-ur-Rehman (IQBAL AND MODERN MUSLIM THOUGHT),
(4) M. Saeed Sheikh (IQBAL AS A MODERN INTERPRETER OF ISLAM),
(5) Abdur Rahman (IQBAL'S PHILOSOPHY OF THE SELF),
(6) M. Rafiuddin (IQBAL'S IDEA OF THE SELF),
(7) Aziz Ahmad (SOURCES OF IQBAL'S PERFECT MAN),

(8) Jamilah Khatoon (IQBAL'S PERFECT MAN),
(9) S.F. Mahmud (THE MAN OF ACTION IN IQBAL'S POETRY),
(10) Mazher-ud-Din Siddiqi (IQBAL'S CONCEPT OF EVOLUTION),
(11) B.A. Dar (IQBAL AND BERGSON),
(12) Hafiz Abbadullah Farooqi (IQBAL AND BERGSON ON TIME),
(13) Niaz Erfan (IQBAL AND EXISTENTIALISM),
(14) Taj Muhammad Khayal (IQBAL'S CONCEPTION OF SATAN AND HIS PLACE IN IEDAL SOCIETY),
(15) B.A. Dar (THE IDEA OF SATAN IN IQBAL AND MILSTON),
(16) Muhammad Munawwar (HARMONY IN IQBAL'S THOUGHT),
(17) Dr Miss Kazimi (IQBAL'S REVOLT),
(18) Chaudhri Muhammad Ali (WHAT AILS THE SPIRIT OF THE EAST?),
(19) Hafiz Abbadullah Farooqi (IQBAL'S CONCEPT OF STATE),
(20) James B. Prior (IQBAL'S VIEW OF "ISLAMIC NATIONALISM" IN *JAVID NAMAH*),
(21) M.M. Sharif (IQBAL'S THEORY OF BEAUTY),
(22) id. (IQBAL'S THEORY OF ART),
(23) Dr Andalib Shadani (IQBAL'S CONCEPTION OF ART),
(24) Sir Abdul Qadir (THE INFLUENCE OF IQBAL ON URDU LITERATURE),
(25) S.A. Vahid (IQBAL'S ELEGIES).
All contributions are discussed under their respective authors - qv.
Variant name: SHEIKH, Saeed A.

2124. **SHERAZI, Fakhirah**, "A COMPARATIVE STUDY OF NIETZSCHE'S SUPERMAN AND IQBAL'S PERFECT MAN", University of the Punjab, Dept. Philosophy, 1967. 95 pp.
M.A. Philosophy; promoter: Abdul Khaliq.
Contents: (1) Introduction, (2) Nietzsche's Superman, (3) Iqbal's Perfct Man, (4) A comparative study of Nietzsche's Superman and Iqbal's Perfect Man, and (5) Conclusion with Abstracts.

2125. **SHERWANI, Latif Ahmad**, "ON IQBAL: HIS POLITICAL IDEAS AT CROSSROADS", *IQBAL REVIEW* 24, no. 1: April (1983): pp. 45-48.

2126. **SHERWANI, Latif Ahmed**, "ALLAMA IQBAL AND THE PAKISTAN MOVEMENT", *IQBAL REVIEW* 24, no. 1: April (1983): pp. 1-20.

2127. **SHERWANI, Latif Ahmed K.**, comp. / ed., *SPEECHES, WRITINGS AND STATEMENTS OF IQBAL*, 3rd revised and enlarged ed., Lahore: Iqbal Academy, 1977.

263 pp.

2128. **SHIBLI, M. Siddiq**, "IQBAL'S DOCTORAL THESIS", *IQBAL REVIEW* 30, no. 1: April-June (1989): pp. 45-53.

2129. **SHINOZANI, Syed Fazal Abbas**, "HIS CRUSADE AGAINST FALSE VALUES", *PAKISTAN TIMES*, 21 April 1974, p. 2.

2130. **SHUKUROV, S.**, "BEDIL AND IQBAL", *THE WORK OF MUHAMMAD IQBAL: ARTICLES BY SOVIET SCHOLARS*, Abdur Rauf MALIK (ed.), Lahore: People's Publishing House, 1983, pp. 138-52.

2131. **SIDDIQ[I], Kalim M.**, mon., *PAKISTAN: A CULTURAL SPECTRUM*, Lahore: Arslan Publications, 1973. xi+235 pp.
Cf. esp. pp. 176-179, 195-199, 211-217.

2132. **SIDDIQ, Muhammad**, "IQBAL'S BORROWINGS FROM ENGLISH POEMS", *JOURNAL OF THE RESEARCH SOCIETY OF PAKISTAN* 14, no. 4: October (1977): pp. 23-34.

2133. **SIDDIQ(U)I, Marghub**, "DICHOTOMY IN IQBAL", *CIVIL AND MILITARY GAZETTE* (Lahore), 21 April 1952, p. 2.

2134. ———, "IQBAL REPRESENTS CULTURAL DEADLOCK", *CIVIL AND MILITARY GAZETTE* (Lahore), 21 April 1954.

2135. **SIDDIQ(U)I, Mazharuddin, and Marghub**, "IQBAL'S PHILOSOPHY OF POWER", *DAWN* (Karachi), 21 April 1960, p. 5.

2136. **SIDDIQI, Hamidullah**, "IQBAL ON MAN, FREEDOM AND DESTINY", *AL-ISLAM* 4, no. [?]: May (1957): pp. 157.

2137. ———, "IQBAL'S LEGAL PHILOSOPHY AND THE RECONSTRUCTION OF ISLAMIC LAW", *IQBAL REVIEW* [?], no. [?]: April (1960).
Originally in: *PROGRESSIVE ISLAM* (Amsterdam), 1955, pp. 3-4; also published in *ISLAMIC LITERATURE* (Lahore), April 1956, pp. 5-22; and in *AL-ISLAM* 3, no. 24: September (1955), pp. 108-112.
Text of a paper read at the Iqbal Day meeting held in the University of Karachi under the

auspices of the Iqbal Academy, Karachi on 23 April 1955.

2138. **SIDDIQI, M. Raziuddin**, "IQBAL AND FREE WILL", *PAKISTAN QUARTERLY* 4, no. 3: August (1954): pp. 12-23, 50-52 // 19-23.   Independence   Anniversary Number.

2139. ———, "IQBAL AND THE PROBLEM OF FREE WILL", *IQBAL STUDIES*, Muhammad Ziaul ISLAM (ed.), Karachi: Bazm-i-Iqbal, 1949.

2140. ———, ed., *IQBAL AS A THINKER (ESSAYS BY EMINENT SCHOLARS)*, 2nd ed., Lahore: Sheikh Muhammad Ashraf, 1952. 304 pp.
The original edition (1944) has viii+300 pp.; the 3rd edition (1960) has 304 pp.
Contents:
(1) M. Razi-ud-Din Siddiqi, IQBAL'S CONCEPTION OF TIME AND SPACE,   (2)
K.G. Saiyidain, PROGRESSIVE TRENDS IN IQBAL'S THOUGHT
(3) M.M. Sharif, IQBAL'S CONCEPTION OF GOD
(4) Khalifa Abdul Hakim, RUMI, NIETZSCHE AND IQBAL
(5) Fazl-ur-Rahman, IQBAL AND MYSTICISM
(6) M. Aziz Ahmad, IQBAL'S POLITICAL THEORY
(7) Kalim-ud-Din Ahmad, IQBAL'S CONCEPTION OF ART
(8) Fayyaz Mahmood, IQBAL'S ATTITUDE TOWARDS GOD
The title on the front cover reads *IQBAL AS A THINKER. A collection of essays on Iqbal by eight scholars of eminence presenting his diverse facets*, whereas that on the title page is as indicated above.

2141. ———, "IQBAL'S CONCEPTION OF TIME AND SPACE", *IQBAL AS A THINKER - EIGHT ESSAYS BY EMINENT SCHOLARS*, Taj Muhammad KHAYAL (ed.), Lahore: Shaikh Muhammad Ashraf, 1944, pp. 1-38.
Starting from poems and lines of poems by Iqbal, the author examines Iqbal's views on the concepts of *time* and *space*, with respect to (1) the commonsense view of time and space, (2) the conception of time and space held by the ancient Greek philosophers Plato and Zeno, (3) the concept of time and space held by the different schools of Muslim thinking, and represented by Al-Ashari, Ibn Hazm, Tusi and Iraqi, and (4) the changing concepts of time and space in modern philsophical and scientific developments (Descartes, Newton, Nietzsche, and Einstein's theory of relativity).
Variant: Hyderabad, Deccan (Hyderabad Academy), Serial No. 6 (1944), Art. No. 7.
Reprinted in Khawaja Abdur RAHIM (ed.), *IQBAL, THE POET OF TOMORROW*, Karachi, n.d., pp. 23[29]-53, where, on p. 29, it is indicated that this paper was originally read as presidential address at Iqbal Day on 21 April 1952 at Y.M.C.A. Hall, Lahore.

2142. **SIDDIQI, Mazharuddin**, "AN HISTORICAL STUDY OF IQBAL'S VIEWS ON SUFISM", *ISLAMIC STUDIES* 5, no. 4: December (1966): pp. 411-27.

2143. ———, "IQBAL'S PRINCIPLE OF MOVEMENT AND ITS APPLICATION TO THE PRESENT MUSLIM SOCIETY", *ISLAMIC STUDIES* 5, no. 1: March (1966): pp. 9-42.

2144. **SIDDIQI, Mazheruddin**, mon., *CONCEPT OF MUSLIM CULTURE IN IQBAL*, Islamic Research Institute Publication 15, Islamabad: Islamic Research Institute, 1983. viii+144 pp.
Chapters: (1) Anti-Classicism of the Qur'an, (2) Iqbal on Muslim Rationalism, (3) Iqbal on Islamic Mysticism, (4) Iqbal on Islamic Democracy, (5) Iqbal on the problem of Ijtihad, (6) Islamic legalisation in the Modern World; bibliography included. Cf. also SIDDIQUI, M., same title, but published in 1993 (later edition?).

2145. ———, mon., *THE IMAGE OF THE WEST IN IQBAL*, Lahore: Bazm-i-Iqbal, 1965. 132 pp. // 148 pp.
The first part of this book offers an analysis of Iqbal's reactions to the socio-political aspects of Western civilisation, and more in particular his stands towards (1) modern nationalism, (2) the Western concept of *democracy*, (3) the emergence of socialism, and (4) the *westernisation* of the new muslim generation. All these seem to be heavily criticised by Iqbal, both in his poetical work and in his essays - whereas Iqbal was unquestionably an admirer of Western philosophy, as the author amply illustrates in the second part of this book. Here the author exemplifies Iqbal's admiration for the Western tradition of *reason*, which brougt about a remarkable tension between *reason* at the one hand, and the traditional Muslim concept of *'ishq* (*love*) at the other.
In his conclusion, Siddiqi asserts that the whole of Iqbal's poetry and philosophy represents the tensions and conflicts of an age of transition in Muslim society, from *medievalism* to *modernism*. 'The Western dominance, according to Iqbal, is not unmerited', he states, because the Muslim world used to be on a par level with the West as far as dynamism and moralism is concerned, but somehow the Muslim world stranded in stagnation. It is now a task for the new generation to overcome this.
But however much Iqbal was ready to aknowledge Western superiority to a certain degree, he never hesitated to criticise certain aspects of Western society, such as its imperialism, its nationalism, its capitalism, and its loss of certain moral values (for instance: the *false notion of equality which disregards the nnatural and beneficial difference between men and women*).
The deeper reasons for Iqbal's criticism of the West, says Siddiqi, are to be found in the fact that (1) *Iqbal was a humanist in the best tradition of Western thougt, and was surprised to find that the Europe of his day did not push this humanism to its logical concl;usion, and reserved it for the people of the West only* - and (2) *Iqbal believed with a deep and abiding conviction in the spiritual character of life.*

Variant: SIDDIQUI, Mazharruddin, 1964.

2146. ———, "IQBAL'S POLITICAL PHILOSOPHY", *ISLAMIC STUDIES* (Karachi) 15, no. 3 (1976): pp. 195-200.

2147. **SIDDIQI, Muhammad Mazharud-Din**, "IQBAL'S CONCEPT OF EVOLUTION", *IQBAL* (Lahore) 2, no. 3: January (1954): pp. 19-61.
Variant title: IQBAL'S CONCEPTION OF EVOLUTION.
An exhaustive analysis of Iqbal's views on the concept of evolution, portraying Iqbal's Islamic answer to the barrier-breaking theories of (a.o.) Darwin and Bergson, and to the theory of social evolution as propounded by McDougall.
This article was reproduced in SHEIKH, M. Saeed, *STUDIES IN IQBAL'S THOUGHT AND ART*, Lahore 1972, pp. 144-190.

2148. **SIDDIQI, Muhammad Shamsuddin**, "105TH BIRTH ANNIVERSARY: IQBAL, THE PROPHETIC POET", *THE MUSLIM* (Islamabab), 9 November 1984.

2149. **SIDDIQI, Nazeer**, "BHARTRIHARI: A FAVOURITE POET OF IQBAL", *IQBAL* (Lahore) 36, no. 2 (1989): pp. 16-26.

2150. ———, "IQBAL'S JOURNEY FROM NEGATION TO AFFIRMATION", *IQBAL* 37, no. 1-2 (1990): pp. 26-32.

2151. **SIDDIQI, Rihana Anwar**, "IQBALIANA - ABSTRACTS, SERIAL No. 1, ARTICLES ON IQBAL AND HIS THOUGHT, PUBLISHED IN PAKISTAN TIMES, LAHORE ", *IQBAL REVIEW* 13, no. 3: October (1972): pp. 69-92.

2152. **SIDDIQUE, Abdul Hameed**, "IQBAL'S CONTRIBUTION TO ISLAMIC RENAISSANCE", *PAKISTAN TIMES*, 21 April 1965, p. 1.

2153. **SIDDIQUE, Abu Lais**, "CULTURAL HERITAGE OF ISLAM AS IQBAL SAW IT", *DAWN* (Karachi), 9 November 1977.

2154. **SIDDIQUE, Muhammad**, mon., *DESCRIPTIVE CATALOGUE OF IQBAL'S PERSONAL LIBRARY*, Lahore: Iqbal Academy, 1983

2155. ———, "IQBAL'S CONTRIBUTION TOWARDS THE CREATION OF PAKISTAN", University of the Punjab, 38 pp.
M.A. Political Science; Promoter: Munir-ud-Din Chughtai.

Contents: (1) Man and environment, (2) Iqbal as an Indian, (3) Iqbal and Muslim politics, and Conclusion.

2156. **SIDDIQUI, Abdul Hamid**, "IQBAL'S CONTRIBUTION TO ISLAMIC RENAISSANCE", *IQBAL: A CRITICAL STUDY*, Misbah-ul-Haq SIDDIQUI (ed.), Lahore: Farhan Publishers, 1977, pp. 16-25.
Short essay on (I) THE RECONSTRUCTION OF RELIGIOUS THOUGHT IN ISLAM.

2157. **SIDDIQUI, F. A.**, "POETIC ART OF ALLAMA IQBAL", *DAWN* (Karachi), 21 April 1948, p. 10.
variant name: SIDDIQUE, F.A.

2158. **SIDDIQUI, Hamidullah**, "IQBAL'S LEGAL PHILOSOPHY AND RECONSTRUCTION OF ISLAMIC LAW", *AL-ISLAM* 3, no. 24: September (1955): pp. 108-12.

2159. ————, "IQBAL'S LEGAL PHILOSOPHY AND RECONSTRUCTION OF ISLAMIC LAW", *TIMES OF KARACHI*, 14 August 1955, p. 4.

2160. ————, "SUMMARY OF IQBAL'S PHILOSOPHY", *AL-ISLAM* 4 and 9, no. 3: 1 September, no. 4: 15 September, no. 5: 1 October, no. 6: 15 October and no. 7: 1 November (1956): pp. 21-22, 31-32, 37-38, 47-48, 52, [??] resp.

2161. **SIDDIQUI, I. R. Arsh & A. B. ASHRAF**, eds., *IQBAL AUR QUAID-I- A'ZAM - IQBAL AND QUAID-I-AZAM - SEMINARS HELD ON 25 AND 26 DECEMBER 1977*, Multan: University of Multan, 1978. 112+150 pp.
Papers on Jinnah and Iqbal, both in Urdu and in English, with bibliographical references. U-E.

2162. **SIDDIQUI, Kalim**, mon., *CONFLICT, CRISIS AND WAR IN PAKISTAN*, London: Macmillan, 1972. xiii+217 pp.
Cf. esp. pp. 32*f.*, 39-46, 49, 112-114, 158*f.*

2163. **SIDDIQUI, M.**, mon., *CONCEPT OF MUSLIM CULTURE IN IQBAL*, Chicago: Kazi Publications, 1993. 240 pp.
A re-issue of an undated booklet (cf. SIDDIQI, Mazheruddin) with the same name, edited by the Islamic Research Institue, Islamabad - qv.

2164. **SIDDIQUI, M. A.**, "IQBAL AND RELEVANCE TO OUR TIMES", *DAWN*, 21 April

1974, p. 7.

2165. **SIDDIQUI, M. H.**, "IQBAL AND MODERN PROBLEMS", *IQBAL: A CRITICAL STUDY*, Misbah-ul-Haq SIDDIQUI (ed.), Lahore: Farhan Publishers, 1977, pp. 150-155.
A short survey of some of Iqbal's opinions on the problems of his times, with emphasis on his views on Islamic socialism, his condemnation of fascism, his politico-philosophical realism, his progressivism in literature, his quintessential Muslim-hood and his role in the genesis of Pakistan as an independent nation.

2166. ———, "IQBAL'S PALESTINE STATEMENT", *IQBAL: A CRITICAL STUDY*, Various authors (mon.), Lahore: Farhan Publishers, 1977, pp. 156-60.
A short introduction on the history of Palestine is followed by Iqbal's statement, read at a public meeting held under the auspices of the Punjab Muslim League on July 27th 1937.

2167. **SIDDIQUI, Marghub**, "IQBAL AS A LIBERAL DEMOCRAT", *PAKISTAN TIMES*, 21 April 1963, p. 2.

2168. ———, "IQBAL'S CONCEPT OF RELIGIOUS CULTURALISM", *THE PAKISTAN TIMES* (Rawalpindi), 2 December 1977.

2169. ———, "IS IQBAL'S CONCEPT OF SUPERMAN AN EVIL INFLUENCE ON PUBLIC MORALS?", *CIVIL AND MILITARY GAZETTE*, 21 April 1956, p. 3.

2170. **SIDDIQUI, Misbah-ul-Haq**, ed./comp., *IQBAL: A CRITICAL STUDY*, various authors (mon.), Lahore: Farhan Publishers, 1977. viii+227 pp.
A collection of 27 essays on various aspects of Iqbal and his work, 'taken from old files of periodicals and newspapers which are out of reach of an ordinary reader', with a brief introduction by the editor and a foreword by K.A. Rashid.
Of articles 1 to 10, no reference to the original publication is given. Contributions include:
(1) Abdul Aziz Mir (THE POET AND KASHMIR),
(2) Abdul Hai (THE MESSAGE OF IQBAL),
(3) Abdul Hamid Siddiqui (IQBAL'S CONTRIBUTION TO ISLAMIC RENAISSANCE),
(4) Aftab Iqbal (IQBAL'S MESSAGE TO MANKIND),
(5) id. (IQBAL WAS BORN AHEAD OF HIS TIMES),
(6) Peter Avery (IQBAL IN THE EYES OF OTHERS),
(7) Syed Zia-ul-Islam Ayan (IQBAL'S CONCEPT OF 'ISHQ),
(8) M.A. Harris (IQBAL'S CONCEPTION OF ART),
(9) Alam Khurshid (THE VISION OF UTOPIA IN JAVEED NAMA),
(10) Syed Mahbub Murshed (IQBAL: SOME ANNIVERSARY MUSINGS),
(11) Ch. Muhammad Ali (HOW TO RELEASE [THE] SPIRIT OF THE EAST?),

(12) A.T.M. Mustafa (IQBAL'S INTERPRETATION OF LIFE),
(13) Niaz Muhammad Khan (JAVEED NAMA: IN IQBAL'S OWN WORDS),
(14) Nusrat Rauf Khwaja (IQBAL'S IDEA OF WOMANHOOD),
(15) R.A. Rashid (IQBAL AND HIS PHILOSOPHY OF SELF),
(16) Riffat Hasan (IQBAL AND SOCIALISM),
(17) Syed Sajjad Hussain (UNDERSTANDING OF IQBAL),
(18) M. Saraf Yusaf (IQBAL'S ROLE IN KASHMIR'S STRUGGLE),
(19) Annemarie Schimmel (WESTERN INFLUENCE ON IQBAL'S THOUGHT),
(20) Sheen Kaaf (IQBAL AND PUNJABI),
(21) M.H. Siddiqui (IQBAL AND MODERN PROBLEMS),
(22) Id. (IQBAL'S PALESTINE STATEMENT),
(23) NN (A Student of Literature) (IQBAL: "THE POET-PHILOSOPHER OF ISLAM" -
A CRITIQUE),
(24) Sundar Das (THE PHILOSOPHY OF SIR MOHAMMAD IQBAL),
(25) NN (NOTES ON THE DEATH OF ALLAMA IQBAL),
(26) Roop Krishna (IQBAL, POET AND PREACHER),
(27) M.D. Taseer (IQBAL AND COSMOPOLITAN CALLERS).
All articles are described under their respective authors.

2171. **SIDDIQUI, Naeem**, *SAYARA: IQBAL NUMBER*, Lahore, 1963

2172. **SIDDIQUI, Naim**, tr., *BAAL-I-JIBREEL: A VERSE TRANSLATION*, Fremont (USA):
Naim Siddiqui, 1996. 160 pp.

2173. ———, "MIRZA, Taqi Ali, IQBAL'S BAL-I-JIBREEL: A VERSE TRANSLATION",
ISLAMIC CULTURE: AN ENGLISH QUARTERLY 71, no. 3 (1997): pp. 95-96.

2174. **SIDDIQUI, Nazeer**, mon., *IQBAL AND RADHAKRISHNAN*, New Delhi: Apt Books -
Sterling Publishers, 1989. 160 pp.
Also appeared in Pakistan (Pak. American Commercial, Rawalpindi 1989), sub-titled "A
COMPARATIVE STUDY".

2175. **SIDDIQUI, Ovais Sualeh**, "IQBAL AND IRAN", *EDUCATION RESEARCH
BULLETIN* [vol. ?], no. [?]: December (1977): pp. 19-24.

2176. **SIDDIQUI, Raziuddin**, "ALLAMA IQBAL AS A BELIEVER", *INDUS TIMES*, 14
August 1962, p. 4.

2177. ———, "IQBAL CRITIQUE OF NATIONALISM", *PAKISTAN TIMES* (Lahore), 21

April 1950, pp. 5, 8.

2178. **SIDDIQUI, Rihana Anwar**, "SIR MUHAMMAD IQBAL", *PAKISTAN TIMES*, 21 April 1977, p. 2.
Reproduction of an obituary note published in the May 1938 issue of the *INDIAN REVIEW OF CALCUTTA*.

2179. ———, "SOME REFLECTIONS FROM THE POEMS OF IQBAL", *ISLAMIC REVIEW AND ARAB AFFAIRS* 58, no. 7-8: July-August (1970): pp. 29, 30.

2180. **SIMNANI, 'Ala'ud-Dawlah**, mon., *OPERA MINORA*, W. M. Jr. THACKSTON (ed.), Cambridge (Mass.), 1988

2181. **SINGH, Amarjit**, "IQBAL AND GANDHI IN ANAND'S NOVELS", *JOURNAL OF THE RESEARCH SOCIETY OF PAKISTAN* 17, no. 2: April (1980): pp. 1-12.

2182. **SINGH, Har Gobind**, "IQBAL'S NATIONAL POETRY", *OASIS* (Bahawalpur), April 1941, pp. 148-53.

2183. **SINGH, Iqbal**, mon., *THE ARDENT PILGRIM. AN INTRODUCTION TO THE LIFE AND WORK OF MUHAMMAD IQBAL*, London / New York / Toronto: Longmans, Green and Co., 1951. vi+246 pp.
Contents: (I) Father and son, (II) The age of reason, (III) Cities of the West, (IV) In search of a faith, (V) The time of unveiling, (VI) Message of the East, (VII) A chapter of deeds, (VIII) The Dead Sea fruit, (IX) The book of eternity, (X) The lost melody, (XI) To sum up; and a Short Bibliography.
2nd, revised edition: Delhi: Oxford UP, 1997, 183 pp.

2184. ———, "MUHAMMAD IQBAL - STUDY IN A PARADOX", *THE ILLUSTRATED WEEKLY OF INDIA*, 12 December 1954, pp. 38-39.

2185. **SINGH, Jogendra**, "FRIEND'S MEMORIES", *CIVIL AND MILITARY GAZETTE* (Lahore), 21 April 1960, p. 1.

2186. **SINGH, Jogindar**, "A FRIEND'S MEMOIR", *THE CIVIL AND MILITARY GAZETTE* (Lahore), 29 November 1938, p. 2.

2187. ———, "SIR MUHAMMAD IQBAL", *CIVIL AND MILITARY GAZETTE*, 21 April

1960.

2188. **SINGH, Khushwant**, tr./intr, *SHIKWA AND JAWAB-I-SHIKWA. COMPLAINT AND ANSWER: IQBAL'S DIALOGUE WITH ALLAH*, Delhi: Oxford UP, 1981/1993. 96 pp.
English translation of (I) SHIKWA and (I) JAWAB-I-SHIKWA, with parallel text, and with an introduction by the translator and a foreword by Rafiq Zakaria.

2189. **SINGH, Mohan**, "TAGORE, PURAN SINGH AND IQBAL", *SIKH REVIEW* 18, no. [?]: May (1969): pp. 36-37.

2190. **SINGH, Sardar Mohan**, "SOME CHARACTERISTICS AND TENDENCIES OF MODERN URDU POETRY", Calcutta University, 1931.
Published by: Lahore Electric Press.

2191. **SINGH, Sardar Umrao**, tr., *A VOICE FROM THE EAST: THE POETRY OF IQBAL*, Lahore: Mercantile Electric Press, 1922. vi+47 pp.
English translation of selected Urdu and Persian poetry, with texts.

2192. **SINHA, Sachchidananda**, mon., *IQBAL: THE POET AND HIS MESSAGE*, Mirza Samiullah BEG (Nawab Yar Jung BAHADUR) (intr.), Allahabad: Ram Narain Lal, 1947. 2+xliii+512 pp.
A very interesting book, written by a Hindu author five years after Iqbal's death, and published in the year of independence, as the time had arrived to attempt a critical appraisal *... I do not expect that all readers of this thesis will agree with everything that is said in it, but I trust that ... it may contribute towards a juster appreciation of Iqbal, as a poet and a thinker, than has been possible hitherto, for want of a proper critical standard among others(?) in Iqbal* (Preface, p. i). Because of the lucid views expressed in the book, we give the complete list of topics discussed:
1) What is critical appraisal? Explanatory and Introductory, 2) Iqbal's career, works and personality, 3) the greatness of Iqbal: some testimonies and comments, 4) Iqbal as "a poet of India", 5) Iqbal's religious background, 6) Iqbal's philosophical background, 7) Iqbal's political background, 8) Iqbal's basic sentiments, 9) Some samples of Iqbal's sentiments, 10) The literary value of Iqbal's Persian poetry, 11) The literary value of Iqbal's Urdu poetry, 12) A study of Iqbal's philosophical theories, 13) Iqbal's attitude towards mysticism or Sufism, 14) Iqbal's works and non-Muslim readers, 15) Iqbal's legacy and its future, 16) Ghalib, Hali, and Iqbal compared, 17) Iqbal and some great poets, 18) Differences due to divergence in interpretation, 19) The author's interpretation of Islam, 20) Iqbal's interpretation of Islam, 21) Some critical estimates of Iqbal, 22) Iqbal's position as a poet-philosopher, 23) Iqbal and the cultural unity of India, 24) Iqbal and patriotism, 25) Iqbal and the Indo-Muslim renaissance, 26) Iqbal and humanism, 27) The popularity of Iqbal,

28) Last words: truth, tolerance, and unity; Appendices: 1) Iqbal and Sir Fazle Hussain, 2) A study in "Uncritical Laudation", 3) Bibliography.

2193. **SLOMP, Jan**, "THE TRIANGLE: HAFIZ, GOETHE, AND IQBAL", *MAIN CURRENTS OF CONTEMPORARY THOUGHT IN PAKISTAN*, Hakim Muhammad SAID (ed.), Karachi: Hamdard Academy, 1973, pp. 388-414.

2194. **SMITH, Wilfred Cantwell**, "IQBAL", *MODERN ISLAM IN INDIA*, Wilfred Cantwell SMITH (mon.), Lahore: Minerva Book Shop, 1943.
Re-issued in Lahore: Rippon Press, 1947, pp. 114-166; and London: Victor Gollancz, 1946, pp. 114-115.

2195. ———, mon., *MODERN ISLAM IN INDIA, A SOCIAL ANALYSIS*, Lahore: Ripon Printing Press, 1947. 475 pp.
On Iqbal, see pp. 4, 38, 51, 110, 147, 156-174, 177, 220, 235, 268, 285, 307, 313, 390, 421, 423, 431.

2196. **SOLBRIG, Ingeborg H.**, "DIE REZEPTION DES GEDICHTS 'MAHOMETS-GESANG' BEI GOETHES ZEITGENOSSEN UND IN DER MODERNEN PERSISCHEN ADAPTION MUHAMMAD IQBALS (1923)", *GOETHE-JAHRBUCH* (Weimar) 100, (1983): pp. 111-26.

2197. **SOOD, R. P.**, "IQBAL: THE POET-PHILOSOPHER", *TRIBUNE*, 2 May 1959.

2198. **SORLEY, Herbert Tower**, "IQBAL", *MUSA PERVAGANS*, Aberdeen: Aberdeen University Press, 1953, pp. 169-203.
English translation of selected poems.

2199. **SPRENGLING**, "THE RECONSTRUCTION OF RELIGIOUS THOUGHT IN ISLAM", *CHRISTENDOM* (Chicago) 45, (1936).
Review of Iqbal's THE RECONSTRUCTION etc.

2200. **SPRENGLING, M.**, "A TONAL TRIBUTE TO IQBAL", *PAKISTAN QUARTERLY* 6, no. 2: Summer (1956): pp. 11-14.

2201. **STATHOPOULOS, Demetrios L.**, "E UPO TOU MUHAMMAD IQBAL (1873-1938): SYNXRONOS THRESKEIOFILOSFIKE THEORESIS KAI ANANEOSIS TOU ISLAM, SYMBOLE EIS TEN EREUNAN TES ISLAMIKES THRESKEIAS [CONTEMPORARY RELIGIOUS AND PHILOSOPHICAL RENOVATION OF

ISLAM]", *LEIMONARION, PROSFORAS EIS TON KATHEGETEN N.B. TOMADAKEN*, Athena: Adelfon Myrtide, 1973, pp. 326-54.
Paper on Iqbal's main aim, the Muslim Renaissance, primarily based on the poet-philosopher's Six Lectures on the Reconstruction of Religious Thought in Islam. Gr.

2202. **STEPANYANTS, M.**, "THE CONCEPT OF THE PERFECT MAN IN THE WORK OF JALAL AD-DIN RUMI AND MUHAMMAD IQBAL", *THE WORK OF MUHAMMAD IQBAL: ARTICLES BY SOVIET SCHOLARS*, Abdur Rauf MALIK (ed.), Lahore: People's Publishing House, 1983, pp. 118-37.

2203. **STEPANYANTS, M. T.**, "THE DEMISE OF FATALISM", *IQBAL: POET-PHILOSOPHER OF PAKISTAN*, Hafeez MALIK (ed.), New Delhi / New York: Columbia UP, 1971.

2204. ———, "PROBLEMS OF ETHICS IN MOHAMMAD IQBAL'S PHILOSOPHY", *IQBAL REVIEW* 14, no. 1: April (1973): pp. 1-8.
A short essay on Iqbalian ethics and philosophy, with reference a.o. to Iqbal's partly admiring Nietzsche, for giving him a model to create *a Muslim philosophy of action that would suit the aims of the national-liberation movement*, and at the same time his rejecting Nietzsche's apparent atheism and cynical aristocratism. Re-issued in [Various authors], *SELECTIONS FROM THE IQBAL REVIEW*, Waheed Qureshi (ed.), Lahore, 1983, pp. 337-344.

2205. **STEPHENS, Ian**, "IQBAL - SOME REMINISCENCES", *IQBAL* 42, no. 2 (1995): pp. 17-22 or 96-91.
A slightly abridged version of an address delivered at the Centenary Celebrations of the birth of Iqbal, held jointly by the Pakistan Association and the Faculty of Oriental Studies at Cambridge on 19 November 1977.

2206. ———, "MEMORIES OF AN EVENING WITH IQBAL", *PAKISTAN TIMES*, 16 September 1977, p. 4.

2207. **SUBHAN, Abdus**, "RELEVANCE OF IQBAL'S MESSAGE TO INDIA", *INDIAN AND FOREIGN REVIEW* 13, no. 14: May (1976): pp. 22-23.

2208. **SUD, K. N.**, "GERMAN INFLUENCE ON IQBAL", *INDIAN AND FOREIGN REVIEW* (New Delhi) 16, no. 14 (1979): pp. 18-19.

2209. ———, "IQBAL AND PAKISTAN", *MAINSTREAM* 7, no. 33: 19 April (1969): pp. 32-33.

2210. ———, tr., *SELECTIONS FROM GHALIB AND IQBAL*, New Delhi, 1978. English translation of selected passages from the works of Ghalib and Iqbal; re-issued by Ind.-US Inc (East Glastonbury, U.S.A., 1978).

2211. **SUHARWARDY, Shaista Ikramullah**, "A CRITICAL APPRECIATION OF IQBAL'S POEMS", *THE CIVIL AND MILITARY GAZETTE* (Lahore), 21 April 1951, pp. 2-4.

2212. **SUKHOCHEV, A.**, "[AN OUTSTANDING URDU POET]", *UCHITELSKAYA GAZETA*, 19 April 1958.
Article on the occasion of the 20th death anniversary of Muhammad Iqbal. R.

2213. **SUKHOCHEV, A. S.**, "RESEARCH INTO IQBAL'S LIFE AND WORKS IN THE SOVIET UNION", *IQBAL COMMEMORATIVE VOLUME*, Ali Sardar JAFRI & K.S. DUGGAL (eds.), New Delhi: All India Iqbal Centenary Celebrations Committee, 1977, pp. 167-74.
The considerable popularity of [...] Asian poets in the Soviet Union and, in particular, such Persian language poets of India as Mirza Bedil, Amir Khusro Dehlevi, Mirza Ghalib, and others prepared the ground for an understanding and spreading of Iqbal's poetry in the Soviet Union and, above all, in the territory of the Central Asian republics (p. 167), where, of course, there was no obvious language barrier. The author surveys Soviet research into Iqbal into two stages: the acquaintance of a comparatively broad range of readers with samples of Iqbal's poetry and the basic landmarks of his life (pp. 168-169), and the profound study of the problems Iqbal's works dealt with (pp. 169-174).

2214. **SUKHOTCHEV, A.**, "MUHAMMAD IQBAL AS SEEN BY PROGRESSIVE WRITERS IN INDIA AND PAKISTAN", *THE WORK OF MUHAMMAD IQBAL: ARTICLES BY SOVIET SCHOLARS*, Abdur Rauf MALIK (ed.), Lahore: People's Publishing House, 1983, pp. 219-35.

2215. ———, "NAZIR AHMAD AND MUHAMMAD IQBAL", *THE WORK OF MUHAMMAD IQBAL: ARTICLES BY SOVIET SCHOLARS*, Abdur Rauf MALIK (ed.), Lahore: People's Publishing House, 1983, pp. 184-99.

2216. **SULTAN[A], Farrukh**, "A STUDY IN IQBAL'S MORAL PHILOSOPHY", University of the Punjab, Dept. of Philosophy, 1965. 140 pp.

M.A. Philosophy; promoter: M. Saeed Sheikh.

2217. **SULTAN KHAN**, "IQBAL ON DEMOCRACY", *IQBAL REVIEW* 33, no. 1: April (1992): pp. 63-101.

2218. ———, "IQBAL'S CONCEPT OF MILLAT", *IQBAL* 38 and 39, no. 4: October and 1: January (1991-1992): pp. 8-36.

2219. **SULTAN, Muhammad**, tr., *THE COMPLAINT AND THE ANSWER*, Rangpur, 1959. Bengali translation of BANG-I DARA.
Beng.

2220. **SULTANA, Farrukh**, "ALLAMA IQBAL, THE POET-PHILOSOPHER", *THE PAKISTAN TIMES* (Rawalpindi), 21 April 1983.

2221. ———, "IQBAL ON REFORM AND PROGRESS", *PAKISTAN REVIEW* (Lahore) 19, no. 4 (1971): pp. 35-39.
Special Iqbal Number.

2222. ———, "IQBAL ON SOCIAL RECONSTRUCTION", *ISLAMIC LITERATURE* 12, no. 4: April (1966): pp. 27-32.

2223. ———, "IQBAL'S APPROACH TO SOCIAL PROBLEMS", *PAKISTAN TIMES*, 21 April 1966, p. 4.

2224. ———, "IQBAL'S CONCEPT OF POWER", *PAKISTAN REVIEW* 14, no. 11: November (1966): pp. 6-8.
Variant title: ... CONCEPTION ...
Published earlier in *IQBAL* 15, no. 1: July (1966), pp. 65-69.

2225. ———, "STATUS OF WOMEN IN IQBAL'S THOUGHT", *PAKISTAN REVIEW* 16, no. 5: May (1968): pp. 35-36.
Published also in *ISLAMIC LITERATURE* 17, no. 1: January (1971), pp. 49-54.

2226. **Sunday Post** (red.), "THE FILM THAT INSULTS ALLAMA IQBAL", *SUNDAY POST* 1, no. 27: 8 June (1958): pp. 1.

2227. **SUROOR, A. A.**, ed., *MODERNITY AND IQBAL*, Srinagar: Iqbal Institute, University of

Kashmir, 1985.
Contents:
S.C. DUBE, Modernization (pp. 9-12); Balraj PURI, Modernization of Islamic Tradition by Iqbal (pp. 13-37); K.R. BOMBWAL, Modernity and Modernization (pp. 38-50); P.N. PUSHP, Modernity in Iqbal's Verse (pp. 51-61); G.R. ABDULLAH, Modern Education in Iqbal's Perspective (pp. 62-70); Salim KIDWAI, Iqbal and Democracy (pp. 71-78); G.R. MALIK, Iqbal and Materialism (pp. 79*ff.*).

2228. **SUVOROVA, A.**, "IQBAL'S *JAVID-NAMA* AND DANTE", *THE WORK OF MUHAMMAD IQBAL: ARTICLES BY SOVIET SCHOLARS*, Abdur Rauf MALIK (ed.), Lahore: People's Publishing House, 1983, pp. 166-83.

2229. **SVENNING, Carl Elof**, intr./tr., *IQBAL, SKALDEN SOM SKAPADE PAKISTAN, EN PRESENTATION OCH ETT DIKTURVAL*, Muhammad IQBAL (mon.), INTERNATIONELLA BOKKLUBBENS BOKGAVA 1, Lidingo: Internationella Bokklubben, 1956. 63 pp.
Titleless introduction by Abdur Rauf Khan, ambassador of Pakistan to Sweden, on (numberless) p. 2.
Includes a preface (Forord), introduction (Inledning) and anthology of Iqbal's works, namely "Kortare Dikter" (Din Inre Kraft, Varen, Ensamhet, Angslan, Taj Mahal, Manskomakt, Tankelyrik, Sub Specie Aeternitatis, Karlekens Lov, Fyra Smadikter [1-4], Osterland), Jagets Hemligheter Larodikt (chap. I and III completely, short extracts from chap. II), and bibliography.
S.

2230. **SYED, Anwar H.**, "ALLAMA IQBAL AND THE QUAID-I-AZAM ON ISSUES OF NATIONHOOD AND NATIONALISM", *PAPERS PRESENTED AT THE INTERNATIONAL CONGRESS ON QUAID-I-AZAM (19-25 DECEMBER 1976)*, Various authors (mon.), Islamabad: Quaid-i-Azam University, 1976, Vol. 4 [of 4], pp. 167-214.
Essay on the question of nationhood and nationalism, centered (as far as Iqbal is concerned) on the idea that Iqbal, in reconciling the ideal on the drawing board with the empirical reality, was more successful than his predecessors Ghazali and Ibn Jama'a.

2231. **SYED, J. W.**, "POETRY: AN EXPRESSION OF SELF", *IQBAL REVIEW* 2, no. 3: October (1961): pp. 71-78.

2232. ———, "RENAISSANCE: THE CULTURAL REBIRTH OF EUROPE", *IQBAL REVIEW* 3, no. 1: April (1962): pp. 65-87.

2233. **SYED, Sher Muhammad**, "DANTE AND MUHAMMAD (PEACE BE UPON HIM)", *IQBAL REVIEW* 28, no. 1: April-June (1987): pp. 77-85.

2234. **SYED, Yehia**, "IQBAL'S VISIT TO CORDOVA MOSQUE", *MORNING NEWS*, 3 May 1959.

2235. **SYMONDS, Richard**, *THE MAKING OF PAKISTAN*, London: Faber and Faber, 1951. Re-issued in Karachi: National Book Foundation, 1976, 231 pp. Cf. esp. pp. 38-41.

2236. **TABBASUM, S. G. M.**, "IQBAL'S CONTRIBUTION TO URDU LITERATURE", *IQBAL DAY SPEECHES*, Lahore, 1954.

2237. **TABRIZI, G. R. Sabri**, "IQBAL'S RELEVANCE TO THE PRESENT-DAY WORLD: PERSIAN WRITINGS OF IQBAL", *IQBAL, COMMEMORATIVE VOLUME*, Ali Sardar JAFRI & K.S. DUGGAL (eds.), New Delhi: All India Iqbal Centenary Celebrations Committttee, 1977, pp. 31-42.
Although Iqbal *revolted against imperialism, colonialism, and all sorts of exploitation of Man by Man*, the author observes that, after his death, his writings are *used by the conservative governments and ruling interests in order to win the support of the people and, at the same time, to defuse his revolutionary and progressive ideas which ultimately can endanger the interests of the ruling class. Thus Iqbal's ideas are distorted and his poetry is reduced to fit merely ceremonial occasions* (pp. 41-42).

2238. **TAFFAREL, G.**, "NOTIZIE BIOGRAFICHE SU MOHAMMAD IQBAL", *ORIENTE MODERNO* (Roma) 17, (1938): pp. 322-23 / 122-123.
I.

2239. **TAHAWAR ALI KHAN**, "POET OF THE EAST", *BIOGRAPHICAL ENCYCLOPAEDIA OF PAKISTAN*, TAHAWAR ALI KHAN (ed.), 1960-1961, pp. 1.

2240. **TAHIR, Parvez**, "ON REMOVING POVERTY", *THE MUSLIM* (Islamabad), 21 April 1980.

2241. **TAJUDDIN, Pir**, "IQBAL'S POLITICAL CAREER", *PAKISTAN TIMES* (Lahore), 21 April 1951.

2242. **TALIB, Gurbachan Singh**, "IQBAL'S POETIC ACHIEVEMENT: AN ESTIMATE",

INDIAN P.E.N. 41, no. 2 (n.d.): pp. 6-9.

2243. **TAQI, S. Mohammad**, "DYNAMIC CONCEPTION OF THE WEST AND THE PHILOSOPHY OF SELF", *IQBAL REVIEW* 5, no. 1: April (1964): pp. 59-64.
Short treatise on the the *dynamic interpretation of reality*, and more in particular on the concepts of *change*, *time* and *space* in the modern philosophies of science. Re-issued in [Various authors], *SELECTIONS FROM THE IQBAL REVIEW*, ed. Waheed Qureshi, Lahore, 1983, pp. 101-106.

2244. **TARIQ, A. R.**, tr., *LONGER POEMS OF IQBAL*, Lahore: Shaikh Ghulam Ali, 1978

2245. ———, tr., *RUBAYIAT OF IQBAL* (RUBAYIAT), Lahore: Shaikh Ghulam Ali & Sons, 1973. xxiv+220 pp.
English translation of (I) RUBAYIAT.

2246. ———, tr. P/E, *SECRETS OF COLLECTIVE LIFE, BEING A DESCRIPTIVE AND COMPREHENSIVE TRANSLATION OF ALLAMA IQBAL'S RUMUZ-I-BEKHUDI*, Lahore: Islamic Book Service, 1977. xii+231 pp.
An English verse translation of (I) RUMUZ-I-BEKHUDI, with a short preface by the translator.

2247. ———, tr. P/E, *SECRETS OF EGO - BEING A DESCRIPTIVE AND COMPREHENSIVE TRANSLATION OF ALLAMA IQBAL'S ASRAR-I-KHUDI*, Lahore: Islamic Book Service, 1977. 227 / 228 pp.
English verse translation of (I) ASRAR-I-KHUDI, with an elaborate introduction on the concept of *khudi* in Iqbal's poetical works and in the Quran.

2248. **TARIQ, A. Rehman**, comp., *SPEECHES AND STATEMENTS OF IQBAL*, Lahore: Shaikh Ghulam Ali, 1973. xxix+246 pp.
A collection of 43 of Iqbal's political addresses and 6 short pieces on questions regarding Islam, not very critically introduced by A.R.Tariq (preface, pp. i-xxiii). The pieces are printed without critical apparatus, and, even more regrettably, without an index. The work is divided in three parts:
(I) Addresses and Speeches: one delivered at the All-India Muslim League, one at the All-India Muslim Conference, and eight at the Punjab Legislative Council, representing a fairly general idea of Muhammad Iqbal's statesmanship, and his rhetorics on local affairs, including:
(1) *Presidential address delivered at the annual session of the All-India Muslim League at Allahabad, December 29th 1930,*
(2) *Presidential address delivered at the annual session of the All-India Muslim*

Conference at Lahore, March 21st 1932,

(3) *Speech on the budget, 1927-1928, delivered in the Punjab Legislative Council, March 5th 1927,*

(4) *Speech on the cut motion Government's demand for grant under Education, delivered in the Punjab Legislative Council, March 10th 1927,*

(5) *Speech on the motion for adjournment regarding communal riots, delivered in the Punjab Legislative Council, July 18th 1927,*

(6) *Speech on the resolution regarding filling of post by open competitive examination, delivered in the Punjab Legislative Council, July 19th 1927,*

(7) *Speech on the resolution regarding Yunani and Ayurvedic systems of medicine, delivered in the Punjab Legislative Council, February 22nd 1928,*

(8) *Speech on the resolution regarding application of the principles of assessment of income-tax to the assessment of land revenue, delivered in the Punjab Legislative Council, February 23rd 1928,*

(9) *Speech on the budget, 1929-1930, delivered at the Punjab Legislative Council, March 4th 1929,*

(10) *Speech on the budget, 1930-1931, delivered at the Punjab Legislative Council, March 7th 1930.*

(II) Letters, articles and notes on *Islam and Qadianism* (nrs. 11-14) and on modern Muslim thought (nrs. 15-16), including:

(11) QADIANIS AND ORTHODOX MUSLIMS, on the necessity of considering and declaring the Qadiani's a seperate religious community,

(12) REJOINDER TO THE "LIGHT", a reply of Iqbal's to the Qadiani weekly THE LIGHT, in which he had been accused of *not believing in the communion of man with God through the instrumentality of what is known as verbal revelation,*

(13) A LETTER TO THE "STATESMAN", once more in reply to an editorial regarding his *Qadiani Statement* (cf. nr. 11),

(14) REPLY TO QUESTIONS RAISED BY PANDIT J.L. NEHRU, an elaborate and interesting piece, in which Iqbal explains the reasons for the spiritual unrest in the Muslim Community (with regard to a.o. the Qadiani question) to the Hindu J.L. Nehru,

(15) McTAGGART'S PHILOSOPHY, a short philosophical essay linking the philosophy of McTaggart with Muslim thought,

(16) SOME STUDY NOTES, more or less randomly collected, but centred on the idea of resurrection and unity among Muslims.

(III) Some *"Miscellaneous statements"* from between 1928 and 1938, including letters, extracts from letters, statements and articles, chronologically arranged. The sequence of the chosen pieces offers a fairly detailed report of, amongst others, the problematic All-India Muslim Conference of the summer of 1932, and the consecutive negotiations with the Sikh Community (nrs. 21-26), the Kashmir disturbances of 1933 (nrs. 34-37), the Round Table Conference (nrs. 30 and 42), and the Palestinian question (nrs. 44-46):

(17) *Letter of resignation of the office of Secretary of the All-India Muslim League,*

published June 24th 1928,

(18) *Extracts from a letter to Sir Francis Younghusband, taken from* CIVIL AND MILITARY GAZETTE, *July 30th 1931,*

(19) *Statement on impressions of the World Muslim Congress, published January 1st 1932,*

(20) *Statement on the Report of the Indian Franchise Committee, published June 5th 1932,*

(21-22) *Statements explaining the postponement of the meeting of the Executive Board of the All-India Muslim Conference, issued June 29th 1932 and July 6th 1932,*

(23) *Statement on the reported split in the All-India Muslim Conference, issued July 1932,*

(24) *Statement on the Sikh demands, issued July 25th 1932,*

(25) *Statement on Sir Jogendra Singh's proposal for Sikh-Muslim negotiations, published August 4th 1932,*

(26) *Statement explaining the resolution passed by the Working Committee of the All-India Muslim Conference regarding Sikh-Muslim Conversation, issued August 10th 1932,*

(27) *Statement on the Communal Award, issued August 24th 1932,*

(28) *Statement on the Lucknow Conference of the Nationalist Muslim leaders, issued October 8th 1932,*

(29) *Statement on the resolution passed at the Lucknow Conference of Nationalist Muslim leaders, issued October 17th 1932,*

(30) *Statement on the constitution emerging from the Round Table Conference, issued February 26th 1933,*

(31) *Statement on the conditions prevailing in Europe, issued February 26th 1933,*

(32) *Statement on the constitution outlined in the White Paper, issued March 20th 1933,*

(33) *Statement on the rebellion in Chinese Turkestan, published May 16th 1933,*

(34) *Statement on the disturbances in Kashmir State, issued June 7th 1933,*

(35) *Statement on resignation of the office of President of the All-India Kashmir Committee, issued June 20th 1933,*

(36) *Statement on rejection of the office of Presidentship of the Tehrik-i-Kashmir, issued October 22nd 1933,*

(37) *Statement on the administrative reforms in Kashmir, issued August 3rd 1933,*

(38) *Statement on the Punjab Communal Formula, issued July 14th 1933,*

(39) *Statement explaining Sir Fazl-i-Hussain's observation in the Council of State regarding Pan-Islamism, issued September 19th 1933,*

(40) *Statement on the proposed Afghan University, published October 19th 1933,*

(41) *Statement on the conditions in Afghanistan, issued November 6th 1933,*

(42) *Statement explaining the attitude of Muslim delegates to the Round Table Conference, issued December 6th 1933,*

(43) *Statement explaining the Congress attitude towards the Communal Award, issued*

June 19th 1934,

(44) *Letter to Miss Ferguharson, containing views on the Palestine Report, dated July 20th 1937,*

(45) *Statement on the Report recommending the partition of Palestine, read at a public meeting held under the auspices of the Punjab Provincial Muslim League at Lahore, July 27th 1937,*

(46) *Letter to Miss Ferguharson on Palestine, dated September 6th 1937,*

(47) *Statement urging the creation of a Chair for Islamic Research, published December 10th 1937,*

(48) *New Year's Message, broadcast from the Lahore Station of the All-India Radio, January 1st 1938,*

(49) *Statement on Islam and Nationalism, in reply to a statement of Maulana Hussain Ahmed, published in* EHSAN, *March 9th 1938.*

2249. **TARIQ, A. S.**, "THE JAVEDNAME", *PAKISTAN QUARTERLY* 6, no. 4 (n.d.): pp. 29-32.

2250. **TARIQ, Abdur Rashid**, "IQBAL AND NATIONALISM", *PAKISTAN REVIEW* 15, no. 4: April (1967): pp. 13-17.

2251. ——, "IQBAL IN THE PERSIAN SPEAKING WORLD", *PAKISTAN REVIEW* (Lahore) 15, no. 4: April (1967): pp. 12-15, 27.

2252. **TARIQ, Abdur Rehaman & Aziz Ahmad SHEIKH**, mon., *THE RENAISSANCE OF ISLAM: IQBAL'S "TULU-E-ISLAM"*, Lahore: Pan Islamic Publications, 1966

2253. **TARIQ, Ali Asghar**, "POETICAL ART AND STYLE OF IQBAL", *THE PAKISTAN TIMES* (Rawalpindi), 1 April 1985.

2254. **TARIQ AZIZ**, tr. U/E, *THE GUIDE* (KHIZR-E-RAAH), IQBAL (mon.), Chicago: Kazi Publications, 1985. 44 pp.
Also published in Lahore: Pan-Islamic Publications, 1965.

2255. ——, tr., *GUIDING CRESCENT*, Chicago: Kazi Publications, 1985. 50 pp.

2256. **TARIQ, Hameed**, "IQBAL'S CONCEPT OF REVOLUTION", *PAKISTAN TIMES*, 15 July 1966, p. 2.

2257. **TARIQ, Khwaja Mahmood**, tr., *IQBAL: RHYMED TRANSLATIONS OF SELECTED*

POEMS, Chakwal: Dhan Kahoon Publications, 1996. xviii+203 pp.

2258. **TARLAN, Ali Nihad**, tr. P/T, *ESRAR VE RUMUZ. ESRAR-I HODI, 'BENLIGIN SIRLARI'* (ASRAR-I-KHUDI), IQBAL (mon.), Istanbul: Yenilik Basimevi, 1958. 60 pp. Turkish translation of ASRAR-I-KHUDI.
T.

2259. ———, tr. P/T, *SARKTAN HABER* (PAYAM-I-MASHRIQ), TURKIYE-PAKISTAN KULTUR CEMIYETI ISTANBUL SUBESI NESRIYATI 1, Istanbul: Ahmed Said Matbaasi, 1963. 130 pp.
Turkish prose translation of (I) PAYAM-I-MASHRIQ. The volume includes, apart from an introduction, Ithaf, Tur Lalesi (163 Rubai), Fikirler, Sarab-i Baki (Gazeller), Garpli Ruhu, and a concluding chapter (Ikbale'e Dair Bilgiler) on the composer.
T.

2260. **TARLAN, Ali Nihat**, tr. P/T, *RUMUZ-I-BEKHUDI*, Istanbul, 1959.
Turkish translation of (I) RUMUZ-I-BEKHUDI.
T.

2261. **TASEER. M.D.**, "IQBAL AND GHAZIL", *THE ILLUSTRATED WEEKLY OF PAKISTAN*, 29 March 1953.
Re-issue of an article from *PAKISTAN QUARTERLY* 1, no. 1 (1949/1951), pp. 28-40 - qv.

2262. **TASEER, M. D.**, "IQBAL AND MODERN PROBLEMS", *THE PAKISTAN TIMES* (Lahore), 21 April 1948, pp. 5, 6.
Also published in *THE CIVIL AND MILITARY GAZETTE*, 21 April 21 1948, p. 6; and in *THE PAKISTAN TIMES*, 21 April 1948 [and 1952], pp. 5-6.

2263. ———, "IQBAL AND THE GHAZIL", *PAKISTAN QUARTERLY* 1, no. 1: April (1949): pp. 28-40.   Variant   date: 1951.

2264. ———, "IQBAL HAD COSMOPOLITAN CALLERS", *IQBAL: A CRITICAL STUDY*, Misbah-ul-Haq SIDDIQUI (ed.), Lahore: Farhan Publications, 1977.
Biographical anecdotes and rememberings, taken from *THE CIVIL AND MILITARY GAZETTE* (Lahore), 21 April 1954.

2265. ———, "IQBAL'S CONCEPTION OF PERFECT MAN", *PAKISTAN CALLING* 4, no.

263

8: 1 April (1951): pp. 7-8.

2266. ———, "IQBAL'S THEORY OF ART AND LITERATURE", *PAKISTAN QUARTERLY* 1, no. 3 (1949/1952): pp. 15-71.

2267. ———, "IQBAL - THE POET OF ISLAM: BASIC CONCEPTION OF GREAT MAN'S WRITINGS", *CIVIL AND MILITARY GAZETTE* (Lahore), 21 April 1950, p. 2.

2268. ———, "IQBAL: THE UNIVERSAL POET", *PAKISTAN QUARTERY* 5, no. 3: 14 August (1955): pp. 35-36 or 40-41 [?].
Independence Anniversary Number.
Also published in Lahore: Munib Publishers, 1977.

2269. ———, "SOME THOUGHTS ON FIRST IQBAL DAY", *CIVIL AND MILITARY GAZETTE* (Lahore), 21 April 1960, pp. 3-5 or viii [?].

2270. **TASEER, Muhammad Din**, mon., *IQBAL: THE UNIVERSAL POET*, Lahore: Munib Publications, 1977. 75 pp.

2271. **TAWFIK, Yaqoob**, comp., *SPEECHES AND ARTICLES OF IQBAL DAY 1967*, Karachi: Iqbal Council, 1968. iii+51 pp.
Iqbal tributes, pp. 3-24; Iqbal and Rumi, pp. 38 *f*.; Iqbal poetry: history and criticism, pp. 42-45.

2272. **THAPAR, Romila**, "MUHAMMED IQBAL", *EASTERN WORLD* (London) 9, no. 8: August (1955): pp. 35-36.

2273. **The Times** (red.), "OBITUARY NOTE", *THE TIMES* (London), 22 April 1938.

2274. **THOMAS, Henry**, "MUHAMMAD IQBAL", *LIVING BIOGRAPHIES OF GREAT PHILOSOPHERS*, Henry THOMAS (ed. or mon. [?]), New york: Perma Giants, 1941.

2275. **TIRKMEN, Erkan**, "MUHAMMAD IQBAL AND MEHMED AKIF'S CONCEPT OF FREEDOM", *ISLAMIC CULTURE* 28, no. 3: October-December (1987): pp. 15-24.

2276. **TIRMIZEY, Muhsin**, "IQBAL'S PERSONAL FILE IN THE LAHORE HIGH COURT", *CIVIL AND MILITARY GAZETTE*, 21 April 1955, pp. 5, 6.
Variant name: TIRMIZI, Muhsin.

Published also in *THE PAKISTAN TIMES*, 21 April 1955, pp. 5-6.

2277. **TOMIMAN**, "IQBAL'S FIRST APPEARANCE BEFORE LAHORE AUDIENCE", *PAKISTAN TIMES*, 21 April 1952, p. 7.

2278. **TRITTON, A. S.**, "SIR MOHAMMAD IQBAL. THE RECONSTRUCTION OF RELIGIOUS THOUGHT IN ISLAM (Book Review)", *BULLETIN OF THE SCHOOL OF ORIENTAL AND AFRICAN STUDIES* 7, no. 3: pp. 693-95.

2279. **TUCCI, G.**, "ADDRESS, IQBAL DAY AT ROME", *IQBAL REVIEW* 8, no. 1: April (1967): pp. 28-30.

2280. **TUFAIL, Mian Muhammad**, mon., *IQBAL'S PHILOSOPHY AND EDUCATION*, Lahore: Bazm-i-Iqbal, 1966. xii+144 pp.
Variant title: *Iqbal's Philosophy of Education*.

2281. **ULLAH, Nagib**, "IQBAL'S POLITICAL PHILOSOPHY: DERVED FROM THE QURAN", *THE MUSLIM* (Islamabad), 11 June 1982.

2282. **UMAR, Muhammad Suheyl**, "CONTOURS OF AMBIVALENCE, IQBAL AND IBN 'ARABI IN HISTORICAL PERSPECTIVE", *IQBAL REVIEW* 34 and 35, no. 1: April, no. 3: October and no. 3: October (1993 and 1994): pp. 21-50, 13-49 and 39-54 resp.
Paper originally presented at the Iqbal Conference held in Cordoba (Spain), November 1991. Analysis of Iqbal's objections against the thought and praxis ascribed to Ibn 'Arabi. Part III focuses on the questions of detrimental effects of the Persian poets and the concept of *fana* (annihilation) as the conclusion of the second phase of Iqbal's relationship with Ibn 'Arabi's ideas; the rest of the article deals with Iqbal's later attitude (1920-1938) towards the philosopher he originally admired. Cf. also, by the same author and under the same title, *STUDIES IN TRADITION* (Karachi) 1, no. 2: April-June (1992), pp. 67-87 and vol. 1, no. 3: July-September (1992), pp. 75-88.

2283. ――――, ed., *IQBAL'S CONTRIBUTION TO LITERATURE & POLITICS*, Brochure Series 1, Lahore: Iqbal Academy Pakistan, 1987. 30 pp.
A short introduction to Iqbal's life and works, and his role in the genesis of Pakistan, with special reference to his relation to the Quaid-i-Azam. Illustrated with original photographs. Published with the courtesy of the Information, Culture & Tourism Dept., Govt. of the Punjab.

2284. ――――, mon., *'THAT I MAY SEE AND TELL'. SIGNIFICANCE OF IQBAL'S WISDOM*

POETRY, Brochure Series 2, Lahore: Iqbal Academy Pakistan, 1997. 27 pp.

2285. ———, "UNDERSTANDING THE RATIONALE OF SHAH WALI ULLAH, SHIBLI AND IQBAL", *IQBAL REVIEW* 37, no. 1: April (1996): pp. 121-25. On the origin of Iqbal's thesis on "the Principle of Movement in the Structure of Islam" (lecture VI of his Reconstruction of Islamic Law) in a key-concept borrowed from Shah Wali Ullah on the authority of Shibli Nu'mani's Al-Kalam.

2286. **UPPAL, J. S.**, "IQBAL - A POET OF INDIA AND PAKISTAN", *UNIVERSITY COLLEGE QUARTERLY* (East Lansing, MI) 12, no. 3 (1967): pp. 24-30.

2287. **UPPAL, Narinjan Singh**, "IQBAL: POET OF HUMANISM", *NATIONAL HERALD*, 1 September 1957.

2288. **'USMAN, M.**, "SOME ECONOMIC PROBLEMS IN IQBAL", *IQBAL* 5, no. 4: April (1967).

2289. **USMANI, M. A.**, mon., *KHUDI THROUGH SEX AND OTHER PHILOSOPHICAL ESSAYS*, Lahore: Philosophical Publications, 1967. 159 pp. On Iqbal philosophy, see pp. 21-35.

2290. **USMANI, Muhammad Adil & Fatima NASIM**, comp., *BOOKS ON ALLAMA IQBAL IN UNIVERSITY LIBRARIES OF PAKISTAN*, Karachi: Dr. Mahmud Husain Library (University of Karachi), 1977. ix+24+62 pp. Allama Iqbal Birth Centenary Celebrations 1977.

2291. **'UWAIDA, Kamil Muhammad Muhammad**, *MUHAMMAD IQBAL*, 1994

2292. **VAHID AL-DIN, Faqir Syed**, mon., *IQBAL IN PICTURES. A PICTORIAL BIOGRAPHY OF THE FAMOUS POET DR. SIR MUHAMMAD IQBAL*, Karachi: Lion Art Press, 1965. 55 or 60 pp. [?]

2293. **VAHID, Syed Abdul**, "A COMPARATIVE STUDY OF THE APPROACHES OF MILTON AND IQBAL TO THE PROBLEM OF THE FALL OF MAN", *ISLAMIC REVIEW AND ARAB AFFAIRS* 47, no. [?]: July-August (1959): pp. 28-30.

2294. ———, "DATE OF IQBAL'S BIRTH", *IQBAL REVIEW* (Karachi) 5, no. 3: October (1964): pp. 21-32. Contribution to the discussion about Iqbal's date of birth, with facsimile reproduction of documents; re-issued as part of S.A. Vahid's *GLIMPSES OF IQBAL*, Karachi, 1974, pp. 191-197.

2295. ———, "DEVELOPMENT OF IQBAL'S GENIUS", (1950): pp. 8.
Starting from a quote from Iqbal's letters to Atiya Begum (*I shall like to meet the Creator and call upon Him to give me a rational explanation of my mind - which I am sure will not be an easy task for Him to do*), Vahid sets forth to reconstruct the growing genius of Iqbal's throughout his career, and focuses in particular on the years 1911-1912, as *the years in which Iqbal saw the light, and thought out his philosophy Ego* [by which] *he came to believe in Spiritual Pluralism*. Includes quotations from several poems, with English translation.
Re-issued as part of S.A. Vahid's *GLIMPSES OF IQBAL*, Karachi, 1974, pp. 68-77.

2296. ———, "DEVELOPMENT OF IQBAL'S THOUGHT", *MORNING NEWS*, 17 April 1966, pp. 1, 2.

2297. ———, "GABRIEL'S WING", *VOICE OF ISLAM*, June 1963.

2298. ———, mon., *GLIMPSES OF IQBAL*, L. MASSIGNON (intr.), Karachi: Iqbal Academy, 1974. 240 pp.
A collection of 19 essays by S.A.Vahid, *written at odd moments over the last few years* [sic], some of which are published here for the first time:
(1) IQBAL AND HIS POETRY,
(2) IQBAL AND ITALY,
(3) IQBAL: A BRIDGE BETWEEN EAST AND WEST,
(4) IQBAL IN POLITICS,
(5) IQBAL: THE POET OF PAKISTAN,
(6) IQBAL AND WESTERN THOUGHT,
(7) DEVELOPMENT OF IQBAL'S GENIUS,
(8) IQBAL AS A LYRIC POET,
(9) IQBAL AS A TEACHER,
(10) ON TRANSLATING IQBAL,
(11) IQBAL AND PAKISTAN,
(12) IQBAL AND HIS CRITICS,
(13) IQBAL AND AFGHANISTAN,
(14) IQBAL: THE ARCHITECT OF PAKISTAN,
(15) IQBAL: A SURVEY OF HIS WORK,
(16) IQBAL: THE SPIRITUAL FATHER OF PAKISTAN,
(17) IQBAL - A HUMANIST,
(18) DATE OF IQBAL'S BIRTH,

(19) A.J. ARBERRY: A GREAT STUDENT OF IQBAL.
Appended to these is an English translation of L. Massignon's Preface to Mrs.
Meyerovitch's French translation of Iqbal's RECONSTRUCTION OF RELIGIOUS
THOUGHT IN ISLAM (qv.), a bibliography, and an index.
*References to the original publication of Vahid's articles are wanting. All articles are
described under their respective titles - and insofar as possible, the original publication
references are given under the same headings.*

2299. ———, "THE GREATNESS OF IQBAL", *IQBAL REVIEW* 15, no. 1: April (1974): pp.
8-12.
A short note, presenting Iqbal as one of the few poets who have achieved to excel in both
main aspects of real poethood, viz. the prophetic and the artistic.

2300. ———, mon., *INTRODUCTION TO IQBAL*, Karachi: Pakistan Publications, 1954. 57 or
67 pp. [?].
Contents: (I) Biographical Sketch, (II) His Poetry, (III) Iqbal as Thinker, (IV) Iqbal as
Architect of Pakistan, (V) The Reconstruction of Religious Thought in Islam, and (VI)
Iqbal in Foreign Lands.

2301. ———, "IQBAL - A BRIDGE BETWEEN EAST AND WEST", *EMBASSY BULLETIN*
(Washington) (1964).
Short essay on Iqbal's merging modern Muslim philosophy with Western thought.
Re-issued as part of S.A. Vahid's *GLIMPSES OF IQBAL*, Karachi, 1974, pp. 24-34.

2302. ———, "IQBAL - A HUMANIST", *GLIMPSES OF IQBAL*, Syed Abdul VAHID (mon.),
Karachi: Iqbal Academy, 1974, pp. 187-90.
Brief note on Iqbal as a humanist - with reference to the adagium *Homo sum, et nihil
humanum a me alienum puto.*

2303. ———, "IQBAL: A SURVEY OF HIS WORK", *GLIMPSES OF IQBAL*, Syed Abdul
VAHID (mon.), Karachi: Iqbal Academy, 1974, pp. 170-178.
Short note on Iqbal's poetical and philosphical works, deploring the fact that Iqbal's
popularity spread more rapidly in non-Arabic countries, but applauding the recent interest
in Iqbal in Arabic countries, due to the efforts of mainly *Al Bashir*, the Arabic magazine of
Pakistan, and Hasan-ul-Azmi, the pioneer in translating Iqbal's works into Arabic.
Published earlier in *IQBAL REVIEW* 14, no. 1: April (1973), pp. 61-68.

2304. ———, "IQBAL, AN ESTIMATE OF HIS WORK", *THE ISLAMIC REVIEW* (Woking)
34 or 39 [?], no. 3-4 (1951): pp. 21-23.

Also published in *DAWN*, 21 April 1968, pp. 5-10.

2305. ———, "IQBAL AND AFGHANISTAN", *PAKISTAN REVIEW* 15, no. 3: March (1967): pp. 17.
Collection of quotations, with English translation, from Iqbal's poetical work, inspired by Afghanistan and Afghan history.
Re-issued as part of S.A.Vahid's *GLIMPSES OF IQBAL*, Karachi, 1974, pp. 131-136.

2306. ———, "IQBAL AND BROWNING", *IQBAL REVIEW* 6, no. 1: April (1965): pp. 73-95.

2307. ———, "IQBAL AND DANTE", *PAKISTAN QUARTERLY* 1, no. 6 (n.d.): pp. 51-54.

2308. ———, "IQBAL AND HIS CRITICS", *GLIMPSES OF IQBAL*, Syed Abdul VAHID (mon.), Karachi: Iqbal Academy, 1974, pp. 118-30.
A short history of criticism on Iqbal, starting with Iqbal's position between the so-called Lucknow and Delhi Schools of Urdu poetry, followed by the heavy attacks of Sufi Schools on Iqbal's lines on Hafiz in ASRAR-I-KHUDI; and a short survey of Western reviews and criticism of Iqbal's works in general.
Previously published in *IQBAL REVIEW* 4, no. 1: April (1964), pp. 1-13.

2309. ———, "IQBAL AND HIS GREATNESS", *PAKISTAN TIMES* (Lahore), 21 April 1961, p. iii.
Iqbal Day Supplement.

2310. ———, "IQBAL AND HIS POETRY", *THE ISLAMIC REVIEW* (Woking) 13 or 42 [?], no. 4: April (1954): pp. 30-34 or 31-33 [?].
Brief treatment of Iqbal's *Poetry for Life*, as opposed to *Art for Art's Sake*, with quotations from different works and English translation.
Re-issued in S.A. Vahid's *GLIMPSES OF IQBAL*, Karachi, 1974, pp. 1-15.

2311. ———, "IQBAL AND HYDERABAD", *IQBAL* [vol. ?], no. [?]: April (1961).

2312. ———, "IQBAL AND ITALY", *MORNING NEWS* (Karachi), 21 April 1964.
Brief notes on Iqbal's link with Italy, and more in particular with the historical persons Machiavelli and Dante, and Iqbal's contemporaries Joseph Mazzini and Mussolini (both of whom Iqbal personally met). Contains quotation of part of Iqbal's poem on Sicily, with English translation.
Reprinted in *PAKISTAN REVIEW* (Lahore) 15, no. 4: April (1967), pp. 9-11, 31; and re-

issued as part of S.A. Vahid's *GLIMPSES OF IQBAL*, Karachi, 1974, pp. 16-23.

2313. ———, "IQBAL AND MILTON", *PAKISTAN QUARTERLY* 7, no. 2: Summer (1957): pp. 52-54/55.

2314. ———, "IQBAL AND PAKISTAN", (1965).
A short note on Iqbal as the inspirator of the nation of Pakistan: (...) *When Mountbatten and those of his school say today that it was a mistake to concede Pakistan, they forget that Pakistan was not a present by the Hindus or the British handed over on a silver salver for the Muslims - it was attained by the Muslims after great sacrifices and hard struggle as a result of the inspiration provided by Muhammad Iqbal, under the leadership of Quaid-i-Azam Muhammad Ali Jinnah.*
Re-issued as part of S.A.Vahid's *GLIMPSES OF IQBAL*, Karachi, 1974, pp. 113-117.

2315. ———, "IQBAL AND (THE) U.S.", *THE MORNING NEWS* (Karachi), 2 July 1961, p. ii.

Pak.-US Co-operation 10th Anniversary Supplement.

2316. ———, "IQBAL AND THE U.S.A.", *MORNING NEWS*, 6 December 1969.

2317. ———, "IQBAL AND WESTERN POETS", *PAKISTAN TIMES*, 21 April 1967, p. 2.

2318. ———, "IQBAL AND WESTERN POETS", *IQBAL - POET PHILOSOPHER OF PAKISTAN*, Hafeez MALIK (ed.), New York, 1971, pp. 347-82 [?].

2319. ———, "IQBAL AND WESTERN THOUGHT(S)", *PAKISTAN TIMES* (Lahore), 21 April 1966, p. 4.
A short survey of Iqbal's pre-eminent influences from Western philosophy; re-issued as part of S.A. Vahid's *GLIMPSES OF IQBAL*, Karachi, 1974, pp. 63-67.

2320. ———, "IQBAL AS A LYRICAL POET", *IQBAL STUDIES*, Muhammad Ziaul ISLAM (ed.), Karachi: Bazm-i-Iqbal, 1949.
Brief note on Iqbal's conception of art, and Iqbal as a lyricist; re-issued as IQBAL AS A LYRIC POET, the 8th essay in S.A. Vahid's *GLIMPSES OF IQBAL*, Karachi, 1974, pp. 78-83.

2321. ———, "IQBAL AS A POET", *PAKISTAN QUARTERLY* 1, no. 2: September (1948/1951): pp. 12-25.

Including an English rendering by G. Ahmad of two (I) poems by Iqbal.

2322. ———, "IQBAL AS A POET", *THE MORNING NEWS* (Dacca), 25 April 1954, p. 4.
Cf. also the article of the same title in *PAKISTAN QUARTERLY* 1, no. 2 (1948).

2323. ———, "IQBAL AS A POLITICIAN", *PAKISTAN TIMES* (Lahore), 21 April 1964.

2324. ———, "IQBAL AS A POLITICIAN, HE STOOD LIKE A ROCK AND NEVER FLINCHED - QUAID-I-AZAM", *DAWN*, 23 April 1967, p. 9.

2325. ———, "IQBAL AS A SEER", *THE PAKISTAN TIMES* (Lahore), 21 April 1963, p. 1.

2326. ———, "IQBAL AS A SEER", *IQBAL, THE POET OF TOMORROW*, Khawaja Abdur RAHIM (ed.), Lahore: Abdul Hameed Khan at Ferozsons Ltd., n.d., pp. 201[205]-212.
In order to perform his true role, a prophetic poet, known in Persian and Urdu as *Ilhami Shair*, must be a seer. The gift of vision is prominently found in Iqbal.
Cf. also the article of the same title in *THE PAKISTAN TIMES*, 21 April 1963.

2327. ———, "IQBAL AS A TEACHER", *GLIMPSES OF IQBAL*, Syed Abdul VAHID (mon.), Karachi: Iqbal Academy, 1974, pp. 84-91.
Short article on Iqbal's career as a teacher - with particular reference to his appointment (1899) as *McLeod Punjab Arabic Reader* at the University of Punjab, his later steps in the teaching profession, and the open question as to what made Iqbal decide to give up the profession.

2328. ———, mon., *IQBAL - HIS ART AND THOUGHT*, Hyderabad / London: John Murray, 1959. xv+265 pp.
Originally published in Lahore: Sheikh Muhammad Ashraf, 1944; re-issued in 1948, and reprinted by Oxford UP (1969); extent of work varying between 254 and 304 pp.

2329. ———, "IQBAL: HIS LIFE", *THE PAKISTAN STANDARD* (Karachi), 24 April 1955.

2330. ———, "IQBAL IN ENGLAND", *IQBAL REVIEW* 17, no. 1: April (1976): pp. 1-6.

2331. ———, "IQBAL IN POLITICS", *GLIMPSES OF IQBAL*, Syed Abdul VAHID (mon.), Karachi: Iqbal Academy, 1974, pp. 35-45.
Starting from a historical survey of twelve centuries of Muslim contact with the Indian subcontinent (from the Conquest of Sind, 712 AD onwards), the author proceeds to modern history, presenting Syed Ahmad Khan as *the founder of the Muslim integration in*

the subcontinent. A brief discussion of the Morley-Minto Reforms (1909) and the Montague Chelmsford Reforms (1919) then brings the author to Iqbal, and his role in the emancipation of Islam in the Indian subcontinent, followed by the origin of the two-nation theory and the instalment of Pakistan as a seperate nation. *It is true that Iqbal did not take any active part in the politics of the sub-continent for a long time*, the author admits, [but at that time] *he was busy in creating political consciousness and a sense of integration amongst his people*. Later on, emphasis is laid on Iqbal as the man who in 1932 brought the two branches of the *Muslim League* together, and then persuaded the *Muslim Conference* to become amalgamated with the unified *League*.

2332.   ———, "IQBAL'S CONTACT WITH WESTERN CULTURE", *PAKISTAN TIMES*, 18 April 1976, p. 1.

2333.   ———, "IQBAL'S ELEGIES", *IQBAL* (Lahore) 6, no. 3: January (1958): pp. 1-18.

2334.   ———, "IQBAL'S PAYAM-I-MASHRIQ", *THE DAWN* (Karachi), February 1951, sec. Magazine Section, p. 12.

2335.   ———, "IQBAL'S POETRY", *ILLUSTRATED WEEKLY OF PAKISTAN*, 16 April 1950, p. 12.

2336.   ———, "IQBAL: THE ARCHITECT OF PAKISTAN", *GLIMPSES OF IQBAL*, Syed abdul VAHID (mon.), Karachi: Iqbal Academy, 1974, pp. 137-69.
A well-documented introduction into the works, the philosophy and the political meaning of Muhammad Iqbal. The poetic section of the article offers a wide range of extracts in English translation, regrettably without mention of their exact source. The philosophy section is mainly on the philosophy of *khudi* and the development of the human ego, whereas the political section emphasises Iqbal's views on *Ijtehad* and the genesis of the two-nation theory.

2337.   ———, "IQBAL: THE POET OF PAKISTAN", *GLIMPSES OF IQBAL*, Syed Abdul VAHID (mon.), Karachi: Iqbal Academy, 1974, pp. 46-62.
A portrait of Iqbal and the *prodigious versatility of his genius* - with reference to the philosophy of the Self (*khudi*), and the development of human ego; to the expressionism of his poetry (Iqbal is said to have subscribed to the last two of Croce's tenets in full, and on the second partially - the 4 tenets of Croce being (1) *Art is an autonomous activity free from ethics*, (2) *Artistic activity is distinct from the activity of the intellect*, (3) *Art consists in unfolding the personality of the artist*, and (4) *Appreciation is the reliving of the artist*); to his *synthesis of classicism and romanticism*; and to his symbolism and mysticism. The article concludes with a brief survey of Iqbal's major epic, metaphysical and philosophical

poetry.

2338. ———, "IQBAL THE SATIRIST", *THE DAWN* (Karachi), 21 April 1947/1949, p. 7.
Iqbal Day Supplement.

2339. ———, "IQBAL: THE SPIRITUAL FATHER OF PAKISTAN", *GLIMPSES OF IQBAL*,
Syed Abdul VAHID (mon.), Karachi: Iqbal Academy, 1974, pp. 179-86.
Short survey of the history of Muslim contacts with the Indian subcontinent, followed by
an appraisal of Iqbal's role in the genesis of Pakistan as a separate Muslim nation.

2340. ———, "IQBAL WAS MESSAGE OF RESURGENT HOPE", *PAKISTAN REVIEW* 2,
no. 4 (1954): pp. 24, 26, 36.

2341. ———, "A.J. ARBERRY: A GREAT STUDENT OF IQBAL", *GLIMPSES OF IQBAL*,
Syed Abdul VAHID (mon.), Karachi: Iqbal Academy, 1974, pp. 198-211.
Short biographical note on A.J. Arberry, published earlier in *IQBAL REVIEW* 13, no. 1:
April (1972), pp. 37-50; with excerpts from his translation of Iqbal's ASRAR-I-KHUDI,
together with the original text.

2342. ———, "THE LYRIC POET", *PAKISTAN TIMES*, 21 April 1968, p. 3.

2343. ———, "THE MESSAGE OF IQBAL FOR OUR TIME(S)", *THE PAKISTAN AFFAIRS*
(Washington) 12, no. 9: 21 April (1959): pp. 2-3.
Iqbal Day Issue.
Published also in *PERSPECTIVE* 2, no. 10: April (1969), pp. 7-11.

2344. ———, "ON TRANSLATING IQBAL", *JOURNAL OF THE INSTITUTE OF ISLAMIC
STUDIES* (Delhi) [vol. ?], no. [?]: January (1967).
Treatment of translations of Iqbal's works into various languages, with particular emphasis
on the works of Nicholson, Arberry, Mahmud Ahmad, Kiernan, Schimmel, Bausani,
Meyerovitch, Hasan-al-Azami, and Abdul Wahhab Azzam. With elaborate quotations and
examples, most of all from Arberry.
Re-issued in *PAKISTAN REVIEW* 15, no. 10: October (1967), pp. 28-34; in *STUDIES IN
ISLAM* 5, July (1968), pp. 129-145; and also as part of S.A.Vahid's *GLIMPSES OF
IQBAL*, Karachi, 1974, pp. 91-112.

2345. ———, "PREFACE, TO THE FRENCH TRANSLATION OF IQBAL'S
RECONSTRUCTION OF RELIGIOUS THOUGHT IN ISLAM", *IQBAL* 15, no. 3:

January (1967): pp. 61-67.

2346. ———, mon., *STUDIES IN IQBAL*, 2nd ed., Lahore: Shaikh Muhammad Ashraf, 1976. xii+364 / viii+345 pp.
Contents: (I) Art in His Poetry, (II) Main Trends of His Thought, (III) Iqbal and Goethe, (IV) Iqbal and Rumi, (V) Iqbal and Dante, (VI) Nature in Iqbal's Poetry, (VII) Iqbal and Browning, (VIII) Iqbal in His Letters, (IX) Iqbal as a Politician. The exhaustive bibliography (pp. 305-354) was published also by Kazi Publications, Chicago, 1985.

2347. ———, ed., *THOUGHTS AND REFLECTIONS OF IQBAL*, Muhammad IQBAL (mon.), Lahore: Shaikh Muhammad Ashraf, 1973/1980. xvi+381+6 pp.
Also published by Kazi Publications (Chicago, 1985).
Contents:
Part I - Miscellaneous (1900-1937) includes THE DOCTRINE OF ABSOLUTE UNITY AS EXPOUNDED BY ABDUL KARIM AL-JILANI; LEBENSLAUF; ISLAM AS A MORAL AND POLITICAL IDEAL; POLITICAL THOUGHT IN ISLAM; STRAY THOUGHTS (i-iii); LETTER TO DR. NICHOLSON; SOME THOUGHTS ON ISLAMIC STUDIES; SELF IN THE LIGHT OF RELATIVITY; McTAGGARTS PHILOSOPHY; KHUSHHAL KHAN KHATTACK; FOREWORD TO "MURAQQA-I-CHUGHTAI"; A PLEA FOR DEEPER STUDY OF THE MUSLIM SCIENTISTS; FOREWORD TO "PERSIAN NAVIGATION"; PRESIDENTIAL ADDRESS DELIVERED AT THE ANNUAL SESSION OF THE ALL-INDIA MUSLIM LEAGUE AT ALLAHABAD ON 29 DECEMBER 1930; PRESIDENTIAL ADDRESS DELIVERED AT THE ANNUAL SESSION OF THE ALL-INDIA MUSLIM CONFERENCE AT LAHORE ON 21 MARCH 1932; SOME STUDY NOTES; "JAVID NAMA" WITH A NOTE BY N.M. KHAN; INTRODUCTION TO "MODERN AFGHANISTAN"; INTRODUCTION TO THE STUDY OF ISLAM; NOTE ON NIETZSCHE.
Part II - Islam and Qadianism, includes: QADIANIS AND ORTHODOX MUSLIMS; REPLY TO QUESTIONS RAISED BY PANDIT JAWAHARLAL NEHRU; A LETTER TO THE 'STATESMAN'; REJOINDER TO "THE LIGHT"; STATEMENT ON HIS RESIGNATION OF THE OFFICE OF THE ALL-INDIA KASHMIR COMMITTEE, ISSUED ON 20 JUNE 1933; STATEMENT ON HIS REJECTION OF THE OFFER OF PRESIDENTSHIP OF THE "TEHRIK-I-KASHMIR", ISSUED ON 2 OCTOBER 1933; LETTER TO PANDIT JAWAHARLAL NEHRU, DATED 21 JUNE 1936
Part III - Speeches in the Punjab Legislative Council
Part IV - Statements.

2348. **VAHIDUDDIN, S.**, "GLIMPSES OF IQBAL'S MIND AND THOUGHT BY DR. H.H.

BILGRAMI", *ISLAMIC CULTURE* 31, no. 1 (1957).

2349. ———, "GOETHE, HAFIZ AND IQBAL: A COMPARATIVE STUDY IN THEIR CREATIVE LIFE-STYLES", *ISLAMIC CULTURE: AN ENGLISH QUARTERLY* 69, no. 4 (1995): pp. 1-14.

2350. ———, "THE PHILOSOPHY OF MUHAMMAD IQBAL", *THE ARYAN PATH* (Bombay) 28, no. 12: December (1957): pp. 546.

2351. ———, "TRADITION AND MODERNITY IN IQBAL'S PHILOSOPHICAL THOUGHT", *ISLAMIC CULTURE* (Hyderabad) 61, no. 3: July (1987): pp. 1-29.

2352. **VAHIDUDDIN, Syed**, "IQBAL AND MYSTICISM", *STUDIES IN ISLAM* 5, no. 2-3: April-July (1968): pp. 180-187.

2353. **VAJDA, G.**, "M. IQBAL: RECONSTRUIRE LA PENSÉE RELIGIEUSE DE L'ISLAM, TR. DE E. MEYEROVITCH (Book Review)", *REVUE DE L'HISTOIRE DES RELIGIONS* 150, (1956): pp. 123.
F.

2354. **VALIUDDIN, Mir**, "IQBAL'S CONCEPT OF LOVE AND REASON", *STUDIES IN ISLAM* 5, no. 2-3: April-July (1968): pp. 83-113.

2355. **VASILYEVA, L.**, "ALTAF HUSSAIN HALI - MUHAMMAD IQBAL'S PREDECESSOR", *THE WORK OF MUHAMMAD IQBAL: ARTICLES BY SOVIET SCHOLARS*, Abdur Rauf MALIK (ed.), Lahore: People's Publishing House, 1983, pp. 200-218.

2356. **VENKATA RAO, P. K.**, "THE SECRETS OF THE SELF: A STUDY OF IQBAL'S POEM ASRAR-I KHUDI", *TRIVENI* (Bangalore) 14, no. 4 (1942): pp. 246-49.
Variant name: RAS, Venkata.

2357. **VERMA, Rajinder Singh**, "IQBAL FOR EVERYONE", *IQBAL* 37, no. 1-2 (1990): pp. 9-25.
Translation of seven QUATRAINS (Ruba'iyat), the poems BELOVED GUEST, INDIA'S ARTISTS, CENSURE, NEW SHRINE, INDIA'S NATIONAL ANTHEM, three GHAZALS, the ANTHEM OF INDIAN CHILDREN, and the QUINTESSENCE OF BEAUTY.

2358. ———, "RAJINDER SINGH VERMA TRANSLATES THREE POEMS OF DR. IQBAL", *IQBAL* (Lahore) 38 and 39, no. 4: October and 1: January (1991-1992): pp. 37-44.
Translation of the poems "Houri and Poet", "Chorus of the stars" and "Nanak", which are also given in the original.

2359. **VIQAR AZIM, Sayyid**, "IQBAL: POET AND PHILOSOPHER", *THE CIVIL AND MILITARY GAZETTE*, 21 April 1962, pp. 1, 2.

2360. **von VELTHEIM-OSTRAU, Hans-Hasso**, "IQBAL'S LAST VISITOR", *TAGEBÜCHER AUS ASIEN*, Various authors (mon.), Hamburg: Classes Verlag, 1956, Vol. I, pp. 138, 145, 162.

2361. ———, "LETZTE BEGEGNUNG MIT IQBAL", *MUHAMMAD IQBAL UND DIE DREI REICHE DES GEISTES*, Wolfgang KOEHLER (ed.), Hamburg: Deutsch-Pakistanisches Forum, 1977, pp. 63-66.
G.

2362. **von VELTHEIM-OSTRAU, Hans-Otto**, "TAGEBÜCHER AUS ASIEN (EXTRACT)", *MUHAMMAD IQBAL: POET AND PHILOSOPHER, A COLLECTION OF TRANSLATIONS, ESSAYS AND OTHER ARTICLES, PRESENTED BY THE PAKISTAN-GERMAN FORUM*, Karachi: Din Mohammad Press, 1960.
G.

2363. **VV.AA.**, mon., *ASPECTS OF IQBAL: A COLLECTION OF SELECTED PAPERS*, M. D. TASEER (ed.), Lahore: Intercollegiate Muslim Brotherhood, 1938

2364. **WADIA, A. R.**, "IQBAL: POET AND PHILOSOPHER (Book Review)", *ARYAN PATH* 16, no. 11: November (1945): pp. 429.

2365. **WAHEED, Ahmad**, ed., *LETTERS OF MIAN FAZL-I-HUSAIN*, Lahore: Research Society of Pakistan, University of the Punjab, 1976. 672 pp.
On Iqbal, see pp. 13, 26, 111, 128, 141, 213, 280sq., 287, 290, 296, 310, 317, 325, 333, 357, 383, 510, 533sq., 536, 601, 605, 637-639.

2366. **WAHEED, Khwaja Abdul**, comp., *A BIBLIOGRAPHY OF IQBAL*, Karachi: Iqbal Academy, 1965. iii+224 pp.

2367. ———, "CAN REALITY BE UNDERSTOOD WITH THE AID OF SCIENCE

ALONE?", *AL-ISLAM* 1, no. 9: 1 August (1953): pp. 65, 66.

2368. ———, "A DOCUMENT OF GREAT HISTORICAL IMPORTANCE COMES TO LIGHT, IQBAL'S FAMOUS INDICTMENT OF QADIANISM", *AL-ISLAM*, 1 October 1958.

2369. ———, "HE PREACHED A UNIVERSAL ORGANISATION", *DAWN*, 21 April 1952, p. 6.

2370. ———, "IJTIHAD IN ISLAM ACCORDING TO IQBAL", *AL-ISLAM* 3, no. [?]: 15 June (1954): pp. 88, 89.

2371. ———, "IN IQBAL'S COMPANY FOR THIRTY YEARS", *THE PAKISTAN TIMES* (Rawalpindi), 9 November 1977.

2372. ———, "IQBAL", *CALCUTTA REVIEW* 110, no. 2 (1949): pp. 89-95.

2373. ———, "IQBAL", *PAKISTAN TODAY* 2, no. 8 (1949): pp. 423-27.
Variant name: WADUD, K.A.

2374. ———, "IQBAL AND THE WEST", *AL-ISLAM*, 15 June, 1 and 15 July 1915.
Three parts.

2375. ———, "IQBAL DENOUNCES THE WEST AND ITS WAYS", *AL-ISLAM* (Karachi) 2, no. 2: 15 January (1954): pp. 1.

2376. ———, "IQBAL'S ELEGIES", *AL-ISLAM* 6, no. 3: January (1951): pp. 1, 18.

2377. ———, "IQBAL: THE POET WHO CONCEIVED PAKISTAN", *AL-ISLAM* 3, no. 8: 15 April (1955): pp. 60.

2378. ———, "MISCHIEVOUS", *AL-ISLAM* 1, no. 18: 15 November (1953): pp. 123. Criticism of the article IQBAL AND MULLA by Dr. Khalifa Abdul Hakim, published in quarterly *IQBAL* (Lahore), and later on published as an anonymous pamphlet.

2379. ———, "THE MULLA IN IQBAL'S POETRY", *AL-ISLAM* 2, no. 1: 1 January (1954): pp. 147.

2380. ———, "PAKISTAN: THE REALIZATION OF IQBAL'S DREAM", *PAKISTAN CALLING* 6, no. 8 (1952): pp. 9-10.

2381. ———, "REALITY, SCIENCE AND RELIGION", *AL-ISLAM* 3, no. 12: 1 July (1955): pp. 89.

2382. ———, "THE ROLE OF IQBAL IN THE ESTABLISHMENT OF PAKISTAN", *AL-ISLAM* 1, no. 6: 15 June (1953): pp. 47.

2383. ———, "SCIENCE CANNOT COMPREHEND LIFE - SAYS IQBAL", *AL-ISLAM* 5, no. 20: 15 May (1958): pp. 153-55.

2384. ———, "SPIRITUAL ROOTS OF POLITICS", *AL-ISLAM* 3, no. 4: 15 February (1955): pp. 25.

2385. ———, "WAS IQBAL INSPIRED BY THE WEST?", *PAKISTAN TIMES* (Rawalpindi), 3 and 9 January 1977, p. 1 and 1 resp.

2386. ———, "ZARB-I-KALIM", *ISLAM* 2, no. 6: 22 August (1936): pp. 41, 42.
Editorial note on the book ZARB-I-KALIM.

2387. **WAHEED-UZ-ZAMAN**, "JINNAH AND IQBAL, FROM CONFRONTATION TO MUTUAL ADMIRATION", *THE PAKISTAN TIMES* (Rawalpindi), 9 November 1977.

2388. **WAHEED-UZ ZAMAN**, mon., *TOWARDS PAKISTAN*, Lahore: Publishers United, 1969. 252 pp.
Iqbal philosophy, pp. 123-147; Iqbal and nationalism, pp. 125-129, 146; Iqbal - presidential addresses, pp. 130-134, 137; Iqbal - correspondence with Jinnah, pp. 139-142.

2389. **WAHID-UD-DIN**, "IQBAL - A RECOLLECTION", *ROZGAR-E-FAQIR* (Karachi) 1, (1965): pp. 38-40.

2390. ———, "IQBAL'S DATE OF BIRTH", *ROZGAR-E-FAQIR* (Karachi) 1, (1965): pp. 229-43.

2391. **WALIULLAH**, "HE WAS OF ALL RACES AND ALL COUNTRIES", *ILLUSTRATED WEEKLY OF PAKISTAN*, 16 April 1950, p. 22.

Iqbal Number.

2392. **WAQAR AHMAD, K.**, "IQBAL'S CONCEPT OF GOD AS THE ULTIMATE EGO", *PAKISTAN TIMES*, 21 April 1977, p. 1.

2393. **WAQAR-UR-RAHMAN**, "IQBAL'S ROLE IN THE PAKISTAN MOVEMENT", *PAKISTAN REVIEW* 16, no. 6: June (1968): pp. 14-18.

2394. **WASTI, S. Razi**, "DR. MUHAMMAD IQBAL. FROM NATIONALISM TO UNIVERSALISM", *IQBAL REVIEW* 18, no. 4: January (1978): pp. 25-35.

2395. **WASWANI, K. N.**, "IQBAL: AN APPRECIATION", *TRIVENI* (Bangalore) (NS) 11, no. 11: May (1939): pp. 18-23.

2396. **WAUGH, Earle**, "M.S. RASCHID, "IQBAL'S CONCEPT OF GOD" (Book Review)", *JOURNAL OF RELIGION* 65, no. 3: July (1985): pp. 443.

2397. **WAUGH, Earle H.**, "IMAGES OF MUHAMMAD IN THE WORK OF IQBAL: TRADITION AND ALTERATIONS", *HISTORY OF RELIGIONS* 23, no. 2 (1983): pp. 156-68.
Iqbal applied his philosophical and religious system to the prophet's life.

2398. **WEIDEMANN, Diethelm**, "ZUM 100. GEBURTSTAG VON ALLAMA IQBAL", *ASIEN - AFRIKA - LATEINAMERIKA* (Ost-Berlin) 6, no. 2 (1978): pp. 251-58.

2399. **WEISCHER, Bernd Manuel**, "SOME REMARKS ON THE 'NIETZSCHE-CONCEPTION' IN THE WORKS OF MOHAMMED IQBAL", *STUDIEN ZUR GESCHICHTE UND KULTUR DES VORDEREN ORIENTS: FESTSCHRIFT FÜR BERTOLD SPULER ZUM SIEBZIGSTEN GEBURTSTAG*, Hans R. ROEMER & Albrecht NOTH (eds.), Leiden: Brill, 1981.

2400. **WERLY, Richard**, *IQBAL, L'ENFANT ESCLAVE*, Paris: Fayard, 1995

2401. **WHEELER, Richard S.**, "THE INDIVIDUAL AND ACTION IN THE THOUGHT OF IQBAL", *MUSLIM WORLD* (Hartford, Conn.) 52, no. 3: July (1962): pp. 197-206.
Re-issued in *IQBAL REVIEW* 38, no. 1: April (1997), pp. 1-15.

2402. **WHITTEMORE, Robert**, "IQBAL'S PANENTHEISM", *REVIEW OF METAPHYSICS*

9, no. [?]: September (1955/1956): pp. 681.
An interesting analysis of the philosophy of Muhammad Iqbal, with reference to Western thinkers, philosophies and philosophic vocabulary. The author considers *Iqbal's philosophy* to be the point of view expressed in his later poems THE SECRETS OF THE SELF and THE COMPLAINT AND THE ANSWER, together with his major prose work THE RECONSTRUCTION OF RELIGIOUS THOUGHT IN ISLAM. *This limitation is necessary*, he states, *since Iqbal's philosophy encompasses a development from the aesthetic pantheism characteristic of his early poetry (...) to the personalistic panentheism of those later writings.* The article concludes with the statement that *the measure of Iqbal's contribution to Western thought is, in large part, his success in showing that the proper understanding of meaning and relation of religion, philosophy and science will be attained only when men come to realise that each is only a perspective - but a perspective for the lack of which Reality would be less.*
Re-issued in *IQBAL REVIEW* 7, no. 1: April (1966), pp. 63-77; and once more in [Various authors], *SELECTIONS FROM THE IQBAL REVIEW*, ed. Waheed Qureshi, Lahore, 1983, pp. 257-271.

2403. ———, "PANENTHEISM", *THE CIVIL AND MILITARY GAZETTE*, 21 April 1961, pp. 3-5.

2404. **WHITTEMORE, Robert C.**, "THE PROCESS PHILOSOPHY OF SIR MUHAMMAD IQBAL", *TULANE STUDIES IN PHILOSOPHY* 24, (1975): pp. 113. Published under the heading "STUDIES IN PROCESS PHILOSOPHY II".

2405. **WICKENS, G. M.**, "MOHAMMED IQBAL: "RECONSTRUIRE LA PENSÉE RELIGIEUSE DE L'ISLAM". TRADUCTION DE EVA MEYEROVITCH (Book Review)", *BULLETIN OF THE SCHOOL OF ORIENTAL AND AFRICAN STUDIES* 19, no. 1 (1957): pp. 179.

2406. **WIJEYERATNE, Tissa**, "THE LEADER OF A NEW MUSLIM RENAISSANCE", *IQBAL REVIEW* 8, no. 1: April (1967): pp. 24-27.

2407. **WIJSYERATNE, Tissa**, "IQBAL: THE LEADER OF A NEW MUSLIM RENAISSANCE", *IQBAL REVIEW* 8, no. 1: April (1967): pp. 23-27.
This article, specially written for the Iqbal Day celebrations, is printed on pp. 24-27; pp. 23-24 contain a survey of the celebrations in Colombo, Ceylon.

2408. **WILLIAMS, L. F. Rushbrook**, ed., *GREAT MEN OF INDIA*, Bombay: Times of India,

1941

2409. **WILLIAMS, Rushbrook**, "ADDRESS, IQBAL DAY AT LONDON", *IQBAL REVIEW* 8, no. 1: April (1967): pp. 13-16.
Address on the occasion of the Iqbal Day celebration held at the Islamic Cultural Centre, London.

2410. **WILSON, C. E.**, tr. P/E, *THE MASNAVI*, Karachi: Indus Publications, 1976

2411. **YA'ACOB, Tunku His Excellency PMN CMG**, "HOMAGE TO IQBAL", *ASIAN REVIEW* (NS) 57, no. 211: July (1961): pp. 199.

2412. **YAHYA, Al-Khash-Shab**, "IQBAL", *IQBAL REVIEW* 16, no. 1: April (1975): pp. 66-70.
English translation of the article published in *AL-AHRAM* of 26 May 1972.

2413. ———, "MOHAMMAD IQBAL", *IQBAL REVIEW* 8, no. 1: April (1967): pp. 94-97.
Iqbal Day in Cairo, address.

2414. **YAHYA, Syed**, "RATION IQBAL ON THE AIR", *THE CIVIL AND MILITARY GAZETTE* (Lahore), 21 April 1953, pp. 3-4.

2415. **YARSHATER, Ehsan**, "IQBAL: THE LIFE AND THOUGHT OF RUMI (Book Review)", *MIDDLE EAST JOURNAL* 14, (1960): pp. 227.

2416. **YASAMEE, Abdullah**, "IQBAL'S CONCEPTION OF HIS ROLE AS POET", *IQBAL REVIEW* 8, no. 1: April (1967): pp. 17-22.

2417. **YASAMEE, Abdullah Khan**, "HIS ROLE AS A POET", *THE PAKISTAN TIMES* (Islamabad), 9 November 1987.

2418. **YUNUS SARAF M.**, "IQBAL'S ROLE IN KASHMIR STRUGGLE", *PAKISTAN TIMES* (Lahore), 21 April 1952, pp. 5-8.

2419. **YUSUF AZMI, M.**, "CONCEPT OF MAN IN IQBAL", *IQBAL REVIEW* 33, no. 1: April (1992): pp. 9-18.

2420. **YUSUF, S. M.**, "IQBAL'S HUMANITARIANISM AND UNIVERSALISM", *IQBAL* 25,

no. 1: January (1978): pp. 65-68.
This paper is the gist of a lecture delivered at a meeting held in Jos, Nigeria, to celebrate the centenary of Iqbal's birth. The author claims that *Pakistan, according to his [Iqbal's] vision, was to be a laboratory where the social, political and economic systems of Islam will be revived, reactivated and developed according to their own nature in the modern conditions to be presented to the entire world in a spirit of humility and fraternity* (p. 68).

2421.   ————, mon., *STUDIES IN ISLAMIC HISTORY AND CULTURE*, Lahore: Institute of Islamic Culture, 1970. v+232 pp.
Iqbal and religion, pp. 208-218.

2422.   ————, "A STUDY OF IQBAL'S VIEWS ON 'IJMA'", *IQBAL REVIEW* 3, no. 3: October (1962): pp. 17-25.
Analysis of the concepts of *Ijtihad* and *Ijma* according to Iqbal, based on the sixth lecture from (I) THE RECONSTRUCTION OF RELIGIOUS THOUGHT IN ISLAM. Re-issued as part of [Various authors], *SELECTIONS FROM THE IQBAL REVIEW*, ed. Waheed Qureshi, Lahore, 1983, pp. 123-131.

2423.   **YUSUF SARAF, M.**, "IQBAL'S ROLE IN KASHMIR'S STRUGGLE", *IQBAL: A CRITICAL STUDY*, Various authors (mon.), Lahore: Farhan Publishers, 1977, pp. 128-36.

A short survey of Kashmir's history since the Sikh conquest of 1819, and some quotations from Iqbal's works, bring the author to a general conclusion about Iqbal's feelings towards his home-land, which were *pessimistic, certainly*, he says, *but a pessimism related only to the present and not to the future*. Article taken from *THE PAKISTAN TIMES*, 21 April 1952.

2424.   **Z.I.A.**, "LITERATURE ON IQBAL", *IQBAL REVIEW* 1, no. 3: October (1960): pp. 79-80.
Review of Qazi Ahmad Mian Akhtar Junagarhi, *IQBALIYAT KA TANQIDI JA'IZAH*, Karachi: Iqbal Academy, 1955, 102 pp.

2425.   **ZAFAR, Yousouf**, "IQBAL AN ARTIST", *PAKISTAN TIMES* (Lahore), 21 April 1955, p. 5.

2426.   **ZAFAR, Yusuf**, "IQBAL AS AN ART ARTIST", *PAKISTAN TIMES*, 21 April 1955, pp. 5-7.

2427.   **ZAHUR-UL-HAQUE**, "ALLAMA IQBAL'S IDEAS ON ECONOMIC ISSUES", *THE*

MUSLIM (Islamabad), 20 April 1984.

2428. **ZAHUR-UL-HAQUE, M.**, "IQBAL ON REDEFINING MUSLIM LAW", *THE PAKISTAN TIMES* (Lahore), 6 November 1992.

2429. **ZAIDI, N. H.**, "IQBAL'S VIEW OF ART", *PAKISTAN REVIEW* 7, no. [?]: October (1958): pp. 43-44.

2430. **ZAIDI, Nazir Hasan**, "IQBAL'S CONCEPTION OF ART", *PAKISTAN TIMES*, 27 March 1977, p. 1.

2431. **ZAIDI, Zahida**, "NATURE IN IQBAL'S POETRY", *IQBAL COMMEMORATIVE VOLUME*, Ali Sardar JAFRI & K.S. DUGGAL (eds.), New Delhi: All India Iqbal Centenary Celebrations Committee, 1977, pp. 150-166.
Although a reconstruction of Iqbal's philosophy of nature in his poetry appears to be quite difficult, influences of various philosophical schools (like Naturalism, Pantheism, Mysticism, Transcendentalism, Unityism and Theism) can easily be detected. Iqbal's artistic and philosophical treatment of nature is subsequently illustrated in his poetry, leading to the conclusion that the poet showed a deep involvement in Nature.

2432. **ZAKARIA, Rafiq**, mon., *IQBAL: THE POET AND THE POLITICIAN*, Khushwant SINGH (intr.), London / New Delhi: Viking Penguin, 1993.   xxii+189 pp.
Contains 16 pages of plates, and bibliographic references.

2433. **ZAMAN, Mukhtar**, "DWAZDEH MANZIL - THE SITE OF 1930 LEAGUE SESSION", *THE PAKISTAN TIMES* (Rawalpindi), 2 December 1977.

2434. ———, "IQBAL'S MESSAGE OF ACTIVISM", *DAWN* (Karachi), 9 November 1985.

2435. **ZAMAN, S. M.**, "IQBAL AND THE FUNDAMENTALS OF ISLAM", *IQBAL REVIEW* 36, no. 3: October (1995): pp. 105-13.

2436. **ZENO**, "A BIOGRAPHY OF IQBAL BY HIS SON", *DAWN* (Karachi), 28 June 1985.

2437. ———, "IQBAL: POET AND PHILOSOPHER", *PAKISTAN TIMES*, 14 July 1977, p. 4.

2438. ———, "IQBAL'S LITERARY IDEAL", *PAKISTAN TIMES*, 21 April 1977, p. 4.

2439.   ———, "ISLAM IS A SOCIALISTIC RELIGION", *PAKISTAN TIMES*, 21 April 1976, p. 4.
The daring statement of the title was made by Iqbal on the eve of his departure for London in 1931, to attend the second Round table Conference.

2440.   ———, "REALITY - FICTIONAL AND SPIRITUAL", *ANNUAL OF URDU STUDIES* 7, (1990): pp. 49-52.

2441.   **ZIA**, "IQBAL'S THOUGHT LIES IN ETERNAL TRUTH OF ISLAM", *THE NATION* (Lahore), 9 November 1986.

2442.   ———, "ISLAMIC ORDER BEST HOMAGE TO IQBAL", *THE PAKISTAN TIMES* (Rawalpindi), 9 November 1980.

2443.   **ZIA, 'Aisha**, "THE CONCEPTS OF INDIVIDUALITY IN IQBAL AND KIERKEGAARD", University of the Punjab, 1971. 126 pp.
Cf. esp. chapter IV: Iqbal on the concept of individuality.
Promoter: Naeem Ahmad.

2444.   **ZIAUDDIN, Ahmad**, "IQBAL: A PIONEER OF MUSLIM RENAISSANCE", *DAWN* (Karachi), 9 November 1977.

2445.   ———, "IQBAL AND THE WEST", *THE PAKISTAN TIMES* (Islamabad / Lahore), 9 November 1986.

2446.   ———, "IQBAL AS AN ARTIST", *THE NATION*, 22 April 1950.
Published also in *THE CIVIL AND MILITARY GAZETTE*, 21 April 1951, p. 3.

2447.   ———, "IQBAL, HIS MIND AND ART", *THE ONWARD*, 31 May 1943.

2448.   ———, "IQBAL'S CONCEPT OF DERACIALISATION", *ISLAMIC LITERATURE* [vol. ?], no. [?]: August (1956): pp. 23-27.
Also published in *DAWN*, 21 April 1956.

2449.   ———, "IQBAL'S CONCEPT OF PAKISTAN", *DAWN* (Karachi), 9 November 1992.

2450.   ———, "IQBAL'S CONCEPT OF STATE", *IQBAL REVIEW* 4, no. 3: October (1963):

pp. 32-47.

2451. ——, "IQBAL'S CONCEPT OF THE PERFECT MAN", *THE DAWN* (Karachi), 21 April 1955, p. 6.

2452. ——, "IQBAL'S CONCEPTION OF ISLAMIC POLITY", *PAKISTAN HORIZON* 34, no. 2 (1981): pp. 44-58.

2453. ——, "IQBAL'S CONCEPTION OF UNIVERSAL BROTHERHOOD", *ILLUSTRATED WEEKLY OF PAKISTAN*, 29 April 1951/1961, pp. 27-30.

2454. ——, "IQBAL'S PHILOSOPHY AND MESSAGE", *THE SIND OBSERVER* (Karachi), 21 April 1950-23 April 1950.

2455. ——, "IQBAL: THE POET AND PHILOSOPHER", *THE STAR* (Allahabad), 31 May 1938.

2456. ——, "IQBAL: THE POET-PHILOSOPHER OF ISLAM", *VISHVABHARATI QUARTERLY* (Santiniketan) (NS) 4, no. 1: May-July (1938): pp. 39-54.

2457. ——, "IQBAL, THE PROPONENT OF PAKISTAN IDEA", *DAWN* (Karachi), 9 November 1984.

2458. ——, "NATURE OF ART ACCORDING TO IQBAL", *IQBAL REVIEW* 4, no. 4: April (1964): pp. 49-58.

2459. ——, "THE POET AS A POLITICAL THINKER", *THE DAWN* (Karachi), 21 April 1950, pp. 10-11.
Special Suppl.

2460. **ZOTOVA, I.**, "INTERPRETATION OF THE SUFI THEME OF 'JOURNEY' IN M. IQBAL'S MATHNAWI 'THE NEW GARDEN OF MYSTERY'", *THE WORK OF MUHAMMAD IQBAL: ARTICLES BY SOVIET SCHOLARS*, Abdur Rauf MALIK (ed.), Lahore: People's Publishing House, 1983, pp. 98-117.

2461. **ZUBAIR, T.**, "IQBAL'S CONCEPTION OF KNOWLEDGE", *DECCAN TIMES*, 7 November 1954.

2462. **ZULFIQAR, Ali**, *THE POETRY OF IQBAL*, Lahore: Aziz Publishers, 1977

2463. **ZULFIQAR, Ghulam Hussain**, "INFLUENCE OF IQBAL ON MUSLIM COUNTRIES", *IQBAL* 43, no. 1 (1996): pp. 57-70.

2464. ———, "IQBAL IN ORIENTAL COLLEGE", *IQBAL* 10, no. 4: April (1962).
On Iqbal's career as a teacher at the University of Punjab (1899 onwards).

2465. ———, "IQBAL'S MESSAGE OF HOPE TO THE NEW WORLD", *JOURNAL OF THE RESEARCH SOCIETY OF PAKISTAN* (Lahore) 29, no. 2: April (1992): pp. 35-54.

2466. ———, "IQBAL'S MESSAGE TO THE YOUTH", *THE PAKISTAN TIMES* (Rawalpindi), 9 November 1987.

2467. ———, "THE ROAD TO FREEDOM", *IQBAL* 44, no. 3-4: July-October (1997): pp. 1-153.
Special Supplement: Golden Jubilee Number.
A brief history of the struggle for Independence, and making of Pakistan, as narrated by Quaid-i-Azam Muhammad Ali Jinnah in some of his Speeches, Interviews and Messages: 1) an idea by Allama Sh. Muhammad Iqbal, 2) realised by Quaid-e-Azam Muhammad Ali Jinnah.
Included are Iqbal's LETTERS to Mr. Jinnah, pp. 6-11.

2468. **ZUMURUD MASAR, Mahmud and Muhammad YUSUF**, eds., *ALLAMA MUHAMMAD IQBAL - KITABIYAT*, Islamabad: Allama Iqbal Open University, Central Library, 1994.
A detailed bibliography of books and articles on Muhammad Iqbal, kept in the Iqbal Dept. of the Central Library, Allama Iqbal Open University, Islamabad - both in Urdu and in foreign languages.
U.

SUBJECT INDEX

Titles of works *by* Allama Muhammad Iqbal are printed in capitals.

BAL-I JIBRIL (part)   7, 387, 799, 830, 1184, 1185, 1189, 1317, 1459, 2048, 2049, 2050, 2052, 2245
BANDAGI-NAMAH   474, 668, 673, 824, 828, 955, 1707
BANG-I-DARA   1843, 2219
BANG-I-DARA (part)   216, 401, 460, 491, 701, 816, 941, 1227, 1228, 2252
Bedil   762, 763, 2130
BEDIL IN THE LIGHT OF BERGSON   762, 763
Bengal   32, 33, 940, 954
Bengali   13, 34, 191, 286, 291, 1667
Bergson   82, 206, 531, 592, 651, 664, 739, 762, 763, 1559, 1610, 1611, 2021, 2088, 2147
Bhagavad Gita   567
Bhartrihari   2149
bibliography   59, 200, 202, 205, 228, 325, 426, 463, 522, 643, 654, 656, 786, 787, 788, 789, 874, 1165, 1166, 1387, 1582, 1664, 1755, 1904, 1922, 1924, 1983, 1998, 1999, 2035, 2151, 2154, 2290, 2303, 2304, 2366, 2468
biography   8, 61, 85, 91, 96, 98, 116, 147, 153, 167, 177, 180, 193, 201, 232, 235, 246, 249, 285, 290, 425, 427, 452, 495, 504, 507, 522, 543, 544, 547, 548, 549, 550, 609, 610, 631, 641, 701, 702, 706, 709, 779, 785, 794, 796, 838, 874, 875, 876, 880, 890, 931, 964, 1006, 1024, 1098, 1104, 1105, 1141, 1154, 1158, 1251, 1267, 1269, 1278, 1327, 1362, 1363, 1377, 1397, 1407, 1427, 1455, 1470, 1482, 1534, 1535, 1596, 1624, 1625, 1643, 1703, 1767, 1776, 1823, 1846, 1857, 1875, 1891, 1928, 1940, 1948, 1949, 1958, 1965, 1975, 1996, 1998, 1999, 2007, 2008, 2031, 2032, 2037, 2039, 2041, 2043, 2044, 2045, 2046, 2071, 2086, 2092, 2101, 2176, 2183, 2185, 2186, 2206, 2234, 2238, 2239, 2241, 2264, 2274, 2276, 2277, 2292, 2294, 2295, 2304, 2311, 2323, 2324, 2327, 2329, 2330, 2332, 2360, 2361, 2371, 2390, 2400, 2408, 2436, 2464
Bradley   1358
Browning, Robert   1328, 1329, 1331, 2306
Buber, Martin   1446, 1861, 1866
Buddhism   741, 1869
CALL FROM THE MINARET; A MUSLIM FAMILY IN BRITAIN   1036
capitalism   841, 1127
child labour   871
children   1533, 1824
China   1270, 1271, 1272
Chinese   1344
[CHRESTHOMATHY]   348, 642, 1002, 1665, 2015
[CHRESTHOMATHY (discourses)]   1627, 1892, 2248
[CHRESTHOMATHY (essay)]   917, 1110, 1692, 2072, 2127, 2248, 2347
[CHRESTHOMATHY (lectures)]   351, 1380, 1382, 1675
[CHRESTHOMATHY (letters)]   157, 213, 429, 544, 671, 861, 900, 917, 931, 1041, 1045, 1050, 1064, 1065, 1093, 1173, 1176, 1460, 1637, 1641, 1876, 1901, 1963, 2042, 2047, 2100,

ORIENTALIA LOVANIENSIA
ANALECTA

44. E. LIPIŃSKI (ed.), Phoenicia and the Bible.
45. L. ISEBAERT (ed.), Studia Etymologica Indoeuropaea Memoriae A.J. Van Windekens dicata.
46. F. BRIQUEL-CHATONNET, Les relations entre les cités de la côte phénicienne et les royaumes d'Israël et de Juda.
47. W.J. VAN BEKKUM, A Hebrew Alexander Romance according to MS London, Jews' College no. 145.
48. W. SKALMOWSKI-A. VAN TONGERLOO (eds.), Medioiranica.
49. L. LAUWERS, Igor'-Severjanin, His Life and Work — The Formal Aspects of His Poetry.
50. R.L. VOS, The Apis Embalming Ritual. P. Vindob. 3873.
51. Fr. LABRIQUE, Stylistique et Théologie à Edfou. Le rituel de l'offrande de la campagne: étude de la composition.
52. F. DE JONG (ed.), Miscellanea Arabica et Islamica.
53. G. BREYER, Etruskisches Sprachgut im Lateinischen unter Ausschluß des spezifisch onomastischen Bereiches.
54. P.H.L. EGGERMONT, Alexander's Campaign in Southern Punjab.
55. J. QUAEGEBEUR (ed.), Ritual and Sacrifice in the Ancient Near East.
56. A. VAN ROEY-P. ALLEN, Monophysite Texts of the Sixth Century.
57. E. LIPIŃSKI, Studies in Aramaic Inscriptions and Onomastics II.
58. F.R. HERBIN, Le livre de parcourir l'éternité.
59. K. GEUS, Prosopographie der literarisch bezeugten Karthager.
60. A. SCHOORS-P. VAN DEUN (eds.), Philohistor. Miscellanea in honorem Caroli Laga septuagenarii.
61. M. KRAUSE-S. GIVERSEN-P. NAGEL (eds.), Coptology. Past, Present and Future. Studies in Honour of R. Kasser.
62. C. LEITZ, Altägyptische Sternuhren.
63. J.J. CLÈRE, Les Chauves d'Hathor.
64. E. LIPIŃSKI, Dieux et déesses de l'univers phénicien et punique.
65. K. VAN LERBERGHE-A. SCHOORS (eds.), Immigration and Emigration within the Ancient Near East. Festschrift E. Lipiński.
66. G. POLLET (ed.), Indian Epic Values. Rāmāyaṇa and its impact.
67. D. DE SMET, La quiétude de l'Intellect. Néoplatonisme et gnose ismaélienne dans l'œuvre de Ḥamîd ad-Dîn al-Kirmânî (Xᵉ-XIᵉ s.).
68. M.L. FOLMER, The Aramaic Language in the Achaemenid Period. A Study in Linguistic Variation.
69. S. IKRAM, Choice Cuts: Meat Production in Ancient Egypt.
70. H. WILLEMS, The Coffin of Heqata (Cairo JdE 36418). A Case Study of Egyptian Funerary Culture of the Early Middle Kingdom.
71. C. EDER, Die Ägyptischen Motive in der Glyptik des Östlichen Mittelmeerraumes zu Anfang des 2. Jts. v. Chr.
72. J. THIRY, Le Sahara libyen dans l'Afrique du Nord médiévale.
73. U. VERMEULEN - D. DE SMET (eds.), Egypt and Syria in the Fatimid, Ayyubid and Mamluk Eras. Proceedings of the 1st, 2nd and 3rd International Colloquium organized at the Katholieke Universiteit Leuven in May 1992, 1993 and 1994.
74. P. ARÈNES, La déesse Sgrol-Ma (Tara). Recherches sur la nature et le statut d'une divinité du bouddhisme tibétain.
75. K. CIGGAAR - A. DAVIDS - H. TEULE, East and West in the Crusader States. Context - Contacts - Confrontations. Acta of the Congress Held at Hernen Castle in May 1993.
76. M. BROZE, Mythe et Roman en Egypte ancienne. Les Aventures d'Horus et Seth dans le papyrus Chester Beatty I.
77. L. DEPUYDT, Civil Calendar and Lunar Calendar in Ancient Egypt.
78. P. WILSON, A Ptolemaic Lexikon. A Lexicographical Study of the Texts in the Temple of Edfu.
79. A. HASNAWI - A. ELAMRANI - M. JAMAL - M. AOUAD (eds.), Perspectives arabes et médiévales sur le tradition scientifique et philosophique grecque.
80. E. LIPIŃSKI, Semitic Languages. Outline of a Comparative Grammar.